New York Eats

NEW YORK
E~A~T~S

The Food Shopper's Guide to the Freshest Ingredients;
the Best Gourmet, Take-Out, and Baked Goods; and the
Most Unusual Marketplaces in All of New York

ED LEVINE

PHOTOGRAPHS BY PETER CUNNINGHAM
AND HILDA BIJUR

St. Martin's Press   New York

Design by Susan Hood

Library of Congress Cataloging-in-Publication Data
Levine, Ed, 1952–
New York eats / Ed Levine.
p.   cm.
Includes index.
ISBN 0-312-06981-2
1. Marketing (Home economics)—New York Metropolitan Area—Guide-books. 2. Grocery trade—New York Metropolitan Area—Guide-books. 3. New York (N.Y.)—Description—1981—Guide-books. I. Title.
TX356.L48   1992
381'.456413'00257471—dc20   91-41547
CIP

First Edition: April 1992
10   9   8   7   6   5   4   3   2

For Vicky and William,
whom I love more than food.

Acknowledgments

There are many people who made working on this book a pleasure, and whom I would like to thank for their help. First, there is Vicky Bijur, the best agent/wife/taster any food-loving writer could have. The unflagging enthusiasm and helpful suggestions of my editor, Barbara Anderson, played a major role in keeping this mammoth project on track. The glorious images of Peter Cunningham, friend and photographer, bring the book to life in a way that my text alone could not. The book is additionally enhanced by the images of Hilda Bijur, first-class photographer and one of the great mothers-in-law of all time, whose tolerance and patience for my obsession knows no bounds. My brother Mike Levine and his friend Alan Schwartz shed great insight into the particulars of many of the wine stores covered in the book. My sister-in-law Carol Levine traveled all over Manhattan with me in search of the perfect kitchenware store. My cousins Sam and Terry Sadin never passed an interesting store without telling me about it. Thanks go to my brother Jesse Levine; his wife, Lynn Silverstein; my brother-in-law Arthur Bijur; and my cousins Bob and Meryl Meltzer, who almost always let me bring dessert. The laughter and support of my friends Steve Braun, Peter Demy, Howie Klar, and Bob Rosen kept me going through the rough parts. Our friend Betsy Amster encouraged me to write the book in the first place, and then played a significant role in shaping the proposal and subsequent manuscript. My former employers, Fred Seibert and Alan Goodman, who were very understanding in giving me the leeway to write this book while working for them. My colleague and friend Tom Barreca had an eye for new food stores even more acute than my own. Lou Baur, Paula Brinkman, Troy Ellen Dixon, Noel Frankel, Dave Landesberg, Rich Mines, Nancy Nalven, Jessica Wolf, Yvette Yasui, Bob Zeltmann, and all the other current and former Fred/Alan employees, tasted more of the food mentioned in this book than they care to remember. Ed Schoenfeld, Vincent Orgera, Scott Campbell, and David Raymer of Vince & Eddie's helped in many ways, not least by loving to talk about and eat food as much as I do. The assistance and hard work of Andrea Casson and Rie Yamaguchi kept me going through the late stages of the book. Elliot Krowe, a friend and colleague, helped me through innumerable computer crises. Jeffrey Berlin of the Laptop Shop was there every time I had a computer catastrophe. Our friend Sue Weiner contributed endless suggestions to help me through various logistical problems. All of my advertising clients, including Rick Hill, Rich Cronin, Harriet Seitler, and Leslye Schaeffer, helped by understanding that though their advertising needs were important to me, food was a matter of life and death. Finally, thanks to all my friends and family for their love and support . . . and the use of their taste buds.

CONTENTS

Introduction

I am an unabashed lover of New York's food and the people who make and sell it. For eighteen years I have been relentless in my pursuit of the ultimate nosh. Some people count sheep when they can't sleep. I call 24-hour diners to find out what their specials are that night or what kind of pie they're serving. My wife claims I choose my friends by the neighborhood they live in and what they know about food there. I say that's a major contributing factor, but certainly not the only one. When I meet someone at a party, I don't ask him what he does for a living or what his sign is. I ask him where he lives and then where he shops for food.

I regard every walk from a bus or subway stop as an opportunity for food adventure. When I find myself with a rented car on my hands after a business meeting, I use it to explore a bakery or food store someone has told me about. Whenever I take my son to a play date, I plot the food possibilities on the way. I know I'm often late for business and social appointments as a result, but my wife, friends, and colleagues have come to be understanding about my obsession. It's only the people at my destination that occasionally get upset about my resultant lateness. But once they find out why I'm late, they want to know what's in the box or bag I'm carrying. Like most New Yorkers—and like most people who visit New York—they are fascinated by and have a deep passion for food.

It is this passion that I encountered again and again while researching this book. I found it in John Fretta and his cohorts, who welcomed me to the back of their wonderful sausage store with a plate of pasta and a glass of wine to watch the Italians play in the World Cup. I found it again in Cambria Heights, a Queens neighborhood that, with its boccie court, pork store, *salumeria*, and Italian-ices joint, could have just as easily been in Sicily as New York. I found it in the voices of second- and third-generation store owners who told me, sadly, that no one in the family was interested in learning the family trade and taking over the store. I found it in every single manager, stock person, and checkout clerk during my five-hour guided tour of Balducci's magical emporium.

New York and the wondrous variety of food that her citizens create are my passions, too. In this book I have tried to convey my enthusiasm and that of the dozens of bakers, butchers, importers, fishmongers, spice and cheese merchants, chocolate dippers, ice cream vendors, pizza and pasta makers, greenmarket farmers, sandwich and take-out servers, caterers and caviar kings who invited me into their stores. Their willingness to share information, stories, philosophy, technique, and even recipes was both gratifying and inspiring. Each foray into a new neighborhood brought joyful discoveries and unexpected eating pleasures. New York is an unending adventure in food. It is my hope that this book will in itself provide pleasure and that it will guide you toward new discoveries of your own.

How to Use This Book

Each *New York Eats* chapter discusses a different category of food shopping, and each category is divided into neighborhoods. New York's neighborhoods have been broken down as follows:

West Harlem
Above 125th Street
Fifth Avenue to Riverside Drive

East Harlem
Above 96th Street
First Avenue to Fifth Avenue

Upper West Side
59th Street to 125th Street
Central Park West to Riverside Drive

Upper East Side
59th Street to 96th Street
First Avenue to Fifth Avenue

Midtown West
34th Street to 59th Street
Fifth Avenue to Eleventh Avenue

Midtown East
34th Street to 59th Street
First Avenue to Fifth Avenue

Chelsea
14th Street to 34th Street
Fifth Avenue to Eleventh Avenue

Kips Bay/Gramercy Park
14th Street to 34th Street
East River to Fifth Avenue

West Village
14th Street to Houston Street
East River to Fifth Avenue

Downtown
Houston Street to Battery Park

Bronx

Queens

Brooklyn

Within each neighborhood, the stores are listed alphabetically. Stores that carry more than one kind of food are cross-referenced in the appropriate chapters. As an example, Balducci's entire entry is in the Mega-Store chapter. But the store is cross-referenced in twelve other chapters: Appetizers and Smoked Fish; Baked Goods; Bread; Cheese; Chocolates, Candy, and Nuts; Coffee, Tea, and Spices; Ethnic Markets; Fish; Meat and Poultry; Pasta; Produce; and Take-out and Prepared Food. A store like Neuman & Bogdonoff, which deals primarily in take-out food, has its entire entry in the chapter on prepared food. But it also carries enough high-quality baked goods to justify a cross-reference in Baked Goods. Each cross-reference appears in the appropriate chapter under the appropriate neighborhood heading. It will guide you to the main entry for the store.

At the end of each entry you'll find the essential information for that store, including the store's full name, its address (including cross streets and zip code) and phone number (area code first), closest subway stop(s) to the store, store hours, delivery information, forms of payment accepted, and mail-order information. While this information was correct at press, it's always a good idea to call a particular store to verify that they're still in business and still in the same location with the same hours, before you head out the door.

I'm sure that each reader will have a favorite store or stores that did not get an entry in this book. It may be that the store is new or was simply overlooked in my research; New York is a big place and its food scene is constantly growing and changing. More likely, though, is that the store did not meet my criterion for inclusion: that it must sell or make at least one item that is distinctive and special. If I've missed a place you feel should be included, write to me c/o St. Martin's Press, 175 Fifth Avenue, New York, NY 10010. I'll check out your suggested store, and if it's as good as expected, I'll try to include it in the next edition of the book.

1

APPETIZERS AND SMOKED FISH

The smoked fish counter has a long and glorious tradition in New York. One of my earliest New York food memories is of my father giving me a few dollars every Sunday morning and asking me to buy Nova, bagels, and cream cheese. I would ride my bike to Rothenberg's, take a number, and, when my number was called, ask for a quarter pound of Nova Scotia lox, sliced thin, please.

Then the fun would really begin. One of the countermen would begin slicing my fish ever so adroitly, while at the same time barraging me with questions and comments about my family. He would ask me about my Little League exploits, my father's health, and my brothers' latest academic and artistic achievements. Though I sometimes wished I could buy my smoked fish in quiet anonymity, I treasured both the sense of community these exchanges gave me and the samples of lox and whitefish doled out by the countermen.

Old-fashioned smoked fish counters are still very much in evidence in New York today. Places like Barney Greengrass and Russ & Daughters still have the wisecracking countermen capable of psychoanalyzing you in a matter of moments. They still have the long glass shelves filled with smoked salmon, baked salmon, sable, whitefish, and sturgeon, with the fish eyes staring at you like an unwanted intruder.

The only thing that has changed is the ever-widening selection of smoked salmon. While my choices as a child were the regular, salty belly lox and the much less salty Nova Scotia salmon (pronounced "novee" in Russian Jewish households) as well as kippered salmon and sable, today's shopper is confronted with eight or ten kinds of smoked salmon, not to mention smoked tuna, mackerel, bluefish, and trout. (See the accompanying interview with Russ & Daughters for some help in understanding the differences among all these smoked fish.)

𝒰PPER WEST SIDE

59TH STREET TO 125TH STREET
CENTRAL PARK WEST TO RIVERSIDE DRIVE

Barney Greengrass the Sturgeon King ~ Before Zabar's was even a gleam in Saul Zabar's eye, the place to go on the Upper West Side for smoked fish was Barney Greengrass. Three generations of Greengrasses have been slicing sturgeon, Nova Scotia salmon, and whitefish since 1908 for loyal customers like the late Groucho Marx and Calvin Klein. The sturgeon here is a work of art; the smoked salmon is beyond reproach; and the homemade borscht, pickled herring, and chopped liver are all first-rate. Even the whitefish salad, made with onion, celery, and green pepper, is mostly whitefish, a far cry from the mayonnaise-dominated concoctions at many other stores. The cream cheese is just fine, but if you're in the neighborhood you'll do better at Fairway buying the homemade cream cheese from Ben's (see page 221).
Note: When shopping here, don't be put off by the line for the restaurant. The wait at the fish counter is actually quite short compared to the wait at Zabar's.

Barney Greengrass the Sturgeon King
541 Amsterdam Avenue (between 86th and 87th streets)
New York, NY 10024
PHONE: (212) 724-4707
SUBWAYS: 86th Street station on the following lines: Broadway–Seventh
    Avenue No. 1 and 9; Eighth Avenue C and Sixth Avenue B.
HOURS: 8:30 A.M. to 6 P.M. Tuesday through Sunday; closed Monday.
Deliveries made up to 4 P.M.
No credit cards.
Mail-order catalog available.

Fairway ~ See page 221.

Murray's Sturgeon Shop — I was worried when I read three years ago that Murray's Sturgeon Shop had been sold yet again. I knew that the original owner, Murray Bernstein, had sold the business in 1974 to Artie Cutler, now a partner in Docks, Carmine's, and Ollie's Noodle Shop, three of the West Side's best and most popular restaurants. Cutler in turn took in another partner, Heshy Berliner, in 1979. Together they succeeded in maintaining the standards for smoked fish that Bernstein had set. But I just didn't know if Murray's could withstand still another ownership change. I needn't have worried. New owners Ira Goller and Kenneth Yevia realize what a treasure they have on their hands and treat Murray's like the endangered species it is. The smoked salmon is still silky, the sturgeon still rich and flavorful, and the pickled herring still sweet as can be. Murray's whipped tuna salad is so good that Robert Duvall had Cutler send Tom Cruise ten pounds to sustain the two movie stars during their *Days of Thunder* shoot in Florida. The whitefish salad is too sweet for me, and the vegetarian chopped liver lacks flavor, but the egg-and-mushroom salad with bits of sweet onion could not be improved upon.

Note: Murray's has terrific bagels, slightly chewy, full of flavor, and always fresh, from Columbia Hot Bagels (See page 46). But Murray's prices are even higher than Barney Greengrass's, which is saying something.

Murray's Sturgeon Shop
2429 Broadway (between 89th and 90th streets)
New York, NY 10024
PHONE: (212) 724-2650
SUBWAYS: 86th Street station on the following lines: Broadway–Seventh
   Avenue No. 1 and 9; Eighth Avenue C and Sixth Avenue B.
HOURS: 8 A.M. to 7 P.M. Sunday, Tuesday through Friday; 8 A.M. to 8 P.M.
   Saturday; closed Monday.
Deliveries available all over Manhattan.
Catering and platters available.
Cash and personal checks only.

Zabar's — See page 237.

*U*PPER EAST SIDE

59TH STREET TO 96TH STREET
FIRST AVENUE TO FIFTH AVENUE

Bloomingdale's — See page 212.

Caviarteria — I thought I was going to get a heavy dose of East Side snootiness the first time I walked into Caviarteria. I couldn't have been more wrong. This appropriately tiny place (given what it sells) has warm, knowledgeable salespeople who are more than happy to give tastes and accompanying explanations about everything they sell. They carry twelve kinds of caviar, from beluga malossol to imperial golden. Try the American trout, an inexpensive, tasty roe. Caviarteria also sells wonderful foie gras and okay, but not great, Scotch smoked salmon.

Caviarteria
29 East 60th Street (between Madison and Park avenues)
New York, NY 10022
PHONE: (212) 759-7410
SUBWAYS: Fifth Avenue station on the Broadway N and R lines; Lexington
    Avenue station on the Sixth Avenue B and Q lines; 59th Street station on
    the Lexington Avenue No. 4, 5, and 6 lines.
HOURS: 9 A.M. to 6 P.M. Monday through Saturday; closed Sunday.
Deliveries in Manhattan.
All major credit cards accepted.
Mail-order catalog available.

Fraser-Morris ~ See page 301.

Grace's Marketplace ~ See page 225.

Sable's ~

I chuckled when I saw Sable's orange-and-white sign, which looks exactly like the Zabar's logo. I guess Sable's owner Kenny Sze wants to remind potential customers that he ran the appetizer department at Zabar's for eleven years before opening his own store in 1991. He apparently learned his lessons well, because Sable's smoked fish is every bit as good as Zabar's. I've sampled the Scottish salmon, the eastern Nova, and the smoked peppered salmon, and all were fresh and beyond reproach. His homemade whitefish salad tastes of whitefish, mayonnaise, and not much else. Kenny even learned how to make first-rate pickled herring in a luscious cream sauce. His chopped liver is wonderful, and I'm not much of a chopped liver lover.

Sable's
1489 Second Avenue (between 77th and 78th streets)
New York, NY 10021
PHONE: (212) 249-6177
SUBWAY: 77th Street station on the Lexington Avenue No. 6 line.
HOURS: 9 A.M. to 8 P.M. Tuesday through Friday; 8 A.M. to 9 P.M. Saturday; 8
    A.M. to 6 P.M. Sunday.
Deliveries in the neighborhood.
Cash and personal checks only.
Platters and catering available.

William Poll ~

William Poll is best known as the appetizer, hors d'oeuvres, and tea-sandwich supplier of choice for some of Manhattan's old-money residents. Fearing that the store's success was based more on prestige than taste, I was surprised to find many good items on sale here. Several of the dips, which can be sampled before buying, are quite fine, especially the cucumber, sun-dried tomato, eggplant, and watercress varieties. Unfortunately, there was not the slightest bit of lobster flavoring in the lobster dip. The smoked salmon is first-rate, even though it is presliced; the soups are not boldly seasoned; the sandwiches are tasty if overpriced.

William Poll
1051 Lexington Avenue (between 74th and 75th streets)
New York, NY 10021
PHONE: (212) 288-0501
SUBWAY: 77th Street station on the Lexington Avenue No. 6 line.
HOURS: 9 A.M. to 6 P.M. Monday through Saturday; closed Sunday.
Deliveries available.
All major credit cards accepted.
Mail-order catalog, picnic and gift baskets, and catering available.

IDTOWN WEST

34TH STREET TO 59TH STREET
FIFTH AVENUE TO ELEVENTH AVENUE

Macy's Cellar Marketplace ~ See page 229.

Petrossian ~ I know Petrossian is synonymous with high-toned appetizer eating in New York. I also know they carry first-rate smoked salmon, foie gras, and caviar in the small portion of its restaurant (located in the gorgeous Alwyn Court building) devoted to retail. Last, I know I can get equally high-quality D'Artagnan foie gras (which I prefer), Scotch salmon, and caviar at many other places around the city at almost half Petrossian's prices. So why does anyone shop at Petrossian's retail store? So they can walk around town with the cool shopping bags with the Petrossian logo.

Note: Petrossian also carries first-rate French chocolates and a small selection of high-quality packaged goods, all at prices that would have made even Donald Trump blush in his salad days. Try the carrot mousseline, which makes a tasty, rich, and quick cream of carrot soup.

Petrossian
182 West 58th Street (at Seventh Avenue)
New York, NY 10019
PHONE: (212) 245-2217
SUBWAYS: 57th Street station on the Broadway N and R lines and the Sixth
    Avenue B and Q lines.
HOURS: 11 A.M. to 9 P.M. Monday through Friday; 1 P.M. to 6 P.M. Saturday
    and Sunday.
Deliveries available.
All major credit cards accepted.
Mail-order catalog.

*M*IDTOWN EAST

34TH STREET TO 59TH STREET
FIRST AVENUE TO FIFTH AVENUE

Nancy's Gourmet Popcorn --- See page 166.

*K*IP'S BAY/GRAMERCY PARK

14TH STREET TO 34TH STREET
EAST RIVER TO FIFTH AVENUE

Todaro Brothers --- See page 233.

*W*EST VILLAGE

14TH STREET TO HOUSTON STREET
FIFTH AVENUE TO WEST STREET

Balducci's --- See page 205.

Dufour Pastry Kitchens --- Seven years ago classical concert promoters Carla Krasner and Judi Arnold decided they wanted to cater (no pun intended) to their own egos instead of performers'. So they started Dufour Pastry Kitchens, which makes puff-pastry appetizer logs so delicious that I've had guests unable to eat their dinners after the appetizer course. The slice-and-bake logs come in thirteen varieties, including a phenomenal sweet-onion-and-parmesan and a nutty mushroom-pâté. Only the smoked-salmon disappointed, and that could be because I've never had a heated smoked-salmon preparation I've liked. They also sell what they call party lites, made with margarine instead of butter.

Note: Stores like Macy's, Balducci's, and Dean & DeLuca also carry a limited selection of Dufour items.

Dufour Pastry Kitchens
808 Washington Street (between Horatio and Gansevoort streets)
New York, NY 10014
PHONE: (212) 929-2800
SUBWAYS: 14th Street station on the Eighth Avenue A, C, and E lines;
    Eighth Avenue station on the 14th Street–Canarsie L line.
HOURS: 8 A.M. to 5 P.M. Monday through Friday; call for Saturday hours;
    closed Sunday.
No delivery.
No credit cards.
Mail order available.

$\mathscr{E}$ AST VILLAGE

4TH STREET TO HOUSTON STREET
EAST RIVER TO FIFTH AVENUE

Knish Nosh ~~~ The concept of a knish having flavor would have been foreign to my ancestors, because most knishes taste like bad mashed potatoes with a little chicken fat thrown in. Knish Nosh's potato and kasha knishes have flavor and texture. The casings are actually flaky and have some taste. In order to keep up with our health-conscious times, Knish Nosh is now also making carrot, broccoli, and spinach knishes. Besides the normal-sized knishes, one of which makes a fine lunch along with the Hebrew National hot dog you can buy here, Knish Nosh makes cocktail knishes, preferred by people who like their knishes in small doses.

Note: I was thrilled when Knish Nosh opened its Manhattan location in 1987. Before that I had a hard time convincing friends that it was worth a trip to Queens just to get a knish.

Knish Nosh
145 Fourth Avenue (between 13th and 14th streets)
New York, NY 10003
PHONE: (212) 529-4910
SUBWAYS: 14th Street–Union Square station on the following lines:
    Lexington Avenue No. 4, 5, and 6; Broadway N and R; 14th Street–
    Canarsie L.

Smoked fish counter at Russ & Daughters.

HOURS: 9 A.M. to 7 P.M. Monday through Friday; closed Saturday and
   Sunday.
Delivery available on orders of $20 or more.
No credit cards.
Mail order by individual request.

OTHER LOCATION: 101-02 Queens Boulevard
Forest Hills, NY 11375
(718) 897-5554

Russ & Daughters ⸺ Besides getting first-rate smoked fish, pickles, and dried
fruit at Russ & Daughters, you'll also engage in one of the Lower East Side's
oldest traditions: counter repartee. Walk into Russ & Daughters on a Sunday
morning; order some silky, rich Gaspé smoked salmon or some of the best sour
or half-sour pickles in town; and steady yourself. These countermen will, in the
course of getting you a quarter of a pound of smoked salmon, examine every facet
of your life. It's cheaper than therapy, and you walk out with great food.

Note: Buy your bagels here, too. It used to be that the bakery two doors down
from Russ & Daughters made the best hand-formed pumpernickel-onion bagels
in the city. But they stopped making them in 1989, and now there's no reason
not to buy Russ & Daughters' good, crusty commercially made bagels. Buy your
cream cheese next door at Ben's Cheese Shop.

Russ & Daughters
179 East Houston Street (between Allen and Orchard streets)
New York, NY 10002
PHONE: (212) 475-4880
SUBWAY: Second Avenue station on the Sixth Avenue F line.
HOURS: 9 A.M. to 6 P.M. Monday through Wednesday; 9 A.M. to 8 P.M.
   Thursday through Sunday.
Delivery available.
No credit cards.
Mail order available.

Yonah Schimmel's Knishes Bakery ⸺ Yonah Schimmel's has been in business
since 1910. The old-fashioned dumbwaiter still carries the kasha, potato, and
fruit-and-cheese knishes from the basement kitchen to the street-level store. It
has tin ceilings, antique food cases, and lots of atmosphere. What it doesn't have
is great knishes. They're okay, but they're on the dry side and have even less
flavor than other knishes. I debated excluding this entry, but how can anyone
write a New York food book and not include Yonah Schimmel's? What the hell;
it's worth a trip if only for the nifty dose of old New York.

Yonah Schimmel's Knishes Bakery
137 East Houston Street (between First and Second avenues)
New York, NY 10002
PHONE: (212) 477-2858
SUBWAY: Second Avenue station on the Sixth Avenue F line.
HOURS: 8 A.M. to 6 P.M. seven days a week.
No deliveries.
No credit cards.
Mail order available.

Yonah Schimmel storefront on Houston Street.

𝒟OWNTOWN

HOUSTON STREET TO BATTERY PARK

Dean & DeLuca ⁓ See page 214.

Gertel's ⁓ Although Gertel's is a bakery, I can't wholeheartedly recommend any of their regular baked goods. The jelly donuts are quite good, and the apple strudel's decent, but, for the most part, Gertel's makes typically heavy, standard

Jewish baked goods. The real reason to go to Gertel's is for the potato kugel, the usually bland potato pudding that every Jewish grandmother serves to her grandchildren. Gertel's potato kugel is a peppery, garlicky wonder, and although it's not exactly a light, nouvelle kind of dish, at least Gertel's version isn't the superheavy lumpen sod most potato kugels are.

Gertel's
53 Hester Street (between Ludlow and Essex streets)
New York, NY 10002
PHONE: (212) 982-3250
SUBWAY: East Broadway station on the Sixth Avenue F line.
HOURS: 7 A.M. to 5 P.M. Sunday through Wednesday; 6:30 A.M. to 5 P.M.
    Thursday; 6:30 A.M. to 3 P.M. Friday; closed Saturday.
No deliveries.
Cash only.

Guss Pickles ⚋ Waiting on line at the Essex Street outdoor stand that is Guss Pickles, I realized I was participating in a Jewish tribal rite that has not changed in eighty-two years. Guss sells wonderful sour, half-sour, and hot pickles plucked from barrels right before your eyes. They also sell terrific sauerkraut, sweet kraut, and pickled tomatoes, and superb grated horseradish. Even if you don't particularly like pickles, you must experience Guss.

Note: For all the New Yorkers you know who have fled the city and then had the nerve to complain about the paucity of real pickles in their new locale, please note that Guss will ship pickles UPS anywhere in the continental United States.

Note: Guss Pickles has officially changed its name to Essex Street Pickles, but everyone still refers to it as Guss.

Pickles, sauerkraut, and pickled tomatoes at the Essex Street outdoor stand of Guss Pickles.

Guss Pickles
35 Essex Street (just north of Hester Street)
New York, NY 10002
PHONE: (212) 254-4477
SUBWAY: East Broadway station on the Sixth Avenue F line.
HOURS: 9:30 A.M. to 6 P.M. Sunday through Thursday; 9:30 A.M. to 2 P.M.
   Friday; closed Saturday.
No deliveries.
Credit cards accepted on orders of $25 or more (that's a lot of pickles).
Mail order available.

$\mathscr{B}$RONX

Teitel Brothers ～ See page 134.

$\mathscr{Q}$UEENS

Greek House Foods ～ See page 139.

Knish Nosh ～ See page 7.

Mediterranean Foods ～ See page 139.

Titan Foods ～ See page 139.

$\mathscr{B}$ROOKLYN

Hirsch's Knishes ～ See page 142.

A Russ & Daughters Primer on Smoked Salmon

"There's an old joke in the smoked fish business that tells you what this business is all about." Mark Federman, third-generation family owner of Russ & Daughters, is discussing the vagaries of the smoked salmon business in his tiny, cluttered office. He's drinking his second cup of coffee of the day while I contentedly chomp away on Nova and cream cheese on a bialy. "An old woman," he continues, "comes into her regular smoked fish store and announces to the counterman, 'I need an eighth of a pound of lox.' The counterman starts to cut, counts out five or six slices and says to the woman, 'Is that enough?' 'Keep going,' she replies without hesitation. He cuts a few more slices and says, 'How about that?' The old woman shakes her head and says 'Keep cutting.' The counterman shakes his head and continues to cut. By now he's cut about five pounds of salmon. Finally he gets to the tail of the salmon and cuts off two more slices. The woman nods and smiles and says, 'Now give me those two slices.' "

The fact that Mark is smiling as he tells this story indicates that he is a worthy successor to the two previous generations of his family that ran Russ & Daughters. His grandfather, Joel Russ, started in the appetizer business selling dried Polish mushrooms from a pushcart in 1900, shortly after he came to America to avoid the military draft in Galicia. By 1914 he had graduated to an Orchard Street storefront called Russ's Cut Rate Appetizers. Now, more than seventy-five years and two generations later, the store still has the look and feel of a classic Lower East Side smoked-fish and appetizer store. Immediately on your left as you walk in are barrels of pickles and baskets of bagels, bialys, and *pletsls*, which are old-fashioned Jewish onion flatbread. On your right are shelves brimming with dried fruits, nuts, and candy of all sorts, including half a dozen varieties of halvah. Past the bagels on the left are the old-style display cases filled with fresh, glistening smoked fish.

With the Lower East Side no longer the epicenter of Jewish life in New York, Russ & Daughters' customer base has broadened considerably. In the ninety minutes I was there, a Montreal restaurateur came by to pick up ten pounds of smoked fish for his restaurant, a truck driver came in to order half a pound of tuna fish, a middle-aged woman stopped in and asked in a heavy Eastern European accent, "Mark, how is your mother feeling?" and a young couple arrived with their two kids to buy some halvah. As Mark himself says, "The store has come full circle. Now it's the neighborhood artists who buy a quarter or an eighth of a pound."

Though Mark feels it is difficult to generalize about the differences in the flavor and texture of the many varieties of smoked fish, he did offer the following observations:

1. Scotch salmon is slightly smokier and leaner than other smoked salmon. He described it as moderately salty.
2. Gaspé, an Altantic salmon, has a delicate flavor. It is the mildest, least salty smoked salmon, with the finest texture—"like silk," according to Mark.

3. Western Nova, a Pacific salmon, is also fairly mild but is saltier than Gaspé. It can be either line-caught or net-caught, with line-caught preferred, he said, because the fish doesn't lose oil and moisture the way it does when it flops around in a net. The best Western Nova is Chinook, or king, salmon.

4. Icelandic smoked salmon has a nice lusty, smoked flavor.

Mark says it's also important to know, as the little old Jewish ladies have found out over the years, that different parts of a smoked salmon taste different. The tail, the thinnest part of the fish, picks up the most salt in the curing process, and is therefore leaner, drier, and saltier than other parts of the fish. Conversely, as you get closer to the head of the fish, it becomes less salty, fattier, and juicier.

When I asked Mark to explain the enduring popularity of Russ & Daughters, he thought for a moment and said, "We do things the same way my grandfather did. The food we sell is direct food. People feel good about eating it."

Best of Smoked Fish and Appetizers

Best all-around freestanding smoked fish and appetizer store: Russ & Daughters

Best caviar store: Caviarteria
Best egg salad: Murray's Sturgeon Shop
Best hot hors d'oeuvres: Dufour Pastry Kitchens
Best knishes: Knish Nosh; Hirsch's
Best pickled herring: Sable's
Best pickles: Guss Pickles
Best smoked salmon: Russ & Daughters
Best smoked tuna: Macy's Cellar Marketplace
Best sturgeon: Barney Greengrass the Sturgeon King
Best tuna salad: Murray's Sturgeon Shop
Best value: Zabar's
Best whitefish salad: Barney Greengrass the Sturgeon King

2

BAKED GOODS: PASTRIES, CAKES, PIES, AND COOKIES

Bakeries are wonderful places. Where else in New York can you buy something for a dollar that brings instant gratification and can even cure a depression? Baked goods are a lot cheaper than psychotherapy, and provide faster, more easily discernible results.

New York is bakery heaven. Its status as a magnet for immigrants means that from babka to Italian cheesecake, New York has every kind of baked good imaginable. Warning: Bakeries, like people, do some things better than others. So don't assume that because I've mentioned a store, everything it carries is worthy of purchase. Where appropriate, I've noted the highlights of each place and warned you off certain other items.

*W*EST HARLEM

ABOVE 125TH STREET
FIFTH AVENUE TO RIVERSIDE DRIVE

Better Crust Bakery ᨆ A friend of mine whose food instincts I trust told me her father used to stop here on his way home the day before Thanksgiving to pick up the Dixon family's pies. So I commandeered a friend's car, went up to Better Crust, and shoved enough money through its bulletproof Plexiglas pay window for one apple, one sweet-potato, and one peach pie. The verdict: Better Crust Bakery is aptly named; its crusts are flaky wonders. The apple pie is densely packed with apples, the sweet-potato pie is redolent of cinnamon and vanilla, and only the peach pie disappointed with its canned peach filling. I've yet to try their mince and pecan pies. The non-pie baked goods I've tasted here are eminently skippable. Oh yes, prices here (like those at my other Harlem entries) are really cheap: $6.25 for a large pie.

Better Crust Bakery
2380 Adam Clayton Powell Boulevard (Seventh Avenue between 139th and
    140th streets)
New York, NY 10030
PHONE: (212) 862-0291
SUBWAYS: 135th Street station on the Broadway–Seventh Avenue No. 2 and
    3 lines.
HOURS: 8 A.M. to 9 P.M. seven days a week.
No deliveries.
Cash only.

Georgie's Pastry Shop ᨆ About 1:30 every day a line starts to form at Georgie's Bake Shop that starts in his postage-stamp-sized store and ends up snaking down the block. Experienced Georgie's shoppers know that's when Georgie's amazing disappearing glazed and jelly donuts come out. A hot Georgie's donut is simply one of New York's great eating experiences. I call them disappearing because every time I've put Georgie's donuts out, even avowed health-food fanatics break down and gobble one up. Georgie's also makes wonderful sweet-potato and coconut pies, and a simple pound cake that is made to go with a scoop of vanilla ice cream. Georgie's apple pie has just a tad too much clove and nutmeg in it for my taste.

Note: If you get to Georgie's and there's no line, in all likelihood the donuts aren't out yet. There may be donuts from the previous day, but the gracious women behind the counter will tell you they're from yesterday. One other note about Georgie's: This may be the cheapest bakery in New York. The donuts are forty cents each, and a ten-inch apple pie is $6.50.

Georgie's Pastry Shop
50 West 125th Street (between Fifth Avenue and Malcolm X Boulevard)
New York, NY 10027
PHONE: (212) 831-0722
SUBWAYS: 125th Street station on the Broadway–Seventh Avenue No. 2 and
    3 lines.

HOURS: 10 A.M. to 7 P.M. Tuesday through Saturday; closed Sunday and
    Monday.
No deliveries.
Cash only.

$\mathscr{U}$PPER WEST SIDE

59TH STREET TO 125TH STREET
CENTRAL PARK WEST TO RIVERSIDE DRIVE

Barcelona Pastry ⚬ See page 19.

Fairway ⚬ See page 221.

William Greenberg Jr. Desserts ⚬ See page 23.

Grossinger's Bakery ⚬ For fifty-five years Herb Grossinger has been selling his
justly famous praline ice-cream cake to New Yorkers. It's sweet, goopy, creamy,
and satisfying, even to a confirmed non–praline eater like myself. He also makes
a huge Hungarian scone, extremely moist and flavorful, the likes of which I
haven't seen anywhere else in the city. His cream cheese cake is my favorite Upper
West Side cheesecake. Last, he makes a cinnamon stick, a kind of stick-shaped
cinnamon doughnut, which is habit-forming. Everything else I've tasted here is
pretty standard.
    Note: The Grossinger's on 75th Street and Columbus Avenue closed recently
to make way for another clothing store . . . just what we need.

Grossinger's Bakery
570 Columbus Avenue (between 87th and 88th streets)
New York, NY 10024
PHONE: (212) 362-8672 or (212) 874-6996
SUBWAYS: 86th Street station on the following lines: Broadway–Seventh
    Avenue No. 1 and 9; Eighth Avenue C and Sixth Avenue B.
HOURS: 7:30 A.M. to 7 P.M. Monday through Thursday; 7:30 A.M. to one half
    hour before sundown Friday (it's Kosher); 8 A.M. to 6 P.M. Sunday; closed
    Saturday.
DELIVERIES: Weekdays only, $20 minimum.
Cash only.

Pâtisserie Les Friandises ⚬ My friends Paul and Susan used to live a couple of
blocks from Les Friandises and, knowing my obsession with food, often implored
me to try it. I resisted for a long time, thinking that because of their normally

low-fat diet, their taste buds would be different from mine when it came to baked goods. But I now know never to doubt them again. After one bite of Les Friandises' *tarte tatin*, buttery and filled with calvados-infused apple chunks, I was in bakery heaven. Simple French bakery items like croissants, brioches, and rolls, which are often butchered in New York, are superb here. Owner Jean Kahn is equally adept at elaborate mousse preparations. Her passion-fruit Miroir, a mousse separated by two layers of vanilla *génoise*, is intensely flavored and ethereally light. Her chocolate-mousse cake should not be left alone in a house with any serious chocoholics. Her brownies are (along with Sarabeth's) the West Side's best. Only her apple and pumpkin pies fall short of the mark. I can think of two reasons Les Friandises is not better known. The first is its unlikely upper Amsterdam Avenue location. The second is its very high prices, given its neighborhood. A six-inch chocolate-mousse cake here is $19.70.

Pâtisserie Les Friandises
665 Amsterdam Avenue (between 92nd and 93rd streets)
New York, NY 10025
PHONE: (212) 316-1515
SUBWAYS: 96th Street station on the following lines: Broadway–Seventh
    Avenue No. 1, 2, 3, and 9; Eighth Avenue C and Sixth Avenue B.
HOURS: 8 A.M. to 6 P.M. Tuesday through Saturday; 8:30 A.M. to 3 P.M. Sunday.
Deliveries in the neighborhood.
American Express accepted.
Also located on Upper East Side, 972 Lexington Ave, (212) 988-1616.

Original Royale Pastry Shop ⚬⚬⚬ Most New York breakfast muffins are so big and heavy that they can cause damage if accidentally dropped. But the corn, bran, and carrot muffins at Royale are positively feathery. The corn muffins, especially, are moist, flavorful wonders, with a unique lemony glaze. The other must-buy here is the Jewish-style corn rye bread. Dense and packed with flavor, it makes the best toast in the universe. Royale, overall, is one of the last bastions of Jewish-bakerydom left in Manhattan. That means the usual rules of thumb concerning Jewish bakeries hold true: count on great cheese, fruit, and cinnamon danish; decent rugelach; and chewy challah. Mocha éclair fans should note that the custard-filled version here is surprisingly good for a bakery that doesn't specialize in this kind of thing. The layer and mousse cakes, however, are too sweet and insubstantial. You know you're holding a less-than-great cake if it doesn't weigh enough in the box.

Original Royale Pastry Shop
237 West 72nd Street (between Broadway and West End Avenue)
New York, NY 10023
PHONE: (212) 874-5642
SUBWAYS: 72nd Street Station on the Broadway–Seventh Avenue No. 1, 2, 3,
    and 9 lines.
HOURS: 6 A.M. to 8 P.M. Monday through Friday; 7 A.M. to 8 P.M. Saturday
    and Sunday.
No deliveries.
No credit cards.
Mail order available.

Sarabeth's Kitchen ~ Sara Levine of Sarabeth's Kitchen is one of New York's great bakers. She started the homey but serious baked goods craze in New York almost ten years ago, and nobody's caught up to her yet. Her sticky buns, though downsized from their original humongous form, are still the standard by which all others in the city are measured. Her scones are so rich and flavorful they don't need butter or jam. Her Budapest coffee cake is just about my favorite coffee cake in New York. Her chocolate-soufflé cake is an intense bittersweet-chocolate experience, as are the chocolate cookies she calls chubbies. Her chocolate-chip cookies are light, almost meringuelike. Her brownies are right up there with the best in the city. During apple season her caramel apples, made with Granny Smith apples and homemade superrich, buttery caramel, are an incredibly indulgent treat, because there's no way to eat one without getting it on your clothes and destroying your teeth. Her jams are so chunky and wonderful they can be eaten straight from the jar. The only things I've found disappointing at Sarabeth's are her Thanksgiving pies, which are unbelievably expensive and just not worth it.

Sarabeth's Kitchen
423 Amsterdam Avenue (between 80th and 81st streets)
New York, NY 10023
PHONE: (212) 496-6280
SUBWAYS: 79th Street station on the Broadway–Seventh Avenue No. 1 and 9
   lines; 81st Street station on the Eighth Avenue C and Sixth Avenue B
   lines.
HOURS: 8 A.M. to 5:30 P.M. and 6 P.M. to 10:30 P.M. Monday through Friday;
   9 A.M. to 5:30 P.M. Saturday and Sunday.
No deliveries.
All major credit cards accepted.
Mail order for her amazing jams only.

The Silver Palate ~ See page 297.

Soutine ~ It's easy to miss this postage-stamp-sized bakery tucked away on a side street between Columbus Avenue and Broadway. And if you did, you would miss sampling three of New York's finest baked goods. Soutine makes exquisitely light pear-walnut muffins filled with big chunks of pear; tangy, crunchy cheddar-cheese rolls that can be a meal in themselves; and what could be New York's ultimate chocolate cake, a twenty-dollar creation called a Chocolate Concord that is an extraordinary combination of chocolate mousse and chocolate meringue. After taking one bite of this cake, my friend Joe said, "Now I know what I want on my birthday for the next forty years." Soutine's owner Madge Rosenberg also bakes beautiful personalized Valentine's Day cookies.

Her cheese Danish are buttery yet surprisingly light, with a barely sweetened cheese filling. She even makes a no-fat, no-sugar fruit roll that actually tastes good. If you're a plum-pudding fan (I'm not), the version they make here during holiday season is the real deal, filled with suet, dried currants, raisins, almonds, and spices. Only the soggy broccoli- , asparagus- , and cheese-stuffed breads disappointed me here.

Soutine
104 West 70th Street (between Columbus Avenue and Broadway)
New York, NY 10023
PHONE: (212) 496-1450
SUBWAYS: 72nd Street station on the following lines: Broadway–Seventh
   Avenue No. 1, 2, 3, and 9; Eighth Avenue C and Sixth Avenue B.
HOURS: 8 A.M. to 7 P.M. Monday through Friday; 9 A.M. to 5 P.M. Saturday; 9
   A.M. to 3 P.M. Sunday; closed Sunday during July and August.
Deliveries in the neighborhood.
Cash and personal checks only.
Mail order available.

Zabar's ⸺ See page 237.

$\mathcal{U}$PPER EAST SIDE

59TH STREET TO 96TH STREET
FIRST AVENUE TO FIFTH AVENUE

Barcelona Pastry ⸺ Most New York apple muffins should be forced to carry the
label "apple-flavored" for all the actual apple you find in them. I happened upon
the Barcelona patisserie one day strolling down Lexington with my cousin Sam.
Sam said, "Let's try the apple muffin." We did, and damned if this apple muffin,
full of apples and made with a cakelike batter, wasn't so good that two blocks
farther south we had to turn around and get another one. Another big winner
here is the Catalonian custard cake, a rectangular *crème brûlée* that is sweet and
rich without being cloying. Barcelona's owner, Joseph Boujol, is a Spaniard who
trained in Switzerland and can therefore make everything from Sacher tortes to
cannoli. Though I'm impressed with his range, you'd do best sticking to the above-
mentioned items, the surprisingly good chocolate-truffle cake, and any of the
other Spanish specialties.

Note: Barcelona Pastry is a good source for decent birthday cakes for kids.
They're all very sweet, but surprisingly moist.

Barcelona Pastry
1440 Lexington Avenue (between 93rd and 94th streets)
New York, NY 10128
PHONE: (212) 369-2914
SUBWAY: 96th Street station on the Lexington Avenue No. 6 line.
HOURS: 6:45 A.M. to 8 P.M. Monday through Friday; 8 A.M. to 8 P.M.
   Saturday; 9 A.M. to 7 P.M. Sunday.
No deliveries.
Cash only.

OTHER LOCATION:
Barcelona Dessert
2534 Broadway (between 94th and 95th streets)
New York, NY 10025
(212) 666-9292

Bloomingdale's ~ See page 212.

Bonté Patisserie ~ Mrs. Bonté and her husband have baked cakes for royalty and presidents, and although nobody ever accused Queen Elizabeth and LBJ of having any taste, in Bonté's case they did. The Bontés make four kinds of occasion cakes: chocolate, Grand Marnier, mocha, and cassis. They're all works of art, so good I've twice carried Bonté cakes to weddings three hours from New York at the request of the bride and groom. Mrs. Bonté's Danish could bring tears of joy to the most stoic person's eyes, and she makes a terrific ready-made French toast I've not seen elsewhere in the city. Her croissants are so meltingly good that Mimi Sheraton deemed them not only wonderful tasting but also of perfect size. Of course, most of us didn't know there was a perfect size for a croissant. Mimi Sheraton says that to measure a croissant you place your two big toes approximately 4½ inches apart. If the tips of the croissant touch each big toe, go ahead and eat the sucker. Otherwise, you must either return it or throw it out.

Warning: The Bontés and their employees can, on occasion, be quite snooty. But a frosty greeting is a small price to pay for baked goods this delicious.

Bonté Patisserie
1316 Third Avenue (between 75th and 76th streets)
New York, NY 10021
PHONE: (212) 535-2360
SUBWAY: 77th Street station on the Lexington Avenue No. 6 line.
HOURS: 9 A.M. to 6 P.M. Monday through Saturday; closed Sunday.
No deliveries.
Cash and personal checks only.

Budapest Pastry ~ I got nervous when, in 1989, I heard that my favorite place for cheese Danish in New York had been sold to a Lebanese man. I just couldn't imagine someone from Beirut baking a mean cheese Danish. But the new owner learned how much his customers loved the cheese Danish, so he apprenticed with the Hungarian couple who sold him the shop. The result is a bizarre Hungarian–Middle Eastern hybrid bakeshop. Only in New York could one bakery turn out quintessential cheese Danish *and* great baklava. I usually don't care for Middle Eastern sweets, but the ones here are light, intriguingly flavored, and not syrupy sweet. The strudels here were never so terrific to begin with, and the new owner hasn't improved upon them. Ditto the mediocre sticky buns.

Note: The new owner also makes pretty good Middle Eastern sandwiches, such as falafel, baba ghanouj, and the like.

Budapest Pastry
207 East 84th Street (just east of Third Avenue)
New York, NY 10028
PHONE: (212) 628-0721
SUBWAYS: 86th Street Station on the Lexington Avenue No. 4, 5, and 6
    lines.
HOURS: 7:30 A.M. to 7:30 P.M. Monday through Friday; 8:30 A.M. to 7:30 P.M.
    Saturday; 10 A.M. to 5 P.M. Sunday.
Deliveries in the neighborhood.
Cash only.

Canard and Company ~~ See page 299.

Choco Rem ~~ I'm not saying it was the only contributing factor, but Choco Rem's black-and-white loaf, a dark-and-white-chocolate mousse wrapped in chocolate leaves, with two tiny layers of biscuit to hold it together, enabled the various warring factions of my family to get along, at least for one afternoon. This cake is so dazzling that it moved my excessively verbal family to silence when I carried it out of the kitchen. I served Choco Rem's capuccino tart along with it, just in case some of the guests weren't up for a rich dessert. Of course, the cappuccino tart turned out to be a round, half-inch-deep slab of chocolate and cappuccino, with a whipped-cream squiggle on the top and a thin butter crust on the bottom. But it wasn't as rich as the black-and-white loaf.

Choco Rem is a sliver of a shop run by Marilyn Miller, a former Playboy bunny who is as sassy and idiosyncratic as any store proprietor I've met. The first time I walked into the store, I asked to purchase one of the cakes I had eyed in her display case. She wouldn't sell it to me because it had been baked the day before. Now that's my kind of baker.

Her baked goods and candies are kosher, because, she says, "when I opened up, my son had a kosher friend, and he wanted his friend to be able to eat here." The day I met her, she was on her way to Houston, Texas, to deliver cakes and candy for a bar mitzvah. Though she occasionally has cakes on hand, most of the time they are available by special order only. That's because the bulk of her business is selling to restaurants. Among her better-known clients are Sistina, Firenze, and Brandywine.

In addition to the black-and-white loaf and the cappuccino tart, Marilyn makes fruit tarts, pecan tarts, linzer tartes, mousse cakes of every imaginable variety, and chocolates so rich I couldn't tell they were kosher. As she presented different pieces of candy to try, she noted with great satisfaction that the raspberry-liqueur-filled chocolate is Nancy Reagan's favorite. After biting into it, I realized that for the first time in my life I actually agreed about something with Nancy Reagan.

Choco Rem
303 East 81st Street (between First and Second avenues)
New York, NY 10028
PHONE: (212) 988-4711
SUBWAY: 77th Street station on the Lexington Avenue No. 6 line.
HOURS: 10 A.M. to 6 P.M. Monday through Saturday; closed Sunday.
American Express accepted.
Mail order available for the chocolates only.

Choco Rem's Cappuccino Tart

1 9-inch tart shell
1 quart heavy cream
3 ounces sugar
1 tablespoon instant espresso
¼ teaspoon vanilla

8 ounces semisweet chocolate
1 ounce unsweetened chocolate
12 egg yolks

Whipped cream for garnish
Chocolate shavings for garnish

1. Steep cream, sugar, espresso, and vanilla at 190°F.
2. In the top of a double boiler, melt all the chocolate.
3. In a large mixing bowl, beat egg yolks, then slowly wisk in cream mixture. Strain, mix in chocolate, and set aside to cool.
4. Preheat over to 350°F.
5. Pour cooled mixture into a 9-inch tart shell. Bake until set, about 10 minutes. When tart has cooled, garnish with whipped cream and chocolate shavings.

Yield: One 9-inch tart

Colette — I've always imagined heaven to be a place where you could eat as many buttery French baked goods as you wanted. If that were true, I'd bet on Colette to win the bakery concession in the hereafter. Assuming I made it there, too, I'd then have unlimited access to her insanely buttery and flavorful Danish and her large and puffy yet surprisingly light plain croissants. She's even made a believer out of me with her almond croissants, and I don't like marzipan flavoring very much. Colette sold the store six years ago, but the new owner, Sophie Cowan, never missed a beat. The quiches here will restore your faith in that hopelessly clichéd preparation. Her fruit tarts and more elaborate mousse cakes are also quite good, but the *pièce de résistance* in the serious dessert category is the Trianon cake, an incredibly rich and butter-infused chocolate loaf made with three kinds of Belgian chocolate. About the only thing I wasn't wild about is Colette's individual pizzas, which were tasty but heavy.

Colette
1136 Third Avenue (between 66th and 67th streets)
New York, NY 10021
PHONE: (212) 988-2605
SUBWAYS: 68th Street–Hunter College station on the Lexington Avenue No.
    6 line; Lexington Avenue station on the Sixth Avenue B and Q lines.
HOURS: 7:30 A.M. to 7 P.M. Monday through Saturday; closed Sunday.
Deliveries in Manhattan.
American Express accepted.
Mail order available.

Dumas Patisserie ∼ When I think about pecan rings, I think about those flavorless, dry masses found in conference rooms preceding morning business meetings. But Dumas's pecan ring is so intense, so buttery, so jammed with pecans, and so distracting that senior managers have banned them from conference rooms all over the city. Dumas also makes what may be the city's finest napoleon, sinfully rich and deeply satisfying. Everything else I've tried here, including the famous fruit strips and apple turnovers, has been okay, but not up to the pecan ring.

Warning: On Saturdays at Dumas, retail customers will feel they're in the way of the Dumas employees trying to get all the wholesale orders out. It's better to go on the weekdays, but even then you may not get an overly friendly reception.

Dumas Patisserie
1378 Lexington Avenue (at the corner of 91st street)
New York, NY 10128
PHONE: (212) 369-3900
SUBWAYS: 86th Street station on the Lexington Avenue No. 4, 5, and 6 lines.
HOURS: 8 A.M. to 6:30 P.M. Monday through Saturday; closed Sunday.
No deliveries.
All major credit cards accepted.

E.A.T. ∼ See page 300.

Fraser-Morris ∼ See page 301.

Grace's Marketplace ∼ See page 225.

William Greenberg Jr. Desserts ∼ In a city full of high-priced bakeries, Greenberg's wins the prize as New York's most expensive cake, pie, and cookie joint. Nobody but Greenberg's would have the nerve to charge more than two dollars for a Danish or more than three dollars for a three-bite apple tart. So it's a good thing that Greenberg's might be New York's best all-around bakery. The list of top-rank Greenberg's treats is long: sticky buns, or *schnecken* as they're called in the old country; fruit pies, especially the sour-cherry; butter cookies that literally melt in your mouth; cheesecake with a dusting of toasted almond on top; strawberry shortcake; the aforementioned Danish, with fresh blueberries in blueberry season. Curiously, where Greenberg's falls down occasionally is with chocolate desserts. The two-dollar brownies can be dry if they're not fresh (I don't care if they wrap them in cellophane, it's when they bake them that counts). The all-chocolate cake has a moist, bittersweet icing, but the cake itself is often dry. Also, Greenberg's babka sometimes suffers from dryness, a cardinal sin in a baked item whose quality depends almost exclusively on moisture.

William Greenberg Jr. Desserts
1377 Third Avenue (between 78th and 79th streets)
New York, NY 10021
PHONE: (212) 535-7118

SUBWAY: 77th Street station on the Lexington Avenue No. 6 line.
HOURS: 8:30 A.M. to 6 P.M. Monday through Friday; 8:30 A.M. to 5:30 P.M.
   Saturday; closed Sunday.
No deliveries.
All major credit cards accepted.

OTHER LOCATIONS:
518 Third Avenue (between 34th and 35th streets)
New York, NY 10016
(212) 686-3344

2187 Broadway (between 77th and 78th streets)
New York, NY 10024
(212) 580-7300

1100 Madison Avenue (between 82nd and 83rd streets)
New York, NY 10028
(212) 744-0304

G & M Pastries ~ I admit it. I had forgotten about G & M until a casual conversation with a friend reminded me that while there are thousands of marble pound cakes made in America every day, there is only one G & M. Sold by the slab, G & M's pound cake belies the humdrum status pound cake occupies in the world of baked goods. G & M also makes a mocha éclair that I used to buy right before a weekly basketball game in the neighborhood. It did slow me down some, but it was worth it. The buttery apple turnovers are terrific. The Danish and pecan rings are excellent, if not up to the city's best. But as Shakespeare said, the pound cake's the thing.

   Note: G & M is one of my favorite sources for birthday cakes. They're moist, not too sweet, and full of flavor.

G & M Pastries
1006 Madison Avenue (between 77th and 78th streets)
New York, NY 10021
PHONE: (212) 288-4424
SUBWAY: 77th Street station on the Lexington Avenue No. 6 line.
HOURS: 7 A.M. to 7 P.M. Monday through Saturday; 7 A.M. to 6 P.M. Sunday.
No deliveries.
Cash only.

Les Délices Guy Pascal ~ There are only a few cakes made in New York bakeries that are so extraordinary they've caused me to commit numerous traffic violations to obtain one. Guy Pascal's Délice cake is one of them. It's got layers of whipped cream and chocolate mousse separated by hazelnut meringue, all topped with a layer of toasted almonds. There are other good things to be had at Guy Pascal, including a first-rate lemon tart that causes my friend Dale to walk her poor dog forty extra blocks to buy one once a week. Guy Pascal's mixed fruit tart has slice after slice of fresh kiwi and strawberries on it, and his chocolate-mousse cake is intensely chocolaty and surprisingly light. His buttery cookies are feathery and yet vividly flavored. About the only things I've consistently been disappointed with here are the dull Danish and the dry pecan rings.

Note: Les Délices Guy Pascal is a spacious, extremely pleasant place to sit and have cake and coffee.

Les Délices Guy Pascal
1231 Madison Avenue (corner of 89th Street)
New York, NY 10128
PHONE: (212) 289-5300
SUBWAYS: 86th Street station on the Lexington Avenue No. 4, 5, and 6 lines.
HOURS: 7 A.M. to 9 P.M. Monday through Friday; 8 A.M. to 8 P.M. Saturday
  and Sunday.
No deliveries.
American Express and Diner's Club accepted.

Neuman & Bogdonoff ~~ See page 303.

Rigo ~~ To my wife's way of thinking, a Dobos torte, a mocha seven-layer cake with a hardened caramel exterior, is as good as cake gets. Rigo makes the best version I've found in the city. Therefore I go to Rigo every year on my wife's birthday. My wife also loves Linzer tortes, those large, round, jam-filled cookies that mostly come in leaden versions. Rigo makes wonderful sour-cherry and poppy-seed Linzer tortes. So I end up going to Rigo a lot more than once a year, which is okay with me because when you walk into Rigo you enter a warm, homey, Hungarian time warp. Rigo makes a first-rate chocolate-mousse cake and solid if unspectacular babkas and Danish. Its strudel is also fine, though with the untimely demise of Mrs. Herbst's ten years ago, New York lacks a truly great strudel emporium.

Rigo
314 East 78th Street (between First and Second avenues)
New York, NY 10021
PHONE: (212) 988-0052
SUBWAY: 77th Street station on the Lexington Avenue No. 6 line.
HOURS: 8 A.M. to 4 P.M. Monday; 8 A.M. to 6 P.M. Tuesday through Saturday;
  9 A.M. to 4 P.M. Sunday.
No deliveries.
Cash only.

Sant Ambroeus Ltd. ~~ Sant Ambroeus is part bakery, part cappuccino bar, part Italian restaurant, and part gelateria. I've never eaten at the restaurant, but the cappuccino is fine, the bakery makes unbelievably gorgeous and ornate cakes, and the gelati and sorbeto, are excellent. The only problem with the elaborate cakes is that sometimes they don't taste as good as they look. The cappuccino-mousse cake is terrific, however—not sweet at all and surprisingly light. The napoleons are also good. The cookies are mediocre at best, and the fruit tarts are heavy and uninteresting.

Warning: Unless you are somehow related to an Italian industrialist, or at least look like you are, you may be in for a chilly reception here.

Sant Ambroeus Ltd.
1000 Madison Avenue (between 77th and 78th streets)
New York, NY 10021
PHONE: (212) 570-2211
SUBWAY: 77th Street station on the Lexington Avenue No. 6 line.
HOURS: 9:30 A.M. to 10:30 P.M. Monday through Saturday; 10:30 A.M. to 6:30
    P.M. Sunday.
Deliveries made all over Manhattan, except Sunday.
All major credit cards accepted.

Word of Mouth ~ See page 305.

Yura ~ See page 306.

$\mathscr{M}$IDTOWN WEST

34TH STREET TO 59TH STREET
FIFTH AVENUE TO ELEVENTH AVENUE

Between the Bread ~ I confess to a bias against muffins that weigh more than a quarter of a pound. Between the Bread's larger-than-life muffins (weighing in at around six ounces), however, are moist and flavorful enough to overcome their girth. The cranberry muffins are appropriately tart, the blueberry muffins are not cloyingly sweet, and the apple-cinnamon muffins are laced with plenty of cinnamon. The store uses only real fruit or high-quality preserves in its batters, so you never get that artificial flavor found in coffee-shop muffins. My current favorite, and certainly the most unusual the store bakes, is the cappuccino muffin; the coffee flavor is strong without being bitter. The only muffins not to my liking here are the healthful muffins made with bran. They're heavy and flavorless and have the texture of pressboard.

Between the Bread
145 West 55th Street (between Sixth and Seventh avenues)
New York, NY 10019
PHONE: (212) 581-1189
SUBWAYS: 57th Street station on the Broadway N and R lines and the Sixth
    Avenue B and Q lines.
HOURS: 7:30 A.M. to 2:30 P.M. Monday through Friday; closed Saturday and
    Sunday.
Deliveries throughout Manhattan.
Cash only at store.
Mail-order brochure available.

OTHER LOCATION:
141 East 56th Street (between Lexington and Third avenues)
New York, NY 10022
(212) 888-0449

Corrado Kitchen ~ See page 285.

Cupcake Café ~ Birthday cakes have never been high on my list of fine foods. While everybody else is singing "Happy Birthday," I'm always thinking about where the cake came from, and how it's going to be too sweet, too dry, and too encased in frosting. Ever since I was a kid, I've requested *not* to get the piece of cake with the flower on it, because all that spun sugar made the cake inedibly sweet. But then I had a chocolate birthday cake with mocha icing made by Ann Warren, co-owner of the Cupcake Café. The cake was moist and intensely chocolaty. The mocha icing was the best icing I'd ever tasted on a birthday cake, smooth and buttery with a strong coffee flavor. The cake tasted so good I didn't even mind that it was studded with tiny, gorgeous purple flowers. If you don't like chocolate cake, Ann also offers vanilla, orange, and Bohemian (maple-walnut) cakes. The icing options (besides mocha) are vanilla, chocolate, orange, and Bohemian. Ann will decorate it with anything you want. When I finished writing this book, I ordered a cake that had the words "It's done" and a book on top. Ann is an artist, one of the last of a dying breed of cake decorators. Besides occasion cakes, the Cupcake makes wonderful, eggy coffee cake, terrific dough- nuts, and some of the best pies in the city. The crumb pies in particular, with their crunchy streusel toppings, are superb (try the apple or the peach).

Note: Don't be put off by the Cupcake's eclectic furnishings or its rather seedy Ninth Avenue location. The weird vibes of the nearby Port Authority Bus Terminal are more than offset by the warm welcome you'll receive here.

Cupcake Café
522 Ninth Avenue (corner of 39th Street)
New York, NY 10018
PHONE: (212) 465-1530
SUBWAYS: 42nd Street–Port Authority Bus Terminal station on the Eighth
    Avenue A, C, and E lines.
HOURS: 7 A.M. to 7:30 P.M. Monday through Friday; 8 A.M. to 6 P.M.
    Saturday; 10 A.M. to 5 P.M. Sunday.
Deliveries on large orders only.
No credit cards.

William Greenberg Jr. Desserts ~ See page 23.

J.P.'s ~ See page 30.

The Little Pie Company ~ Don't let the cutesy name fool you. These people make grown-up pies, maybe the most sophisticated in the city. I've tried five that merit induction to the Pie Hall of Fame: Coconut-banana-cream, Key lime, ched- dar-crust apple, pear-apple crumb, and the store's signature sour-cream apple- walnut. The pumpkin and the old-fashioned apple pies are merely good and solid.

Apple pies fresh from the oven of The Little Pie Company.

Note: These guys love apples—to the point that they put apples in their brownies. Now I love apple desserts as much as anyone, but there ought to be a USDA rule forbidding the inclusion of apples in a brownie recipe.

Note: If you want Little Pie Company pies for Thanksgiving, you have to call and reserve them approximately two weeks in advance; otherwise, you're doomed like I was three years ago to wait on line outside on Thanksgiving morning hoping for a shot at the baking overrun.

The Little Pie Company
424 West 43rd Street (between Ninth and Tenth avenues)
New York, NY 10036
PHONE: (212) 736-4780
SUBWAYS: 42nd Street–Port Authority Bus Terminal station on the Eighth
    Avenue A, C, and E lines.
HOURS: 8 A.M. to 7:30 P.M. Monday through Friday; 10 A.M. to 6 P.M.
    Saturday; noon to 5 P.M. Sunday.
No deliveries.
Visa and MasterCard accepted.

Macy's Cellar Marketplace ⟿ See page 229.

Poseidon Bakery ⟿ The Fable Brothers have been making and selling Greek pastries for more than sixty years. I only wish they had discovered a way to make nouvelle Greek pastries in that time. The baklava, bird's nest, and other Greek pastries are quite good if you like that kind of thing. They're heavy and sweet, and, unlike other Greek pastry you get around New York, they're also fresh. I prefer the savory pastries here, such as the tangy, flaky spinach or cheese pies. But the true prize at Poseidon is the phyllo dough, which they both sell and use in making their pastries. It's light, hand-rolled, and wonderfully textured, so good that many first-rate restaurants and food shops around the city use it in their own kitchens. Poseidon also makes frozen Greek hors d'oeuvres such as miniature spinach-and-cheese pies. They're tasty, but it always makes me nervous when the instructions on the package tell you to wipe off the excess oil.

Poseidon Bakery
629 Ninth Avenue (at 44th Street)
New York, NY 10036
PHONE: (212) 757-6173
SUBWAYS: 42nd Street–Port Authority Bus Terminal station on the Eighth
   Avenue A, C, and E lines.
HOURS: 9 A.M. to 7 P.M. Tuesday through Saturday; 10 A.M. to 4 P.M. Sunday;
   closed Monday.
Cash only.
Mail-order catalog available.

Remi to Go --- See page 307.

ⵊⵊIDTOWN EAST

34TH STREET TO 59TH STREET
FIRST AVENUE TO FIFTH AVENUE

Between the Bread --- See page 26.

La Boulange --- La Boulange's owner, Pierre Weber, is the third generation of his family to become a pastry chef. His father and grandfather owned a pastry store in Paris, but luckily for New Yorkers Pierre took several of his family's recipes and came to New York to seek fame and fortune. His chocolate Truffon cake, made with a light chocolate mousse and chocolate sponge cake, is one of New York's great chocolate desserts. His Trio cake, alternating layers of dark-, milk-, and white-chocolate mousse with white-chocolate shavings on top, is one of those rare visually resplendent cakes that actually tastes terrific. I think his Vosgienne cake, made of chocolate sponge, whipped cream, and fresh raspberries, is a bit too sweet. If you're looking for something less rich, try his simple bread pudding, which is moist, hearty, and filling.

La Boulange
712 Third Avenue (between 44th and 45th streets)
New York, NY 10017
PHONE: (212) 949-7454

SUBWAYS: 42nd Street–Grand Central on the following lines: Lexington
   Avenue No. 4, 5, and 6; Flushing No. 7; 42nd Street Shuttle.
HOURS: 7 A.M. to 6 P.M. Monday through Friday; closed Saturday and
   Sunday.
Deliveries in the neighborhood.
Cash only.

OTHER LOCATION:
J.P.'s
4 West 55th Street (between Fifth and Sixth avenues)
New York, NY 10019
(212) 765-7575

$\mathscr{K}$IPS BAY/GRAMERCY PARK

14TH STREET TO 34TH STREET
EAST RIVER TO FIFTH AVENUE

The City Bakery ⁓ I was skeptical the minute I walked into the City Bakery. A minimalist food display in the window was echoed by a minimalist but beautiful decor: high ceilings; a frosted, windowed Japanese-style wall separating the dining area from the kitchen; and an array of cakes and individual tarts that were even more minimalist and beautiful than the space. They looked like Mondrian paintings. Clearly, I thought, they're using minimalist display techniques to hide the fact that their stuff just doesn't taste very good. Boy, was I wrong. Only the look is minimalist. The passion-fruit tart with a raspberry polka dot is simultaneously sweet, tart, and buttery. The chocolate tart, with a milk chocolate and caramel filling, tastes like the ultimate Heath Bar. The cane-sugar *crème brûlée* tart is a more subtle pleasure than the other two tarts, but just as good. The double-chocolate-mousse cake is one of New York's finest, although its brownie crust doesn't have much flavor. In the morning there are first-rate flaky croissants, *pains au chocolat*, and raspberry turnovers bursting with raspberry jam.

The City Bakery
22 East 17th Street (between Fifth Avenue and Broadway)
New York, NY 10003
PHONE: (212) 366-1414
SUBWAYS: 14th Street–Union Square station on the following lines:
   Lexington Avenue No. 4, 5, and 6; 14th Street Canarsie L; Broadway N
   and R.
HOURS: 7:30 A.M. to 12 midnight Monday through Saturday; 9 A.M. to 6 P.M.
   Sunday.
Deliveries in neighborhood.
All major credit cards accepted.

Friend of a Farmer ⁓ When I saw its cutesy ersatz farmhouse look, I was prepared to hate Friend of a Farmer. But when I tasted the cherry-walnut square, with its firm cherries, chunks of walnuts, streusel topping, and intensely buttery shortbread crust, I forgave all the taffeta. Friend of a Farmer makes superb breads. The cinnamon-raisin bread is terrific for French toast, and its regular white bread makes excellent toast. The strudels and turnovers are more doughy than flaky, but they're loaded with fresh firm fruit, nuts, and aromatic cinnamon. The muffins are moist and flavorful, if a little sweet for my taste. The apple cake was delicious the first time I tried it but had virtually no apple in it the next time. The deep-dish pies contain generous amounts of fresh fruit but have a less-than-mediocre crust. Friend of a Farmer does a huge brunch business on Saturdays and Sundays, so be prepared for a mob scene if you go there on those days to buy baked goods.

Friend of a Farmer
77 Irving Place (between 18th and 19th streets)
New York, NY 10003
PHONE: (212) 477-2188
SUBWAYS: 14th Street–Union Square station on the following lines:
    Lexington Avenue No. 4, 5, and 6; Broadway N and R; 14th Street–
    Canarsie L.
HOURS: 8 A.M. to 10 P.M. Tuesday through Saturday; 9:30 A.M. to 3:30 P.M.
    Sunday; closed Monday.
No deliveries.
No credit cards.

Gindi Cafe ~ My wife, who's a heckuva lot more sophisticated than I am, introduced me to Dacquoises, layers of nut-flavored meringue filled with whipped cream or buttercream, when we lived in the Village. We lived next door to a wholesale dessert maker and caterer who put these extraordinary hazelnut fingers in his store window to cool. He worked late, so whenever we got the late-night munchies we would knock on his door and buy one of his wondrous creations. He went out of business and we moved uptown, so I was relieved when I discovered a bakery, Gindi, that made sufficiently authentic Dacquoises to feed my wife's Dacquoise craving. Gindi's Dacquoises come in four flavors: mocha, chocolate, lemon, and raspberry. I prefer the mocha, but then again I never met a mocha anything I didn't like. Gindi also makes a wonderful brownie-nut pie, creditable blueberry and apple-crumb pies, and a homemade version of a Yankee Doodle made with lots of whipped cream and drizzled with chocolate ganache. The cookies are okay—nothing special—and the layer cakes are too sweet for my taste. The leaden raspberry tart is the only real loser here.

Note: Although Gindi originally opened as a bakery, it has now become a decent neighborhood spot for soups, sandwiches, salads, and the like, many of which are vegetarian.

Gindi Cafe
935 Broadway (between 21st and 22nd streets)
New York, NY 10010
PHONE: (212) 505-5502
SUBWAYS: 23rd Street station on the Broadway N and R lines and the
    Lexington Avenue No. 6 line.
HOURS: 8 A.M. to 9 P.M. Monday through Friday; 10:30 A.M. to 6 P.M.
    Saturday and Sunday.
Deliveries available.
Cash and personal checks only.

Todaro Brothers ∿ See page 233.

*W*EST VILLAGE

14TH STREET TO HOUSTON STREET
FIFTH AVENUE TO WEST STREET

Balducci's ∿ See page 205.

Patisserie J. Lanciani ∿ When I lived in the western section of Greenwich Village, I found it excruciatingly painful to walk past this palace of caloric sin on my way to the subway each morning. Mr. Lanciani makes an excellent if expensive brownie that's dense, incredibly chocolaty, and filled with walnuts. Lanciani's also has great Danish, buttery fruit tarts and strips, and a white-chocolate-mousse cake built with ladyfingers and called a Gâteau Charlene Blanche, which I often fantasize about when I can't sleep. Lanciani also has a number of tables and chairs, so you can buy a piece of cake, sip some cappuccino, and while away countless hours.

Patisserie J. Lanciani
271 West Fourth Street (between Perry and 11th streets)
New York, NY 10014
PHONE: (212) 929-0739
SUBWAYS: Christopher Street–Sheridan Square station on the Broadway–
    Seventh Avenue No. 1 and 9 lines.
HOURS: 8 A.M. to 9 P.M. Monday; 8 A.M. to 11 P.M. Tuesday through
    Thursday; 8 A.M. to midnight Friday and Saturday; 8 A.M. to 10 P.M.
    Sunday.
$10 fee for deliveries.
American Express accepted.

Priscilla's ∿ Priscilla Ribero comes from a whole family of cooks. One bite of her apple *kuchen*, a kind of eggy German coffee cake, and I found myself wishing I, too, had grown up a Ribero. Priscilla's makes terrific cinnamon pull-aparts that taste like French toast. Her brioches with Gruyère are cause for celebration, and her sticky buns are very good, if not among the city's best. I found her muffins too healthy tasting, except for the delicious orange-pecan entry. Her cookies, though, are worth a special trip. Her benne wafers are chewy-dense with brown sugar and sesame seeds. Once you've tasted her ginger snaps, you'll never be able to eat the store-bought variety again. Last, her flaky, crusted apple pie is filled with cinnamon and apples. The pumpkin pie, alas, is just another pumpkin pie. Priscilla's also makes sandwiches, salads, and other take-out food, but it's definitely not up to the level of the baked goods.

Priscilla's
35 Jane Street (between Hudson Street and Eighth Avenue)
New York, NY 10014

PHONE: (212) 255-0952
SUBWAYS: 14th Street station on the Eighth Avenue A, C, and E lines; 8th
   Avenue station on the 14th Street–Canarsie L line.
HOURS: 8 A.M. to 8 P.M. Monday through Friday; 9 A.M. to 8 P.M. Saturday;
   closed Sunday.
Local deliveries for individual orders.
Visa and MasterCard accepted.

Taylor's ~ After happening upon Taylor's and being knocked out by its zebra brownies, I called to find out more about the store. "Can you call back in a few minutes? We're jammin'," the man answering the phone explained. All I can say is that if owner Cindy Taylor's recipes are improvised, she's the Charlie Parker of baked goods. Her muffins are full of flavor, reasonably light, and bursting with fresh ingredients. Her chocolate-soufflé cake is airy, studded with walnuts, and quite chocolaty. Her homemade hot dog buns with mustard and onion would make even Perdue chicken franks an inviting lunch. Her perfect praline cookies are an explosion of chocolate, praline, and pecans. In fact, her oversized cookies in general are the best in New York. She also makes the only iced cinnamon bun I've ever really loved, and a bacon-and-cheese biscuit that when heated in the store's microwave becomes a perfect walking lunch. Taylor's soups, sandwiches, and take-out entrées are all quite good but not quite up to the standard of the baked goods.

Taylor's
523 Hudson Street (between 10th and Charles streets)
New York, NY 10014
PHONE: (212) 645-8200
SUBWAYS: Christopher Street–Sheridan Square station on the Broadway–
   Seventh Avenue No. 1 and 9 lines.
HOURS: 6 A.M. to 7 P.M. Monday through Friday; 8 A.M. to 6 P.M. Saturday;
   11 A.M. to 6 P.M. Sunday.
Local deliveries only.
Cash only.

Taylor's Praline Cookies

1½ pounds butter	1 pinch salt
2¼ cups light brown sugar	4 teaspoons baking soda
2¼ cups white sugar	7½ cups flour
1 tablespoon vanilla extract	6 cups chocolate chips
6 eggs	3 cups walnuts (optional)

TOPPING

3 cups of whole pecan halves
Brown sugar
Butter

1. Preheat oven to 350°F. Lightly grease a large baking sheet.
2. In a large bowl and using an electric mixer set on high, cream butter. Add sugars and vanilla and continue beating together until smooth. Stir in eggs.
3. Add salt, soda, and flour to the bowl and stir until well blended.
4. Mix in chocolate chips (and walnuts).
5. Using a small scoop, place balls of dough on prepared baking sheet. Press down lightly on the dough with water-moistened fingers.
6. Top each ball of dough with a pecan half and a pinch of brown sugar, then dot with butter.
7. Bake for 10 to 12 minutes. The sugar and butter should be caramelized and golden brown around the edges.

Yield: 9 dozen cookies
Note: Recipe can be halved for home use.

Taylor's Bacon-Cheese Biscuits

6 cups flour	¾ pounds butter
½ tablespoon baking soda	3 cups buttermilk
1 tablespoon plus ¾ teaspoon baking powder	2 cups shredded cheddar cheese
	1 cup crumbled cooked bacon
1 teaspoon salt	

1. Preheat oven to 450°F.
2. In a large bowl, combine flour, soda, baking powder, and salt. With a pastry blender cut in the butter until mixture resembles coarse crumbs.
3. Add buttermilk to flour mixture and mix lightly with a fork until the

mixture clings together and forms a ball of soft dough. Knead gently 5 or 6 times.

4. With a floured rolling pin, roll the dough to ½-inch thickness. Sprinkle center third of dough with cheese and bacon. Fold the top layer over the bacon and cheese, then fold up the bottom layer.

5. With a floured 2-inch cutter, cut the dough into rounds. Place rounds 1 inch apart on an ungreased baking sheet. Put the dough scraps together, reroll, and cut out more biscuits.

6. Bake for 10 to 12 minutes or until biscuits are light brown.

Yield: 18 biscuits

*E*AST VILLAGE

14TH STREET TO HOUSTON STREET
EAST RIVER TO FIFTH AVENUE

Black Hound ⤳ Most flourless chocolate cakes are superrich, butter-suffused droplets that look like hockey pucks. They're invariably good, but after a few bites you feel like you've swallowed a small car. Black Hound's flourless chocolate cake contains cocoa, chocolate, a little sugar, and lots of eggs. The result is an intensely chocolaty, ethereally light dessert. Serve it with whipped cream and even people who claim they don't like chocolate desserts will walk away from your table happy. Black Hound's cookies are also extraordinary—buttery and highly flavored—and its chocolate truffles are as good as or better than the ones sold at big-name chocolate stores. Black Hound's chocolate-raspberry cake has been written up a few times, but I found it to be dry and not at all up to the store's best efforts.

Black Hound
149 First Avenue (between 9th and 10th streets)
New York, NY 10003
PHONE: (212) 979-9505
SUBWAYS: First Avenue station on the 14th Street–Canarsie L line; Astor
   Place station on the Lexington Avenue No. 6 line.
HOURS: Noon to 7 P.M. Monday through Saturday; closed Sundays; closed
   Saturdays during July; closed entire month of August.
Deliveries in Manhattan with a $50 minimum.

De Robertis Pasticceria ⤳ For nearly nine decades, couples in the East Village have settled their differences over fig tarts and espresso at the nifty little booths at the back of this incredibly friendly Italian bakeshop. The fig tarts are what a Fig Newton should taste like. The pignoli cookies are a superior version of that Italian cookie standard. The chocolate-covered canollis have crisp shells and very smooth filling. The strawberry shortcake is only passable, but as New York isn't much of a strawberry shortcake town, it will definitely do if you're in the neighborhood.

De Robertis Pasticceria
176 First Avenue (between 10th and 11th streets)
New York, NY 10003
PHONE: (212) 674-7137
SUBWAYS: First Avenue station on the 14th Street–Canarsie L line; Astor
   Place Station on the Lexington Avenue No. 6 line.
HOURS: 9 A.M. to 11 P.M. Sunday through Thursday; 9 A.M. to Midnight
   Friday and Saturday.
Deliveries in the immediate neighborhood.
Cash only.

Encore Patisserie ~~ The Encore Patisserie's chocolate-truffle cake has just the right ratio of intense bittersweet chocolate icing, chocolate mousse, and sponge cake; that is, it's 25 percent frosting, 60 percent mousse, and 15 percent cake. So the fact that the sponge-cake portion is dry doesn't ruin the cake. Encore also makes a first-class key-lime tart that is as tart as a dessert can be, and a pesto-mozzarella bread that tastes much better than it looks. The exotic-sounding Polish donuts turn out to be the standard jelly variety, so maybe that's where jelly donuts came from.

Encore Patisserie
141 Second Avenue (between 8th and 9th streets)
New York, NY 10003
PHONE: (212) 505-1188
SUBWAY: Astor Place station on the Lexington Avenue No. 6 line.
HOURS: 7 A.M. to 9 P.M. Monday through Saturday; 8 A.M. to 6:30 P.M.
   Sunday.
Deliveries in the neighborhood.
Cash only.

Veniero Pasticceria ~~ In general, Italian pastries and cookies leave me cold. But this venerable New York institution makes a ricotta cheesecake so sublime one can easily imagine mobsters from competing crime families declaring Veniero's a demilitarized zone. It sells the light and lemony cheesecake in rectangular slabs by the pound to go or by the piece to stay along with a cappuccino or espresso. In the summer, Veniero's serves up flavorful homemade Italian ices. Its gelati, however, are nothing special. The rest of the cakes and cookies are pretty standard too—heavy, old-style Italian fare.

Veniero Pasticceria
342 East 11th Street (between First and Second avenues)
New York, NY 10003
PHONE: (212) 674-7264 or (212) 674-4415
SUBWAYS: First Avenue station on the 14th Street–Canarsie L line; Astor
   Place Station on the Lexington Avenue No. 6 line.
HOURS: 8 A.M. to midnight seven days a week.
Delivery available.
No credit cards.

Downtown

HOUSTON STREET TO BATTERY PARK

Barocco Alimentari ~ See page 311.

Caffè Roma ~ Whenever friends from out-of-town ask me where to go for cappuccino and Italian pastries in Little Italy, I steer them to Caffè Roma. Since the turn of the century, Caffè Roma has been serving crunchy cannolis, Italian cheesecake, and strong espresso and cappuccino. With its green-painted tin ceilings and its old-fashioned pastry cases, Caffè Roma will have you thinking you're an extra in a Martin Scorcese film. The *biscotti* are pretty dry, but they taste great dipped in espresso or cappuccino. The lemon ices are just tart enough, and the Sambuca ice will get you tipsy if you eat more than one.

Caffè Roma
385 Broome Street (between Mulberry and Mott streets)
New York, NY 10012
PHONE: (212) 226-8413
SUBWAYS: Spring Street station on the Lexington Avenue No. 6 line; Grand
    Street station on the Sixth Avenue B, D, and Q lines.
HOURS: 8 A.M. to midnight every day.
No deliveries.
No credit cards.

The Cleaver Company ~ It was a colleague who sent me on an exploratory trip to The Cleaver Company. She said she'd never been inside but that everything looked good and there was always a line. After sampling its individual pear-currant tart with a brown-sugar crumb topping, I'm ready to queue up with everybody else; pear and currant turn out to be perfectly complementary flavors. Try Cleaver's sticky buns, too. Filled with cinnamon and pecans, these rich but not too sweet creations deserve consideration in the New York City Sticky Bun Contest. Cleaver's triangular scones are also extraordinary, moist, full of flavor, and, unlike the snowball-sized scones sold in many other places in the city, actually light. However, the chocolate-lemon yogurt pound cake is a misbegotten combination of flavors, and the fruit in the apple-cherry-blueberry minipie was too finely chopped for my taste.

The Cleaver Company
229 West Broadway (corner of White Street)
New York, NY 10013
PHONE: (212) 431-3688
SUBWAYS: Franklin Street station on the Broadway–Seventh Avenue No. 1
    and 9 lines.
HOURS: 8 A.M. to 5:30 P.M. Monday through Friday; closed Saturday and
    Sunday.
Deliveries free in the neighborhood.
No credit cards.
Mail order available.

Dean & DeLuca ~ See page 214.

Eileen's Special Cheesecake ~ Eileen's Special Cheesecake represents the ultimate in genetic engineering; it's the happy result of an Italian man and a Jewish woman who met, fell in love, married, and exchanged cheesecake recipes. This culinary joining created phenomenally light cream cheesecake with a graham-cracker crust. Eileen's makes thirteen flavors, including such exotica as butter pecan and amaretto. The chocolate lacked real chocolaty flavor, and the blueberry and cherry cheesecakes are made with preserves instead of fresh fruit, but cheese-cake afficionados know a great cheesecake is meant to be eaten plain and un-adorned. Though cheesecake is the store's reason for being, Eileen's has gradually expanded into other baked goods. Her Granny Smith apple pie is quite good, if not up to the city's best.

Eileen's Special Cheesecake
17 Cleveland Place (corner of Kenmare Street)
New York, NY 10012
PHONE: (212) 966-5585
SUBWAY: Spring Street station on the Lexington Avenue No. 6 line.
HOURS: 8 A.M. to 7 P.M. Monday, Wednesday, and Friday; 8 A.M. to 6 P.M.
    Tuesday and Thursday; 10 A.M. to 6 P.M. Saturday and Sunday.
$5 charge for delivery in Manhattan on a $10 minimum order.
Visa and MasterCard accepted.
Mail order available.
Will ship via Federal Express anywhere in the U.S.A.

Ferrara's ~ To some people Ferrara's is the quintessential Little Italy pastry and espresso place. To me it's an overpriced, excessively glitzy joint, with a few decent pastries and substandard gelati and Italian ices. Ferrara's *biscotti* are acceptable, but they pale in comparison to the ones made at Ecce Panis. The regular and chocolate-covered cannolis are okay, but sometimes they're soggy. My two favorite pastries here are the Croccante, a chocolate-nut roll filled with chocolate custard, and the Parigina, a hazelnut-cream-filled ladyfinger dipped in French chocolate. The lemon ices taste like unmixed frozen lemonade, and I failed to detect much chocolate flavor in the chocolate gelato.

Ferrara's
195 Mulberry Street (between Mulberry and Mott streets)
New York, NY 10012
PHONE: (212) 226-6150
SUBWAYS: Spring Street station on the Lexington Avenue No. 6 line; Grand
    Street station on the Sixth Avenue B, D, and Q lines.
HOURS: 7 A.M. to midnight Sunday through Thursday; 7 A.M. to 1 A.M.
    Fridays and Saturdays.
Deliveries made throughout the five boroughs.
All major credit cards accepted for table service only.
Mail-order catalog available.

Houghtaling Mousse Pie Ltd. ⁓ There's chocolate mousse, that humdrum dessert served at every French restaurant, and then there's Sue Houghtaling's chocolate mousse, which is so rich, light, and flavorful that eating it is truly a sensuous experience. She puts her mousse into ten varieties of mousse pies and sells it frozen in purple cardboard containers, calling it "Loose Moose." Sue Houghtaling also makes six kinds of truffle cake, a sinful hybrid of cake and mousse. Her chocolate creations, with their incomparable chocolate-and-ground-nut crusts, are extraordinary. Her fruit and nut desserts, like her lemon-mousse and hazelnut-mousse pies, are also very good, although I wish the fruit flavoring were more vivid.

Note: "Loose Moose" can also be found at Dean & DeLuca.

Houghtaling Mousse Pie Ltd.
235 Mulberry Street (between Prince and Spring streets)
New York, NY 10012
PHONE: (212) 226-3724
SUBWAY: Spring Street station on the Lexington Avenue No. 6 line.
HOURS: 9:30 A.M. to 6 P.M. Monday through Friday; open Saturdays before
    major holidays; closed Sunday.
Deliveries are made on Monday, Wednesday, and Friday with a $20
    minimum order.
Cash and personal checks only.
Mail order available.

ℬRONX

Madonia Brothers ⁓ See page 134.

ℬROOKLYN

Faith's Bakery ⁓ Greenmarket manager Joel Petraker was the first person to tip me to Faith's. I resisted the long trip to Park Slope, however, until I found out that half the baked goods I like at Dean & Deluca came from Faith's. I was now looking for an opportunity to go, and it came when my family was invited to a friend's wedding reception at the Ethical Culture Society in Park Slope. I struck up a conversation with someone from the area who started rhapsodizing about Faith's and informed me it was ten blocks away from where we were. I grabbed my son, persuaded my wife's brother and his girlfriend to give us a ride, and off we went. Faith's turns out to be a tiny, immaculate sliver of a store. I knew I was in the right place when I saw Faith's miraculous fruit tarts, each with chunks of fresh fruit, a very thin layer of pastry cream, and—this is what makes them extraordinary—a layer of hazelnut *génoise* (a moist sponge cake). I spotted four other confections I'd sampled and swooned over at D & D: a tart cream-lime pie, a silky tart made with enough chocolate mousse to drown a bison, an ethereal coconut angel food cake, and a slablike chocolate-soufflé cake. I scoured the pastry case for a couple of items I hadn't tried at Dean & Deluca's. The deep-dish strawberry-rhubarb pie had loads of fresh strawberries and tart rhubarb, a tasty streusel top, and an okay if not great crust. The raspberry-pear tart had big chunks of pears, swirls of fresh raspberry, and an extremely buttery crust. My son's chocolate-chip cookie was nothing to write home about, and neither was a banana–chocolate-chip muffin. I left vowing to come back and try one of Faith's cheesecakes.

Faith's Bakery
1112 Eighth Avenue (between 11th and 12th streets)
Brooklyn, NY 11215
PHONE: (718) 499-8108
SUBWAY: Seventh Avenue–Park Slope station on the Sixth Avenue F line.
HOURS: 8 A.M. to 7 P.M. Tuesday through Friday; 9 A.M. to 6 P.M. Saturday;
   closed Monday.
No deliveries.
Cash and personal checks only.

Junior's Restaurant --- Almost twenty years ago, when I first came to New York, I thought nothing of getting into my car, making the forty-five-minute trek from my Upper West Side apartment to Junior's, eating a slice of their cheesecake, and coming back. Although I no longer have the time to make that pilgrimage on a regular basis, a recent visit to Junior's told me that the cheesecake is still re-markable enough to warrant such excursions. Junior's cheesecake is so unbe-lievably rich and heavy that it positively oozes cream cheese in the center. It has only enough crust to keep its shape. Junior's makes ten kinds of cheesecake, from praline to pineapple, but serious Junior's devotees know that the plain cheesecake is the way to go. I know Junior's has other baked goods, but I don't know anyone who's ever tasted them. Junior's restaurant food is fairly standard Jewish deli fare, with its chief advantage being its late hours.

Note: Junior's now ships its cheesecakes all over the country, even to Manhattan.

Junior's Restaurant
386 Flatbush Avenue Extension (corner DeKalb Avenue)
Brooklyn, NY 11201
PHONE: (718) 852-5257
SUBWAYS: DeKalb Avenue station on the Broadway R and Sixth Avenue D
   lines.
HOURS: 6:30 A.M. to 1 A.M. Saturday through Thursday; 6:30 A.M. to 3 A.M.
   Friday.
Deliveries for catering only.
All major credit cards accepted.
Mail order available.

Leske's --- I've found that one sure sign of a bakery's quality is the size of the line at the counter on weekdays. The Friday I went to Leske's there was a line out the door. What everyone was patiently waiting for were the Scandinavian baked goods the store has been making for nearly six decades. These include white mountain bread, a traditional white bread dusted with flour, which tastes wonderful in sandwiches or as toast; limpa, a rye bread made with molasses and raisins; and Danish that would be eligible for the Danish pantheon if it weren't for their too-sweet white frosting. (There should be a law prohibiting the use of white frosting on Danish.) Leske's is one of those places I pray won't change no matter how small the Scandinavian community becomes in Bay Ridge.

Leske's
7612 Fifth Avenue (between 76th and 77th streets)
Brooklyn, NY 11220
PHONE: (718) 680-2323
SUBWAY: 77th Street station on the Broadway R line.
HOURS: 6 A.M. to 6:30 P.M. Tuesday through Friday; 6 A.M. to 6 P.M.
   Saturday; 6 A.M. to 3 P.M. Sunday; closed Monday.
No deliveries.
No credit cards.

Best of Baked Goods

Best angel food cake: Faith's Bakery; Yura
Best apple cobbler: Yura
Best apple pie: Taylor's; Priscilla's
Best apple-crumb pie: Cupcake Café
Best apple turnover: G & M Pastries
Best babka: none
Best banana-cream pie: Sarabeth's Kitchen
Best bran muffin: Royale Pastry Shop
Best brownies: Sarabeth's Kitchen; Corrado Kitchen; Patisserie Les Friandises
Best sour-cherry pie: William Greenberg Jr. Desserts
Best cheesecake (all-around): Eileen's Special Cheesecake
Best cheesecake (Italian): Veniero Pasticceria
Best cheesecake (Jewish): Junior's Restaurant
Best chocolate-soufflé cake: Taylor's
Best chocolate cake (specialty): Soutine's chocolate concorde
Best chocolate-chip cookie: Taylor's
Best coconut-banana-cream pie: The Little Pie Company
Best coffee cake: Neuman & Bogdanoff; Cupcake Café
Best cookies (oversized): Taylor's
Best cookies (small): William Greenberg Jr. Desserts
Best corn muffin: Royale Pastry Shop
Best crumb buns: Hahn's (available at Bloomingdale's, Canard and Company, and Fairway)
Best Dacquoise: Gindi Café
Best Danish (cheese): Budapest Pastry
Best Danish (fruit): Colette; William Greenberg Jr. Desserts; Bonté Patisserie

Best of Baked Goods, continued

Best doughnuts: Georgie's Pastry Shop
Best eclairs: Bonté Patisserie; G & M Pastries
Best fruit tarts: Faith's Bakery
Best individual tarts and cakes: The City Bakery
Best-looking cake that also tastes incredible: Choco Rem's black-and-white
    loaf; La Boulange's trio cake
Best ice-cream cake: Grossinger's Bakery
Best Key lime pie: The Little Pie Company; Faith's Bakery
Best marble pound cake: G & M Pastries
Best muffins (over all): Taylor's; Yura
Best occasion cakes: Cupcake Café
Best pecan ring: Dumas
Best pumpkin pie: Better Crust Bakery
Best rugelach: Zabar's
Best *schnecken* (small pecan-raisin sticky buns): William Greenberg Jr.
    Desserts
Best specialty cake: Guy Pascal's Délice cake
Best sticky bun: Sarabeth's Kitchen
Best strawberry shortcake: Taylor's; William Greenberg Jr. Desserts
Best (and only good) sugarless dessert I've ever had: Sugarless apple pie from
    The Bakery in Mamaroneck (sold at Todaro Brothers)
Best sweet-potato pie: Better Crust Bakery
Best *tarte tatin*: Patisserie Les Friandises

3

BREAD

B uying a great bread is perhaps the easiest and least expensive way to make any meal a treat. Even the most expensive breads to be had in New York cost less than fifteen dollars. A three-dollar focaccia makes an exciting two-person lunch when topped with fresh mozzarella cheese.

There are two kinds of terrific bread bakers in New York: first, the traditional Italian and Jewish bakers, like Morrone's and Orwasher's, that make bread in brick ovens the way their parents and grandparents did around the turn of the century; and, second, the Eli Zabars of the world, who became obsessed with bread fairly recently and experimented with doughs and ovens until they were absolutely satisfied with their products.

Ask Eli Zabar, who makes Eli's breads, or Noel Comess of Tom Cat Bakery a question about bread and be prepared for an answer suffused with love and reverence for the sanctity of bread baking. Serious bread bakers are students of yeasts and oven temperatures and starter dough. Because most great bread bakers make up their dough every morning, experienced bread mavens can sometimes detect subtle differences in a baker's breads from day to day. This is especially true of sourdough bread.

There is no excuse for not eating superior bread in New York, where lucky New Yorkers reap the benefits of a score of first-rate bread bakers that distribute their loaves and rolls to hundreds of delis and gourmet markets. Eli Zabar's baguettes and rolls are available at Zabar's, Grace's Marketplace, Nature's Gifts, and dozens of other stores. Hoboken's trio of Italian bakeries, Antique, Dom's, and Marie's (all descendents of the Policastro family), sell their bread to Bruno the King of Ravioli, Dean & Deluca, The Silver Palate, and LaMarca, among others. Stores like Dean & Deluca and Fairway have constantly expanding bread selections that make each store visit a bread adventure.

But in spite of the wide distribution of superb bread in the city, there is nothing like entering one of New York's classic ethnic bakeries like Morrone's or Orwasher's and being enveloped in that wonderful fresh bread smell.

*E*AST HARLEM

ABOVE 96TH STREET
FIRST AVENUE TO FIFTH AVENUE

La Tropézienne — Tropézienne makes perhaps my favorite old-fashioned French baguette in the city. It's crisp, light, and full of flavor. The fact that you have to travel to East Harlem to buy one may deter some people, but not me—because if you get there early enough, you can snare one of owner Roger Bransol's first-rate croissants fresh from the oven. If they're out of plain croissants, you'll have to settle for a croissant filled with cream cheese, which is essentially one of the city's lightest and best cheese Danish. And if you're feeling truly wicked you can get a Tropézienne, a triangular wedge of extraordinarily light cake filled with a frothy, sweet egg custard. If you're on your way out of town via the Triboro Bridge, La Tropézienne is the perfect pit stop.

La Tropézienne
2131 First Avenue (between 109th and 110th streets)
New York, NY 10029
PHONE: (212) 860-5324
SUBWAY: 110th Street station on the Lexington Avenue No. 6 line.
HOURS: 6 A.M. to 5 P.M. Tuesday through Friday; 6 A.M. to 4 P.M. Saturday;
    6:30 A.M. to 1 P.M. Sunday.
No deliveries.
Cash only.

Morrone & Sons Bakery — You're headed to Long Island to visit friends or in-laws, you're wisely taking the Triboro Bridge to avoid Midtown Tunnel gridlock,

Exquisite, hearty breads at Morrone & Sons Bakery.

and then you realize in a panic that you're going to arrive empty-handed. Don't worry. Stop at Morrone's for some of the best bread in New York. In their seventy-year-old brick ovens, the Morrone family make not only great Italian white, whole wheat, and semolina loaves in every shape imaginable but also terrific sandwich-sized baguettes and the city's best onion rolls. Morrone's prosciutto bread, filled with prosciutto, salami, and cheese, is out of this world, a meal in itself. One stop at Morrone's, and you won't even mind dinner with the in-laws.

Note: You must go early if you want the onion rolls here. The last time I went they were sold out by 11:00 A.M.

Morrone & Sons Bakery
324 East 116th Street (between First and Second avenues)
New York, NY 10029
PHONE: (212) 722-2972
SUBWAY: 116th Street station on the Lexington Avenue No. 6 line.
HOURS: 6 A.M. to 6 P.M. Tuesday through Sunday; closed Monday.
No deliveries.
Cash only.

𝒰PPER WEST SIDE

59TH STREET TO 125TH STREET
CENTRAL PARK WEST TO RIVERSIDE DRIVE

Bagels on Second ⁓ See page 48.

Columbia Hot Bagels ~ I was about to give up. I had searched high and low for a truly great bagel and had come up empty. H & H's are too heavy and sweet (and expensive), Bagels on the Square are very good but far from perfect, and Bagels on Second are hand rolled but just too big. Shortly before finishing this book, I happened to buy a couple of absolutely wonderful bagels at Murray's Sturgeon Shop. I knew that Arthur Cutler, the former owner of Murray's, owned Columbia Hot Bagels, so I set out one Sunday morning with my son (a reliable bagel tester if there ever was one), and went up to Columbia Bagels. I ordered a dozen assorted, and as soon as we left the store, we started taking bites out of each one. It was bagel heaven. These were perfect bagels, chewy but not too hard, flavorful without being too sweet (they're made with barley malt instead of sugar), and not big enough to double as an inner tube. The rye bagels were a revelation, the cinnamon-raisin had plenty of plump raisins and a strong cinnamon flavor, and the egg bagels were light and yet still strongly textured. We made our way down to the bottom of the bag. The salt bagels had just enough salt, the onion had plenty of crunchy onions, and the sesame and poppy were excellent. Finally, my search for the quintessential bagel in the bagel capital of the world had ended.

Note: Even though the bagels here are normally machine made, hand-rolled bagels are available on request at no extra charge. The only other retail outlet for Columbia Hot Bagels, besides Murray's, is Zabar's.

Columbia Hot Bagels
2836 Broadway (between 110th and 111th streets)
New York, NY 10025
PHONE: (212) 222-3200
SUBWAYS: 110th Street–Cathedral Parkway station on the Broadway–
   Seventh Avenue No. 1 and 9 lines.
HOURS: Twenty-four hours a day, seven days a week.
Cash only.

Fairway ~ See page 221.

H & H Bagels ~ The founder of H & H Bagels should be given a MacArthur Foundation Genius Award for opening up his first bagel store across the street from Zabar's, merely the leading smoked fish retail store in America. Like zombies, people walk out of Zabar's, arms laden with shopping bags, and head to H & H. To complete the ritual, they then rip off a piece of one of the hot bagels they just bought and munch on it as they walk down Broadway. Yet as someone who's completed that ritual hundreds of times over the last twenty years I have to say that H & H Bagels ain't that great. Yes, they're invariably hot and fresh, but they have so little crunch and so much air in them that I hear a whooshing sound every time I take a bite. I also find the dough to be too sweet, not just in the cinnamon-raisin bagels, but also in the plain, sesame, poppy, even the onion bagels. In fact, my favorite H & H bagel these days is the sourdough variety because it's not as sweet as the others.

Note: I find H & H's prices to be unconscionable. Their current 65-cent price is almost double that of most competitors. Also, H & H Bagels East is unrelated to the West Side store. The East's bagels are mediocre and characterless.

H & H Bagels
2239 Broadway (corner of 80th Street)
New York, NY 10024
PHONE: (212) 595-8000
SUBWAYS: 79th Street station on the Broadway–Seventh Avenue No. 1 and 9
    lines; 81st Street station on the Eighth Avenue C and Sixth Avenue B
    lines.
HOURS: Twenty-four hours a day, seven days a week.
Deliveries on orders of ten dozen or more.
Cash only.
Mail order available by calling 1 (800) NYBAGEL.

Pâtisserie Les Friandises ⁓ See page 16.

Original Royale Pastry Shop ⁓ See page 17.

Sarabeth's Kitchen ⁓ See page 18.

The Silver Palate ⁓ See page 297.

Soutine ⁓ See page 18.

Zabar's ⁓ See page 237.

𝒰PPER EAST SIDE

59TH STREET TO 96TH STREET
FIRST AVENUE TO FIFTH AVENUE

Bagelry ⁓ The book was put to bed, no more last minute entries allowed, when I met someone at a party who told me that his brother-in-law, a bagel purist had just opened a bagel store in Manhattan. Since he and his wife seemed to be as food-obsessed as I am, I excused myself from the gathering and found my way to Bagelry. Bagelry's bagels were terrific, crunchy on the outside, chewy on the inside, not pumped up with air, and small enough to fit into the palm of your hand. In fact, these bagels were the best I found in the city, the equal of Columbia Hot Bagels (and a little smaller to boot). In fact, just like Columbia Hot Bagels, Bagelry uses malt instead of sugar in its recipe. It's heartening to know that someone is still interested in making bagels the old-fashioned way. Besides the world-class bagels and bialys, Bagelry also carries high-quality smoked fish from Duck Trap River Farms in Maine.

Bagelry
1324 Lexington Avenue (between 88th and 89th streets)
New York, N.Y. 10128
PHONE: (212) 996-0567
SUBWAY: 86th Street on the Lexington Avenue No. 4, 5 and 6 lines.
HOURS: 6:30 A.M. to 7 P.M. seven days a week.
Free delivery in the neighborhood.
Cash only.
Mail order available by calling 800-43-BAGEL.

Bagels on Second ⋙ Bagel elephantiasis has shown itself to be a continuing problem on the New York foodscape. But Bagels on Second's giganto bagels are actually chewy and flavorful. They're handmade, so sometimes they're slightly misshapen. (I happen to like slightly misshapen food, because at least then I know a person and not a machine made it.) Bagels on Second makes the standard variety of bagels: plain, poppy, sesame, onion, garlic, salt, whole-wheat, and cinnamon-raisin. They also make a kitchen-sink bagel they call the everything bagel, which never should have made it out of their test oven. Bagels on Second also sells just about anything anyone's thought to put on a bagel, from Black Forest ham to Genoa salami to the more standard items like whitefish salad and smoked salmon.

Bagels on Second
1475 Second Avenue (between 76th and 77th streets)
New York, NY 10021
PHONE: (212) 794-2850
SUBWAY: 77th Street station on the Lexington Avenue No. 6 line.
HOURS: 7 A.M. to 9 P.M. Monday through Friday; 7 A.M. to 8 P.M. Saturday; 7
   A.M. to 6 P.M. Sunday.
Free delivery.
All major credit cards accepted.
Platters and catering available.

OTHER LOCATION:
Bagels on Second
2170 Broadway (between 76th and 77th streets)
New York, NY 10023
PHONE: (212) 595-7549

Bloomingdale's ⋙ See page 212.

Bonté Patisserie ⋙ See page 20.

Canard and Company ⋙ See page 299.

Colette ⋙ See page 22.

Ecce Panis, perhaps the finest bread store in all of New York.

E.A.T. ⁓ See page 300.

Ecce Panis ⁓ See below.

Ecce Panis

There are certain food stores in New York that are so good they force me to expand my idea of just what constitutes a New York neighborhood. Ecce Panis, the jewel of a bread bakery at 65th Street and Third Avenue, is one of them. This neighborhood expansion takes the following form: It's a Saturday afternoon, and my wife and I have taken our son, William, to visit her aunt and uncle at 92nd Street and Fifth Avenue. As we're hailing a cab to take us home, I say, "Hey, Ecce Panis is right in the neighborhood; let's stop and get some bread on the way home."

Ecce Panis opened in February 1989 under the same ownership as the restaurants Sign of the Dove, Contrapunto, Arizona 206, and Yellowfingers. Those restaurants are the only places you can obtain this exceptional bread outside of the store itself. To call the incredible loaves that come out of Ecce Panis's ovens "bread" is like calling Michelangelo's Sistine Chapel ceiling an illustration. The sweet focaccia, studded with sour cherries and raisins, is

Ecce Panis, continued

irresistible. The onion loaves and sun-dried-tomato loaves are short, oblong focaccia-type creations that have whole sun-dried tomatoes and strands of onion on top. They're so good they make a meal by themselves. The "regular" sourdough and the sourdough rye are great soup or sandwich breads. The chocolate bread, made only on Fridays and Saturdays, is a round chocolate-brown sourdough bread made with lots of bittersweet chocolate. It makes extraordinary French toast. Ecce Panis also makes four kinds of biscotti—pistachio-almond, chocolate–macadamia nut, bourbon-pecan, and chocolate-hazelnut—that are so good they've turned me around about that mundane form of cookie. And, in one of the most insidious yet delightful marketing schemes ever, Ecce Panis puts out baskets of bite-sized chunks of all the breads they're selling on a given day.

The baker responsible for this bread nirvana is Paula Oland, an attractive, self-effacing Canadian who became interested in bread while attending art school in Los Angeles. She says she "likes the integrity of bread baking. Plus, the moment you think it's simple, it gets complicated. Because when you bake bread, you're playing with the weather, you're playing with something wild."

According to Oland, the bread-baking process she employs at Ecce Panis is not that complicated. It is certainly painstaking and time consuming. An Ecce Panis loaf has its genesis in what's called starter, the leavening mixture that makes bread rise and gives it bite. The next step is to create a sponge, a combination of yeast, flour, salt, water, and whatever else goes into a particular bread. This sponge sits and ferments for up to twelve hours. Then the dough is made and aged for ten to twelve hours. The individual loaves are weighed out and shaped by hand and then retarded, so that the dough doesn't rise prematurely. Finally, the breads are baked in stone-hearth ovens at 450° F for forty minutes. This twenty-four- to thirty-six-hour process generates a very low yield of a maximum of twelve hundred loaves a day. A typical state-of-the-art commercial bakery bakes half a million loaves a day.

What separates Ecce Panis bread from most other breads in the city is the depth of flavor Oland achieves. You taste one thing in a loaf of her bread, and then a split second later you taste something else. What gives Ecce Panis bread its flavor depth? According to Oland it's very simple. "Time," she says, "is equivalent to flavor in breads."

Ecce Panis
1120 Third Avenue (between 65th and 66th streets)
New York, NY 10021
PHONE: (212) 535-2099
SUBWAY: 68th Street–Hunter College station on the Lexington Avenue No.
   6 line.
HOURS: 10 A.M. to 7 P.M. Monday through Friday; 10 A.M. to 6 P.M. Saturday
   and Sunday.
Cash only.

Tips on Making a Natural Starter, from Ecce Panis

Bread made with natural starter has a more complex, wheaty flavor than bread made with commercial yeasts. It also has superior keeping qualities.

Starter is essentially a flour-and-water mixture that attracts and grows *airborne* yeast cells. It will, with nothing else added and fed daily with fresh unbleached bread flour and water, develop into a bubbling starter within a week or two if left out in the open. The flavor of a starter can be enhanced by adding a few pieces of unwashed and untreated, that is, organic, fruit to the flour-and-water mixture. (Grapes and organic raisins work especially well for this purpose.) The natural yeast cells present on the fruit will feed on the flour in the water and reproduce.

Initially, you will probably want to use spring water because, depending on where you live, the chemicals in your tap water could destroy the fragile young yeast cells. The ratio of flour to water need not be exact, but a good starting proportion would be 1 part water to 1 part flour. By and by, your starter will become stronger and you may want to experiment with using local water. If it becomes less active with regular use, switch water sources. A healthy starter at room temperature will have a clean, tangy smell—more like wine than beer. It should be somewhat light with bubbles. If the smell is overwhelming and the starter heavy and lifeless, dump most of it and refresh it with lots of new flour and water. It should be in much better shape in six to eight hours. If not, feed again.

It is really difficult to kill all those yeast cells unless you leave the starter unattended for weeks at a time. By the way, if you do leave it, keep it refrigerated for more stability.

Paula Oland's Sourdough Crumpets

The starter in these crumpets gives them a slightly sour flavor that contrasts nicely with breakfast accompaniments such as sweet butter and maple syrup. The honeycomb surface of the crumpets is perfect for holding these sweet toppings.

1 tablespoon fresh yeast (or 1
   package dry yeast)
2 tablespoons lukewarm water
1 cup unbleached all-purpose flour
1 cup unbleached pastry flour
1/3 cup sourdough starter

1/3 cup yogurt
2/3 cup cold water
3/4 teaspoon salt
1/2 teaspoon baking soda activated in 2
   tablespoons hot water

1. Dissolve yeast in the lukewarm water.
2. Put the flour in a bowl and add yeast mixture, starter, yogurt, and cold water. Beat with a wooden spoon for a few minutes to develop the gluten. Add salt and mix well. Cover and allow the batter to rise until it falls when agitated. This could take 2 to 3 hours.
3. Add activated baking soda. Stir to combine and allow to rise for 30 to 45 minutes.
4. Crumpets are cooked slowly on a heavy griddle greased with butter. The batter can be poured into round cookie cutters or rings such as those used for English muffins, or they can be poured free-form onto the griddle as thin pancakes. For either method, heat a heavy griddle and grease it with butter. If you use a cookie cutter or rings, grease those, too, and pour batter into them to a depth of 3/8 inch. Cook slowly for 5 minutes and turn to brown lightly on the other side. Wrap when cool. Toast before serving.

Yield: Approximately 12 crumpets

Fraser-Morris ⬧ See page 301.

Glendale Bake Shop ⬧ When I was a kid, my family used to go to a neighborhood delicatessen, Wilshire's, for dinner every other Sunday night. Wilshire's pastrami and corned beef were just fine, but what I most remember about the place were the incredible pretzel rolls they served with the meal. My parents were constantly admonishing me not to fill up on them. Having lost all hope of finding a new source for these memorable oblong miniloaves, I was delighted when I walked past the Glendale Bake Shop and saw pretzel rolls being sold. Glendale's pretzel rolls are New York's finest—the best and lightest soft pretzel you've ever tasted.

You'll find every baked good imaginable at the Glendale Bake Shop, from cheesecake to chocolate layer cake to rye bread. They even make their own bagels, highly unusual in this day and age. But it's all pretty standard stuff other than those pretzel rolls.

Glendale Bake Shop
1290 Lexington Avenue (corner of 87th Street)
New York, NY 10128
PHONE: (212) 410-5959
SUBWAYS: 86th Street station on the Lexington Avenue No. 4, 5, and 6 lines.
HOURS: 6 A.M. to 8 P.M. Monday through Saturday; 6 A.M. to 4 P.M. Sunday.
Deliveries in the neighborhood.
Cash only.

OTHER LOCATION:
1319 First Avenue (corner of 71st Street)
New York, NY 10021
(212) 861-2300

Grace's Marketplace ⏤ See page 225.

Orwasher's Bakery ⏤ In the late 1970s I had a job I absolutely despised except that each day it took me to East 78th Street, near Orwasher's Bakery. In its old-fashioned brick ovens, Orwasher's makes bread by hand, the same way they've been making it there for seventy-six years. Although pumpernickel-raisin bread has become a cliché in New York, Orwasher's version, with just the right number

Abram Orwasher shows off the bread ovens of Orwasher's Bakery.

of raisins and the proper chewy texture, still sets the standard. Louis Orwasher and his son Abram also turn out a cinnamon-raisin bread perfect for making French toast, and a first-class Irish soda bread among the thirty kinds of bread and rolls they sell daily.

Warning: For some misguided reason, Orwasher's has taken to slicing its bread and putting it in unperforated plastic bags. This destroys the texture of the bread, so ask them to put your unsliced bread in a paper bag. There's a reason the French guys in the movies all carry their bread unadorned under their arms. It's the best way to maintain a bread's texture.

Orwasher's Bakery
308 East 78th Street (between First and Second avenues)
New York, NY 10021
PHONE: (212) 288-6569
SUBWAY: 77th Street Station on the Lexington Avenue No. 6 line.
HOURS: 7 A.M. to 7 P.M. Monday through Saturday; closed Sunday.
No deliveries.
Cash only.

ℳIDTOWN WEST

34TH STREET TO 59TH STREET
FIFTH AVENUE TO ELEVENTH AVENUE

A La Russe — See page 121.

Golden Brioche — Before I discovered Golden Brioche, I regarded the brioche as an inferior, bodyless form of French bread to be eaten only when a high-quality croissant wasn't available. But the brioches at Golden Brioche are light, buttery confections that have plenty of flavor and texture. Although the plain brioches here are good enough to stand on their own, I prefer the apple and cinnamon varieties, which have enough of their distinguishing flavors without overwhelming the bread itself. In total the store makes nine kinds of brioches in many shapes and sizes, plus an exceptional, eggy bread-pudding tart. The ham-and-cheese brioche makes a satisfying light lunch, though I admit I've never really understood the concept of a light lunch.

Golden Brioche
1333 Broadway (corner of 36th Street)
New York, NY 10036
PHONE: (212) 629-5544
SUBWAYS: 34th Street station on the Broadway N and R and Sixth Avenue B,
    D, F, and Q lines; 34th Street–Penn Station on the Broadway–Seventh
    Avenue No. 1, 2, 3, and 9 lines.
HOURS: 7:30 A.M. to 7 P.M. Monday through Friday; 10 A.M. to 6:30 P.M.
    Saturday; 10 A.M. to 6 P.M. Sunday.
No deliveries.
Cash only.

57th Street Greenmarket ⸺ See page 275.

Macy's Cellar Marketplace ⸺ See page 229.

$\mathscr{M}$IDTOWN EAST

34TH STREET TO 59TH STREET
FIRST AVENUE TO FIFTH AVENUE

Chez Laurence ⸺ My friends Dale and Peter refer to Chez Laurence as Larry's, because the owner, Lawrence Rosen, is really just Larry from Great Neck, Long Island. It's his wife, Anna, who's French, and she is the one responsible for the delectable croissants and brioches at Chez Laurence. Her croissants are the genuine article—slightly crisp, golden brown, buttery without being soggy, and not so big that you feel bloated after eating one. Her brioches are just about as good, eggy without being heavy. The same brioche dough is used to make the bread that forms the foundation of two excellent sandwiches: tuna salad, which my wife claims is the best in New York (she's never been to Eisenberg's); and mackerel salad with grated carrots, which is so tasty you forget it's mackerel. Chez Laurence's *pains au chocolat* have just the right amount of bittersweet chocolate in them. That means just when you're wondering where that intense chocolate bite is, it arrives. If it had any more chocolate in it, it wouldn't be a suitable breakfast food. Chez Laurence's chocolate- and fruit-based pastries are just fine, but it's the croissants, brioches, and *pains au chocolat* that make the place special.

Chez Laurence
245 Madison Avenue (southeast corner of 38th Street)
New York, NY 10016
PHONE: (212) 683-0284
SUBWAYS: 42nd Street–Grand Central on the following lines: Lexington
    Avenue No. 4, 5, and 6; Flushing No. 7; 42nd Street Shuttle.
HOURS: 7 A.M. to 6:30 P.M. Monday through Friday; closed Saturday and
    Sunday.
No deliveries.
Cash only.

La Boulange ⸺ See page 29.

$\mathscr{K}$IPS BAY/GRAMERCY PARK

14TH STREET TO 34TH STREET
EAST RIVER TO FIFTH AVENUE

The City Bakery ⸺ See page 30.

Ess-A-Bagel ∽ When I was complaining to my friend Karen about the sorry state of bagels in New York, she referred me to her local bagel emporium, Ess-A-Bagel. Ess-A-Bagel's gargantuan bagels look like inner tubes, but at least they have the texture and crunch of real bagels. The pumpernickel-raisin bagels here are terrific, the slightly sour pumpernickel dough offset by the sweetness of the raisins. Ess-A-Bagel makes the standard assortment, including onion, salt, garlic, poppy, sesame, plain, pumpernickel, and the aforementioned pumpernickel raisin. Its only concession to the designer bagel movement is the oat-bran bagel they've started to make. Besides bagels, Ess-A-Bagel makes a variety of fish, cheese, and vegetarian spreads.

Ess-A-Bagel
359 First Avenue (corner of 21st Street)
New York, NY 10010
PHONE: (212) 260-2252
SUBWAY: 23rd Street station on the Lexington Avenue No. 6 line.
HOURS: 6:30 A.M. to 10 P.M. Monday through Saturday; 6:30 A.M. to 5 P.M.
    Sunday.
No deliveries.
Cash only.
Mail order available.

Friend of a Farmer ∽ See page 30.

La Boulangère ∽ La Boulangère owner Linda Blankenhorn was a psychologist before she turned to baking, and after tasting her scrumptious breads, rolls, and French-breakfast baked goods, I am happy to report she made the right career move. Her seven-grain bread is the best I've tasted in the city. It's slightly sweet and full-bodied, with none of the dullness that mars most seven-grain loaves. Her conventional baguettes are light and crunchy, and her sourdough salt baguettes taste like a Parisian pretzel. I like the buttery croissants here, but I wish they had a little more crunch to them. I love La Boulangère's cheese Danish, with its not-too-sweet cheese filling complemented by lots of raisins. Her *pain au chocolat* has that blast of high-quality bittersweet chocolate I like in the middle. The only real loser here is the seven-grain muffin. Unlike the seven-grain bread, it was dry and dull, with an unappetizing texture.

La Boulangère
49 East 21st Street (between Park Avenue South and Broadway)
New York, NY 10010
PHONE: (212) 475-8582.
SUBWAYS: 23rd Street station on the Broadway N and R lines and the
    Lexington Avenue No. 6 line.
HOURS: 7:30 A.M. to 10 P.M. Monday through Friday; 7:30 A.M. to 6 P.M.
    Saturday; 8 A.M. to 5 P.M. Sunday.
Delivery available.
All major credit cards accepted.

LaMarca Cheese Shop ⸺ See page 70.

Todaro Brothers ⸺ See page 233.

Union Square Greenmarket ⸺ See page 275.

$\mathcal{W}$EST VILLAGE

14TH STREET TO HOUSTON STREET
FIFTH AVENUE TO WEST STREET

Bagels on the Square ⸺ Making an old-fashioned, hand-formed bagel that's slightly crisp on the outside and textured on the inside seems to be a lost art these days. Bagels on the Square doesn't make them by hand either, but at least theirs have some crunch and texture to them. Its sesame and poppy bagels are both very good, crunchy enough and coated with seeds. The garlic bagels are intensely garlicky, the onion bagels are right on the mark, and the cinnamon-raisin bagels are fine if you believe in them as a legitimate bagel type (I don't). Even the five-grain bagel, a nineties creation if there ever was one, had terrific flavor, and didn't taste overly healthful. Another bagel creation that would have my parents turning over in their graves is the oat-bran bagel with blueberries and strawberries. It's a bagel nightmare, an ill-conceived bagel form if there ever was one.

Bagels on the Square
7 Carmine Street (between Bleecker Street and Sixth Avenue)
New York, NY 10014
PHONE: (212) 691-3041
SUBWAYS: West Fourth Street–Washington Square station on the following
    lines: Sixth Avenue B, D, F, and Q; Eighth Avenue A, C, and E.
HOURS: Twenty-four hours a day, seven days a week.
No deliveries.
Cash only.
Mail order available.

Balducci's ⸺ See page 205.

Melampo Imported Foods ⸺ See page 292.

Pâtisserie Claude ⸺ I was determined not to include an entry for Pâtisserie Claude because every time I've been in the store I've gotten rude, nasty service. I figured that if I wanted French patisserie snootiness, I could go to Paris to experience it firsthand. Then one morning my assistant brought me a Pâtisserie Claude croissant and brioche, and I realized that an entry had been earned, regardless of the quality of the store's service. Pâtisserie Claude's croissants are light, buttery, and not too big. The brioches are lighter, of course, but just as good. The Danish are mediocre to poor and eminently skippable, but the fruit tarts are first-rate and the hazelnut-chocolate-mousse squares are marred only by a rum-soaked layer of sponge cake on the bottom.

Pâtisserie Claude
187 West Fourth Street (between Sixth and Seventh avenues)
New York, NY 10014
PHONE: (212) 255-5911
SUBWAYS: Christopher Street–Sheridan Square station on the Broadway–
    Seventh Avenue No. 1 and 9 lines; West Fourth Street–Washington
    Square station on the following lines: Sixth Avenue B, D, F, and Q;
    Eighth Avenue A, C, and E.
HOURS: 8 A.M. to 8 P.M. seven days a week.
No deliveries.
Cash only.

Priscilla's ⁓ See page 32.

Taylor's ⁓ See page 33.

A. Zito and Sons Bakery ⁓ I know it's blasphemous to say, but Zito's bread is nowhere near my favorite Italian bread in New York. Don't get me wrong; I like Zito's white and whole-wheat breads. They just don't have the body and texture of a D & G or a Morrone's loaf. But go to Zito's when the bread is hot (8:00 A.M.,

Owner Anthony Zito entices passersby with his fine Italian loaves.

10:00 A.M., and 3:00 P.M. Monday through Friday; 6:00 A.M., 10:30 A.M., and 2:00 P.M. Saturday; and 6:00 A.M. Sunday), and you won't believe or care about what I think. Zito's also sells lard bread, made with prosciutto, provolone, and lard; and semolina bread, a soft, eggy, round loaf that is my favorite Zito's creation.

Note: If you think Zito's sells only bread, you're wrong. On my third visit to the store in a week, I noticed a few cans of imported Italian tomatoes on a shelf. Whether they're for sale or for decoration I don't know.

A. Zito and Sons Bakery
259 Bleecker Street (between Sixth and Seventh avenues)
New York, NY 10014
PHONE: (212) 929-6139
SUBWAYS: Christopher Street–Sheridan Square station on the Broadway–
Seventh Avenue No. 1 and 9 lines; West Fourth Street–Washington
Square station on the following lines: Sixth Avenue B, D, F, and Q;
Eighth Avenue A, C, and E.
HOURS: 6 A.M. to 6 P.M. Monday through Friday; 6 A.M. to 5 P.M. Saturday; 6
A.M. to noon Sunday.
No deliveries.
Cash only.

EAST VILLAGE

14TH STREET TO HOUSTON STREET
EAST RIVER TO FIFTH AVENUE

Black Hound ⁓ See page 35.

Encore Patisserie ⁓ See page 36.

DOWNTOWN

HOUSTON STREET TO BATTERY PARK

Barocco Alimentari ⁓ See page 311.

Dean & DeLuca ⁓ See page 214.

D & G Bakery ⁓ Mary Jackson, the owner of D & G, says the reason her bread tastes extraordinarily good is that "no machines touch our bread; everything is done by hand." Somebody sure has magic fingers, because D & G's bread is so crusty and full of flavor that putting even butter on it is a sin. D & G makes equally good round and long white and whole-wheat breads and rolls. It also turns out a tangy provolone bread and a prosciutto bread that's peppery and moist without being greasy.

Warning: Get to D & G early if you want to make sure they have the breads you want. I've arrived a number of times at noon only to find they were sold out of provolone bread. The smart thing to do is just call ahead the morning you're planning to pick up the bread and reserve some.

Note: You'll also find some, if not all, D & G breads at Fairway, Jefferson Market, Balducci's, and Tutta Pasta, among others.

D & G Bakery
45 Spring Street (Between Mott and Mulberry streets)
New York, NY 10012
PHONE: (212) 226-6688
SUBWAY: Spring Street station on the Lexington Avenue No. 6 line.
HOURS: 8 A.M. to 2 P.M. seven days a week.
No deliveries.
Cash only.

Gertel's ⏤ See page 9.

Kossar's Bialystoker Kuchen Bakery ⏤ At most bagel factories in New York, bialys are an afterthought. I've never understood this, because to me a good bialy is better than a good bagel. It's lighter and has half the calories and more texture and flavor. Kossar's is mecca for bialy lovers like me. They make the best bialys in town, and since bialys are their specialty, they're always fresh. Kossar's makes, to my knowledge, the only garlic bialys in New York, in addition to standard onion bialys, rolls, and onion rounds—flat onion loaves about eight inches in diameter. Oh yes, Kossar's also sells bagels, although buying a bagel at Kossar's is like ordering a steak at a seafood restaurant.

Note: Unlike bagels, bialys must be toasted to be eaten. Do not eat an untoasted bialy. It will taste like uncooked dough.

Kossar's Bialystoker Kuchen Bakery
367 Grand Street (between Essex and Norfolk streets)
New York, NY 10002
PHONE: (212) 473-4810
SUBWAY: East Broadway station on the Sixth Avenue F line.
HOURS: Twenty-four hours a day, seven days a week.
No deliveries.
Cash only.

Texas Tortilla Factory ⏤ Having lived in Los Angeles for a year, I developed a fondness for steaming-hot, fresh-flour tortillas. But until the Texas Tortilla Factory opened in 1990, I had come to regard New York as tortilla hell. Even most of the Mexican restaurants here serve premade, gummy tortillas, with all the flavor of trampolines. There can be no doubt about the freshness of the Texas Tortilla

Factory's tortillas, because you actually see the woman making them in the window as you walk into this tiny storefront. A baker's dozen costs less than $1.50, but you'd better buy two dozen, because the first package won't survive the trip home. In addition to tortillas, the store makes a wide range of Tex-Mex dishes. The white corn tortilla chips are greasy, slightly sweet, and addictive. The pinto beans made from scratch are excellent, and the quesadillas made by grilling two tortillas with a choice of fillings are one of my favorite cheap lunches in New York.

Texas Tortilla Factory
36 Water Street (between Broad Street and Coenties Slip)
New York, NY 10004
PHONE: (212) 952-1465
SUBWAY: Wall Street station on the Broadway–Seventh Avenue No. 2 and 3
    lines; Whitehall Street–South Ferry station on the Broadway R line.
HOURS: 11 A.M. to 8 P.M. Monday through Friday; closed Saturday and
    Sunday.
Delivery available for very large orders.
Cash only.

Vesuvio Bakery — For more than seventy years Anthony Dapolito has been making Italian bread and *biscotti* in his brick oven in Soho. The bread's okay—nothing special—but the plain and peppered *biscotti* and the sesame breadsticks are satisfyingly crunchy. The best reason to come to Vesuvio's is to soak up the atmosphere of bygone New York. From the hand-painted sign out front to the bread piled in the window to the old-fashioned bins containing the *biscotti*, it's as if Vesuvio's has been frozen in time.

Vesuvio Bakery
160 Prince Street (between Thompson Street and West Broadway)
New York, NY 10012
PHONE: (212) 925-8248
SUBWAYS: Spring Street station on the Eighth Avenue C and E lines.
HOURS: 7 A.M. to 7 P.M. Monday through Saturday; closed Sunday.
No deliveries.
Cash only.

𝓑RONX

Addeo's Bakers — See page 134.

𝓑ROOKLYN

Damascus Bakery — Get to the Damascus Bakery at noon, when the baklava comes out of the oven, and you'll discover that baklava doesn't have to be heavy, syrupy, and overly sweet. Damascus Bakery's pistachio baklava is fairly light and densely textured, and doesn't turn the bag it comes in into a soggy mess. The pita bread turned out at Damascus is good enough to be shipped all over the city, but it doesn't compare to that of the Near East Bakery down the street. The pita concoction that's intriguing here is the *lahmajun*, a pita pizza made with ground lamb, lemon juice, curry powder, and tomato sauce.

Note: Damascus's Bread can also be found at Dean & DeLuca, International Grocery, and Canard and Company.

Damascus Bakery
195 Atlantic Avenue (between Court and Clinton streets)
Brooklyn, NY 11201
PHONE: (718) 625-7070
SUBWAYS: Borough Hall station on the following lines: Broadway–Seventh
    Avenue No. 2 and 3, Lexington Avenue No. 4 and 5.
HOURS: 8 A.M. to 7 P.M. seven days a week.
Deliveries in the neighborhood.
Cash only.
Mail order available.

Leske's ~ See page 40.

Near East Bakery ~ When you walk down the stairs from street level to get to the Near East Bakery, you enter a dungeonlike room that feels like the den of hostage-taking international terrorists. But after sampling the slightly crispy, aromatic, and greaseless potato pies and the oniony, lemony spinach pies, I began to fantasize about being held prisoner there. Order a box of six pies, which are so fresh and turn over so quickly they are invariably hot, and try to make it home with that incredible smell emanating from the box. If you make it, you are a pillar of self-discipline and a better person than I am. The only way to get the pie box home intact is also to buy some of the best pita bread (white, whole wheat, or sesame) in the city and munch on that instead. If that doesn't work, the only thing left to try is distracting yourself with *zatar* bread, a flat pita baked with olive oil and *zatar* (wild thyme). That wasn't hot when I bought it, so it actually arrived home intact. Actually, the only way you won't immediately dive into your Near East Bakery goodies is to go next door to Sahadi Importing Company, buy some of the incredible yogurt dip *latany*, and content yourself with thinking about how that spread is going to taste on the bread when you get home.

Near East Bakery
183 Atlantic Avenue (between Court and Clinton streets)
Brooklyn, NY 11201
PHONE: (718) 875-0016
SUBWAYS: Borough Hall station on the following lines: Broadway–Seventh
    Avenue No. 2 and 3, Lexington Avenue No. 4 and 5.
HOURS: 9:30 A.M. to 4:30 P.M. Tuesday through Saturday; 9:30 A.M. to 1 P.M.
    Sunday; closed Monday.
Cash only.

Best of Breads

Best all-around bread bakery (Nuevo Retro): Ecce Panis
Best all-around bread bakery (Italian): Morrone & Sons Bakery
Best all-around bread bakery (Eastern European): Orwasher's Bakery
Best bagels: Bagelry, Columbia Hot Bagels
Best bialys: Kossar's Bialystoker Kuchen Bakery
Best *biscotti* (savory): Vesuvio Bakery
Best *biscotti* (sweet): Ecce Panis
Best brioches: Golden Brioche
Best corn-rye bread: Royale Pastry Shop
Best croissant: Chez Laurence; Bonté Patisserie
Best ficelle: Zabar's (sold in stores all over the city)
Best French baguette (old-fashioned): La Tropézienne
Best focaccia: Melampo Imported Foods
Best Italian bread (old-fashioned): D & G Bakery
Best onion rolls: Morrone & Sons Bakery
Best pita bread: Near East Bakery
Best prosciutto bread: Morrone & Sons Bakery
Best pumpernickel-raisin bread: Orwasher's Bakery
Best rolls (savory): Soutine's cheddar-sourdough rolls
Best rolls (sweet): Zabar's walnut-raisin rolls (made and sold at E.A.T. but
    sold in stores all over the city)
Best rye bread: Orwasher's Bakery
Best sandwich baguette: Morrone & Sons Bakery
Best semolina bread: Morrone & Sons Bakery
Best tortillas: Texas Tortilla Factory

4

CHEESE

New York, and the rest of the country for that matter, has gone cheese crazy. Twenty years ago the cheeses you would find in most New York refrigerators would be Cracker Barrel and Swiss Knight and Wispride. Even ten years ago most New Yorkers knew about only Brie and Edam and maybe Gouda. These days many locals think nothing of going to their neighborhood gourmet store and asking for a New York State *chèvre* or a Massachusetts Camembert. New York is a city of discerning and demanding cheese consumers.

The cheese counters at stores like Balducci's and Fairway offer a staggering array of international cheeses. It's impossible to remember or know each of the hundreds of cheeses these stores have in stock, particularly since new cheeses seem to arrive every week. Even supermarket chains are stocking many more cheeses than they were just a few years ago.

In New York you'll find not only French and Italian and Spanish and Swiss and Dutch cheeses but also domestic cheeses from makers such as Coach (yes, it's the same people that started and sold Coach Leathers) and Goat Folks and Laura Chenel (all high-quality domestic *chèvre* makers). Craigston is another maker whose cheeses (Camembert) stand up very well to their European counterparts.

When shopping for cheese, be adventuresome. Try a new cheese every time you shop for a dinner party. Discovering a new cheese is one of life's simpler pleasures. Don't be afraid to ask for a taste before you buy. Any cheese department or store or counter serious about cheese will be glad to give you one.

Knowledgeable cheese-counter people are getting harder and harder to find in New York. Too often even the mega-stores like Balducci's and Fairway have people working behind the cheese counter who don't know the difference between English farmhouse cheddar and Cracker Barrel. So if you happen upon somebody knowledgeable where you shop for cheese, cultivate a relationship. You'll be rewarded with a cheese education that you couldn't get even at Harvard.

The Ultimate Cheese Maven

I had my first encounter with Steve Jenkins in the early eighties, when he was on his way to becoming a partner at Fairway. I was a regular Fairway shopper then but still a relative cheese neophyte. My mother-in-law and two of her friends were coming over for brunch, and I wanted to impress them with my culinary acumen. I discovered a recipe in the *Silver Palate Cookbook* for a Brie soufflé that I thought was rich enough to mask any other deficiencies in the meal my wife and I were serving.

I waltzed into Fairway, went to the cheese counter, picked up a piece of ripe, conventional, pre-wrapped Brie, and innocently asked Steve Jenkins if the Brie I was showing him would be appropriate for my soufflé. He looked at me with unmasked contempt and said, "I wouldn't. I don't even call that stuff cheese. It's just garbage we sell because some people don't know any better. Try some of this," he said, giving me some raw-milk Brie that had just come in from France. Sure enough, it had an extraordinary texture and flavor, and I made a Brie soufflé that my mother-in-law still talks about.

Like many of the cheeses he sells, Steve Jenkins is an acquired taste. Currently ensconced as the head of the cheese department at Dean & DeLuca, he's still as prickly and bristling with confidence as ever. But he knows cheese, as his membership in the Guilde des Fromages, France's cheese experts' guild, proves. More important, he's never steered me wrong. Most of the cheeses I buy regularly are ones that Steve Jenkins turned me on to.

Steve Jenkins hasn't always known cheese. He came to New York in 1975, armed with a degree from the University of Missouri and a burning desire to

The Ultimate Cheese Maven, continued

be an actor. Quickly tiring of the aspiring actor's sorry lot, he took a job in a now-defunct cheese store at 91st and Madison. But it wasn't until 1977, when he went to work for Giorgio DeLuca at Dean & DeLuca that his cheese education began. He recalls, "I got what we call at the store 'the treatment.' I got roughed up regularly. He called me a meatball at least once a day. But I learned about food in general and cheese specifically—about how it looks and tastes. I read every cheese and food book I could get my hands on."

What did he learn? That "back then there was no real cheese in America that had a finite origin." All the cheese sold in New York was identified only by its country of origin, if at all. Jenkins says that "at the time the conventional wisdom was that cheese had to be sold with its wrapper on. Otherwise customers would think it wasn't fresh. We started cutting [the wheels] in half and putting [them] on display."

From D & D Jenkins moved to what would become a small chain of specialty stores called Pasta & Cheese. There he claims to have introduced New Yorkers to a host of terrific Italian cheeses including Mascarpone, a sinfully rich cream cheese used in making *tiramisu*, and buffalo-milk mozzarella. From there he moved on to Fairway, where he would entice customers with frequently hilarious and always engaging signs describing his latest discoveries. At Fairway he became a partner until he was fired for taking too much credit for the store's success in a *New York Times* article. He then was going to start his own specialty food store in Battery Park City. The financing and other arrangements were in place, but Jenkins pulled out because, as he puts it, "my gut told me I wouldn't get the foot traffic I'd need." Instead he helped open a specialty food store called Sigmund's in Great Neck, Long Island; had a short, unhappy stint at Balducci's; and ended up back at Dean & DeLuca, where he's turned the cheese department into perhaps the finest all-around cheese store in New York.

Steve Jenkins hasn't changed a bit. He still demands a great deal from his employees and his customers. "Who put this *fromage blanc* out this way? Where's the sign for the Mascarpone? You can't sell cheese like this. Man, I'm away three days and the place goes to pieces." And he's still turning me on to cheeses. "Hey, Ed, try this classic blue goat made by these folks in Massachusetts." "Wait until you taste this Fromagerie Belle Chèvre made in Alabama." For the past couple of years Jenkins has been championing the cause of the new generation of American cheese artisans.

No matter how many bumps he's encountered along the way, Steve Jenkins remains the same impassioned, committed zealot he's always been. He says, "We're rushing toward a time where everything is tasteless. We've got to support the artisans. If it looks rough and raw and unrefined, that's the cheese you should pursue, that's what will have the most flavor. You're not a snob because you care about what you eat. You're smart."

*U*PPER WEST SIDE

59TH STREET TO 125TH STREET
CENTRAL PARK WEST TO RIVERSIDE DRIVE

Fairway ～ See page 221.

Zabar's ～ See page 237.

*U*PPER EAST SIDE

59TH STREET TO 96TH STREET
FIRST AVENUE TO FIFTH AVENUE

Fraser-Morris ～ See page 301.

Grace's Marketplace ～ See page 225.

Ideal Cheese Shop ～ In writing this book I learned something that now seems all too obvious: Anybody who has written a book about what he sells is a great and trustworthy source to buy from. The Lobels have written about meat, the Schapiras have written about coffee, and Ed Edelman (along with Susan Grodnick) wrote *The Ideal Cheese Book* (New York: Harper & Row, 1986). Edelman opened

Customer samples a new cheese at the Ideal Cheese Shop.

his store in 1955 after working in his father's dairy shop and at a time when Brie was considered exotic. Responding to customers' requests for cheeses they had eaten abroad, Edelman started working with importers to bring in cheese then considered unusual, such as St. André, Boursin, and Explorateur. Today the Ideal Cheese Shop sells hundreds of cheeses and is a magnet for serious cheese lovers. It must be considered the city's best freestanding cheese store. If you're having a dinner or cocktail party, go to Ideal and put yourself in the hands of Ed Edelman or any of his knowledgeable counterpeople. The last time I did they introduced me to three sublime cheeses: a Reblochon from Savoie; a three-year-old farmhouse extra-aged Gouda; and a Fromage des Vignerons, a strong winy-tasting cow's-milk cheese.

Ideal Cheese Shop
1205 Second Avenue (between 63rd and 64th streets)
New York, NY 10021
PHONE: (212) 688-7579
SUBWAYS: Lexington Avenue station on the Sixth Avenue B and Q lines and
    the Broadway N and R lines; 59th Street station on the Lexington
    Avenue No. 4, 5, and 6 lines.
HOURS: 9 A.M. to 6:30 P.M. Monday through Friday; 9 A.M. to 6 P.M.
    Saturday; closed Sunday.
All major credit cards accepted.
Mail-order price list available.

La Fromagerie ⟿ See page 283.

*M*IDTOWN WEST

34TH STREET TO 59TH STREET
FIFTH AVENUE TO ELEVENTH AVENUE

DiLuca Dairy ⟿ In researching this book, I must have gone to fifteen or twenty stores that made their own mozzarella. There is only one, however, that I've asked my wife to include in my casket to take to the hereafter. That's Diluca Dairy's mozzarella, with its gossamer texture and subtle nutty flavor. The mozzarella at Diluca is so fresh that it's almost always still warm when you buy it. They also make a celestial *bocconcini* with equally extraordinary smoked mozzarella and homemade sun-dried tomatoes. Lastly, Diluca Dairy makes some of the great Italian sandwiches in New York. One of their sandwiches either on a hero roll or, even better, on Italian peasant bread, makes a great lunch for at least two people. It doesn't matter what you ask them to put on your sandwich, so long as you include mozzarella.

DiLuca Dairy
484 Ninth Avenue (between 37th and 38th streets)
New York, NY 10018
PHONE: (212) 563-2774

A truly international array of cheeses can be found at the 9th Avenue Cheese Market.

SUBWAYS: 34th Street–Pennsylvania Station on the Eight Avenue A, C, and
   E lines.
HOURS: 9 A.M. to 6:30 P.M. Tuesday through Saturday; closed Sunday and
   Monday.
Deliveries in the neighborhood.
Cash only.
Mail order available.

Macy's Cellar Marketplace ~ See page 229.

9th Avenue Cheese Market

9th Avenue Cheese Market ~ More than 300 kinds of cheese are crammed into this small Ninth Avenue storefront, and chances are owners Karen and Ando Andonopolo can tell you a story about each one. It's rare to find owners of a store who take so much pleasure in what they do. The Andonopolos are Greeks from Turkey, and though their store has a Middle Eastern slant, they carry a wide range of French, Italian, and American specialties. They carry fifteen kinds of feta cheese and a wide array of Kashkaval and Kasseri, Baltic and Middle Eastern table cheeses. You'll also find Russian sausages and all kinds of dried fruits, breads, olives, and caviars. Their coffee prices, $3.98 a pound for regular, $4.98 a pound for decaf, are among the lowest I've seen in New York.

9th Avenue Cheese Market
525 Ninth Avenue (between 39th and 40th streets)
New York, NY 10018

PHONE: (212) 564-7127
SUBWAYS: 42nd Street–Port Authority Bus Terminal station on the Eighth
Avenue A, C, and E lines.
HOURS: 9 A.M. to 7:30 P.M. Monday through Saturday; closed Sunday.
No deliveries.
Cash only.

$\mathscr{K}$IPS BAY / GRAMERCY PARK

14TH STREET TO 34TH STREET
EAST RIVER TO FIFTH AVENUE

LaMarca Cheese Shop ⁓ Joseph LaMarca's interest in cheese was piqued, claims his daughter, by a book on cheese that she and her mother gave him as a birthday present. It must have been some book, because shortly thereafter Joseph LaMarca gave up his business for the privilege of working for and being tortured by Giorgio DeLuca of Dean & DeLuca fame. In 1975 he opened LaMarca, a cheese and food shop described by staff and customers alike as a family, neighborhood kind of place. LaMarca carries a broad if not exhaustive selection of cheeses. The last time I was there I bought a perfectly ripe Taleggio that was so earthy and pungent that the cab driver asked for a piece of it. LaMarca makes fresh mozzarella every day. I found the regular-sized mozzarella a little hard, but the *bocconcini* with tomatoes were just the right consistency, creamy, and garlicky. LaMarca carries terrific breads, including baguettes from the Tom Cat Bakery and from Marie's in Hoboken and first-rate semolina bread from Grimaldi's. Every day LaMarca makes up four fresh soups. Try the tangy, cream-based tomato or the tortellini in broth, which is made with an excellent chicken stock.

LaMarca Cheese Shop
161 East 22nd Street (NW corner of Third Avenue)
New York, NY 10010
PHONE: (212) 673-7920
SUBWAY: 23rd Street station on the Lexington Avenue No. 6 line.
HOURS: 10 A.M. to 6:45 P.M. Monday through Friday; 10:30 A.M. to 5:30 P.M.
Saturday; closed Sunday.
Deliveries in the neighborhood.
All major credit cards accepted.

Todaro Brothers ⁓ See page 233.

$\mathscr{W}$EST VILLAGE

14TH STREET TO HOUSTON STREET
FIFTH AVENUE TO WEST STREET

Balducci's ⁓ See page 205.

Murray's Cheese Store — Nobody seems to know exactly how long Murray's Cheese Store has been in business, but new owner Rob Kaufelt says the original owner's wife told him the shop opened around 1940. Murray's has prospered all these years by offering friendly service and low prices on high-quality cheeses and pâtés. Every day there is a handwritten list of cheeses that are specially discounted. Though the staff at Murray's claims the list changes, some of those cheeses have been on special for as long as the store's been in business—forever. It doesn't really matter. Even the cheeses *not* on the list are reasonably priced. Besides cheese, Murray's carries a wide array of fresh pastas, sauces, breads, and pâtés.

Note: In 1991 Rob Kaufelt bought Murray's and moved it across the street from its original location. The new store is brighter, the Italian cheese selection is much broader, and, thanks to the aid and advice of cheese whiz Steve Jenkins, all the cheeses in the store are now displayed in mouthwatering fashion. When I showed up to check out the new store, I tried a Tuscan sheep cheese, yolo, that turned out to be an earthy delight.

Murray's Cheese Store
257 Bleecker Street (just west of Sixth Avenue)
New York, NY 10014
PHONE: (212) 243-3289
SUBWAYS: Christopher Street–Sheridan Square station on the Broadway–
    Seventh Avenue No. 1 and 9 lines; West Fourth Street–Washington
    Square station on the following lines: Sixth Avenue B, D, F, and Q;
    Eighth Avenue A, C, and E.
HOURS: 8 A.M. to 6:30 P.M. Monday through Saturday; closed Sunday.
No deliveries.
Cash only.

*E*AST VILLAGE

14TH STREET TO HOUSTON STREET
EAST RIVER TO FIFTH AVENUE

East Village Cheese Store — This tiny storefront is the closest thing you can find to a Zabar's in the East Village. It has a fine, if limited, selection of imported cheeses, a decent array of breads, and assorted items such as coffee, cold cuts, and olive oil, all at East Village prices. The last time I was here I put together a terrific cheese platter comprised of a Huntsman, an English cheese with layers of Stilton and cheddar; two incredibly creamy French *chèvres*, one called a Bellay, the other called simply fresh French goat cheese; and a triple-cream blue cheese called saga blue. Don't expect huge selections of anything at East Village Cheese, or helpful counterpeople, and you'll do very well.

Warning: It can get very crowded in this thin slice of a store. But it does have a number system, and the counterpeople move fast.

East Village Cheese Store
34 Third Avenue (between 9th and 10th streets)
New York, NY 10003

PHONE: (212) 477-2061
SUBWAYS: Astor Place station on the Lexington Avenue No. 6 line; 8th Street
   station on the Broadway N and R lines.
HOURS: 9 A.M. to 6:30 P.M. Monday through Friday; 9 A.M. to 5:30 P.M.
   Saturday and Sunday.
No deliveries.
Cash only.

Russo & Son Dairy Products ⟶ Asked for his guiding philosophy, Jack Russo
smiled impishly and said, "Mozzarella's next to godliness." Russo's makes mozzarella at least three times a day, more if demand warrants it. Both the unsalted
and lightly salted versions are excellent, and Russo's mozzarella rolls with prosciutto and salami are highly flavorful, the sublety of the mozzarella playing off
the intensity of the fillings. The store also carries a selection of pastas, sauces,
Italian cheeses, cold cuts, and good, crusty Italian breads; but mozzarella is king
here.

Russo & Son Dairy Products
344 East 11th Street (between First and Second avenues)
New York, NY 10003
PHONE: (212) 254-7452
SUBWAYS: First Avenue station on the 14th Street–Canarsie L line; Astor
   Place station on the Lexington Avenue No. 6 line.
HOURS: 8 A.M. to 7 P.M. Monday through Saturday; 10 A.M. to 3 P.M. Sunday.
No deliveries.
Cash only.

Sal's Gourmet & Cheese Shop ⟶ Sal's is the quintessential neighborhood cheese
and gourmet shop. Every time I go in, the people behind the counter are engaged
in animated conversation with customers, and they're not even talking about the
food. But if they were, they'd be talking about Sal's first-rate selection of imported
Italian cheeses, or the fresh regular and smoked mozzarella made every day. Or
they might be discussing the crusty semolina bread made especially for Sal's in
a charcoal-fueled brick oven at an undisclosed location in Brooklyn. They might
also be talking about the store's wide range of fresh and dried pastas, some of
which are made on the premises. Sal's homemade marinara sauce is thick and
rich with tomatoes and not at all oily. Although one of my clients swears by Sal's
pesto, I found it tasted overwhelmingly of basil and little else.

Sal's Gourmet & Cheese Shop
169 First Avenue (between 10th and 11th streets)
New York, NY 10003
PHONE: (212) 529-7903
SUBWAYS: First Avenue station on the 14th Street–Canarsie L line; Astor
   Place station on the Lexington Avenue No. 6 line.
HOURS: 9 A.M. to 8 P.M. Monday through Saturday; 9 A.M. to 4 P.M. Sunday.
All major credit cards accepted.
Catering available.

$\mathscr{D}$OWNTOWN

HOUSTON STREET TO BATTERY PARK

Alleva Dairy ~ The pristine, old-fashioned tile floors at Alleva Dairy are the only real clue that the store is nearly one hundred years old. The regular mozzarella here is just fine, but it's the smoked mozzarella that brings me back time after time. It has just the right amount of smokiness so that it doesn't overwhelm the flavor and texture of the fresh mozzarella. Alleva also carries a large selection of Italian cheeses, including a Mascarpone-and-Gorgonzola *torta* with basil I've not found elsewhere in the city.

Note: Like many Italian cheese stores, Alleva sells pasta sauces and dried pasta. The dried pasta is standard, but the fresh tomato sauce is exceptional.

Alleva Dairy
188 Mulberry Street (corner of Grand Street)
New York, NY 10012
PHONE: (212) 226-7990
SUBWAYS: Spring Street station on the Lexington Avenue No. 6 line; Grand
   Street station on the Sixth Avenue B, D, and Q lines.
HOURS: 8:30 A.M. to 6 P.M. Monday through Saturday; 8:30 A.M. to 3 P.M.
   Sunday.
No deliveries.
Cash only.
Mail order available.

Ben's Cheese Shop ~ Ben's homemade cream cheese is to Philadelphia cream cheese what Château Lafitte Rothschild is to Thunderbird. In fact, after sampling some of Ben's cream cheese, you may never be able to eat store-bought cream cheese again. Ben's has no gum, no preservatives, no nothing, so it's made and sold in oblong loaves. It comes in vegetable, garlic-and-herb, and scallion flavors, and they're all good; but I believe that adding anything to Ben's is gilding the lily. The other specialty of the house is baked farmer cheese. Ben's makes ten kinds, including an apple-walnut that's tasty enough to pass for dessert if you're on a diet.

Warning: Sometimes Ben's has been known to unwittingly sell cream cheese past its prime, so ask what's fresh the day you walk in.

Ben's Cheese Shop
181 East Houston Street (between Allen and Orchard streets)
New York, NY 10002
PHONE: (212) 254-8290
SUBWAY: Second Avenue station on the Sixth Avenue F line.
HOURS: 8:30 A.M. to 5:30 P.M. Monday through Thursday; 8:30 A.M. to 3:30
   P.M. Friday; 7:30 A.M. to 6 P.M. Sunday; closed Saturday.
No deliveries.
Cash only.

Dean & DeLuca ~ See page 214.

DiPalo Dairy ⁓ "We're still old-world," Sammy DiPalo replied when asked what makes his sixty-six-year-old store special. "We give our customers the best quality and service." What he serves his customers is silky mozzarella made every day in full view of anyone who wanders in; sweet, creamy ricotta cheese made upstate and trucked into the city because of the New York City ban on making dairy products with raw milk; and smoked mozzarella that is absolutely the smokiest I tasted in researching this book. DiPalo's also carries a full line of Italian cold cuts and cheeses, including an imported mountain Gorgonzola cheese that rendered eight food lovers speechless when served on slices of fresh pear.

Warning: On Saturday and Sunday mornings DiPalo's can get very crowded. I don't mind very much, because there are worse things to do on a weekend morning than watch fresh mozzarella being made and smell aged Parmigiano-Reggiano.

DiPalo Diary
206 Grand Street (corner of Mott Street)
New York, NY 10012
PHONE: (212) 226-1033
SUBWAYS: Spring Street station on the Lexington Avenue No. 6 line; Grand
    Street station on the Sixth Avenue B, D, and Q lines.
HOURS: 8:30 A.M. to 6:30 P.M. Monday through Saturday; 8:30 A.M. to 2 P.M.
    Sunday.
No deliveries.
Cash only.

Joe's Dairy ⁓ Once, when I was waiting for a very late bride at St. Anthony's, the church across the street from Joe's Dairy, I let my baser instincts get the best of me: I bolted out of the pew, scurried over to Joe's, bought a prosciutto-and-mozzarella roll, and came right back. Though some people thought I was rude, the ones who know about Joe's understood perfectly. Joe's mozzarella, made fresh every day, is a heavyweight contender in the New York fresh mozzarella championships. I was worried when Joe Aiello sold the store four years ago, but the new owner, Anthony Campanelli, apprenticed with Joe for four years, thereby ensuring mozzarella continuity. Anthony's smoked mozzarella is also a work of art. On weekends he makes a smoked-mozzarella-and-pepper-cured-prosciutto roll that by itself is worth a special trip to Joe's. His *bocconcini*, small marinated mozzarella balls, are dosed with loads of fresh garlic and red pepper, giving them a real kick; on occasion, however, I've found them way too salty.

Joe's Dairy
156 Sullivan Street (just south of Houston Street)
New York, NY 10012
PHONE: (212) 677-8780
SUBWAYS: Spring Street station on the Eighth Avenue C and E lines;
    Houston Street station on the Broadway–Seventh Avenue No. 1 and 9
    lines.
HOURS: 7:30 A.M. to 6 P.M. Tuesday through Saturday; 9 A.M. to 12:30 P.M.
    Sunday; closed Monday.
Deliveries in Manhattan.
Cash only.

Owner Anthony Campanelli takes a break from making his store's fresh mozzarella.

Anthony Campanelli creates fresh mozzarella for Joe's Dairy.

The tangy, robust Feta Kefalinias at Greek House Foods may be the best feta you'll ever taste.

*B*RONX

S. Calandra & Sons ⸺ See page 134.

*Q*UEENS

Greek House Foods ⸺ See page 139.

Mediterranean Foods ⸺ See page 139.

Titan Foods ⸺ See page 139.

*B*ROOKLYN

M & I International Foods ⸺ See page 142.

Best of Cheeses

Best American cheese selection: Dean & DeLuca
Best cheese department in a mega-store: Dean & DeLuca
Most consistently knowledgeable counter staff: Ideal Cheese Shop
Best cream cheese: Ben's Cheese Shop
Best French cheese selection: Balducci's
Best freestanding cheese store: Ideal Cheese Shop
Best Italian cheese selection: Todaro Brothers
Best Italian cheese store: DiPalo Dairy
Best mozzarella (fresh): DiLuca Dairy
Best mozzarella (smoked): Joe's Dairy
Best ricotta: Alleva Dairy

5

CHOCOLATES, CANDY, AND NUTS

Until recently New York was not in the major leagues for chocolate. Yes, there are New York institutions such as Mondel's and Li-Lac, which have been making chocolates for more than fifty years. But for most New Yorkers, Barton's and Barricini's were the names that came to mind when they thought about chocolate.

My grandmother would bring a box of Barton's every Sunday when she visited us. And the sorry truth about Barton's and Barricini's was that they were merely regional equivalents of Fanny Farmer and Whitman's chocolates. They were great to discover on the coffee table after your parents had a party, but you wouldn't waste your own money on them.

Then, in the 1970s the chocolate scene began to change. We entered the chocolate truffle era. Top-name European chocolatiers such as Teuscher, Neuchatel, and Manon started opening retail outposts in Manhattan, and Tom Kron opened his first Kron Chocolatier in New York in 1972. All of a sudden high-priced, high-quality "designer" chocolates were the rage. Today, there are dozens of these chocolate stores in Manhattan, and every major gourmet store like Balducci's or Bloomingdale's has an extensive selection of chocolates either flown in from Europe once or twice a week or made in America by one of the plethora of excellent chocolatiers born of the candy revolution.

Introducing people to fine chocolate after they've known only Barton's is a lot of fun, and eating a creamy, buttery truffle is even more fun; but there are a couple of things to know before embarking on a chocolate purchase. When you're buying chocolates flown in from Belgium, Switzerland, or France, ask when the candy displayed arrived. Fresher candy tastes better. We all learned that years ago when we bought Mary Janes only to discover that they were so hard we couldn't bite into them. Don't be afraid to ask what's in—and inside—each chocolate. You'll be disappointed if you don't like chocolates with liquor in them and all the chocolates you buy turn out to contain champagne or rum or Cointreau.

$\mathcal{U}$PPER WEST SIDE

59TH STREET TO 125TH STREET
CENTRAL PARK WEST TO RIVERSIDE DRIVE

Fairway ⁓ See page 221.

Godiva Chocolatier ⁓ The Campbell's Soup Company may know how to make a mean bowl of chunky sirloin soup, but it should stay away from chocolates. Before Campbell's took over Godiva in 1967, it was one of the premier Belgian chocolate makers. Now almost the entire Godiva line is made in Reading, Pennsylvania, and though I don't know how close Reading is to Hershey, there is no denying that Godiva is tasting more Pennsylvanian than Belgian at this point. Godiva's recent chocolates are just too sweet. Even the truffles don't have the luxuriant taste and texture they should.

Godiva Chocolatier
245 Columbus Avenue (between 71st and 72nd streets)
New York, NY 10023
PHONE: (212) 787-5804
SUBWAYS: 72nd Street station on the following lines: Broadway–Seventh
    Avenue No. 1, 2, 3, and 9; Eighth Avenue C and Sixth Avenue B.
HOURS: 10 A.M. to 10 P.M. Monday through Friday; 11 A.M. to 10 P.M.
    Saturday; noon to 7 P.M. Sunday.
No deliveries.
All major credit cards accepted.

OTHER LOCATIONS:
793 Madison Avenue (between 67th and 68th streets)
New York, NY 10021
(212) 249-9444

85 Broad Street
New York, NY 10005
(212) 514-6240

560 Lexington Avenue (between 50th and 51st streets)
New York, NY 10022
(212) 980-9810

33 Maiden Lane (between Nassau and William streets)
New York, NY 10038
(212) 809-8990

701 Fifth Avenue (between 55th and 56th streets)
New York, NY 10022
(212) 593-2845

2 World Financial Center
New York, NY 10048
(212) 945-2174

Mondel's Homemade Chocolates ⁓ Though I admit I never met a truffle I didn't like, sometimes I get the urge for the candy I grew up with—things like butter crunch and almond clusters. To satisfy these urges I head for Mondel's, truly an old-fashioned neighborhood candy store run by Florence Mondel, daughter of the founder. For almost fifty years Columbia University students and locals have been crowding eight at a time into this tiny store jam-packed with chocolate and candy of every size and shape imaginable. The bittersweet dark-chocolate almond clusters, held together with a layer of caramel, are a dreamy comfort food, as is the butter crunch. The caramels, while not having that luxurious mouth feel some of the upscale chocolatier caramels have, are nonetheless a terrific antidote to whatever anxiety you're trying to cope with. Mondel's also makes nifty tiny mint-chocolate cups I've not seen elsewhere. Besides a seemingly infinite variety of chocolates, Mondel also carries things like lollipops, jellybeans, candy corn, and sucking candies.

Note: Unlike the salespeople at many of the upscale truffle joints described in this chapter, the people who wait on you at Mondel's are usually pleasant and helpful. What a radical concept.

Mondel's Homemade Chocolates
2913 Broadway (at 114th Street)
New York, NY 10025
PHONE: (212) 864-2111
SUBWAYS: 116th Street–Columbia University station on the Broadway–
    Seventh Avenue No. 1 and 9 lines.
HOURS: Noon to 6:30 P.M. Monday through Saturday; call ahead at holiday
    time; closed Sunday.
No deliveries.
American Express accepted.
Mail order available.

The Silver Palate ⁓ See page 297.

Zabar's ～ See page 237.

𝒰PPER EAST SIDE
59TH STREET TO 96TH STREET
FIRST AVENUE TO FIFTH AVENUE

Bloomingdale's ～ See page 212.

Elk Candy Company & Marzipan ～ Marzipan is one of those foods you either love or hate. I happen to despise the stuff, yet I feel compelled to mention the folks at Elk Candy, who are definitely the kings of marzipan in New York. From potatoes to fruit, marzipan here comes in every conceivable shape and color. Besides the marzipan, Elk makes okay chocolate candies—nothing to write home about, but a definite cut above the Whitman's sampler. Nonpareil fans should note that Elk makes a bittersweet variety they call a kringle that is the best-tasting version I've ever had of that prosaic candy.

Elk Candy Company & Marzipan
240 East 86th Street (between Second and Third avenues)
New York, NY 10028
PHONE: (212) 650-1177
SUBWAYS: 86th Street station on the Lexington Avenue No. 4, 5, and 6 lines.
HOURS: 9 A.M. to 6:45 P.M. Monday through Friday; 10 A.M. to 5:45 P.M.
    Saturday and Sunday.
No deliveries.
Cash only.
Mail order available.

Fraser-Morris ～ See page 301.

Godiva Chocolatier ～ See page 79.

Grace's Marketplace ～ See page 225.

La Maison du Chocolat ～ I was thrilled when I heard that famed Parisian chocolatier Robert Linxe was opening a store in New York. After all, Linxe is supposed to be to chocolate what Barney Greengrass is to sturgeon. So I thought up a lame excuse to go over to the East Side, walked into the store, and ordered two assortments of chocolates, some fruit jellies they call fruit pâtés, one champagne truffle, one natural truffle, a small bag of chocolate-covered almonds, and a box of Arribes (bittersweet wafers filled with a thin layer of chocolate ganache). The

Arribes were breathtaking: The bittersweet chocolate was barely sweetened, the ganache smooth and silken. The assorted chocolates were exceptional, richly textured and intensely flavored the way all great chocolates are. The fruit pâtés, specifically the blueberry and passion fruit, were the best fruit jellies I've ever had. The truffles were standard, richer than sin, and very buttery. The chocolate-covered almonds were, well, chocolate-covered almonds; good, but certainly not worth the price of $7.50 for a small bag of perhaps twenty. So in conclusion I would like to extend the warmest of welcomes to Robert Linxe. If he ever needs a place to stay in New York, he's always welcome at our house . . . as long as he brings some chocolate as a hospitality gift.

Note: Be prepared for a little bit of Parisian attitude at La Maison du Chocolat.

La Maison du Chocolat
25 East 73rd Street (just west of Madison Avenue)
New York, NY 10021
PHONE: (212) 744-7117
SUBWAY: 77th Street station on the Lexington Avenue No. 6 line.
HOURS: 10 A.M. to 6 P.M. Monday through Saturday; closed Sunday.
Deliveries made all over Manhattan.
All major credit cards accepted.
Mail order available.

Teuscher Chocolates of Switzerland ⁓ See page 83.

ℳIDTOWN WEST

34TH STREET TO 59TH STREET
FIFTH AVENUE TO ELEVENTH AVENUE

Le Chocolatier Manon ⁓ I don't know if it's the *crème fraîche* fillings or the fact that they're made entirely by hand or the intriguing flavors—all I know is that Manon makes celestial molded chocolates, by far the richest, most sinful in town. Try the Enfant Bruxelles, a combination of coffee and chocolate *crème fraîche*; or the Caramel Noir, made with dark chocolate, *crème fraîche*, and dark caramel cream; or the Bouchon, made with dark chocolate, *crème fraîche*, and cognac-flavored butter cream. But it doesn't matter what you try, they're all terrific.

Warning: Even within the realm of expensive chocolates, Manon's prices are stratospheric. As this book went to press they were $44 a pound. What is amazing is that even at that price Manon could not afford its own tiny storefront at 71st and Madison. In January of 1991 the folks at Manon, unable to deal with a rent increase that brought their rent to four hundred dollars a square foot, had to move to Bergdorf Goodman.

Le Chocolatier Manon
at Bergdorf Goodman, Seventh Floor
754 Fifth Avenue (between 57th and 58th streets)
New York, NY 10022

flavors and textures that are a wonderful complement to the truffles. Try the chopped almond or the walnuts with a ground hazelnut filling.

Note: Friendliness seems to be incompatible with selling chocolates of this quality.

Teuscher Chocolates of Switzerland
670 Fifth Avenue (between 49th and 50th streets in Rockefeller Center)
New York, NY 10020
PHONE: (212) 246-4416
SUBWAYS: 47-50th Streets–Rockefeller Center station on the Sixth Avenue B,
    D, F, and Q lines; 53rd Street station on the Eighth Avenue E line.
HOURS: 10 A.M. to 6 P.M. Monday through Wednesday, Friday, and Saturday;
    10 A.M. to 7:30 P.M. Thursday; closed Sunday.
Deliveries all over Manhattan.
All major credit cards accepted.
Mail order available.

OTHER LOCATION:
25 East 61st Street (corner of Madison Avenue)
New York, NY 10021
(212) 751-8482

✐IDTOWN EAST

34TH STREET TO 59TH STREET
FIRST AVENUE TO FIFTH AVENUE

Fifth Avenue Chocolatière ⸺ Say you've got a friend who's just been named taxidermist of the year and you want to get him a chocolate moosehead to commemorate that fact. Fifth Avenue Chocolatier will make it up for you if you give them two weeks notice. FAC specializes in making chocolate versions of literally anything you can think of, from parakeets to record covers. The great thing is that the chocolate moosehead will actually taste good, as FAC is owned by one of the founders of Kron, the first serious New York chocolatier. Their standard chocolates are good—not great—and their truffles are too buttery for my taste. Their caramels, however, are wonderful, sinfully rich, and smooth.

Fifth Avenue Chocolatière
506 Madison Avenue (between 52nd and 53rd streets)
New York, NY 10022
PHONE: (212) 935-5454
SUBWAYS: Fifth Avenue–53rd Street station on the Eighth Avenue E and
    Sixth Avenue F lines.
HOURS: 9 A.M. to 7 P.M. seven days a week.
$10 charge for deliveries in Manhattan.
All major credit cards accepted.
Mail order available.

OTHER LOCATIONS:
120 Park Avenue (corner of 42nd Street)
New York, NY 10017
(212) 370-5355

Godiva Chocolatier ～ See page 79.

Kalustyan's ～ See page 124.

Neuchatel ～ See page 83.

Teuscher Chocolates of Switzerland ～ See page 83.

$\mathcal{W}$EST VILLAGE

14TH STREET TO HOUSTON STREET
FIFTH AVENUE TO WEST STREET

Balducci's ～ See page 205.

Li-Lac Chocolates ～ I used to manage a jazz club in the West Village, and every time I walked by Li-Lac on my way to work my diet ended. Li-Lac has gone through a few owners since it first opened in 1923, but none foolish enough to

Single-item purchases are definitely allowed at Li-Lac Chocolates.

tamper with the way the chocolates are made. Old-fashioned caramels, first-rate truffles, and filled creams are all made fresh on the premises every day. With its lilac-covered walls and antique candy cases, Li-Lac harkens back to a kinder and gentler time. One particularly endearing thing about Li-Lac: It's the only top-level chocolate store in New York that allows you to buy a single piece of chocolate. No quarter-pound minimum here.

Li-Lac Chocolates
120 Christopher Street (between Bleecker and Barrow streets)
New York, NY 10014
PHONE: (212) 242-7374
SUBWAYS: Christopher Street–Sheridan Square station on the Broadway–
    Seventh Avenue No. 1 and 9 lines.
HOURS: 10 A.M. to 8 P.M. Monday through Saturday; noon to 8 P.M. Sunday;
    hours vary during summer months.
$10.50 charge for deliveries in Manhattan.
All major credit cards accepted.
Mail-order catalog available.
Order by calling 1 (800) 624-4874.

$\mathcal{E}$AST VILLAGE

14TH STREET TO HOUSTON STREET
EAST RIVER TO FIFTH AVENUE

Black Hound ⎯ See page 35.

$\mathcal{D}$OWNTOWN

HOUSTON STREET TO BATTERY PARK

Bazzini ⎯ Bazzini has been roasting nuts at this location for more than 100 years, but up until two years ago you could buy them retail only in five-pound lots. Now I love fresh-roasted nuts as much as anyone, but five pounds is too many nuts even for me. With the influx of new businesses and residents in the area, Bazzini has opened a nifty little store that sells its nuts in one-pound lots along with coffee, baked goods, and assorted gourmet items. Bazzini's fresh roasted cashews are to Planter's what chateaubriand is to a Big Mac. Their butter-toffee peanuts are sinfully addictive, and they make several kinds of satisfying crunches, including a delicious nut brittle called Bazittle.

Bazzini
339 Greenwich Street (corner of Jay Street)
New York, NY 10013
PHONE: (212) 227-6241

SUBWAYS: Chambers Street station on the Broadway–Seventh Avenue No. 1,
2, 3, and 9 lines and the Eighth Avenue A and C lines.
HOURS: 8 A.M. to 7 P.M. Monday through Friday; 10 A.M. to 6 P.M. Saturday;
closed Sunday.
Delivery available for large orders.
Cash only.
Mail order available.

Dean & DeLuca — See page 214.

Economy Candy — A penny candy store at 78 RPM is the best way to describe
this Lower East Side institution. Economy Candy carries hundreds of kinds of
penny candies, nuts, dried fruits, and chocolates. Some are standard items you
can get anywhere, like M&Ms and licorice. Others, such as Pixie sticks, those
straws filled with powdered candy you devoured as a child, are blasts from the
past I've not seen elsewhere in the city. It's great fun to go into Economy Candy,
pick up an empty plastic bag, and wander around dumping into it whatever strikes
your fancy.

Note: Though it is quite hectic in Economy Candy, service is helpful and prompt.

Economy Candy
108 Rivington Street (between Essex and Ludlow)
New York, NY 10002
PHONE: (212) 254-1832
SUBWAYS: Delancey Street station on the Sixth Avenue F line; Essex Street
station on the Nassau Street J, M, and Z lines.
HOURS: 8 A.M. to 5:30 P.M. Sunday through Friday; 10 A.M. to 5 P.M.
Saturday.
No deliveries.
All major credit cards accepted.
Mail-order catalog available.

Godiva Chocolatier — See page 79.

Neuchatel — See page 83.

The Sweet Life — When I was a kid, my grandmother took great pride in serving
us garishly colored, artificially flavored fruit slices after stuffing us with potato
pancakes and blintzes. The Sweet Life is a candy, nut, and dried fruit store that
carries eight kinds of fruit slices, including flavors I'd never seen before, like pink
grapefruit and watermelon. It also sells ten kinds of halvah from all over the
world on any given day, including a delicious one imported from Israel in non-
summer months only. The Sweet Life's selection of nuts and dried fruits is fairly
standard, with dried apricots and roasted almonds and the like predominating.
Its non–fruit slice candy varieties include a credible butter crunch (not made on
the premises) and lots of hard candies.

The Sweet Life
63 Hester Street (corner of Ludlow Street)
New York, NY 10002
PHONE: (212) 598-0092
SUBWAY: East Broadway station on the Sixth Avenue F line.
HOURS: 9 A.M. to 6 P.M. Sunday through Friday; closed Saturday.
Cash only.
Mail order available.

Wolsk's ⏤ For more than fifty years Wolsk's has been a terrific source for high-quality nuts and dried fruits sold at very low prices. Almost all the nuts sold here are roasted on the premises, and that combined with the high turnover guarantees freshness. The dried fruit is equally good. Try the no-sugar-added dried pineapple. It's incredibly ugly and looks like something you'd eat only on an Outward Bound trip, but it actually tastes wonderful.

Wolsk's
81 Ludlow Street (just south of Delancey)
New York, NY 10002
PHONE: (212) 475-0704
SUBWAYS: Delancey Street station on the Sixth Avenue F line; Essex Street
    station on the Nassau Street J, M, and Z lines.
HOURS: 8 A.M. to 5 P.M. Sunday through Thursday; 8 A.M. to 2:30 P.M.
    Friday; closed Saturday.
No deliveries.
Cash only in the store.
Visa and MasterCard accepted for telephone orders.
Mail order available.
Extensive gift basket selection.

$\mathscr{B}$RONX

Hoft's ⏤ See page 178.

$\mathscr{B}$ROOKLYN

Sahadi Importing Company ⏤ See page 140.

Best of Chocolates, Candy, and Nuts

Best all-around candy store: Teuscher Chocolates
Best bonbons: Teuscher Chocolates
Best butter crunch: Mondel's Homemade Chocolates
Best chocolate-covered graham crackers: Hoft's
Best caramels: Fifth Avenue Chocolatièr
Best flavors (chocolate): Le Chocolatièr Manon
Best fruit jellies: La Maison du Chocolat
Best home-style candy: Li-Lac Chocolates
Best intense chocolate hit: Arribes at La Maison du Chocolat
Best marzipan: Elk Candy
Best nonpareils: Elk Candy
Best penny-candy store: Economy Candy
Best roasted nuts: Bazzini
Best truffles: Teuscher Chocolates

6

COFFEE, TEA, AND SPICES

E ven when the rest of America was drinking Maxwell House exclusively, lots of New Yorkers were drinking much more exotic coffee.
Specifically, the center of the New York coffee drinker's universe has always
been Greenwich Village. Bohemians, hipsters, and artists seem to thrive
on coffee (it's those late hours they keep, I think). They drank it at the
turn of the century, and they still drink it now, in coffeehouses such as
Cafe Borgia, Caffè Dante, and the Peacock Caffè. And when they weren't
drinking hot, steaming, full-bodied coffee in cafés, they wanted to drink
it in their apartments and lofts. They were fortunate that three of the
city's four oldest coffee emporiums were located in the Village. McNulty's
on Christopher Street opened for business in 1895, Schapira's (also known
as Flavor Cup) followed suit in 1903, and the Johnny-come-lately Porto
Rico Importing Company jumped on the coffee bandwagon in 1908.

That's not to say that other parts of New York hadn't discovered the
joys of drinking a real cup of coffee. German immigrants populating their
Yorkville neighborhood sated their coffee desires at M. Rohrs, established
in 1896. Paprikas Weiss and the now-gone Bremen House opened on the
Upper East Side in part to meet the coffee needs of the Hungarians and
other middle Europeans who shopped there. Upper West Siders had to

wait for Zabar's to open in 1935 to have a serious coffee store to call their own.

Today there are three distinct kinds of coffee stores serving the needs of New Yorkers. First, there are the aforementioned old-fashioned New York coffee stores. They've been around for nearly a century, and I can't imagine the city without them. Then there are the first-rate coffee departments of the mega-stores such as Zabar's, Balducci's, Dean & DeLuca, and Grace's Marketplace. Though their selection and price may vary greatly, their sales volume dictates tremendous turnover, the one absolutely indispensable key to ensuring great coffee. Lastly, there are the newest generation of coffee merchants. People like Oren Bloostein of Oren's Daily Roast treat coffee with such reverence, love, and respect that they're injecting new life into New York's coffee-selling community.

There are a couple of crucial things to know when buying coffee in New York. New York's strict health codes and environmental laws make it virtually impossible for anyone to roast his own beans in New York. The only exception to that is Schapira's, which has a grandfather clause in its lease that allows them to roast beans right on the premises. In fact, they'll let you come watch them roast if you call first to let them know you're coming. Oren Bloostein roasts his own beans in New Jersey and brings them into his three Manhattan locations every day. Everybody else with the exception of Zabar's uses the same classic triumverate of coffee wholesalers-roasters: White House, First Colony, and Gillies 1840. Murray Klein and Saul Zabar of Zabar's have their own roaster who roasts exclusively for them.

As I stated earlier, freshness, and therefore turnover, is the key to obtaining great coffee. Zabar's sells thirty thousand pounds of coffee a week, so you know their beans are impeccably fresh. Even if one of the reputable wholesalers supplies your local deli, it means nothing if the coffee sits there for weeks at a time.

Once you buy it, keep coffee in an airtight container in the refrigerater or freezer. Ground coffee will keep in a freezer for three weeks before you'll start to notice a deterioration in taste. That doesn't mean you can't drink it after three weeks. It just means the coffee will begin to lose some of its flavor and distinctive qualities. Unground beans will last two months, again stored in an airtight container.

Although coffee has been taken seriously by New Yorkers for a long time, the same cannot be said for tea. Until ten years ago, Gothamites, like Americans everywhere, had to content themselves with Lipton and Tetley, with herbal tea drinkers opting for Celestial Seasonings. Even the radical-fringe tea drinkers only went as far as Earl Grey and Darjeeling. Now, every serious coffee retailer I talked to mentioned the increasing popularity of loose teas. Places like Porto Rico and the Sensuous Bean carry up to fifty kinds of loose tea. New Yorkers interested in Chinese teas can now satisfy their curiosity at Ten Ren Tea and Ginseng Company. Those of us interested in French aromatic teas can now buy them at Danal.

With the healthy-food movement exploding all over the world, it's not surprising that New Yorkers have gotten interested in herbs and spices as low-calorie ways to flavor food. Even ten years ago we contented ourselves with curry powder and fresh garlic as exotic herbs and spices of choice. Who would have thought that today people in the city can buy oregano still on the branch or fresh coriander virtually year-round.

UPPER WEST SIDE

59TH STREET TO 125TH STREET
CENTRAL PARK WEST TO RIVERSIDE DRIVE

Adriana's Bazaar ~ See page 116.

Azteca Deli Grocery ~ See page 116.

Fairway ~ See page 221.

Kalpana Indian Groceries and Spices ~ See page 117.

The Sensuous Bean ~ When Joe Pumphrey left his corporate law job to open the Sensuous Bean in 1976, the legal profession's loss became the West Side coffee drinker's gain. Joe sold out in 1990 to Lucretia and Dorothy LaMura, but I haven't seen any discernible loss in service or quality. Fifty kinds of coffee and twenty-eight kinds of tea can be blended in any configuration you want at this extremely civilized and unpretentious place. The coffees run the gamut from the exotic (toasted praline) to the refined (the Swiss coffee La Semeuse, served at Lutèce). The teas range from orange pekoe to strawberry kiwi. The Sensuous Bean is a true specialty store; all it carries is coffee, tea, coffee and tea makers, and their accompanying materials. No lox, no whitefish, not even a coffee cake.

The Sensuous Bean
66 West 70th Street (between Columbus and Central Park West)
New York, NY 10023
PHONE: (212) 724-7725
SUBWAYS: 72nd Street station on the following lines: Broadway–Seventh
    Avenue No. 1, 2, 3, and 9; Eighth Avenue C and Sixth Avenue B.
HOURS: 10 A.M. to 7 P.M. Monday through Friday; 9:30 A.M. to 7 P.M.
    Saturday; noon to 6 P.M. Sunday.
All major credit cards accepted.
Mail order catalog available.

Stop One Supermarket ~ See page 117.

Zabar's ~ See page 237.

*U*PPER EAST SIDE

59TH STREET TO 96TH STREET
FIRST AVENUE TO FIFTH AVENUE

Bloomingdale's ~ See page 212.

Grace's Marketplace ~ See page 225.

M. Rohrs ∼ Since 1896, M. Rohrs has been selling coffee out of its gorgeous antique red-and-gold coffee tins to loyal customers from all over the Upper East Side. Dennis Smith, the store's current owner, isn't even distantly related to the Rohrs family, but he is just as committed to selling fresh, high-quality coffee at a fair price. Choose from almost forty kinds of beans that you can either bring home unground or have Dennis grind in his old-fashioned grinder. I'm partial to both the strong Ethiopia Yrgachese and the woody-tasting Tanzania Peaberry. M. Rohrs carries almost twenty kinds of loose tea, including a delicious cinnamon tea my whole family loves. It also carries coffeepots and filters, and tea pots and strainers.

M. Rohrs
1692 Second Avenue (between 87th and 88th streets)
New York, NY 10128
PHONE: (212) 427-8319
SUBWAYS: 86th Street station on the Lexington Avenue No. 4, 5, and 6 lines.
HOURS: 9:30 A.M. to 6:30 P.M. Monday through Friday; 9 A.M. to 6 P.M.
   Saturday.
No deliveries.
Cash only.
Mail order and shipping available.

Oren's Daily Roast ∼ The three Oren's Daily Roast stores are perhaps the most user-friendly coffee stores in the city. The help is knowledgeable and friendly, the coffee is beautifully displayed in glass cannisters, and the stores are filled with helpful pamphlets that tell you anything you want to know about coffee. The coffee itself is incredibly fresh, as Oren Bloostein roasts it himself in small batches in New Jersey two or three times a week. The selection is varied, featuring many unusual African and Central and South American beans. Try the Arabian mocha mattari or the Zimbabwe 053. What he doesn't carry is flavored coffees, so you won't find vanilla fudge twirl coffee at Oren's.

Oren's Daily Roast
1574 First Avenue (between 81st and 82nd streets)
New York, NY 10028
PHONE: (212) 737-2690
SUBWAYS: 86th Street station on the Lexington Avenue No. 4, 5, and 6 lines.
HOURS: 7 A.M. to 8 P.M. Monday through Friday; 10 A.M. to 6 P.M. Saturday;
   10 A.M. to 5 P.M. Sunday.
All major credit cards accepted.
Mail order available.

OTHER LOCATIONS:
434 Third Avenue (between 30th and 31st streets)
New York, NY 10016
(212) 779-1241

1144 Lexington Avenue (between 79th and 80th streets)
New York, NY 10021
(212) 472-6830

Paprikas Weiss ∼ See page 120.

ℳIDTOWN WEST

34TH STREET TO 59TH STREET
FIFTH AVENUE TO ELEVENTH AVENUE

Empire Coffee and Tea ⁓ If you're shopping the Ninth Avenue food axis, this store is worth a visit. Its principal advantage is variety. Seventy kinds of coffee can be found here, including exotic types like Peruvian and chocolate-macadamia nut. Empire also carries seventy varieties of loose tea, including such exotica as Russian wine, lychee black tea, and Assam, an Indian tea. Prices are reasonable, if not dirt cheap, but the service can be slapdash and not terribly friendly.

Empire Coffee and Tea
592 Ninth Avenue (between 42nd and 43rd streets)
New York, NY 10036
PHONE: (212) 586-1717
SUBWAYS: 42nd Street–Port Authority Bus Terminal station on the Eighth
    Avenue A, C, and E lines.
HOURS: 8:30 A.M. to 7 P.M. Monday through Friday; 9 A.M. to 6:30 P.M.
    Saturday; closed Sunday.
Delivery available between 14th and 86th streets.
All major credit cards accepted.

International Grocery ⁓ See page 122.

Macy's Cellar Marketplace ⁓ See page 229.

9th Avenue Cheese Market ⁓ See page 69.

𝒞HELSEA

14TH STREET TO 34TH STREET
FIFTH AVENUE TO ELEVENTH AVENUE

Kitchen Food Shop ⁓ See page 308.

𝒦IPS BAY/GRAMERCY PARK

14TH STREET TO 34TH STREET
EAST RIVER TO FIFTH AVENUE

Kalustyan's ⁓ See page 124.

Oren's Daily Roast — See page 94.

Spice and Sweet Mahal — See page 125.

Todaro Brothers — See page 233.

*W*EST VILLAGE

14TH STREET TO HOUSTON STREET
FIFTH AVENUE TO WEST STREET

Aphrodisia — Browsing through an herb-and-spice store can be a daunting experience for the uninitiated. After all, who knows how to pronounce fenugreek, much less use it. Aphrodisia, however, makes it somewhat easier with its complete reference library in the back of the store. The store carries five hundred different kinds of herbs and spices, so the library comes in handy. If you want to buy whole allspice berries to grind yourself, you'll find them here. About half the store's inventory is for cooking. The rest are medicinal herbs, hence the primary purpose for the reference library: it's illegal for the store to dispense herbal medicinal advice so the owners figure the best they can do is let you read about it.

Note: Aphrodisia carries no fresh herbs.

Aphrodisia
282 Bleecker Street (between Sixth and Seventh avenues)
New York, NY 10014
PHONE: (212) 989-6440
SUBWAYS: Christopher Street–Sheridan Square station on the Broadway–
Seventh Avenue No. 1 and 9 lines; West Fourth Street–Washington
Square station on the following lines: Sixth Avenue B, D, F, and Q;
Eighth Avenue A, C, and E.
HOURS: 11 A.M. to 7 P.M. Monday through Saturday; noon to 5 P.M. Sunday.
All major credit cards accepted.

Balducci's — See page 205.

Hot Stuff Spicy Food Store — Though I like hot and spicy food just fine, I'm not one of the gluttons for punishment who goes out of his way to pick out and eat the Szechuan peppers at a Chinese restaurant. So I was a little bit wary when Hot Stuff proprietor David Jenkins offered me a taste of something called Melinda's XXXTRA Hot Sauce, made with habañero peppers, merely the hottest peppers to be found on this earth. I took just the tiniest dab of it, about the amount of perfume a tasteful woman wears, and put it on a tortilla chip. It was so hot my mouth tingled for a full five minutes. As is evidenced by the store name, Hot Stuff carries incendiary sauces from all over the world. You'll find everything from sambals, those piquant relishes served at an Indonesian Fijsttafel feast, to Inner Beauty Hot Sauce, a Caribbean concoction that tastes great on chicken. You'll also find all kinds of hot Indian, West African, and Caribbean sauces and condiments. Many of the products have wonderful names like Hot Sauce from Hell and Satan's Revenge. In season, Jenkins carries fresh New Mexican chilies. At Hot Stuff there are cookbooks with titles like *Hotter Than Hell*, chili pepper wreaths (which are actually quite handsome), and chili pepper lights to put on your Christmas tree. Even if you're not so obsessed with hot food as Jenkins, Hot Stuff is a fun store to browse. He's always got a dozen sauces that he puts out for tasting. Some of them aren't even that hot.

Hot Stuff Spicy Food Store
227 Sullivan Street (between Bleecker and West 3rd Streets)
New York, N.Y. 10012
PHONE: (212) 254-6120
SUBWAY: West Fourth Street-Washington Square station on the following
  lines: Sixth Avenue B, D, F, and Q; Eighth Avenue A, C, and E.
HOURS: 11 A.M. to 9 P.M. every day.
Delivery by special arrangement only.
All major credit cards.
Mail order available.

McNulty's Tea and Coffee

McNulty's Tea and Coffee — McNulty's has been doing the same thing for nearly 100 years: selling fresh, high-quality coffees and teas in an old-fashioned setting replete with tin ceilings and wooden slat floors and bins. Though the current owner, Tai Lee, has owned the place for only ten years, the store's quality and service standards remain unchanged. On any given day McNulty's has seventy-five kinds of coffee, ranging from the usual Hawaiian Kona and Kenya AA to the obscure Chinese coffee from Yunnan, a sharp, snappy brew, and Indian Mysore, a lighter but still flavorful coffee. One interesting note: McNulty's price for Jamaican Blue Mountain is usually a full $10.00 cheaper per pound than that of its village counterpart, Porto Rico Importing Company.

McNulty's Tea and Coffee
109 Christopher Street (between Bleecker and Hudson streets)
New York, NY 10014
PHONE: (212) 242-5351
SUBWAYS: Christopher Street–Sheridan Square station on the Broadway–
  Seventh Avenue No. 1 and 9 lines.
HOURS: 10 A.M. to 9 P.M. Monday through Saturday; 1 P.M. to 7 P.M. Sunday.
All major credit cards accepted.
Mail-order catalog available

OTHER LOCATION:
247 Columbus Avenue (between 71st and 72nd streets)
New York, NY 10023
PHONE: (212) 362-4700
PHONE ORDERS: (800) 356-5200

Peter Longo sells nearly five dozen types of coffee and more than 140 types of loose tea at Porto Rico Importing Company.

Porto Rico Importing Company ~~~ Of the three old-time Village coffee stores, Porto Rico is the upstart, having been open only eighty-four years. But judging by the lines that form in the store every Saturday, the immediate community doesn't care that it's the new kid on the block. Peter Longo sells 58 coffees and 140 loose teas. It's the only place in the city that carries Panamanian Bouquette, an inexpensive rich, sweet, aromatic coffee. He also carries, much to the chagrin of coffee purists, a full line of flavored coffees, including peaches-and-cream and chocolate-mint. His loose teas include Darjeeling, T.G.F.O.P. Tigerhill, China Lapsang, and Crocodile. The only other thing Porto Rico sells besides coffee and tea is a full line of coffee and tea makers at heavily discounted prices.

Porto Rico Importing Company
201 Bleecker Street (just east of Sixth Avenue)
New York, NY 10012
PHONE: (212) 477-5421
SUBWAYS: West Fourth Street–Washington Square station on the following
    lines: Eighth Avenue A, C, and E; Sixth Avenue B, D, F, and Q.
HOURS: 9:30 A.M. to 9 P.M. Monday through Saturday; noon to 7 P.M.
    Sunday.
No deliveries.
All major credit cards accepted.
Mail-order catalog available.

The sign over the door reads "Flavor Cup," but inside you'll find the coffee domain of Schapira Coffee Company.

OTHER LOCATIONS:
Porto Rico Importing Company
40½ St. Mark's Place (between First and Second avenues)
New York, NY 10003
(212) 533-1982

Auggie's
107 Thompson Street (between Prince and Spring streets)
New York, NY 10012
(212) 966-5758

Schapira Coffee Company ~ One look at, or one whiff of, the inside of Schapira Coffee (also known in the neighborhood as Flavor Cup), and you know its owners are devoted to coffee. Piles of unroasted coffee beans from all over the world lie in burlap bags, awaiting roasting in the old-fashioned coffee-bean roasters located in the back of the store. Immediately on the left as you walk in are bins of coffees and teas for sale. Everything about the store, from the coffee to the wood bins, is a delight to the senses.

You have entered the coffee domain of the Schapira family, who have been selling coffee and tea for nine decades in the same location. Schapira is the only store in Manhattan that roasts its own beans. In fact, if you give them a call, they'll let you come and watch them roast. They do it every day, so you know the coffee is the freshest anywhere.

As could be expected in this caffeine purist's store, the Schapiras don't go in for exotic-flavored coffees. They sell twenty-five varieties, including standards like Colombian, Kenyan, Kona, and mocha java. Try the house-blend brown roast, a light yet full-bodied coffee; or the store's Italian roast, a darker blend of Colombian and other Central American coffees; or, for something different, the Venezuelan coffee, which has a winy, pungent flavor. You won't be disappointed with any of the coffees here.

Note: My friends Karen and Mitchell, coffee lovers to the bone, report that Schapira's mail-order service is the quickest to be found anywhere. If you call and order coffee, it goes out the same day and arrives two days later anywhere in the city or country.

Schapira Coffee Company
(Flavor Cup)
117 West 10th Street (between Greenwich and Sixth avenues)
New York, NY 10014
PHONE: (212) 675-3733
SUBWAYS: Christopher Street–Sheridan Square station on the Broadway–
   Seventh Avenue No. 1 and 9 lines; West Fourth Street–Washington
   Square station on the following lines: Sixth Avenue B, D, F, and Q;
   Eighth Avenue A, C, and E.
HOURS: 9 A.M. to 6:30 P.M. Monday through Friday; 9 A.M. to 5:30 P.M.
   Saturday; 11 A.M. to 4 P.M. Sunday.
Visa, MasterCard and personal checks accepted.
Mail-order catalog available.

*E*AST VILLAGE

14TH STREET TO HOUSTON STREET
EAST RIVER TO FIFTH AVENUE

Angelica's ~ Before I walked into Angelica's, I thought sea salt was sea salt. Silly me. Angelica's carries five kinds of sea salt from different parts of the world, to go along with the hundreds of spices, herbs, and organic foodstuffs they carry. Angelica's carries organically grown grains—everything from quinoa to ten different kinds of organic rice. In the back of the store they have an extensive tea section that features at least fifty teas at any one time. I spotted a mocha tea that smelled so bizarre I couldn't bring myself to buy it. Next to the teas is a terrific sign that says: "Delicious herbal teas. Not medicinal. They taste so good. Just to drink for pure pleasure." Angelica's also carries organically grown dried fruit in oversized metal cannisters in the front of the store. The last time I was there I asked for a quarter of a pound of dried bing cherries, figuring I'd get a hippie version of those wonderful cherries American Spoon Foods sells in upscale markets like Fairway. Imagine my surprise when my dried bing cherries turned out to have the pits still in them. That means of the four ounces of cherries I bought, three ounces were pits. Bummer.

Angelica's
147 First Avenue (corner of 9th Street)
New York, NY 10003
PHONE: (212) 677-1549 or (212) 529-4335
SUBWAY: Astor Place station on the Lexington Avenue No. 6 line.
HOURS: 10 A.M. to 7:45 P.M. Monday through Saturday; 11 A.M. to 6:45 P.M.
   Sunday.
Cash only.

Danal ⁓ Imagine you're visiting a friend's eccentric English grandmother who's lived in the same house for fifty years collecting tchotchkes, and you get an idea what it feels like walking into Danal, the city's only full-time tea salon. Although to truly experience Danal you have to sit down to tea there, you can create your own Danal experience by purchasing some of the wonderful aromatic teas they exclusively import from France. Danal's aromatics are black teas that have been blended with fruits and flowers. They're not herbal or decaffeinated, but they have the same soothing effect. Plus, they smell great. Try the Goût Russe Dutchka, which has a distinct grapefruit, lemon-lime, and orange taste; or the four-red-fruit, which has strawberries, raspberries, red currants, and cherries blended in. I've never had the Mélange Interdit, a blend of tangerine, lavender, vanilla, and grapefruit, but it sounds intriguing. Besides the seventeen aromatics, Danal also carries standard teas such as Earl Grey, Darjeeling, and oolong.

Danal
90 East 10th Street (between Third and Fourth Avenues)
New York, NY 10003
PHONE: (212) 982-6930
SUBWAYS: Astor Place station on the Lexington Avenue No. 6 line; 8th Street
　station on the Broadway N and R lines.
HOURS: 9 A.M. to 6:30 P.M. Tuesday through Friday; 11:30 A.M. to 5:30 P.M.
　Saturday and Sunday; Closed Monday.
No deliveries.
Credit cards accepted.
Mail-order available.

Pete's Spice and Everything Nice ⁓ Before walking into Pete's, I didn't know that there were two kinds of lemongrass: one to make tea with and the other to use in Thai cooking. But Pete's is the kind of store that will teach you everything there is to know about spices, herbs, and grains. From fifteen kinds of rice, including a red Thai rice, to black sesame seeds to Jacobs cattle beans, Pete's has everything. You want pumpernickel flour to make your own pumpernickel bagels, Pete's has it. Not only does Pete's carry everything, but also owner Donald Camy patiently explains how to cook the special foods you've just bought.

Pete's Spice and Everything Nice
174 First Avenue (between 10th and 11th streets)
New York, NY 10003
PHONE: (212) 254-8773
SUBWAYS: First Avenue station on the 14th Street–Canarsie L line; Astor
　Place station on the Lexington Avenue No. 6 line.
HOURS: 10 A.M. to 7:30 P.M. Monday through Saturday; 12:30 P.M. to 5 P.M.
　Sunday.
No deliveries.
Cash only.
Spice catalog available.

Porto Rico Importing Company ⁓ See page 98.

$\mathscr{D}$OWNTOWN

HOUSTON STREET TO BATTERY PARK

Auggie's ⏤ See page 99.

Dean & DeLuca ⏤ See page 214.

Kam Kuo Food ⏤ See page 127.

Kam Man Foods ⏤ See page 127.

Ten Ren Tea and Ginseng Company ⏤ Walking into the soothing environs of Ten Ren after a day of frenetically paced shopping in Chinatown is like finding an oasis in the dessert. You walk in, sit down at a perfect little table for two, and try whatever tea you're considering buying. Ten Ren actually owns its own tea plantations in Taiwan. They'll tell you anything you want to know about their many kinds of conventional and ginseng teas. Besides the teas, which are sold in gorgeous, old-fashioned lacquered bins, Ten Ren also carries lovely, simple Chinese tea sets. Spend a few minutes in Ten Ren, and you will walk out rejuvenated and ready to face the Chinatown throngs once again.

Ten Ren Tea and Ginseng Company
176 Canal Street (between Mott and Elizabeth streets)
New York, NY 10013
PHONE: (212) 925-9822
SUBWAYS: Canal Street station on the following lines: Lexington Avenue No.
   6, Broadway N and R, Nassau Street J, M, and Z; Grand Street station on
   the Sixth Avenue B, D, and Q lines.
HOURS: 10 A.M. to 8 P.M. seven days a week.
All major credit cards accepted.
Mail order available.

$\mathscr{B}$ROOKLYN

Sahadi Importing Company ⏤ See page 140.

Best of Coffee, Tea, and Spices

Best all-around coffee store: Oren's Daily Roast; Schapira Coffee Company
Best prices: Zabar's
Best selection (coffee): McNulty's Tea and Coffee; Porto Rico Importing
    Company
Best selection (tea): Bloomingdale's
Best service: Oren's Daily Roast; Schapira Coffee Company
Best spice store: International Grocery; Kalustyan's; Sahadi Importing
    Company
Best tea (Chinese): Ten Ren Tea and Ginseng Company

7

COOKWARE AND COOKING UTENSILS

B ecause New York is arguably the culinary capital of America, it makes sense that it's also the best place in this country to shop for cookware and cooking utensils. The serious amateur or professional chef will find anything he or she needs in Manhattan. From Japanese ice-sculpture tools to German truffle-carving instruments, New York cookware stores have it all.

Basically, you can divide cooking utensils and cookware into two separate categories. There are the things you need to prepare and cook the food and the things you need to serve and present it. Stores, even large department stores such as Bloomingdale's and Macy's, tend to be thoroughly stocked in either the preparation and cooking items or in the presenting and serving paraphernalia, but not both. So the best way to use the information found in this chapter is to know which of these categories you are interested in before you set out on a shopping expedition.

As in wine stores, price, service, selection, and general attitude are the qualities that distinguish cookware establishments. For example, if you sort of know what you want, but you're not sure, and you're interested in being educated without being bludgeoned or beaten up when you shop, Broadway Panhandler is the store for you. However, if you know exactly what you want and why you want it, and if you're willing to be subjected occasionally to Fred Bridge's abuse, Bridge Kitchenware is the only place to go (see page 109). Again, as with wine stores, if you find a salesperson who's been helpful and steered you right once, stick with the store and that salesperson.

$\mathcal{U}$PPER WEST SIDE

59TH STREET TO 125TH STREET
CENTRAL PARK WEST TO RIVERSIDE DRIVE

Zabar's Housewares — For years now Murray Klein and Saul Zabar have tried to position their housewares and cookware department against the big department stores as the knowledgeable consumer's only logical shopping choice. Though the comparative language they use on the signs in the store can often be hyperbolic and strident, they're right. In terms of price and selection, Zabar's is one of New York's best housewares and cookware stores. Within its chaotic, poorly laid out environs, you can find everything from the sublime and elegant (a copper fish steamer) to the ridiculous and funky (a french-fry refrigerator magnet). Bread machines, pressure cookers, coffee makers, waffle irons, hot plates, rice cookers, Crockpots, bamboo steamers, microwave dishes, salad spinners, toasters, pizza stones, citrus peelers, pepper mills, and egg timers are just a few of the hundreds of items on display and literally hanging from the ceiling in this cook's nirvana. Its cutlery selection includes Henckel, Wusthof, Sabatier, Gerber, and Chicago Cutlery. Zabar's also carries all the major cookware lines, including All-Clad, Calphalon, T-FAL, and Le Creuset, as well as all the significant manufacturers of electrical gadgets for the kitchen, such as Braun, DeLonghi, Gaggia, Krups, and GE. You'll find things you can't find anywhere else, like the German Rosle's Cook Shop line of incredibly heavy-duty, well-made metal kitchen implements. What you often won't find is somebody to help you. When the store is crowded, finding a salesperson is difficult, and finding a knowledgeable salesperson for anything besides the basic electrical gadgets is nearly impossible. You also won't find much of a selection of plates and glasses.

Zabar's Housewares
2245 Broadway (between 80th and 81st streets)
Second floor
New York, NY 10024
PHONE: (212) 787-2000

SUBWAYS: 79th Street station on the Broadway–Seventh Avenue No. 1 and 9
    lines; 81st Street station on the Eighth Avenue C and Sixth Avenue B
    lines.
HOURS: 9 A.M. to 6 P.M. seven days a week.
No deliveries.
All major credit cards accepted.
Mail order available.

𝒰PPER EAST SIDE

59TH STREET TO 96TH STREET
FIRST AVENUE TO FIFTH AVENUE

Bloomingdale's Main Course — With huge selections of designer glassware,
flatware, and plates, the Main Course is every bride's dream. But for the serious
cook, the Main Course isn't all that impressive a place. They carry all the requisite
brands like Calphalon, All-Clad, and Le Creuset, but the selection is often sparse
and the nonsale prices are perilously close to list. They do occasionally carry
brands I've never seen anywhere else. The last time I was there, I bought a heavy-
gauge French nonstick frypan, an Analon, that is guaranteed to keep its nonstick
coating for ten years. The store seems oriented toward gadgetry, which makes
sense, given the store's glitzy, nonutilitarian orientation. What surprises me is
how difficult it is to get a question answered by a salesperson. They're either
nowhere to be found or brusque when you do find them.

Bloomingdale's Main Course
1000 Third Avenue (between 59th and 60th streets)
New York, NY 10022
PHONE: (212) 355-5900
SUBWAYS: 59th Street station on the Lexington Avenue No. 4, 5, and 6 lines;
    Lexington Avenue station on the Sixth Avenue B and Q lines and the
    Broadway N and R lines.
HOURS: 10 A.M. to 9 P.M. Monday and Thursday; 10 A.M. to 6:30 P.M.
    Tuesday, Wednesday, Friday, and Saturday; noon to 6 P.M. Sunday.
Delivery available.
All major credit cards accepted.
Mail-order catalog available.

Kitchen Arts and Letters — When Kitchen Arts and Letters owner Nach Waxman
explained to me that "no book is sold here without a conversation," I realized
that he is as fascinated and obsessed with food as I am. Waxman carries six
thousand titles in his tiny store, all of them related to food. He carries cookbooks,
fiction with food themes, restaurant guides for New York and many other major
cities in the United States and Europe, a comprehensive list of wine books, books
on food agriculture and farming, and (a man after my own heart!) six photo and
essay books on diners. He also carries an extensive selection of books published
abroad as well as lots of food and cooking memorabilia like antique food labels,

restaurant postcards, crate labels, and early food-related print ads. Kitchen Arts and Letters is a store made for browsing, conversing, and, alas, buying. The last time I visited, I ended up staying an hour and a half, and buying seventy-five dollars' worth of books.

Note: Although Waxman has only a couple of shelves of out-of-print books in the store, he has thousands of titles in his basement. He will conduct a free search for any book he doesn't have.

Kitchen Arts and Letters
1435 Lexington Avenue (between 93rd and 94th streets)
New York, NY 10128
PHONE: (212) 876-5550
SUBWAY: 96th Street station on the Lexington Avenue No. 6 line.
HOURS: 1 P.M. to 6 P.M. Monday; 10 A.M. to 6:30 P.M. Tuesday through
    Friday; 11 A.M. to 6 P.M. Saturday; closed Sunday; closed Saturday during
    July and August.
Credit cards and personal checks accepted.
Telephone orders accepted and shipped out upon receipt of check.

Williams-Sonoma — Going from a crowded, chaotic scene like Zabar's to the extremely civilized, genteel halls of Williams-Sonoma can be a shock to the system. When I walked into Williams-Sonoma, a distinguished-looking man dressed in a rather formal suit came up to me and inquired in a nonimperious British accent, "May I assist you with anything?" Williams-Sonoma's laid-back, comfortable environment is the best and perhaps only reason to shop here. It carries a limited selection of high-quality, upscale goods at standard to high prices. You can usually find one brand of whatever it is you're looking for, whether it's cutlery (Wusthof) or cookware (All-Clad) or an espresso maker (Braun). What is surprising about Williams-Sonoma is the number of good values you can find on plates and glasses. You expect to find Portuguese majolica at Williams-Sonoma, but you don't expect to find inexpensive, handsome Blue Wave Chinese tableware and numerous shelves of reasonably priced hand-blown glasses from Hungary. (Maybe it's cross-pollination from the Williams-Sonoma–Pottery Barn merger.) The store also carries a limited selection of cookbooks and gourmet foods. The cookbooks weren't anything special, but the specialty foods—things like Callebaut chocolate and gooseberry preserves from Oregon—were impressive.

Williams-Sonoma
20 East 60th Street (between Madison and Park avenues)
New York, NY 10021
PHONE: (212) 980-5155
SUBWAYS: 59th Street station on the Lexington Avenue No. 4, 5, and 6 lines;
    Lexington Avenue station on the Sixth Avenue B and Q lines; Fifth
    Avenue station on the Broadway N and R lines.
HOURS: 10 A.M. to 7 P.M. Monday through Friday; 10 A.M. to 6 P.M. Saturday;
    noon to 5 P.M. Sunday.
Deliveries by messenger service.
All major credit cards accepted.
Mail order available.

OTHER LOCATION:
110 Seventh Avenue (at 17th Street)
New York, NY 10011
(212) 633-2203

1175-1179 Madison Ave (at 86th Street)
New York, NY 10028

Also, outlet store at
231 Tenth Avenue (between 23rd and 24th streets)
New York, NY 10011
(212) 206-8118

*M*IDTOWN WEST

34TH STREET TO 59TH STREET
FIFTH AVENUE TO ELEVENTH AVENUE

J. B. Prince --- The first time I walked into J. B. Prince, I overheard a friendly discussion between a chef and a caterer over the relative merits of Japanese ice-carving tools. That exchange alone told me that J. B. Prince is for serious chefs only. It was opened twelve years ago by Judy Prince, a dedicated amateur chef who frequently found herself unable to find the tools she needed for a specific recipe. She doesn't bother with everyday pots and pans. You won't find Le Creuset or All-Clad here. What you will find is an incredible selection of things like *tuile* pans—molded pans that can be used only for baking *tuiles*, those U-shaped butter cookies served with dessert in French restaurants. You'll also find handmade truffle cutters from Germany, a full line of chocolate molds and models for making your own candy, and a full line of molds for game pies and pâtés. There's also a selection of unusual books about food, including nifty books about things like Chinese garnish techniques. The last time I was here I bought a terrific book on spices. J. B. Prince is located in a suite of offices on the seventh floor of a Midtown office building, and it's actually more of a showroom for its huge mail-order catalog than a retail store. But it does have loads of interesting, hard-to-find chef's tools on hand. The staff is amazingly friendly and helpful, especially given what they sell and whom they sell it to.

J. B. Prince
29 West 38th Street (between Fifth and Sixth avenues)
Seventh floor
New York, NY 10018
PHONE: (212) 302-8611
SUBWAYS: 34th Street station on the Sixth Avenue B, D, F, and Q and the
    Broadway N and R lines.
HOURS: 9 A.M. to 5 P.M. Monday through Friday; closed Saturday and
    Sunday.
No deliveries.
All major credit cards accepted.
Mail order available (in fact, most of their sales are mail-order).

Macy's Cellar Marketplace ～ Macy's Cellar is basically a better-laid-out Bloomingdale's, with a greater emphasis on less expensive product lines. That means that while they carry high-end brands such as Calphalon and Henckel, they also carry a greater variety of mid-range cutlery and cookware. So you're likely to see more Supra and Farberware pots and pans and Rowenta cutlery. On the other hand, its selection of electric gadgetry is more limited and less toney than that at Bloomie's. The dedicated home chef will find a few more specific kitchen implements, such as garlic presses and pastry bags. Another advantage Macy's has over Bloomie's is that the first-rate gourmet food department is right next to the housewares and cookware section. At Bloomingdale's, they're separated by five floors.

Macy's Cellar Marketplace
151 West 34th Street at Herald Square (the entire block between Broadway
    and Seventh Avenue)
New York, NY 10001
PHONE: (212) 736-5151
SUBWAYS: 34th Street station on the Sixth Avenue B, D, F, and Q and the
    Broadway N and R lines; 34th Street–Penn Station on the Broadway–
    Seventh Avenue No. 1, 2, 3, and 9 and the Eighth Avenue A, C, and E
    lines.
HOURS: 9:45 A.M. to 8:30 P.M. Monday, Thursday, and Friday; 9:45 A.M. to
    6:45 P.M. Tuesday, Wednesday, and Saturday; 10 A.M. to 6 P.M. Sunday.
Deliveries available.
All major credit cards accepted.
Mail order available by calling 1 (800) 446-2297.

ℳIDTOWN EAST

34TH STREET TO 59TH STREET
FIRST AVENUE TO FIFTH AVENUE

Bridge Kitchenware ～ See below.

The Customer Is Always Wrong: The World According to Fred Bridge

"I'm the king of this business," Fred Bridge said, gesturing toward a row of the thousands of pieces of cooking equipment he carries in his store. "Ask anyone, they all come in here," he said pointing to one of at least a dozen yellowed newspaper clippings showing Fred Bridge and one of his famous customers, including Julia Child, the late Danny Kaye, and Lutèce's André Soltner.

The business Fred Bridge is pronouncing himself king of is the

The Customer Is Always Wrong:
The World According to Fred Bridge, continued

kitchenware business. And though Mr. Bridge's statement says at least as much about him as it does about his store, a quick perusal of his premises indicates he just might be right. From pie cutters that automatically and evenly dissect any size of pie to five-hundred-dollar copper pots, Fred Bridge carries everything the amateur or professional chef might employ. You need a specially made, double-thick cookie sheet, he's got it. You need a *sauteuse*, a copper pan that functions as both a frypan and a saucepan, Fred's got it. You need a paella pan, come to Bridge, where Fred Bridge will sell you a paella pan that he himself designed—presuming, of course, that he deems your intentions serious enough that he will let you buy one of his pans.

You see, unlike most other retailers, Fred Bridge feels the retailer is always right. Conversely, the customer is almost always wrong. So you have to be prepared for a full frontal assault if you walk into Bridge Kitchenware and he deigns to wait on you.

I tried to warn my sister-in-law Carol when she walked into Bridge with me one late fall day to inquire about nonstick frypans. "Now, Carol," I said protectively, "don't be upset if he bites your head off when you ask him a question. That's just his manner. He's really okay."

Armed with my warning, Carol proceeded to walk up to Fred Bridge and asked, innocently enough, "Could you please give me some advice on nonstick fry pans? I've been using a T-FAL, but there are a lot of nicks and cuts on the cooking surface, and food is beginning to stick. Is there another brand that's better?" Bridge immediately replied, "T-FAL's the best there is. It shouldn't scratch if you take good care of it. So maybe you're careless."

Attempting to intervene, I said, "Mr. Bridge, I'm Ed Levine, and I interviewed you a couple of months ago for a book I'm writing." "Is she with you?" he asked, pointing to my sister-in-law. I nodded, and he continued, "Well, maybe you can tell me why she's so careless." Being a perservering sort, Carol wouldn't back down. "I'm not careless," she said, "I use only plastic or wood utensils, and I've been using the pan for fifteen years." "You been using this pan for fifteen years?" he said. "Why didn't you say that in the first place. You can't ask for more than that from any pan. You're not careless. Just buy another T-FAL."

Not all interactions with Fred Bridge are so painful. When he does get to know you, he can be downright charming in his own cantankerous way. Many people I know who have shopped at Bridge for years just ignore the man's permanently pained expression.

Fred Bridge and his store are not for everyone. My sister-in-law, for example, is not likely to return anytime soon. But I'm content to wander through his wonderful store, discovering all kinds of zippy cooking items that you can't find anywhere else. After all, Fred Bridge doesn't bite. At least I've never seen him bite anyone.

Bridge Kitchenware
214 East 52nd Street (between Second and Third avenues)
New York, NY 10022
PHONE: (212) 688-4220
SUBWAYS: 51st Street station on the Lexington Avenue No. 6 line;
   Lexington and Third avenues station on the Sixth Avenue F and Eighth
   Avenue E lines.
HOURS: 9 A.M. to 5:30 P.M. Monday through Friday; 10 A.M. to 4:30 P.M.
   Saturday; closed Sunday.
Visa and MasterCard accepted.
Mail order available.

𝒦IPS BAY/GRAMERCY PARK

14TH STREET TO 34TH STREET
FIRST AVENUE TO FIFTH AVENUE

Fishs Eddy ⸺ See page 112.

𝒞HELSEA

14TH STREET TO 34TH STREET
FIFTH AVENUE TO ELEVENTH AVENUE

Chocolate Gallery ⸺ You're one of those compulsive do-it-yourselfers who's decided to make a multicolored, multitiered cake adorned with rhinos using hula
hoops. Don't despair. Head on down to the Chocolate Gallery, the only store in
New York devoted to cake-making supplies. From all kinds of molds and pans to
colored sugars to cartoon-character figurines, the Chocolate Gallery has every
conceivable item related to cake and cookie baking. In addition, if you decide you
want to launch a cake-making career, Chocolate Gallery runs a cake-making and
cake-decorating school. Many of the clerks in the store are friendly and knowledgeable and, if anything, know too much about the art of cake making.

Chocolate Gallery
34 West 22nd Street (between Fifth and Sixth avenues)
New York, NY 10010
PHONE: (212) 675-2253
SUBWAYS: 23rd Street station on the Broadway N and R lines and the Sixth
   Avenue F line.
HOURS: 10 A.M. to 6 P.M. Monday through Saturday; closed Sunday.
No deliveries.
All major credit cards accepted.
Mail order available.

Williams-Sonoma ⁓ See page 107.

*W*EST VILLAGE

14TH STREET TO HOUSTON STREET
FIFTH AVENUE TO WEST STREET

Fishs Eddy ⁓ Fishs Eddy specializes in industrial china—overruns on special-order china designed for institutions such as the government, hotels, cruise lines, country clubs, and restaurants. So if you've always wanted to eat at the Harvard Club but could never figure out how to get in, buy some of the Harvard Club china I saw on my last visit here. Then order some Chinese take-out, put on your Harvard sweatshirt, and you're home free; you won't even have to wear a jacket. Even if you don't want to buy anything, it's fun to browse through all the unusual crockery and gadgetry. For example, I've seen tableware on detour from the U.S. Navy and the International House of Pancakes (IHOP). Fishs Eddy also carries lots of Fiesta Ware, the brightly colored, utilitarian dinnerware from the thirties currently in vogue.

Note: Everything sold at Fishs Eddy is brand new. They will not sell used dishes.

Fishs Eddy
551 Hudson Street (between Perry and 11th streets)
New York, NY 10014
PHONE: (212) 627-3956
SUBWAYS: Christopher Street–Sheridan Square station on the Broadway–
   Seventh Avenue No. 1 and 9 lines.
HOURS: 10 A.M. to 11 P.M. Monday through Saturday; noon to 11 P.M.
   Sunday.
Deliveries in Manhattan.
Visa and MasterCard accepted.

OTHER LOCATION:
889 Broadway (between 19th and 20th streets)
New York, NY 10003
(212) 420-9020

*D*OWN TOWN

HOUSTON STREET TO BATTERY PARK

Broadway Panhandler ⁓ Broadway Panhandler is that retailing rarity in New York, a discount store that prides itself on good service. It sells high-quality merchandise in a relatively uncluttered, almost airy environment. Broadway Panhandler combines the best elements of an old-fashioned country store and an urban cookware emporium, selling everything from mason jars for putting up your own preserves to exquisitely crafted copper cookware. "We're here to guide people," store manager Page Watson commented, and the last time I was in the store I watched Page guide two young women to the back of the store to inspect the many wedding-cake decorations the store carries.

Note: Don't let the sight of numerous tchotchke-like items, such as candles and napkins, convince you the store doesn't sell high-quality merchandise. Although it doesn't have some of the absolutely top-of-the-line, superexpensive kitchenware that Bridge has, it does carry items such as Wusthof cutlery, Gaggia espresso makers, and All-Clad cookware. This particular store just doesn't let snobbery get in the way of serving the needs of many communities.

Broadway Panhandler
520 Broadway (between Spring and Broome streets)
New York, NY 10012
PHONE: (212) 966-3434
SUBWAYS: Prince Street station on the Broadway R line; Spring Street
    station on the Lexington Avenue No. 6 line.
HOURS: 10:30 A.M. to 6 P.M. Monday through Friday; 11 A.M. to 6 P.M.
    Saturday; noon to 5 P.M. Sunday.
No deliveries.
All major credit cards accepted.
Mail order available.

Dean & DeLuca — See page 214.

Hung Chong Import — Hung Chong Import has everything anyone would need for a complete Chinese kitchen, at prices 50 percent below what you would pay uptown. The store carries about twenty-five kinds of woks in every size and material imaginable, including one the size of a wading pool. You'll also find a wide selection of Chinese cleavers and other cutlery, and items like rice steamers and industrial-strength Chinese tea sets. The staff doesn't speak much English here, and you'll be vying for goods with every Chinese-restaurant owner in New York—but these prices make the jousting you'll do worthwhile.

Hung Chong Import
14 Bowery (between Pell and Doyers streets)
New York, NY 10002
PHONE: (212) 349-1463
SUBWAYS: Canal Street station on the following lines: Lexington Avenue No.
    6, Broadway N and R, Nassau Street J, M, and Z; Grand Street station on
    the Sixth Avenue B, D, and Q lines.
HOURS: 9 A.M. to 7 P.M. seven days a week.
No deliveries.
Cash only.
Mail order available.

Matas Restaurant Supply — There are at least fifty restaurant-supply stores on the Bowery between Houston Street and Canal Street, but there are only a couple that actively encourage retail customers. Matas is one of them. Its merchandise

is well displayed, the prices are low, and the men behind the desks are actually friendly. They even let me use their bathroom after spending a princely $1.50 on a tomato corer. Matas, like virtually every other store I visited in this area, carries three brands of pots and pans: Toroware, Supra, and Duraware. If you're looking for Le Creuset or Calphalon, you won't find it on the Bowery. Although the prices down here are low, it should be noted that the Toroware and Supra prices were only a dollar or two lower than at Zabar's. But if it's industrial salt and pepper shakers or industrial china you're looking for, this is where you'll find them.

Matas Restaurant Supply
226-230 Bowery (between Prince and Spring streets)
New York, NY 10002
PHONE: (212) 966-2251
SUBWAYS: Spring Street station on the Lexington Avenue No. 6 line; Second
    Avenue station on the Sixth Avenue F line.
HOURS: 8 A.M. to 5 P.M. Monday through Friday; 10 A.M. to 4 P.M. Saturday;
    closed Sunday.
Deliveries all over the New York area.
Cash and charge accounts only.
No mail order.

Best of Cookware and Cooking Utensils

Best all-around store: Broadway Panhandler
Best Chinese kitchenware store: Hung Chong Import
Best owner: Bridge Kitchenware
Best selection: Bridge Kitchenware
Best selection (exotica): J. B. Prince
Best service: Broadway Panhandler

8

ETHNIC MARKETS

I t is hard to imagine any other city in the world that has New York's array of ethnic markets. With recent immigrants streaming in from Africa, Asia, and Central and South America, it makes sense that markets have sprouted in every corner of the city to meet the food needs of these new New Yorkers. Add these stores to the existing markets opened for the earlier waves of Italian, Chinese, and Eastern European immigrants, and you would be hard-pressed to think of *any* foodstuff that couldn't be found in New York. From the West African Grocery on Ninth Avenue to the Brazilian Food Products store on West 46th Street, New York has virtually everything any homesick foreigner or adventurous cook could want.

Exploring these markets is rewarding and fun, and you don't have to use up any frequent-flyer mileage to do it. What's most enjoyable about going to these places is the warm and friendly reception you are likely to get. No matter how halting my pronunciation of an ingredient was or how sketchy my overall knowledge of a culture's food, I found the vast majority of shopkeepers to be exceedingly helpful and accommodating. They're more than happy to explain how to cook an unfamiliar-looking purchase. Although language barriers can occasionally be a problem, I have found there is almost always someone in the store (or in a neighboring store) who speaks enough English to overcome any communication difficulties.

$\mathcal{U}$PPER WEST SIDE

59TH STREET TO 125TH STREET
CENTRAL PARK WEST TO RIVERSIDE DRIVE

Adriana's Bazaar --- Adriana's Bazaar is the Certs of stores. It's actually two stores in one. First, it's a shop that specializes in spices and difficult-to-locate packaged and dried ingredients, mostly for Asian, Caribbean, Middle Eastern, and Central and South American cuisines. That means you'll find six kinds of *harissa*, the fiery condiment served with couscous. You'll also find jars of hard-to-find ingredients, such as Ras el Hanout, an Indian spice made with dried flowers and used in making curries, and bottles of Outerbridge Sherry Pepper Sauce for use in making Caribbean fish stew. This is also the only store I know that sells Kalustyan's amazing chutneys (see page 124). Not only does Adriana's Bazaar provide a source for all these ingredients, but also it has five hundred recipes on file that tell customers how to use what they've bought. And if owner Rochelle Zabarkes doesn't carry an ingredient you're looking for, she'll conduct a search free of charge.

The other component of Rochelle's store concept is a unique one involving prepared foods. She carries a rotating set of dishes from ten restaurants, caterers, and bakers around the city. The last time I was in the store she had ribs from Sylvia's in Harlem (see page 160), pungent and well-spiced chicken tikka masala from Gaylord's Indian restaurant, extraordinary desserts from the City Bakery (see page 30), and marvelous jerk chicken with an incendiary sauce from Elaine's, a local caterer. Anybody who makes Sylvia's ribs available one block from my apartment is okay with me.

Adriana's Bazaar
2152 Broadway (between 75th and 76th streets)
New York, NY 10023
PHONE: (212) 877-5757
SUBWAYS: 72nd Street station on the Broadway–Seventh Avenue 1, 2, 3, and
    9 lines.
HOURS: 10 A.M. to 9 P.M. Monday through Saturday; 11 A.M. to 7 P.M.
    Sundays.
Delivery available.
All major credit cards accepted.

Azteca Deli Grocery --- New York is not known for its Mexican food sources, so I got excited when my friend and fellow foodie Olga Rigsby told me about Azteca, where she had found many ingredients for a famous visiting Mexican chef. The shop carries a wide assortment of dried chilis, from *ancho* to *chile costeno* to *chile molido*, and dried Mexican herbs such as *tamarindo* and *guaje*, along with fresh flour tortillas made in that bastion of Mexican cooking, Passaic, New Jersey. Looking for quesadilla cheese? This is the place to find it. If you're in the neighborhood and interested in a quick lunch, stop by Azteca for one of its superb soft tacos. Every day they make beef, goat, tongue, and chicken varieties. When I ordered a chicken burrito, the proprietor shredded the chicken off the bone as I watched. Now that's what I call fresh. Wash down your burrito or taco with one of the Jarritos brand Mexican sodas or a bottled nonalcoholic sangria I've never seen anywhere else, Sangría Senoria, and you'll never know you're still on the West Side.

Azteca Deli Grocery
698 Amsterdam Avenue (between 93rd and 94th streets)
New York, NY 10024
No phone.
SUBWAYS: 96th Street station on the Broadway–Seventh Avenue 1, 2, 3, and
    9 lines.
HOURS: 8 A.M. to 11 P.M. every day.
No deliveries.
No credit cards.

Kalpana Indian Groceries and Spices — Kalpana owner Tony Maharaj is an Indian who grew up in Trinidad, which explains why he runs the only store I know of that carries both Indian basmati rice and genuine Jamaican ginger beer. Tony says his goal is to create a truly international food store. In recent years he has expanded into Indonesian, Middle Eastern, and Mexican foods, with a few Chinese and Thai foodstuffs thrown in for variety. His Indian offerings include real Lipton Darjeeling tea, which comes in a beautiful green can, unusual chutneys like cilantro and tamarind, and two kinds of custom-blended curry. His Caribbean items include Ting, a wonderful, somewhat tart grapefruit soda from St. Kitts; many kinds of hot sauces, including Jamaican jerk chicken sauce and a hot papaya sauce; and incendiary fresh peppers called Scotch Bonnets, from Jamaica. Kalpana is also the only Upper West Side store I've come across that carries lemongrass, both the fresh and the dried varieties. The store exudes friendly vibes, and Tony will explain how to use anything in stock. Oh yes, after you've done your food shopping at Kalpana, Tony will be glad to rent you one of the hundreds of Indian movies he keeps in back of the counter.

Kalpana Indian Groceries and Spices
2526 Broadway (between 94th and 95th streets)
New York, NY 10025
PHONE: (212) 663-4190
SUBWAYS: 96th Street station on the following lines: Broadway–Seventh
    Avenue No. 1, 2, 3, and 9; Eighth Avenue C; Sixth Avenue B.
HOURS: 1 P.M. to 8:30 P.M. Monday through Saturday; closed Sunday.
No deliveries.
Cash only.

Stop One Supermarket — At first glance Stop One Supermarket looks like a prototypical bodega. It's got big piles of plantains, a series of big cold cases for beer and soda, and containers of unidentifiable sweets on the counter near the register. But walking through the store you'll discover that, along with Kitchen (page 308), Stop One is the best source for dried Mexican chilies in New York. At any given moment, Stop One carries at least ten varieties, including *ancho, chile pasilla*, and *chile costeno*. Stop One also sells the wonderful Jarritos brand

Mexican tamarind soda, which tastes like a carbonated, not-very-sweet, iced fruit tea. Stop One makes terrific fresh tamales every day and soft tacos on weekends. The last time I was there on a Saturday, there were chicken tacos.

Stop One Supermarket
210 West 94th Street (between Broadway and Amsterdam Avenue)
New York, NY 10025
PHONE: (212) 316-5920
SUBWAYS: 96th Street station on the following lines: Broadway–Seventh
    Avenue No. 1, 2, 3, and 9; Eighth Avenue C and Sixth Avenue B.
HOURS: 8 A.M. to 1 A.M. seven days a week.
Cash only.

$\mathcal{U}$PPER EAST SIDE

59TH STREET TO 96TH STREET
FIRST AVENUE TO FIFTH AVENUE

Grace's Marketplace --- See page 225.

Katagiri --- Imagine your local Gristede's or D'Agostino's, downsize it by half, move it to Tokyo, and you'll get what it feels like to walk into Katagiri. Katagiri is your basic miniaturized Japanese grocery store. It stocks fresh fish, both imported from Japan and local; Japanese packaged goods, including cookies and noodles; Japanese beers and soft drinks; Japanese frozen foods, such as dumplings and TV dinners; and every Japanese foodstuff you could think of. In the back of the store is a full-service Japanese butcher counter that carries, among other things, the thin-sliced beef and pork you use to make sukiyaki. The front of the store has a sushi take-out counter.
    Note: Many of the people who work at Katagiri don't speak much English. But I found that a lot of its clientele, mostly Japanese expatriates or businesspeople stationed here, are more than happy to assist you in any way they can.

Katagiri
224 East 59th Street (between Second and Third avenues)
New York, NY 10022
PHONE: (212) 755-3566
SUBWAYS: 59th Street station on the Lexington Avenue No. 4, 5, and 6 lines;
    Lexington Avenue station on the Sixth Avenue B and Q lines and the
    Broadway N and R lines.
HOURS: 10 A.M. to 7 P.M. Monday through Saturday; 11 A.M. to 6 P.M.
    Sunday.
Deliveries in Manhattan.
Visa and MasterCard accepted.
Mail order available.

Milano Gourmet ~ The Milano Gourmet has the look and feel of a Little Italy grocery store, so I was surprised to find it on the Upper East Side. The Italian heroes here are first-rate, although I wish they were made on better bread. The homemade marinara sauce is a little bland, but for half the price of Contadina's (formerly Pasta and Cheese), it's an incredible bargain. Fresh pasta is made at the store every day, and the fusilli I bought was excellent, firm, and flavorful when I cooked it up. In a sea of pretension, Milano Gourmet is an island of down-to-earthness.

Milano Gourmet
1582 Third Avenue (corner of 89th Street)
New York, NY 10128
PHONE: (212) 996-6681
SUBWAYS: 86th Street station on the Lexington Avenue No. 4, 5, and 6 lines.
HOURS: 6 A.M. to 11 P.M. Monday through Thursday; 6 A.M. to midnight
    Friday and Saturday; 9 A.M. to 9 P.M. Sunday.
Deliveries in the neighborhood.
American Express accepted.

OTHER LOCATION:
120 East 34th Street (between Lexington Avenue and Park Avenue)
New York, NY 10016
(212) 683-5151

Old Denmark ~ For more than fifty years Steen Steensen and his chef Louis Cassiana have been whipping up traditional Danish specialties for homesick Danes and jaded Manhattanites alike. Their homemade pâté is made with veal, pork, and liver and is so good that my friend Seth started eating my portion off my plate after he had finished his. The shrimp and lobster salads are freshly made and simply prepared. Besides all the seafood and smorgasbord dishes, Old Denmark makes traditional Danish foods like meatballs and liver pâté. It also carries Danish packaged goods including fish balls, smoked mussels, and crumbly Danish cheese cookies. If you want to eat your lunch at Old Denmark, there's a terrific back room where the chef or the owner seats you and serves you a plate of food, a buttered Danish bread, and superb Danish pound cake, all for a price—$10.65 —that belies the poshness of the neighborhood you're eating in. The first time I walked into Old Denmark with a friend to eat lunch, we sat down and asked for a menu. Steen Steensen smiled bemusedly, shook his head, and said, "No, we've been here fifty-one years, and that's one thing we don't have here, a menu. But are you hungry? I'll be right back with a plate of food."

Old Denmark
133 East 65th Street (between Park and Lexington avenues)
New York, NY 10021
PHONE: (212) 744-2533
SUBWAYS: 68th Street–Hunter College station on the Lexington Avenue No.
    6 line; Lexington Avenue station on the Sixth Avenue B and Q lines.
HOURS: 9 A.M. to 5:30 P.M. Monday through Saturday; closed Sunday.
Deliveries in the neighborhood.
Cash only.
Mail order available.

Hungarian sausage, spices, and jams are the stars at Paprikas Weiss.

Paprikas Weiss ～ Visualize a Budapest gourmet store in pre-Communist Hungary, and you're seeing Paprikas Weiss. Hungarians and non-Hungarians alike flock to PW for the five different kinds of paprika, the poppy seeds, the many varieties of Hungarian sausage, and the freshly made *lekvar*—the prune or apricot jam Eastern Europeans use for baking. The apricot *lekvar* is so tasty I eat it straight from the jar. Who needs to bake? The store also carries an extensive selection of coffees and teas. Skip the mediocre baked goods. You'll do much better at Rigo, a few blocks away.

Paprikas Weiss
1546 Second Avenue (between 80th and 81st streets)
New York, NY 10021
PHONE: (212) 288-6117
SUBWAY: 77th Street station on the Lexington Avenue No. 6 line.
HOURS: 9 A.M. to 6 P.M. Monday through Saturday; closed Sunday.
No deliveries.
All major credit cards accepted.
Mail-order catalog available.

ᴍIDTOWN WEST

34TH STREET TO 59TH STREET
FIFTH AVENUE TO ELEVENTH AVENUE

A La Russe ⁓ Let's say you've heard about all the great Russian food stores in Brighton Beach but you're one of those hopelessly lazy and jaded Manhattanites who thinks it takes a visa to go to Brooklyn. Well, you're in luck, because Gregory Foreman emigrated from Russia ten years ago and opened A La Russe on West 54th Street in Manhattan. A La Russe has incredible Russian black bread—so flavorful and so dense it's hard to cut. It comes with walnuts and raisins as well as plain. The mushroom-barley soup here is almost as good as the Second Avenue Deli's, which is merely the best in the city. It contains loads of dill, like almost everything else made here. The chicken cutlet reheated in a microwave was moist and tender, and the stuffed cabbage was first-rate. The salads are unusual and superb, including a walnut-spinach salad made with mung beans; an eggplant caviar that's second only to my wife's; a crunchy, oniony string-bean salad; and a mayonnaise-laden Russian chicken-potato salad. The piroshki—filled dough buns—are very good, though after a while it's hard to distinguish among the fillings. A La Russe also sells bags of *pelmeni*—Siberian beef dumplings that make great appetizers at parties—and makes creditable fresh meat sandwiches on exceptional breads. The sweets, ranging from cookies to a chocolate cake, are pretty uninspiring, but whoever heard of Russians making knockout desserts, anyway?

A La Russe
315 West 54th Street (between Eighth and Ninth avenues)
New York, NY 10019
PHONE: (212) 246-6341
SUBWAYS: 50th Street station on the Eighth Avenue C and E lines; 7th
    Avenue station on the Sixth Avenue B and D lines.
HOURS: 10 A.M. to 7 P.M. Monday through Friday; noon to 7 P.M. Saturday;
    closed Sunday.
Deliveries in Manhattan.
Cash only.

Coisa Nossa ⁓ Coisa Nossa's store window looks like that of any other variety store. It's got a big computerized Lotto sign in the window and a few other nondescript items strewn around the edges. But when you walk in you're immediately confronted by a rack of Brazilian newspapers and magazines. Walk past the magazines and newspapers, and you come upon shelves of Brazilian foodstuffs. Items such as manioc, a kind of flour used in Brazilian cooking; guava paste; and unsweetened passion-fruit and cashew juice are lined up as they would be in a store in Rio. There is dried beef, Brazilian sausage, and everything you need to make *feijoada*, the stew that is the national dish of Brazil. There is also a rack of Brazilian teas and coffees, and, in the front of the store, boxes of Brazilian coconut and guava candies, which are too sweet for my taste. Coisa Nossa is a pleasant place, but the times I've been there, no one's spoken enough English to answer my questions.

Coisa Nossa
46 West 46th Street (between Fifth and Sixth avenues)
New York, NY 10036
PHONE: (212) 719-4779
SUBWAYS: 47th–50th Streets–Rockefeller Center station on the Sixth Avenue
    B, D, F, and Q lines.
HOURS: 9 A.M. to 7:30 P.M. seven days a week.
Deliveries in the neighborhood.
Cash only.
Mail order available.

International Grocery and International Food ~ If you want to know how
Marco Polo felt after coming upon the wealth of spices in the East, come down
to International Grocery. There you'll find huge bins of every imported spice you
can think of, from Greek oregano still on the vine (stick) to flax seeds to curry
powder. International also carries fresh feta cheese, dried fruits, a huge selection
of Greek olives and olive oils, and extraordinary homemade Greek halvah. Its
sister store, International Food, also carries a homemade yogurt that thankfully
bears no resemblance to Dannon or Colombo. The yogurt also goes into some
first-rate Greek dips and appetizers. For example, the *tzatziki*, made with dill,
garlic, and lemon, makes the versions you'll find in any restaurant seem pedes-
trian. International Food will, given one day's notice, marinate lamb for you that
will make the best shish kebob you've ever eaten.

Bins of imported spices and grains at International Grocery.

International Grocery and International Food
529 and 543 Ninth Avenue (between 39th and 41st streets)
New York, NY 10018
PHONE: (212) 279-5514 (for the grocery store)
SUBWAYS: 42nd Street–Port Authority Bus Terminal station on the Eighth
    Avenue A, C, and E lines.
HOURS: 8 A.M. to 6 P.M. Monday through Saturday; closed Sunday.
Deliveries in the neighborhood.
Cash only.

Manganaro Foods and Restaurant ~~ When you walk into Manganaro, you'll
swear you've walked onto a movie set (in fact, the famous "You don't have to be
Jewish to eat Levy's" commercial was shot here). From the tin ceiling to the
antique shelves and bins, it looks like nothing's changed since the store opened
in 1893. But luckily for us, the food is real here. In the front there is a huge
selection of imported Italian groceries, including dried pastas and olive oils. In
the back, they make okay Italian sandwiches and various pasta dishes. But the
item to try is the *arancini*, a fried rice croquette oozing with cheese, which they'll
pack up for you with fresh marinara sauce and a couple of pieces of Italian sausage.

Manganaro Foods and Restaurant
488 Ninth Avenue (between 37th and 38th streets)
New York, NY 10018
PHONE: (212) 563-5331
SUBWAYS: 42nd Street–Port Authority Bus Terminal station on the Eighth
    Avenue A, C, and E lines.
HOURS: 8:30 A.M. to 7 P.M. Monday through Saturday; 11:30 A.M. to 4:30 P.M.
    Sunday.
Deliveries in Manhattan.
All major credit cards accepted.
For mail order call 1 (800) 4-SALAMI.

West African Grocery ~~ If you've enjoyed the food at one of the African restaurants cropping up all over New York or if you just want to relive your days as a
Peace Corps volunteer in Kenya, the West African grocery is for you. It stocks
African staples like cocoyams (a kind of white yam), palm wine, and Nigerian
beer. The people who work here are very friendly and will carefully explain how
to cook any of the unfamiliar items you ask them about.

West African Grocery
535 Ninth Avenue (between 39th and 40th streets)
New York, NY 10018
PHONE: (212) 695-6215
SUBWAYS: 42nd Street–Port Authority Bus Terminal station on the Eighth
    Avenue A, C, and E lines.
HOURS: 8:30 A.M. to 8 P.M. Monday through Saturday; closed Sunday.
No deliveries.
Cash only.

$\mathscr{C}$HELSEA

Han Arum ~ If you walk down West 32nd Street between Fifth and Sixth avenues, you'll swear you've taken a very wrong turn and ended up in Seoul. The store signs are in Korean, except those of the Seoul Korea Restaurant and the Industrial Bank of Korea. Halfway down the block, on the north side of the street, you'll spot a big English sign that says, "Supermarket." Inside, you'll find Han Arum, by far the largest Korean supermarket in New York. Here are row after row of Korean foodstuffs—everything from kimchi (pickled cabbage) to Korean noodles to sweetened squid chips, the Korean answer to Ruffles. Items on display that you won't find in your local A & P include bean jelly, cow's knees (for soup), microscopic shrimp, and seasoned hairtail entrails. There's even a salad bar that features twenty distinctly Korean side dishes. Last time I was there, I saw dried sliced squid, coral-colored whiting eggs, hot 'n' salty fish intestines, and whole garlic cloves in broth. For dessert, there's an array of Korean baked goods and cookies. I bought a package of walnut cakes, which turned out to be the greasiest fried crullers I'd ever eaten.

Han Arum
25 West 32nd Street (between Fifth and Sixth avenues)
New York, NY 10016
PHONE: (212) 695-3283
SUBWAYS: 34th Street Station on the Sixth Avenue B, D, F, and Q and the
    Broadway and R lines.
HOURS: 10 A.M. to 9 P.M. every day.
Deliveries available.
All major credit cards accepted ($50 minimum).

$\mathscr{K}$IPS BAY/GRAMERCY PARK

Kalustyan's ~ Like a police dog searching for drugs, I followed the scent of fresh roasted almonds to the back of Kalustyan's, where Lebanese chef Arpiar Afarian was handing out samples of almonds that had just come out of the oven. Kalustyan's carries not only wonderfully fresh roasted nuts but also more unusual snacks such as roasted jumbo red Persian melon seeds, and salted and roasted black watermelon seeds. More than that, the store is a veritable Indian and Middle Eastern marketplace or bazaar transplanted to Manhattan. It blends its own spices, makes four kinds of homemade mango chutney, and carries things I've never seen in the city, such as dried lemons and sun-dried mulberries. In summer the store carries fresh California dates. Chef Afarian makes his own stuffed grape leaves and other assorted Middle Eastern preparations such as baba ghanouj and hummous, which taste fresh and spritely. Only the soggy falafel let me down.

Note: The people who work at Kalustyan's are extremely friendly and will patiently explain what spices like *zatar*, sumac, or cardamom are and how they should be used.

Kalustyan's
123 Lexington Avenue (between 28th and 29th streets)
New York, NY 10016
PHONE: (212) 685-3451
SUBWAY: 28th Street station on the Lexington Avenue No. 6 line.
HOURS: 10 A.M. to 8 P.M. Monday through Saturday; 11 A.M. to 6 P.M.
    Sunday and holidays.
No deliveries.
All major credit cards accepted.
Mail-order catalog available.

Spice and Sweet Mahal ⎯ Although Indian sweets don't exactly thrill me, Spice and Sweet Mahal's *Kheer mohan*, a fried cheese shell with a cream filling, has me rethinking my entire outlook on Indian desserts. Besides the wide selection of Indian sweets, Spice and Sweet Mahal also carries everything an inventive Indian cook would need: hard-to-find spices such as black cardamom, a wide variety of Indian pickles, basmati rice, and even chapati flour for making your own Indian breads.

Spice and Sweet Mahal
135 Lexington Avenue (corner of 29th Street)
New York, NY 10016
PHONE: (212) 683-0900
SUBWAY: 28th Street station on the Lexington Avenue No. 6 line.
HOURS: 10 A.M. to 8 P.M. Monday through Saturday; 11 A.M. to 7 P.M.
    Sunday and holidays.
No deliveries.
All major credit cards accepted.
Mail order available.

Todaro Brothers ⎯ See page 233.

*W*EST VILLAGE

14TH STREET TO HOUSTON STREET
FIFTH AVENUE TO WEST STREET

Balducci's ⎯ See page 205.

Myers of Keswick ⎯ The first time I walked into Myers of Keswick, I thought my journey south of 14th Street had turned into a trans-Atlantic flight. I was the

Myers of Keswick carries an extensive line of British packaged goods.

only customer in the store not speaking with an English accent. The owner, Peter Myers, makes his own English sausages, including a Cumberland sausage from his grandfather's hundred-year-old recipe. I have yet to taste a bad sausage here, but my favorite is the curried lamb concoction, which tastes fabulous grilled. Myers also makes a terrific lard pastry dough he uses in his sausage rolls, steak-and-kidney pies, Cornish pasties, and shepherd's pies. Everything I've tried here has been first-rate, but there is a sameness to it all. Even Peter Myers warns, "Don't overdose on this kind of food. Order a couple of things and come back for more." Myers also carries British packaged goods, such as Heinz of England condiments and a not-too-sweet British fruit soda called a Tizer that I've gone back for several times.

Myers of Keswick
634 Hudson Street (between Horation and Jane streets)
New York, NY 10014
PHONE: (212) 691-4194
SUBWAYS: 14th Street station on the Eighth Avenue A, C, and E lines;
    Eighth Avenue station on the 14th Street–Canarsie L line.
HOURS: 10 A.M. to 7 P.M. Monday through Friday; 10 A.M. to 6 P.M. Saturday;
    noon to 5 P.M. Sunday.
No deliveries.
American Express accepted.

OWNTOWN

HOUSTON STREET TO BATTERY PARK

Italian Food Center ⁓ See page 291.

Aisle cards are in English and Chinese at Kam Kuo Food.

Kam Kuo Food ⁓ The day I walked into Kam Kuo, I noticed they were having a sale on Buddhist shrines. With its aisles labeled in two languages and its fancy plastic shopping bags printed with the store's 800 phone number on it, Kam Kuo Foods is like Gristede's in Peking. Row after row of frozen Chinese foods and packaged goods, including a very large selection of Chinese teas, highlight the store's selections. You'll also find not-so-standard food items such as preserved duck eggs. Though the store has meat and produce sections, don't count on doing one-stop Chinatown shopping here, as the pickings looked quite meager in both. Upstairs Kam Kuo has a wide array of Chinese cooking utensils, plates, woks, tea sets, and rice cookers at what seemed to be reasonable prices.

Note: English is spoken by many people who work here.

Kam Kuo Food
7 Mott Street (corner of Park Row)
New York, NY 10013
PHONE: (212) 349-3097
SUBWAYS: Canal Street station on the following lines: Lexington Avenue No.
    6, Broadway N and R, Nassau Street J, M, and Z; Grand Street station on
    the Sixth Avenue B, D, and Q lines.
HOURS: 9 A.M. to 9 P.M. seven days a week.
Deliveries in Manhattan.
American Express accepted.
For mail order ($200 minimum) call 1 (800) 331-4056.

Kam Man Foods ⁓ When I asked the sales clerk at Kam Man how I would use the ginseng root marked $1,250 a pound, she told me it was used in making soup. Must make a heckuva bowl of soup. Kam Man has a huge selection of dried

Shoppers at Kam Man Foods on Canal Street.

seafood, including scallops, shrimp, oysters, and pollack, to go along with the fresh meat sold in the back of the store. In the store window you'll see the succulent barbecued pork and the extraordinary roasted duck they make on the premises. Kam Man is one of the only places in Chinatown that makes its own *joong*, the Chinese equivalent of tamales, stuffed with rice, black beans, sausage, mushrooms, and pork. There are also rows of big glass jars containing all kinds of Chinese mushrooms, herbs, and roots. English seemed to be at a premium here.

Kam Man Foods
200 Canal Street (between Mott and Mulberry streets)
New York, NY 10013
PHONE: (212) 571-0330
SUBWAYS: Canal Street station on the following lines: Lexington Avenue 6,
   Broadway N and R, Nassau Street J, M, and Z; Grand Street station on
   the Sixth Avenue B, D, and Q lines.
HOURS: 9 A.M. to 9 P.M. seven days a week.
No deliveries.
Visa and MasterCard accepted ($50 minimum).
Mail order available.

The Adventures of Chop Suey Looey

To even the most intrepid food shopper, Manhattan's Chinatown can seem like an impenetrable fortress guarded by the thousands of Chinese-Americans who shop and/or live in the area. I knew there had to be bargains and strange delights galore in Chinatown; I just needed a genie to unlock its mysteries.

Enter Chop Suey Looey, a.k.a. Ed Schoenfeld, a Brooklynite who as a teenager became obsessed with Chinese food. After studying Chinese cooking with the doyenne of Chinese cooking teachers, Grace Chu, Schoenfeld worked for Chinese restaurateur David Keh for three years and then spent five years at the various branches of the esteemed Shun Lee set of upscale, first-rate Chinese restaurants. Having frequented various branches of the Shun Lee restaurants over the last twenty years, I knew that no one could explain the vagaries of shopping in Chinatown better than Ed.

On a dreary May day the two of us set out—I playing hooky from work and Ed taking a few hours off from his latest venture, a West 68th Street restaurant called Vince and Eddie's that serves homey yet sophisticated American food and has quickly become one of the best restaurants on the West Side. Driving like a man with a lot on his mind, Schoenfeld nonetheless managed to point out various sights and landmarks with both hands without totaling the car, its passengers, or any hapless pedestrians that wandered into our path.

Ten minutes later, we arrived at one of those noodle-thin streets in Chinatown that dead-ends two blocks after you get on it. Ignoring the score of No Parking signs, Ed shut down his borrowed red Mazda and announced, "I've been parking and shopping on this block for ten years and I've gotten only one ticket. Just don't print where it is, or I'll never be able to find a spot here."

We walked first to Catherine Street, where Ed pointed to the two strips of stores that lined the sides of the street and said, "I can get almost everything I need on this block." We started at Kam Kee, a produce market that Schoenfeld prizes for its huge shallots, fresh bean sprouts, and ripe wintermelon. Pointing to what looked like cherries with covers he asked, "Have you ever had a fresh lichee? They're better than sex."

At the Catherine Street Meat Market we watched a fine-featured Chinese woman folding and stuffing shrimp and pork dumplings in the window. The store sells them in packages of twelve for $3.50, and Schoenfeld pronounced them wonderful. He explained that when Chinese people eat meat, they eat mostly pork, and this store carries dozens of cuts of pork and pork parts. The Catherine Street Meat Market also sells homemade pork and duck liver sausage, traditional red Chinese sausage, and such exotica as black chickens, which are chickens whose skin is black instead of yellow. Schoenfeld says they are prized for their succulent meat.

At Hoi Sing Seafood, a fish market, Ed sung the praises of the salmon. "See," he said, "that's beautiful Norwegian salmon. Salmon should be

The Adventures of Chop Suey Looey, continued

marbled, almost like good beef, and this salmon is. And check out the price: $5.80 a pound. That's less than half what you'd pay uptown." He was right. I checked Citarella, the top-notch fish store in my neighborhood, and the Norwegian salmon was $13.95 a pound.

We next wandered into the Shun Lee Shin Trading Company, whose shelves were lined with dry goods imported from both Taiwan and mainland China. Schoenfeld stopped to admire the huge bags of dried mushrooms. Every conceivable variety of Chinese mushroom could be found here. "See those," he said, pointing to some dried mushroom caps with white lines on the top. "Those are *foi goo*. They're wonderful, but you should soak them in water for two days before cooking them." After saying good-bye in Chinese to the two people working in the front of the store, he looked back at another set of shelves and noted, "Oh, yeah, sometimes I buy my rice noodles and cellophane noodles here."

After stopping for a cup of coffee and some shrimp balls, we walked around the corner to Ocean Sea Food, where the specialty is live seafood. There were lobsters and carp swimming around in tanks, but what made an indelible impression were the huge live turtles. I'm not talking about the turtles we all had as kids that invariably escaped from their bowls only to be found dead in the living room the next morning. I'm talking about turtles that would force a person to walk on the other side of the street if confronted in a hostile urban environment. I'm talking about turtles that weigh up to ten pounds. Schoenfeld saw me recoil and chuckled, "I don't think you want to stick around and watch them slaughter one of these turtles. It's not a pretty sight."

At an unnamed fish market at 25 Catherine Street, Schoenfeld pointed out the many varieties of clams, oysters, and crabs and noted their freshness. He then asked the man in Chinese if they had any live frogs today. The man pointed to some empty rectangular boxes with wire-mesh covers and said no. As we were leaving, Schoenfeld pointed to an empty stool and said, "Usually there's a woman sitting on that stool cleaning conch. They have great conch here."

We then jumped back into Schoenfeld's car and headed east on East Broadway. Schoenfeld noted that until about twenty years ago East Broadway had been almost completely Jewish, with dairy restaurants and tallis and yarmulke factories abounding. Now it was almost entirely Chinese. Where there had been Hebrew characters painted on buildings there were now Chinese characters. Even the sign on the building that houses the Yiddish newspaper *The Forward* was in Chinese. In fact, as we passed the Westlake Noodle Company at 183 East Broadway, Schoenfeld noted, almost to prove the point, "That's where I get my lo mein and almond cookies."

I realized that we had been in Chinatown for two and a half hours without ever venturing into what I had also thought of as Chinatown—the area bounded by Mulberry Street on the west, the Bowery on the east, Canal

Street on the north, and Walker Street on the south. I mentioned this to Schoenfeld, and he explained that, for him, the old part of Chinatown was just too congested and difficult to get around in, especially since he shopped by car. But my mentioning this to him seemed to spur his imagination, and a few minutes later we ended up at Hung Chong Import on the Bowery. It turned out to be the ultimate Chinese restaurant supply store, thirty kinds of woks piled neatly on one side, surrounded by bamboo steamers of every size and variety. There were knives and cleavers everywhere, enough to prop twenty horror films. "This place is the greatest, isn't it?" Schoenfeld asked rhetorically.

After that Ed divulged his favorite place to buy shrimp, Lobster King, where jumbo shrimp were an astounding $6 a pound, less than half what they cost uptown. Schoenfeld picked up one of the shrimp, nodded approvingly, and motioned for me to smell it. It smelled like the sea, not fishy, but sealike. Schoenfeld explained that since almost all jumbo shrimp is frozen before coming to New York, the ones that smelled like the sea are the freshest, as it means they have not been frozen long.

We then headed uptown, and after a stop at Ed's restaurant, he dropped me off at my office. As I got out and thanked him profusely, he said something that made me realize he was as food-obsessed as I was. "Let me know when you're coming to Brooklyn, and I'll go with you to Eagle Foods. It's a great store. Or Arthur Avenue in the Bronx. I really love Arthur Avenue."

Kam Kee
24 Catherine Street (between East Broadway and Henry Street)
No phone

Catherine Street Meat Market
21 Catherine Street (between East Broadway and Henry Street)
Phone: (212) 693-0494

Hoi Sing Seafood
17–19 Catherine Street (between East Broadway and Henry Street)
Phone: (212) 964-9694

Shun Lee Shin Trading Company
22½ Catherine Street (between East Broadway and Henry Street)
No phone

Ocean Sea Food
19–21 Henry Street (between Catherine and Market streets)
Phone: (212) 227-3067

Unnamed fish market
25 Catherine Street (between East Broadway and Henry Street)

Hung Chong Import
14 Bowery (between Pell and Doyle streets)
Phone: (212) 349-1463

The Adventures of Chop Suey Looey, continued

Lobster King
210 Canal Street (at Mulberry Street)
No phone

CHINATOWN
GENERAL DIRECTIONS
SUBWAYS: Canal Street station on the following lines: Lexington Avenue No.
6, Broadway N and R, Nassau Street J, M, and Z; Grand Street station
on the Sixth Avenue B, D, and Q lines.

$\mathcal{B}$RONX

A Food Lover's Tour of Arthur Avenue

To Sal Calandra, proprietor of the sixty-year-old S. Calandra & Sons cheese
shop on Arthur Avenue in the Bronx, putting mozzarella or ricotta cheese in
the refrigerator is tantamount to committing cheese homicide. "If you put
my cheeses in the refrigerator," he told me, "I take no responsibility for it. If
you paper it, it's also on you. The only reason I paper my cheese is to get my
products to their destination."

I had heard from some food folks whose opinion I respect that shopping
on Arthur Avenue, the Bronx's Little Italy, was like being transported to
another era, and my encounter with Mr. Calandra proved it. Arthur Avenue
and 187th Street are the two main shopping thoroughfares of the
neighborhood called Belmont, immortalized by the 1950s doo-wop group
Dion and the Belmonts. Working people from Calabria, Naples, and Sicily
settled in Belmont in the late 1800s, and although the area now is home to
Albanians, Yugoslavs, and Hispanics as well, it is still Italian enough that
parts of *The Godfather* were filmed here. Although it's bordered on the south
by the urban blight of the South Bronx, Belmont is safe enough that old
ladies still walk the streets at night without fear.

Belmont is a food shopper's paradise. The stores are on two main streets,
everybody is incredibly friendly, and the prices are sometimes half what you'd
pay in Manhattan. I began my exploring at Borgatti's, a fifty-five-year-old
fresh pasta store where the pasta is so fresh it's cut to order. When I asked
for a pound of fettuccini, Mario Borgatti went over to a narrow counter on
the side of the store containing all the pasta dough, took a few sheets, and
put it through a slicer as I watched. He then put some cornmeal on it so
that it wouldn't stick and wrapped it in white paper. Borgatti's ravioli (both
cheese and meat varieties) come wrapped in brown paper bundled by string.

Borgatti's also makes manicotti (the only thing in the store sold frozen), fresh lasagna noodles, and carrot and tomato pastas that are sold dry. "We work the way people would work at home," Mario Borgatti explained to me. After sampling Borgatti's silky pasta, I realized that no matter how many pasta machines we had gotten for our wedding, I was never going to be able to make pasta like this at home.

After leaving Borgatti's, I was unsurprisingly a little hungry, so I was grateful that in front of Cosenza's Fish Market was a man shucking ice-cold clams on the half-shell. The clams were a fitting introduction to Cosenza's, a fish store specializing in Mediterranean fish such as *dorado* and *triglie*. Cosenza's also sells *baccalà*, or dried cod; *rosamalina*, tiny silvery fish eaten raw with oil and vinegar; live lobsters and crabs, at amazingly low prices; and a variety of fresh oysters.

Two stores down from Cosenza's is Teitel Brothers, an old-fashioned Italian deli and specialty store. Teitel's boasts a tantalizing selection of Italian cheeses, olives, and deli meats. They also sell a brand of extra-virgin olive oil, Edda, in a gallon can for $12.99, which Ed Schoenfeld, proprietor of Vince and Eddie's restaurant on Manhattan's Upper West Side, swears is better than some Tuscan olive oils sold elsewhere for three times the price. And if you're into putting up your own olives, Teitel's also sells fresh, uncured olives still on their branches.

The store window at Biancardi's is filled with four or five kinds of fresh sausage and fully dressed rabbits. Being the father of a young boy who's fond of cottontails, I couldn't bring myself to buy a rabbit, especially since these still had a little tail remaining. But it seemed like half of the store's patrons were buying them, so they must be good. I contented myself with buying a pound each of lamb, veal, and sweet-and-hot pork sausage, and then broke down and violated a long-standing, self-imposed sausage limit and bought half a pound of dried sweet sausage that looked positively irresistible hanging on the wall. (The splurge was worth it because the dried sausage was excellent and I was able to invite myself to a friend's house in the suburbs for a barbecue the next weekend, using the sausage as a lure.) The last item I bought before leaving Biancardi's was a beautiful aged shell steak for half what it would have cost at any of my local butchers on the Upper West Side of Manhattan.

No Italian shopping foray is complete without bread and dessert, and Belmont has at least six bakeries. The traditional long Italian breads were a disappointment at Addeo's and Madonia Brothers. But the winner was the *pane di casa*, an oval-shaped white bread with a chewy, burned crust, which you can buy either sliced or unsliced. At Addeo's, the *pane di casa* was so fresh that it was still hot when I got to my car three blocks away. For dessert, I bought a cappuccino cake at Addeo's made with cappuccino butter-cream frosting and chocolate sponge cake. Although I worried about it all the way home because the cake box barely weighed anything, the cake turned

A Food Lover's Tour of Arthur Avenue, continued

out to be fine, with a pleasant, smooth cappuccino flavor. It was not one of my ten favorite desserts of all time, but it was good all the same. Cannoli fans should note that Madonia Brothers is so passionate about cannolis that they stuff them to order to ensure freshness and crispness. Although I usually hate the leaden cookies baked at Italian bakeries, Madonia Brothers also has a deliciously light macaroon called a Mario special, made with egg whites, hazelnuts, coconuts, and chocolate chips.

As I was getting into my car to leave Arthur Avenue, Mario Borgatti's parting words to me were ringing in my ears. He wouldn't let me pay for the last package of ravioli I bought there, and when I protested he waved me off with a beguiling smile on his face. "Don't worry about it. I know you'll be back. You're hooked," he said. He was right. I *was* hooked—on Borgatti's, on Cosenza's, on Biancardi's, and on Arthur Avenue, New York's Little Italy without glitz.

S. Calandra & Sons
2314 Arthur Avenue
Phone: (212) 365-7572

Borgatti's Ravioli and Egg Noodles
632 East 187th Street
Phone: (212) 367-3799

Cosenza's Fish Market
2354 Arthur Avenue
Phone: (212) 364-8510

Teitel Brothers
2349 Arthur Avenue
Phone: (212) 733-9400

Biancardi's
2340 Arthur Avenue
Phone: (212) 733-4058

Addeo's Bakers
2352 Arthur Avenue, or 2372 Hughes Avenue
Phone: (212) 367-8316 or 8888

Madonia Brothers
2348 Arthur Avenue
Phone: (212) 295-5573

ARTHUR AVENUE JAUNT

GENERAL DIRECTIONS

SUBWAY AND BUS: From the Fordham Road station on the Lexington Avenue
No. 4, Eighth Avenue C, or Sixth Avenue D line, take the BX12 bus east
to Arthur Avenue.

Mediterranean Foods, one of the oldest stores in Astoria.

ℚUEENS

Astoria: The Feta the Better

Like most New Yorkers my exposure to Greeks and Greek foods has been
limited to ordering a feta cheese omelette, a Greek salad, or spinach pie at
one of the hundreds of Greek coffee shops that dot the city. I knew that
Astoria had one of the largest Greek populations in the world outside Greece,
and I knew that I liked feta cheese and spinach pie a lot. So one crisp, sunny
April morning, armed with suggestions from a Greek cookbook author, Diane
Kochilas, I set out with my friend Peter Cunningham, a first-rate
photographer, in his dark red 1980 Chevrolet Impala. The car's main feature,
according to Peter, is that it looks so much like an unmarked police car that
nobody messes with the people in it.

We crossed the Triboro Bridge, took the first exit, 31st Street, and turned
right. We found ourselves under the elevated N-train subway track, and yet I
felt as if I had boarded an airliner and landed in Greece. Greek tavernas
dotted every corner and store signs were in Greek and English.

We parked the car and walked into Mediterranean Foods, one of the oldest
stores in the area. I found myself surrounded by a display of Greek-olive-oil
cans piled so high that they blocked the windows. Greek packaged goods
were everywhere, and the whole place smelled like one big olive. I followed
my nose to the cheese and olive counter, where the dried homemade beef
sausages called *loukanika* hung over a wire. There were two signs on the
counter, one listing the five kinds of olives the store carried, the other the

Astoria: The Feta the Better, continued

This small Astoria store carries some of New York's finest feta cheese and halvah.

store's homemade Greek specialty foods. I bought a container of *tzatziki*, the cucumber, yogurt, and garlic dip my wife adores. It turned out to be the most garlicky we'd ever eaten. I also bought a container of *taramosalata*, a fish-egg dip that my wife also loves. It was a little saltier than the store-bought variety we were used to but had a much fresher taste overall. I was about to leave when I decided that I had to have a piece of *loukanika*. I later learned the sausage had lots of paprika in it, giving it the flavor of Hungarian salami.

We walked a couple of doors down to a much smaller storefront, Greek House Foods. Here the olives were on the right and the cheese counter was straight back. The owner, Kosta Dimatis, is a swarthy young man with jet black hair, a heavy beard, and a wonderfully engaging wry smile. He beckoned us to come in and sample a few of his feta cheeses sitting in brine in huge tins and barrels. He gave us a taste of feta Kefalinias, which like all Greek feta cheeses is named after the island or town it comes from. Tangy and robust, it was the best feta I'd ever eaten. We each bought half a pound of it and sampled a few others. Then I inquired about a homemade dessert, halvah Farsalon, that Diane had told us was available there. Kosta told us that his mother stops making it after Easter. We were a couple of weeks too late, and I vowed to be on time next year.

We crossed the street and wandered into the Anestis Fish Market, where we were greeted by hundreds of clear fish eyes staring at us. There were

"Sometimes, when a box of these fish comes in, I love them so much I just put my whole face in the box," says Anestis Fish Market owner Anestis Stefanides (left).

skorpinas, St. Peters, fresh sardines, *seppie*, mullets, and a seemingly endless variety of imported Mediterranean fish. Impeccably clean, almost pristine, Anestis is owned by Anestis Stefanides, a compactly built Greek with short hair and a fisherman's cap. Anestis goes on shopping expeditions to Greece, Italy, and Africa, looking for the best sources of fish. "The fish we import taste and smell very different from American fish," he says. "Sometimes, when a box of these fish comes in, I love them so much I just put my whole face in the box."

We started walking down 31st Street, under the subway track. We stopped in front of Tony's, a renowned gyro and souvalaki joint where a life-sized statue of Tony with one arm torn off beckoned us inside. The proprietor, who was stoking his charcoal souvlaki fire, said the fire wasn't ready yet. We said we'd stop by later.

Several blocks later we happened upon Titan Foods, the largest Greek food store in Astoria and probably the largest Greek supermarket in the country. It has wide aisle after wide aisle of Greek dry goods and groceries. In fact, it looks just like a Gristede's or a D'Agostino's but with aisle signs in Greek instead of English. We headed to the cheese and olive counters in the back of the store, where we introduced ourselves to an extremely friendly young counterman from Araxova in southern Greece. He insisted we try a kind of spreadable feta made there. It was delicious—sort of a feta cream cheese. He also had us sample a superb hard cheese cured in olive oil called *ladotori*. He

Astoria: The Feta the Better, continued

then led us to the olive and brined-vegetable barrels. He told us he didn't care much for olives (in Greece, I thought, that would be grounds for arrest) but he did introduce us to *volvi*, tiny, sweet rose-colored pickled onions.

As we were leaving Titan, I bought a bottle of lemon squash from Cyprus that turned out to be an incredibly tart lemon concentrate perfect for mixing with good old New York seltzer. At the checkout counter, a middle-aged woman implored us to try some hard breads, resembling zwieback, that were made in her hometown in Greece. I broke down and bought a package, and when we opened them at work they were so hard and stale I wondered if the crackers had come over when she did.

Peter and I continued our journey down 31st Street until we arrived at the next main shopping intersection, at 23rd Avenue. There we tried a couple of sweet Greek pastries that were syrupy and pretty standard, as well as a piece of spinach pie that was tasty but oily. We crossed the intersection and saw a sign that caught our eye. "Kiryiako's," it said in wooden letters that were peeling and falling down. It was a tiny store, with bins of nuts and grains crowding both the outside and the inside. We asked Kiryiako Mutofopoulos to recommend a feta cheese. He took out a huge chunk from a barrel, sliced off a large piece, and offered us a taste on the long knife he had cut it with. We paid for our cheese and left. All this noshing was making me hungry, so we had a cab take us back to Tony's, near where we had parked. We ordered a souvlaki and a gyro and watched George, the owner, slice the gyro meat off the spit, put the souvlaki on his now red-hot coal fire, grill the pita bread, and stuff our sandwiches. Both were scrumptious, but Peter and I decided we preferred the souvlaki.

We were already stuffed from all the delectable food we had eaten on our tour of Greek Astoria, but I managed to prevail upon Peter to stop at Rizzo's. A friend of mine had sworn this place served the best Sicilian pizza in the city (see page 260 for more on Rizzo's). After all, Astoria also has a sizable Italian community (as well as a Slavic one, for that matter).

We found Rizzo's easily enough, but we couldn't find a parking space close by. Feeling confident about our ersatz unmarked-police-car status, we parked in a bus stop, dropped into Rizzo's, and had the best Sicilian pizza we'd ever had. We walked out ten minutes later, feeling triumphant and sated after our successful Astoria excursion. My heart sank to the level of the pizza in my stomach when I saw not one but two members of the New York City police force attaching not one but two white slips to our protected car. I told Peter I would pay for the tickets but that next time we should take a subway to go on a food foray.

Anestis Fish Market
31-01 30th Avenue
Phone: (718) 274-7280

Greek House Foods
32-22 30th Avenue
Phone: (718) 545-5252

Kiryiako's Grocery
29-29 23rd Avenue
Phone: (718) 545-3931

Rizzo's
30-13 Steinway Street
Phone: (718) 721-9862

Mediterranean Foods
32-20 30th Avenue
Phone: (718) 728-6166

Titan Foods
25-50 31st Street
Phone: (718) 626-7771

Tony's Souvlaki
28-44 31st Street
Phone: (718) 728-3638

ASTORIA
GENERAL DIRECTIONS
SUBWAY: 30th Avenue (Grand Avenue) station on the Broadway N line.

$\mathscr{B}$ROOKLYN

Fredricksen and Johannesen ~ Besides being the only shop I visited that specializes in traditional Norwegian foods, F & J, in Bay Ridge, is also a J. C. Penney mail-order depot. I can't vouch for the quality of the dry goods, but the Norwegian meat, cheese, and fish specialities were intriguing. There was *oon*, a Norwegian slicing cheese with clove and caraway seeds. I loved the fresh and smoked home-made Norwegian sausage and the smoked ham. There was a combination beef-and-pork meat loaf called a chud pudding that my young son was crazy about. The fish specialties include fish cakes, fish pudding, and lightly smoked Norwegian salmon. On the walls hang dried, cured legs of lamb. They looked great, but you have to buy a whole leg, and I wasn't prepared to make such a commitment. Oh yes, F & J also carries every form of cloudberry and lingonberry imaginable, from whole lingonberries imported from Canada to cloudberry jams to lingonberry juice.

Fredricksen & Johannesen
7719 Fifth Avenue (between 77th and 78th streets)
Brooklyn, NY 11220

PHONE: (718) 745-5980
SUBWAY: 77th Street station on the Broadway R line.
HOURS: 9 A.M. to 6 P.M. Monday through Saturday; closed Sunday.
No deliveries.
All major credit cards accepted.
Mail order available.

Sahadi Importing Company ⁓ You need only breathe deeply once upon entering Sahadi's (as the locals call it) to know you have entered a hallowed food hall. The smell of spices such as cumin and mint and curry overwhelm you immediately. Though the Sahadi brothers have expanded the store to include foods like lox and curried chicken salad, don't let the new items fool you. This is still in many ways the definitive Middle Eastern food store in New York. Old-fashioned bins and barrels filled with spices, rice, lentils, and chickpeas attest to the authenticity of this establishment. There are glass jars displaying every kind of dried fruit and nut imaginable. There are barrels containing twenty different kinds of olives, including a huge purple Chilean variety called an Alphonse that even a confirmed non–olive lover like me could appreciate. Go to the back of the store where the prepared foods are and sample the traditional Middle Eastern spreads and dips. The baba ghanouj, hummous, and tabouli are all spritely, fresh, and well-spiced. The revelation for me was the fresh yogurt concoction called *lebany*, made either with garlic or with mint and apples. Don't buy your pitas here to accompany the dips. Instead, head on down two stores to the Near East Bakery. Sahadi's *lebany* on the Near East Bakery's sesame pita is an extraordinary combination.

Sahadi Importing Company
187 Atlantic Avenue (between Court and Clinton streets)
Brooklyn, NY 11201
PHONE: (718) 624-4550
SUBWAYS: Borough Hall station on the following lines: Broadway–Seventh
    Avenue No. 2 and 3, Lexington Avenue No. 4 and 5.
HOURS: 9 A.M. to 7 P.M. Monday through Friday; 8:30 A.M. to 7 P.M.
    Saturday; closed Sunday.
No deliveries.
Cash and personal checks only.
No mail order.

Brighton Beach Memoir

Turning onto Brighton Beach Avenue from one of the side streets, I though I'd entered a time warp. Thousands of pedestrians speaking Russian and Yiddish made me think I was in the Brooklyn of my parents' time. The only difference I could discern is that today's Russian Jewish immigrants seem to be making a concerted effort to hold onto the old ways, whereas the Russian Jewish immigrants of my parents' generation and their sons and daughters, dived headlong into mainstream American life. With its intense shopping bustle, Brighton Beach these days is a celebration of its residents' new-found American freedom and their Russian heritage.

The first stop on my Brighton Beach gastronomic tour was the boardwalk and Hirsch's Knishes. My friend Peter and I ordered one each of the store's three knishes: potato, kasha, and cherry-cheese. The counterwoman handed us our kasha and potato knishes but shook her head and said there weren't any cheese knishes to be had that day. With that, an elderly man dressed in an old-fashioned undershirt, bermuda shorts, and sandals without socks suddenly appeared from in back of the huge knish oven. He looked at me and said, "Cheese knishes, five minutes."

We walked over to a bench overlooking the ocean, and began eating the potato and kasha knishes, passing them back and forth like two winos sharing a bottle of Thunderbird. With the first bite we realized we were in the presence of knish masters. The dough was flaky, the fillings onion-laced and extremely tasty. These knishes were (gasp) light. We ran the few steps back to the Hirsch's counter to look for any signs of the cherry-cheese knishes. The bermuda-shorted man appeared with a full tray fresh from the oven. With our new prize in hand, Peter and I headed back to Brighton Beach Avenue. Even Peter, a confirmed non–knish lover, admitted that the cherry-cheese knish was an oblong log of perfection. The cherries were tart, the pot cheese filling not too sweet. This was a blintze disguised as a knish.

We turned onto Brighton Beach Avenue, headed east, and soon spotted White Acacia, a grocery store and specialty shop recommended to me by my editor. We were in a grocery store, all right, but somehow we ended up in Odessa instead of Brooklyn. All the signs were in Russian. We looked at the rows of sausages, the containers of salads, the aisles of Russian packaged foods, and the barrels of pickles, peppers, and whole pickled watermelon slices, and didn't know where to turn.

Finally, a young man in his twenties spotted Peter's Baruch College T-shirt and said, "Hey, did you go to Baruch? I just graduated from there." He turned out to be Al Feldman, the owner's son. As his father nodded approvingly, Al steered us toward the stuffed cabbage, the potato-and-vegetable salad, and the Israeli eggplant spread. He told us about the Siberian dumplings, *pilmeni*, sold frozen in five-pound bags, but when we told him we lived an hour away, he said they wouldn't travel well. When I asked father and son what else would they recommend, the father suggested the turkey they smoked on the premises. Sure enough, it was the best smoked turkey I'd ever eaten. Both Feldmans let me know their purview extended well beyond the Brighton Beach axis when they shouted in unison, "It's a lot better than the smoked turkey you get at Zabar's or Balducci's."

A few blocks farther down, we entered M & I International Foods, Brighton Beach's Zabar's. Shiny walls with neon signs blinking the names of the different counters greet customers here. The meat counter had shelf after

Brighton Beach Memoir, continued

shelf of sausages and other smoked and nonsmoked meats. I couldn't get near the cheese and salad counters, although the salad counter, with many unfamiliar items, looked especially promising. I settled in at the end of a long prepared-foods line, thankful for the perusing time I would have until my turn came. I ordered a length of sausage, two kinds of stuffed cabbage, beef stroganoff, veal stuffed with mushrooms, and apple strudel. The sales clerk totaled my purchases, which came to $9.45. When ten dollars buys you enough prepared food to feed four people you know you're not in Manhattan any more.

Peter and I then got in the car and drove ten or fifteen blocks until I saw in plain block letters a sign for Mrs. Stahl's Knishes. Having sampled Mrs. Stahl's knishes when they opened and quickly closed a store on West 72nd Street in 1989, I knew I had to have a knish at the source. Because we were so full we could hardly move, I ordered one each of the fifteen different kinds of knishes they had, ranging from Spanish rice to vegetarian chopped liver to spiced apple, had them boxed, and took them to work the following Monday. I knew I would get an impartial and accurate reading from my coworkers. They disappeared in less than five minutes, a new company record.

Last, we visited the Odessa Gastronome. A friend had tipped me to the chicken Kiev served at this relatively new store, opened in 1988 by two housepainters from Odessa. I was skeptical, thinking there were too many ways for take-out chicken Kiev to go wrong. But when I served it to my guests that evening, there were oohs and aahs all around the table. The clothes of three out of four people actually were ruined by butter spurting from the chicken, a sure sign of chicken Kiev quality.

I came back from Brighton Beach thinking about franchising Hirsch's Knishes and opening an Odessa Gastronome in Manhattan. Then I realized that it would never work, that Hirsch's and the White Acacia and Odessa Gastronome belonged right where they were and nowhere else, a D-train ride and a continent or two away.

Hirsch's Knishes
3145 Brighton 4th Street
(between Coney Island Avenue and Ocean Parkway)
Phone: (718) 332-0341

White Acacia
281 Brighton Beach Avenue
(between 2nd and 3rd streets)
Phone: (718) 648-2525

M & I International Foods
249 Brighton Beach Avenue
Phone: (718) 615-1011

Mrs. Stahl's Knishes
1001 Brighton Beach Avenue
Phone: (718) 648-0210

Odessa Gastronome:
1113 Brighton Beach Avenue
Phone: (718) 332-3223

BRIGHTON BEACH
GENERAL DIRECTIONS

SUBWAYS: Brighton Beach station on the Sixth Avenue D and Q lines.

9

FISH

When I was growing up in the New York area, fish was a low-priced source of protein my parents tried to get us to eat. Whenever we heard there was fish for dinner we would make faces that could politely be described as unattractive.

The fish that invariably caused this reaction was flounder. Fried flounder. Growing up, I was convinced that flounder was the only kind of fish in the ocean. Well, that's not completely true. I knew about flounder, Howard Johnson's fried clam strips, and lox, although I wasn't sure lox came from a fish.

Obviously, many things have changed since then. First of all, fish is no longer cheap. Second, kids don't seem to make the same faces my brothers and I used to make. My son, for example, actually seems to like the taste of fish. Last, the choices available in New York fish stores are mind-boggling. Certain fish markets provide shoppers with nearly 100 different kinds of fish brought in on a daily basis from all over the country and the world. From Hawaiian mahi-mahi to Santa Barbara prawns to Greek scorpio, New Yorkers can find any fish they want.

Rosedale Doc, Mayor of the Fulton Fish Market

It is 3:15 A.M., and Lexington Avenue between 78th and 79th streets is pretty deserted. I am waiting for Robert Neuman, owner of the Rosedale Fish Market and the dean of New York fishmongers. Neuman, who at 75 has been in the fish business for 53 years, is supposed to meet me in front of his store and take me down to the Fulton Fish Market, New York's eighty-five-year-old wholesale fish market. The market is open from 4:00 to 6:00 A.M. Monday through Friday, but any serious restaurateur or fish retailer gets there early for the best possible selection. At 3:35 Neuman still hasn't shown up, so assuming he may have forgotten, I venture down to the market, hoping his legendary status will allow me to ask anyone selling fish where Rosedale Doc (his Fulton Street nickname) is.

There are lots of fish at the Fulton Fish Market—lots of fish in lots of crates being sold by young and old men in parkas and lots of waterproof boots. The market comprises two buildings, one of which opened in 1907, the other in 1936. According to Richard Lord, a consultant to the market and an ichthyologist currently writing a fish encyclopedia, 100 million pounds of fish were sold at the market in 1991 by about seventy-five vendors. A total of 500 species of fish can be found there in the course of a year (up to 75 on any given day), everything from the standard Atlantic salmon to a Caribbean species called doctorfish that Jamaicans make into a fish tea. The bulk of the fish found at the market comes from New England and the Canadian Maritime Provinces, but up to 25 percent of a given day's supply can be imported from places such as Ecuador (giant shrimp) and Scotland (salmon). But even though there are plenty of fish and plenty of men, there is no Robert Neuman. I ask around, and apparently I have just missed him. I do a couple of laps around the market and finally run into a guy who tells me that Neuman has taken the day off and that he is buying for Neuman this morning. I am not happy. It is now 4:30, I have been up for almost two hours, my clothing is suffused with the smell of fish, and I still haven't done the interview.

I head for home and work, and later I call Neuman. In his gravelly Spencer Tracy voice he apologizes profusely, saying he has just gotten back from Santa Fe and decided not to go down to the market today. I tell him that it's okay but that next time he should call to let me know. We agree to wait a couple of weeks (my body needs time to recover from this middle-of-the night jolt) and try again.

Almost a month later I find myself being dropped off by taxi, again at 3:15 A.M., in front of the Rosedale Fish Market. Though I half-expect to renew my acquaintance with the Korean family that runs the twenty-four-hour produce market and deli next door, I am relieved to find the lights on in the Rosedale Fish Market. I approach the store and spot a short, ruddy-faced man with stringy grayish white hair wearing a brown knit cap. It's Neuman going over the previous day's receipts. He looks up, smiles broadly, and comes to the door to let me in.

Rosedale Doc, Mayor of the Fulton Fish Market, continued

We drive down to the fish market in his Buick. Although he appears robust and full of energy, he sounds like a man trapped by his own success. "I'm 72, and I'm weary. I don't have the guts to quit. I've never been able to take any time off. Five days a week, I get up at two A.M., leave the house at three, get to the market by a quarter to four, do my buying, get to the store by seven, open at eight, close the store by six-thirty, go home, eat dinner, and go to sleep by seven-thirty P.M. On Saturdays, there's no market, so I allow myself the luxury of sleeping until five or six. On Sundays I do bookkeeping in the office I built in the basement of my house."

But just then we arrive at the market, and he pulls into the same parking space he's been using for fifty years. All of a sudden his face lights up; he looks like a child coming down the stairs on Christmas morning. "I can't wait for Monday to get started," he announces as he bounces out of his car, fishhook in hand. We walk into the market, and I feel I am accompanying the mayor of the market on a campaign tour. "Heh, Bob, I missed ya, but the market's up today," one wholesaler calls out. Neuman has just returned from a five-day visit to Santa Fe, where one of his sons owns a fish market and restaurant. Neuman nods to him and says to me, "His father was my best friend." He points to a young man in a red hat selling gray sole and says, "I bought my first pound of gray sole from his grandfather a long time ago." I ask him about a recent trend among fish-store owners and restaurateurs to buy their fish direct and bypass the market. "I don't buy anything direct. I might save money, but I'd lose friends, and it's not worth it."

Just then Neuman spots one of his regular suppliers and holds up a small shoebox he's been carrying. He takes out a pair of baby moccasins that he bought in Santa Fe and hands them to the man. "This is for the baby," Neuman says. The man smiles broadly and shakes his head as he examines the moccasins. Neuman introduces me, and the man with the moccasins says, pointing to Neuman, "This guy never quarrels on price—he's a quality man."

We keep walking, and we pass some fish that is clearly past its prime. "I hate to buy ugly fish," he says, shaking his head. I ask Neuman what he looks for when he buys fish. He says, "The eyes should be clear and the flesh should be firm, but mostly I don't worry about the fish. I buy the people. If you trust the people you're buying from, you'll be okay. We pass one of his regular gray sole suppliers, and Neuman spots an undersized gray sole. "Would I buy that crap?" he asks, hooking the fish and examining it closely. The wholesaler laughs as Neuman says, "He calls me the East Coast director of aggravation."

Neuman stops at a concessions truck and purchases two styrofoam containers of coffee. He starts to drink one and walks with the other toward a stall labeled The Blue Ribbon Fish Company. Blue Ribbon, run by Bob and David Samuels, is one of Neuman's regular suppliers and also one of the major fish suppliers for both Le Bernardin and Bouley, two of the half-dozen restaurants awarded four stars by *The New York Times*. Bob Samuels spots Neuman coming, takes the other container of coffee from him and asks, "What about yesterday's coffee?" Neuman asks to borrow a pencil, and Samuels replies, "You want fish or pencils?"

We walk back to the Blue Ribbon Fish Company's office, where a cashier totes up purchases. No cash changes hand at the market. Regulars are billed at the end of the week and are expected to pay a week later. Neuman says, "If you get behind two or three weeks, that can run into a lot of money, and they let you know." We walk into a tiny office adjoining the cashier's space, where there's a run-down couch and a single chair. Neuman sits down and says, "Sometimes I come back here and close my eyes for a few minutes."

"You know," he starts to explain, "if I wasn't doing this I'd spend the rest of my life in the library. I'm kind of a half-assed history buff. Did you notice I have a sign in my store that reads 'A Fish Monger Remembers'? It's a picture of Sacco and Vanzetti, two radical activists executed on August 23, 1927. Every year on that date I put the sign in the window.

"You may not know this, but when Oliver Wendell Holmes retired, he merely told his clerks, 'I won't be down tomorrow.' That's the way to go out. I'd put a sign that says 'I won't be down tomorrow' in the window, and I'd call it a day.

"But if I called it a day, I wouldn't know what to do with myself. Running the store, coming down here, it's an ego trip. My father used to say, 'A one-man business is run by one man.' Now I know what he meant." Just then Neuman gets up to leave. "You know, young fella, business is a matter of tuning and fine-tuning all the time. I guess in that way I'm the Leonard Bernstein of the Rosedale Fish Market."

Touring and Buying at the Fulton Fish Market

The Fulton Fish Market is open to the public Monday through Friday. First-time visitors may be a little intimidated by all the hubbub and macho bantering that goes on, so a guided tour may be your best bet. Richard Lord, ichthyologist and consultant to the Fish Market, gives guided tours for $30 for a minimum of three and a maximum of six persons. Lord is so knowledgeable that you may occasionally find yourself politely cutting him short to complete the tour in under two hours.

With or without Lord, you can buy fish at the Fulton Fish Market from virtually any vendor there. You'll find the best selection on Monday and Thursday (that's when the fish comes in from the Gulf of Mexico and Florida)

Touring and Buying at the Fulton Fish Market, continued

and the lowest prices on Friday (nobody wants unsold fish on their hands over the weekend). Although the market opens at 4:00 A.M., most vendors don't want to deal with the public until 5:30, after their regular wholesale customers have done their buying. The vendors won't break up a whole case of fish to sell you one fish, but they will sell you an individual piece of a fish on display at their stands. Prices are low. A whole bluefish will cost less than a dollar a pound at the market and up to four times as much in an upscale Manhattan fish market such as Citarella. It's romantic to think about haggling over price when buying at the market, but be forewarned that until a vendor gets to know you, bargaining won't do you much good. Also, don't be annoyed if you pay a price that's slightly higher than the one you've just heard a vendor quote one of his regular customers. If you start showing up at 4:00 A.M. five days a week and buying hundreds of dollars' worth of fish, you'll eventually get the lower price, too.

---

*U*PPER WEST SIDE

59TH STREET TO 125TH STREET
CENTRAL PARK WEST TO RIVERSIDE DRIVE

Citarella ⌁ According to reputable New York fish historians, Citarella in the 1970s and 1980s was on its last legs (or fins, as the case may be), the result of its absentee owner's love of the horses. So in 1983 Joe Gurada took over this fifty-year-old upper West Side institution and returned it to its rightful place in the New York fishmonger pantheon. Today Citarella is the standard by which fish markets all over the West Side are judged. In fact, it (along with Fairway) has become part of a weekend-destination food-shopping axis for New York City expatriates who have relocated to Westchester and New Jersey. The store has a terrific selection of both filets and whole fish. You'll find everything from standards (Dover sole, tuna, swordfish, squid, shrimp in various sizes, scallops, bluefish, halibut, scrod, and salmon) to exotica (shad roe, boned shad, soft-shell crab, sea urchin, pompano, mahi-mahi, seafood sausage, orange roughy, and catfish filets). In addition to the store's whimsical and creative window displays, another extremely pleasant feature is the recently constructed shellfish bar. After braving the weekend madness at Fairway, there's no better quick picker-upper than downing a dozen clams or oysters here. The clam selection is limited to littlenecks and cherrystones, but the oyster choices are more varied, with Belons, Wellfleets, Apalachicolas and Cape bluepoints usually available on a given day. The Manhattan clam chowder here is woefully inconsistent. Some days it's a peppery delight, filled with chunks of clams. Other days, it's oversalted, with a real paucity of clams.

Citarella's window displays, created daily by Fernando Lara, are a Westside tradition.

Note: I've heard a couple of complaints in recent months about the fish going downhill here, but I have not noticed any deterioration in quality or freshness. I have, however, had less-than-friendly service here on more than one occasion.

Citarella
2135 Broadway (corner of 75th Street)
New York, NY 10023
PHONE: (212) 874-0383
SUBWAYS: 72nd Street station on the following lines: Broadway–Seventh
   Avenue No. 1, 2, 3 and 9; Eighth Avenue C and Sixth Avenue B.
HOURS: 8:30 A.M. to 7 P.M. Monday through Saturday; 10 A.M. to 6 P.M.
   Sunday.
Delivery available.
Cash or personal checks only.

The Lobster Place ⁓ I figure no one's fussier about food than upscale restaurateurs and their chefs, so when I heard that the Lobster Place supplies restaurants like La Côte Basque and the Tribeca Grill with lobsters, I decided it was the place to go for crustaceans in Manhattan. The Lobster Place has tanks that can hold ten thousand pounds of lobster at any one time. One sure sign of a lobster's quality is how lively it is, and the Lobster Place's lobsters are squirmier than my four-year-old son. They also sell vertebrate fish here, but the place in general does look a little funky, so I'd stick to lobster.

The Lobster Place
487 Amsterdam Avenue (between 83rd and 84th streets)
New York, NY 10024
PHONE: (212) 595-7605

SUBWAYS: 86th Street station on the following lines: Broadway–Seventh
Avenue No. 1 and 9; Eighth Avenue C and Sixth Avenue D.
HOURS: 9 A.M. to 7 P.M. Monday through Friday; 9 A.M. to 6 P.M. Saturday;
closed Sunday.
Deliveries in the neighborhood.
All major credit cards accepted.

$\mathcal{U}$PPER EAST SIDE

59TH STREET TO 96TH STREET
FIRST AVENUE TO FIFTH AVENUE

Baldwin Fish Market --- My friend and colleague Tom, a first-rate marketer if there ever was one, said I had to see the incredibly smart thing the Baldwin Fish Market does as a service for its customers. The idea: photocopies of about twenty fish recipes from *The New York Times*, not only tacked to a bulletin board but also available to take home. The Baldwin Fish Market has a limited selection of very fresh fish, ranging from Dover sole to salmon to tuna. It also has a live lobster tank and a small selection of shellfish. I wish other fish markets would copy the Baldwin's *Times* idea. It probably represents a copyright infringement, but it sure is great for the Baldwin Fish Market's customers (and most likely for the recipe creators as well).

Baldwin Fish Market
1584 First Avenue (between 82nd and 83rd streets)
New York, NY 10028
PHONE: (212) 288-9032
SUBWAYS: 86th Street station on the Lexington Avenue No. 4, 5, and 6 lines.
HOURS: 8 A.M. to 7:30 P.M. Monday through Saturday; closed Sunday.
Deliveries within a twenty-block radius.
Cash only.

Catalano's --- Joe Catalano believes the secret of his store's success is that he tries to keep it a real old-fashioned fish market. Toward that end he filets all of his own fish, carries a large selection of whole fish, and buys his fish with eating rather than appearance in mind. According to him, that means the Georgia Bank flounder he sells may have some dark tissue in it, but it'll taste great. He was right about the flounder I brought home from his store. It was delicious, with firm flesh and, yes, a little bit of dark tissue. Catalano's makes a crabmeat-and-smoked-shrimp salad so delicious that I didn't care if the "crabmeat" was in fact sea leg, the phony crabmeat made out of pollack and cod. Catalano's also makes the best-prepared Manhattan clam chowder I tasted in researching this book. It was properly peppery, with little bits of bacon punctuating each spoonful.

Catalano's
1652 Second Avenue (between 85th and 86th streets)
New York, NY 10028
PHONE: (212) 628-9608

Robert Neuman carries on the tradition of supplying impeccably fresh fish at the Rosedale Fish Market.

SUBWAYS: 86th Street station on the Lexington Avenue No. 4, 5, and 6 lines.
HOURS: 9 A.M. to 7 P.M. Monday through Friday; 9 A.M. to 6 P.M. Saturday; closed Sunday.
Neighborhood delivery available.
Cash and personal checks only.

Rosedale Fish Market ⁓ If high-quality fish is what you want, and money is no object, the Rosedale Fish Market is for you. Seventy-five-year-old legendary fishmonger Robert Neuman and his father before him have been supplying gorgeous, impeccably fresh fish to price-is-no-object Upper East Siders for nearly eighty-five years. Although the selection here is somewhat limited, you can always find Dover sole, salmon, tuna, and the like, unless Neuman, on his daily trek to the Fulton Fish Market, has deemed one of them to be of insufficient quality (see accompanying sidebar). The lobster salad and fresh tuna salad I bought here were okay, nothing more.

Note: If you're stuck for a summertime dinner-party entrée, Rosedale, on twelve hours' notice, will prepare and deliver a cold poached salmon with dill sauce that is simply extraordinary.

Rosedale Fish Market
1129 Lexington Avenue (between 78th and 79th streets)
New York, NY 10021
PHONE: (212) 734-3767
SUBWAY: 77th Street station on the Lexington Avenue No. 6 line.

Fresh fish, reasonable prices at Central Fish Company.

HOURS: 8 A.M. to 6 P.M. Monday through Saturday; closed Sunday.
Deliveries in Manhattan.
American Express accepted.
No mail order, although occasional Federal Express packages will be sent.

ℳIDTOWN WEST

34TH STREET TO 59TH STREET
FIFTH AVENUE TO ELEVENTH AVENUE

Central Fish Company — It's hard to distinguish Central Fish from its Ninth Avenue counterpart, Sea Breeze. Both sell countless varieties of local and imported fish at ridiculously low prices. One item Central Fish carries that Sea Breeze doesn't is politically correct (non–South African) Brazilian lobster tails. They're sold frozen but taste quite good broiled or grilled. Central also sells fresh Maine and Florida shrimp, delicious if smaller alternatives to the frozen Gulf shrimp. Service at Central Fish can be kind of brusque, but inexpensive fresh fish has to be paid for some way.

Central Fish Company
527 Ninth Avenue (at 39th Street)
New York, NY 10018
PHONE: (212) 279-2317
SUBWAYS: 42nd Street–Port Authority Bus Terminal station on the Eighth
    Avenue A, C, and E lines.

HOURS: 7:30 A.M. to 6:30 P.M. Monday through Saturday; closed Sunday.
Deliveries in Manhattan.
Cash only.

Macy's Cellar Marketplace ～ See page 229.

Sea Breeze ～ You've made the wrong-headed decision to serve ten people Dover sole, and you're determined not to file for Chapter 11. Don't despair. Head down to Sea Breeze, or its neighbor Central Fish. There you'll find Dover sole for $7.99 a pound, about half what you'd pay in other parts of town. Besides low prices, Sea Breeze offers a wide variety of domestic and imported fish, from red mullet to scorpio. Just don't expect pristine shopping conditions. You won't find tiled walls or dry floors here.

Sea Breeze
541 Ninth Avenue (corner of 40th Street)
New York, NY 10018
PHONE: (212) 563-7537
SUBWAYS: 42nd Street–Port Authority Bus Terminal station on the Eighth
    Avenue A, C, and E lines.
HOURS: 7:30 A.M. to 6 P.M. Monday; 7:30 A.M. to 6:30 P.M. Tuesday through
    Friday; 7:30 A.M. to 5:30 P.M. Saturday; closed Sunday.
No deliveries.
Cash only.

Pisacane Midtown ～ The entrance to Pisacane is through a thick, gray, refrigerator door with a small circular peephole in it. So it's no surprise that Pisacane sells some of the freshest fish to be had in all of New York. When you order tuna steaks here, they're sliced to order from a large section of tuna. It's one of the few New York fish markets I've encountered that, in season, has a tank full of live Dungeness crabs. Pisacane also sells beautiful Cape scallops still in their shell. The only disappointment here is the quality of the prepared foods. The clam sauces and chowders were bland, the dill-accented shrimp salad was just okay, and the fresh tuna salad was not so fresh the day I bought it.

Pisacane Midtown
940 First Avenue (between 51st and 52nd streets)
New York, NY 10022
PHONE: (212) 355-1850
SUBWAYS: 51st Street station on the Lexington Avenue No. 6 line; Lexington
    and Third avenues station on the Sixth Avenue F and Eighth Avenue E
    lines.
HOURS: 8 A.M. to 6 P.M. Monday through Friday; 9 A.M. to 5 P.M. Saturday;
    closed Sunday.
Deliveries in Midtown only.
Cash only.

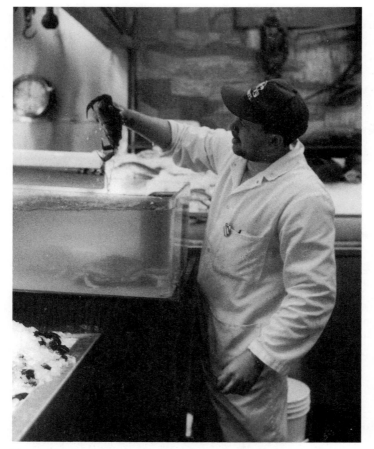

The tank of live Dungeness crab is a special feature at Pisacane Midtown.

$\mathcal{C}$HELSEA

14TH STREET TO 34TH STREET
FIFTH AVENUE TO ELEVENTH AVENUE

Starfish Enterprises ⏤ Walk into Starfish, and you're greeted by a wonderful, briny sea smell that instills confidence that the fish you buy will be fresh. Co-owners Jonathan Lindle and Sandra Soehngen carry a limited but impeccably chosen selection of vertebrate fish such as tuna, swordfish, and Dover sole, at prices at least 30% lower than other fish markets of comparable quality. It's their shellfish, however, that sets them apart from other fish stores. On any given day they carry half a dozen varieties of clams, oysters, and mussels, depending on what's freshest. The last time I was here I picked up six mild Pine Island oysters, which come from North Carolina. Starfish also carries wonderful smoked trout and trout and bluefish pâtés made by Duck Trap Farms in Maine. Everyone who works at Starfish seems to be knowledgeable, friendly, and solicitous of customers. They are glad to answer any questions about their fish and its preparation, and they might even throw in a lemon free of charge, as they did with my purchase of Pine Island oysters.

Note: Prices here are lower than other comparable designer fish markets such as Rosedale and Citarella.

Starfish Enterprises
233 Ninth Avenue (between 24th and 25th streets)
New York, NY 10011
PHONE: (212) 807-8106
SUBWAYS: 23rd Street station on the Eighth Avenue C and E lines.
HOURS: 9 A.M. to 7 P.M. Monday through Friday; 9 A.M. to 6 P.M. Saturday;
   closed Sunday.
Deliveries available.
Visa and MasterCard accepted.
Starfish is the only place I've run into that actually ships fresh oysters and
   clams by mail.

Balducci's Soft-Shell Crabs Meunière

The best way to prepare soft-shell crabs is to clean them right before cooking. A simple step-by-step guide is as follows: Turn crab on its back and remove apron (pointed section in the center). Lift flaps on either side and remove spongy gill tissues (lungs). Cut off eyes at the tip of the head and squeeze until bile sac pops out. Discard sac and pat crabs dry on paper towel. (Do not rinse, or much of the sweet crab juice will wash away.)

If soft-shell-crab cleaning is not your forte, but you're addicted to their flavor, simply order them dressed to start with. In any case, make sure you select real live wires—their claws should be waving and their surface glistening.

¼ cup vegetable oil	*4 tablespoons unsalted butter*
4 soft-shell crabs, cleaned	*2 ounces dry white wine*
½ cup all-purpose flour	*Juice from 1½ lemons*
1 large egg, beaten	*2 tablespoons chopped fresh chives*

1. Heat oil in a medium-sized skillet over medium heat. Dust crabs with flour, then dip in egg. Sauté in oil for 1½ minutes on each side until golden and remove to paper towel. Discard oil.
2. Reduce heat to low and add butter to same skillet. When butter melts, add wine and lemon juice. Place crabs back in skillet and cover. Cook 4 to 5 minutes more over very low heat. Sprinkle with chives and serve in pan juices.

Yield: 2 servings

𝒦IPS BAY/GRAMERCY PARK

14TH STREET TO 34TH STREET
EAST RIVER TO FIFTH AVENUE

Todaro Brothers ～ See page 233.

𝒲EST VILLAGE

14TH STREET TO HOUSTON STREET
FIFTH AVENUE TO WEST STREET

Balducci's ～ See page 205.

Jefferson Market Seafood ～ Although Jefferson Market Seafood is separated from the main store by only two doors, it seems leagues away in terms of presentation. The last time I was here, there was liquid dripping from the scallops onto some other fish on the shelf below in the store window. The fish filets were sloppily laid out, with insufficient ice cover. I know these things are not supposed to make a difference, but in a fish market appearance is 90 percent of the game. It isn't everything, because the tuna I brought home from Jefferson the last time I was there was terrific. The store has a wide selection of fish on any given day, including turbot, orange roughy, mahi-mahi, and monkfish filets. There is also a smaller selection of whole fish, including pompano and brook trout.

Jefferson Market Seafood
455 Sixth Avenue (between 11th and 12th streets)
New York, NY 10011
PHONE: (212) 675-2277
SUBWAY: Christopher Street–Sheridan Square station on the Broadway–
    Seventh Avenue No. 1 and 9 lines; West Fourth Street–Washington
    Square station on the following lines: Sixth Avenue B, D, F, and Q;
    Eighth Avenue A, C, and E.
HOURS: 9 A.M. to 8 P.M. seven days a week.

𝒟OWNTOWN

HOUSTON STREET TO BATTERY PARK

Dean & DeLuca ～ See page 214.

Hoi Sing Seafood ⬥ See page 131.

Lobster King ⬥ See page 132.

Ocean Sea Food ⬥ See page 131.

Petrosino ⬥ When I asked Vincent Petrosino how he got his start in the fish business, he replied, "I was born with scales on me." That was his way of telling me that his father started the store sixty years ago. It's a tiny, dimly lit place, with a wooden model of a boat and a fishing shack in back of the counter. The selection is limited to the standards like gray sole, salmon, scrod, halibut, swordfish, and salmon. The last time I was there I bought a piece of gray sole, didn't cook it for a day, and still found it to be impeccably fresh. Besides the fish, Petrosino's usually has a selection of clams, oysters, and mussels. It also has a small live-lobster tank.

Petrosino
161 Duane Street (between West Broadway and Hudson Street)
New York, NY 10013
PHONE: (212) 732-8131
SUBWAYS: Chambers Street station on the Broadway–Seventh Avenue No. 1,
    2, 3, and 9 lines and the Eighth Avenue A and C lines.
HOURS: 8 A.M. to 5 P.M. Monday through Wednesday; 8 A.M. to 6 P.M.
    Thursday and Friday; closed Saturday and Sunday.
$50 minimum on deliveries.
Cash or personal checks only.

𝓑RONX

Cosenza's Fish Market ⬥ See page 134.

𝒬UEENS

Anestis Fish Market ⬥ See page 138.

Best of Fish

Best all-around fresh fish store: Pisacane Midtown
Best Manhattan clam chowder: Catalano's; Rosedale Fish Market
Best Chinatown fish market: Hoi Sing
Best lobsters: The Lobster Place
Best Mediterranean fish selection: Sea Breeze; Anestis Fish Market
Best prices: Central Fish; Sea Breeze; Hoi Sing Seafood
Best shellfish (mussels, oysters, clams): Starfish Enterprises
Best Value: Starfish Enterprises

10

GOTTA HAVE IT . . . GOTTA HAVE IT NOW

There are certain kinds of New York eating experiences I love that, strictly speaking, either don't really fall within the purview of this book or don't fall neatly into any of the chapters I've included. So after agonizing about this unfortunate state of affairs with my editor, we decided to devote a chapter to all these foods.

We decided to call it "Gotta Have It . . . Gotta Have It Now" because there are times in a person's life when a food craving just cannot go unanswered. I'm not talking about the last months of pregnancy here. I'm talking about those times a vegetarian is walking down the street and is overcome by the urge for a hot dog. I'm talking about those times a person who keeps kosher is struck by the urge for an Italian sausage sandwich or a BLT. I'm talking about the moment you realize you can't go another step without an order of potato pancakes. We all get these urges. We cannot ignore them, or they will just manifest themselves negatively in some other aspect of our lives.

Note: Every food mentioned in "Gotta Have It" is the best in its category in New York, so I've not included a "Best of" page for this chapter.

BARBECUE

Sylvia's Restaurant ~ Normally I regard barbecued ribs baked in a conventional oven with the same scorn I reserve for Stewart sandwiches, those hideous things they microwave at gas stations all over the country. But Sylvia's barbecued ribs are so tangy, so transcendent it doesn't matter where she cooks them. If you order them with rice, to soak up the peppery but sweet sauce, and the candied "sweets" (sweet potatoes), you'll be making annual pilgrimages here, as all the Japanese and European tourists do. You might want to substitute macaroni and cheese for the candied yams, so that for dessert you can have Sylvia's ethereal sweet potato pie, made with more than a hint of vanilla.

Note: Don't let Sylvia's Harlem location deter you from these ribs. If tour operators from all over the world steer their patrons here, you can be reasonably sure of your safety at Sylvia's. Plus, the outside environs are more than made up for by the warmth of both your fellow patrons and the waitresses.

Note: Three times in the last few years our office Christmas party was catered by Sylvia's. Without giving her a shameless plug, I can tell you Sylvia's fried chicken and ribs made it a most soulful holiday season.

Sylvia's Restaurant
328 Lenox Avenue (between 126th and 127th streets)
New York, NY 10027
PHONE: (212) 996-0660
SUBWAYS: 125th Street station on the Broadway–Seventh Avenue No. 2 and
    3 lines.
HOURS: 7:30 A.M. to 10:30 P.M. Monday through Saturday; 1 P.M. to 7 P.M.
    Sunday.
No deliveries.
Cash only.

BLINTZES

Cafe Edison ~ My grandmother's greatest joy was coming over to our house on the weekends, getting up early, and making blintzes for my brothers and our friends. One Saturday morning, we set a family record when the four Levine brothers and our friend Dan ate ninety-seven blintzes among the five of us. It was easy to consume that many, because my grandmother's blintzes were sensational, full of fresh pot cheese and redolent of cinnamon and raisins. They were also slightly asymmetrical—sort of a modern architect's rendering of a blintz. Over the years, I've consumed hundreds of blintzes, looking for a kitchen that made its blintzes in the same slightly misshapen fashion. Finally, I discovered the not-quite-tubular blintzes at Cafe Edison. They arrive at the table crisp but not too crisp, with cheese oozing out of one or more of its corners. Finally, I have achieved blintz closure, and my grandmother can rest in peace knowing there's someone else in the world making perfect, imperfect blintzes.

Cafe Edison
228 West 47th Street (between Seventh and Eighth avenues)
New York, NY 10036
PHONE: (212) 354-0368

SUBWAYS: 50th Street station on the Broadway–Seventh Avenue No. 1 and 9
  lines and the Eighth Avenue C and E lines.
HOURS: 6:15 A.M. to 10:30 P.M. Monday through Saturday; 6 A.M. to 3 P.M.
  Sunday.
Deliveries in the neighborhood.
Cash only.

BREAD PUDDING (EASTERN EUROPEAN STYLE)

Cafe Edison ~ Frances Edelstein has been serving her hearty Eastern European peasant food at this unlikely outpost in the theater district for more than twenty-five years. Habitués refer to it as the Polish Tea Room. Although her soups (of course she serves matzo-ball), blintzes, and latkes are all first-rate, it is her bread pudding I constantly take detours for. It's moist, slightly chewy, and studded with raisins and, believe it or not, maraschino cherries. One slice of this bread pudding and you'll be fortified for whatever New York throws at you.

Note: This unlikely coffee shop is the unofficial lunchtime clubhouse for much of the New York theater world. This means you may occasionally be vying for the last piece of bread pudding with Neil Simon or Manny Azenberg, his producer.

Cafe Edison
228 West 47th Street (between Seventh and Eighth avenues)
New York, NY 10036
PHONE: (212) 354-0368
SUBWAYS: 50th Street station on the Broadway–Seventh Avenue No. 1 and 9
  lines and the Eighth Avenue C and E lines.
HOURS: 6:15 A.M. to 10:30 P.M. Monday through Saturday; 6 A.M. to 3 P.M.
  Sunday.
Deliveries in the neighborhood.
Cash only.

CHINESE DUMPLINGS

Dumpling King ~ Most dumplings in Chinese restaurants require a safecracker to bite all the way through the thick, doughy, pasty casings. But Dumpling King's dumplings are a revelation, by far the best dumplings I've come across in New York. The fried pork variety has a thin, tasty casing that's been fried to a golden brown on both sides. The filling is a wonderful, lean mixture of pork, scallions, and spices. The fried shrimp dumplings have the same wonderful casings and an intriguing creamy minced shrimp and scallion filling. The equally superb steamed shrimp dumplings have just chunks of whole shrimp in them. In general I'm a fried-dumpling fan, but here the incredibly high quality of both preparations makes it difficult to make a choice. Besides pork, shrimp, beef, and crabmeat dumplings, Dumpling King also makes an amazing vegetable dumpling that's just as tasty as the meat and shellfish varieties. Dumpling King, it should be noted, has a large, conventional Chinese-restaurant menu. It's just that I've never felt the need to have anything more than dumplings here.

Dumpling King
1694 Second Avenue (between 87th and 88th streets)
New York, NY 10028
PHONE: (212) 410-2700, 1701, 6654
SUBWAYS: 86th Street station on the Lexington Avenue No. 4, 5, and 6 lines.
HOURS: 11:30 A.M. to 11:30 P.M. Sunday through Thursday; 11:30 A.M. to
    midnight Friday and Saturday.
Delivery in Manhattan.
American Express accepted.

OTHER LOCATION:
Dumpling King II
986 Second Avenue (at 52nd Street)
New York, NY 10022
(212) 759-7070

CHINESE SPARE RIBS

Pig Heaven, Big Wong, and Ollie's — If I were a pregnant woman, I'm sure
one of my food cravings would be Chinese spare ribs. Because even now, I'll be
in a meeting with colleagues or be involved in a "How was your day?" conversation
with my wife when visions of Chinese spare ribs start dancing in my head. My
spare-rib cravings take me all over town. When I'm on the Upper East Side,
visiting my mother-in-law, I'm thinking about Pig Heaven's long, lean, incredibly
meaty spare ribs. When I'm on jury duty or anywhere south of 14th Street, my
mind and heart are at Big Wong's, where the spare ribs are small, sticky, sweet
four-bite jobbies, served the traditional Chinese way, at room temperature. And
when I'm in my apartment or walking anywhere in my Upper West Side neighborhood, I'm dreaming about Ollie's Noodle Shop's transcendent midsize spare
ribs, served sizzling hot to cater to New Yorkers' tastes.

Pig Heaven
1540 Second Avenue (between 80th and 81st streets)
New York, NY 10028
PHONE: (212) 744-4887
SUBWAY: 77th Street station on the Lexington Avenue No. 6 line.
HOURS: 11:30 A.M. to 11:30 P.M. Sunday through Thursday; 11:30 A.M. to
    12:30 A.M. Friday and Saturday.
Deliveries in Manhattan.
All major credit cards accepted.

Big Wong Restaurant
157 Mott Street (corner of Grand Street)
New York, NY 10013
PHONE: (212) 966-6808
SUBWAYS: Canal Street station on the following lines: Lexington Avenue No.
    6, Broadway N and R, Nassau Street J, M, and Z; Grand Street station on
    the Sixth Avenue B, D, and Q lines.
HOURS: 9:30 A.M. to 9 P.M. Tuesday through Saturday; closed Sunday.
No deliveries.
Cash only.

OTHER LOCATION:
67 Mott Street (corner of Canal Street)
New York, NY 10013
(212) 964-0540
This location is open Sunday.

Ollie's Noodle Shop & Grille
2315 Broadway (corner of 84th Street)
New York, NY 10024
PHONE: (212) 362-3712 or (212) 362-3111
SUBWAY: 86th Street station on the following lines: Broadway–Seventh
    Avenue 1 and 9, Eighth Avenue C and Sixth Avenue D.
HOURS: 11:30 A.M. to midnight Sunday through Thursday; 11:30 A.M. to 1
    A.M. Friday and Saturday.
Deliveries in the neighborhood.
All major credit cards accepted.

OTHER LOCATION:
There is another Ollie's at 114th Street and Broadway, but I don't find it to
    be as good as the 84th Street location.

COLD SESAME NOODLES

Hwa Yuan Szechuan Restaurant ～ Cold sesame noodles have become the ultimate throwaway Chinese food in New York. In fact, a host of Chinese restaurants
have started to give them away as premium items to encourage delivery orders.
As a result, most of them taste like a greasy, salty version of a bad Chinese peanut
butter sandwich made with inferior peanut butter. But the chef at Hwa Yuan
Szechuan Restaurant has raised the level of cold sesame noodles to an art form.
He uses real peanut butter, sesame oil, and more than ninety other ingredients
to produce the best cold sesame noodles in New York. The noodles are firm (is
there a Chinese word for *al dente*?), and the sauce is nutty, sweet, and slightly
hot at the same time. They're not even very greasy. An order of cold sesame
noodles and some of the very good fried dumplings makes a satisfying cheap
lunch for two.
   Note: Hwa Yuan Szechuan used to be the ultimate Chinatown hole-in-the-wall.
But a fire forced them to rebuild, and now the place is unsuccessfully trying to
look like one of the new high-tech establishments dotting the Chinatown landscape.

Hwa Yuan Szechuan Restaurant
40 East Broadway (just east of the Bowery)
New York, NY 10002
PHONE: (212) 966-5534, 5535, 5547
SUBWAY: Canal Street station on the following lines: Lexington Avenue No.
    6, Broadway N and R, Nassau Street J, M, and Z; Grand Street station on
    the Sixth Avenue B, D, and Q lines.
HOURS: 11 A.M. to 10 P.M. Sunday through Thursday; 11 A.M. to 11:30 P.M.
    Friday and Saturday.
Free delivery.
All major credit cards accepted.

EGG CREAMS

Egg Cream from Moisha's Luncheonette

Lenny Zabrowsky provides this recipe for authentic egg creams. Lenny was the owner of Moisha's Luncheonette where, until its unfortunate closing in 1991, you could get the best egg creams in the city.

1. Start with an inch of very cold, almost frozen milk.
2. Spritz seltzer into the milk until it fills the glass.
3. Put in Fox's U-Bet Chocolate Syrup, let it settle to the bottom of the glass, then stir it with a long spoon. The chocolate should rise to the top and you should be left with an inch of white foam. Your taste buds will tell you if you've done it right.

EMPANADAS

Ruben's Empanadas ~ Empanadas, or meat pies, have gotten a bad rap in New York because of the flavorless, greasy pockets of meat you get from most street carts. But Ruben's handmade, fresh-baked empanadas have a flaky crust and tasty, nongoopy fillings. I'm partial to the piquant ground beef and the spicy chicken varieties. Even the seafood empanada is made with fresh scrod and real crabmeat, and it's only fifty cents more than the ground beef. A Ruben's empanada makes a great walking lunch. In fact, smart folks pick up a couple of empanadas here and then walk over to explore the South Street Seaport area. That way they avoid the mediocre, cliched foods served at most of the seaport's mall-like food concessions.

Ruben's Empanadas
64 Fulton Street
New York, NY 10038
PHONE: (212) 962-7274
SUBWAYS: Broadway–Nassau Street station on the Eighth Avenue A and C
    lines; Fulton Street station on the following lines: Nassau Street J, M,
    and Z; Lexington Avenue No. 4 and 5; Broadway–Seventh Avenue No. 2
    and 3.
HOURS: 7 A.M. to 7 P.M. seven days a week.
Delivery available.
Cash only.

OTHER LOCATION:
77 Pearl Street (at Coenties Slip)
New York, NY 10038
(212) 509-3825

FALAFEL

Falafel 'N' Stuff ⁓ In New York, Falafel is too often synonymous with soggy chickpea balls served hours or even days after they were cooked. At Falafel 'n' Stuff you have to wait a little while for your falafel because they cook it to order. The result is the perfect sandwich: crispy, fresh chickpea balls laden with intriguing spices, lettuce and tomato, and a homemade tahini sauce that's doused liberally throughout a fresh pita bread. Falafel 'n' Stuff is an authentic, inexpensive Middle Eastern restaurant that serves nothing but impeccably fresh vegetarian dishes like baba ghanouj, hummous, and tabouli as well as simple grilled meats like shish kebab and chicken.

Falafel 'N' Stuff
1586 First Avenue (between 82nd and 83rd streets)
New York, NY 10028
PHONE: (212) 650-9530 or (212) 879-7023
SUBWAYS: 86th Street station on the Lexington Avenue No. 4, 5, and 6 lines.
HOURS: Noon to midnight seven days a week.
Deliveries in the neighborhood.
All major credit cards accepted.

FRIED CHICKEN

M & G Diner ⁓ Fried chicken is one of my comfort foods, which I turn to in times of stress. So when my anxiety-level meter is pinned to the red, I head to the M & G Diner on 125th Street. I order the fried chicken, white meat please. Then I head to the juke box, plunk in two quarters for "Rainy Night in Georgia" and "(Can I) Change My Mind," and take my seat at the counter. Just as Tyrone Davis is winding down, my chicken arrives. It's perfect: golden-brown and crispy on the outside, tender and juicy inside. You get your choice of two vegetables, and being a starch freak, I opt for the macaroni and cheese and the candied yams. Normally I would choose mashed potatoes in these circumstances, but alas, at M & G they use the instant variety. Two perfect mini–corn muffins round out the meal. The rest of the soul food at M & G is first-rate, and the welcome you'll get at this unprepossessing place is just as warm as the food.

M & G Diner
383 West 125th Street (between St. Nicholas Avenue and Morningside
   Drive)
New York, NY 10027
PHONE: (212) 864-7326
SUBWAYS: 125th Street Station on the Eighth Avenue A and C lines and the
   Sixth Avenue B and D lines.
HOURS: Twenty-four hours a day, seven days a week.
No deliveries.
Cash only.

GOURMET POPCORN

Nancy's Gourmet Popcorn ~~ When I was growing up, one of my favorite experiences was eating a box of Cracker Jacks. I liked the popcorn just fine, but I absolutely craved the peanuts. Nancy's has come up with the ultimate adult equivalent of Cracker Jacks, macadamia-nut caramel popcorn with coconut shreds. The caramel popcorn has real caramel flavor, and with every other handful you get a macadamia nut or two. Unlike that of a lot of other gourmet popcorn places, Nancy's popcorn tastes like it was popped on the same day you bought it. She makes nine powdered flavors, everything from garlic-and-herb to garden-salad. Among her eight glazed flavors are an irresistable butterscotch and a surprisingly appetizing piña colada made with banana chips, coconut shreds, and pineapple. Her chocolate fudge popcorn is made with real chocolate.

Nancy's Gourmet Popcorn
700 Third Avenue (between 43rd and 44th streets)
New York, NY 10017
PHONE: (212) 370-4480
SUBWAYS: 42nd Street–Grand Central on the following lines: Lexington
    Avenue No. 4, 5, and 6; Flushing No 7; 42nd Street Shuttle.
HOURS: 10:30 A.M. to 6:10 P.M. Monday through Friday; 11 A.M. to 4 P.M.
    Saturday (except summer months); closed Sunday.
Delivery available.
Visa and MasterCard accepted.
Mail order available by calling 1 (800) 7-NANCYS.

HAMBURGERS

Corner Bistro ~~ The Corner Bistro is a classic New York bar. It has a resident cat and plain brown booths in the back with thousands of initials carved in the tables, and it is dark even at two in the afternoon. You'll find the cover of darkness to be a plus when you're eating the restaurant's huge, juicy Bistro burger—which is merely the best burger in New York—because when it's this dark, you can't see the incredible mess you're making while trying to eat it. You can't see the ketchup, the cheese, and the meat juice spurting out onto your clothes as you try to put this wondrous burger in your mouth. You can taste, however, that the burgers are made with impeccably fresh meat and then simply broiled under an old-fashioned broiler. No mesquite grills, no charcoal flavor, no nothin'. Order french fries to go with it, and you get a mountain of freshly cooked matchstick potatoes. When you need an inexpensive red-meat fix, this is the place to go.

Corner Bistro
331 West Fourth Street (Corner of Jane Street)
New York, NY 10014
PHONE: (212) 242-9502
SUBWAY: 14th Street station on the Eighth Avenue A, C, and E lines and the
    Broadway–Seventh Avenue No. 1, 2, 3, and 9 lines; Eighth Avenue
    station on the 14th Street–Canarsie L line.
HOURS: 11:30 A.M. to 4 A.M. Monday through Saturday; noon to 4 A.M.
    Sunday.
No deliveries.
Cash only.

HEALTH FOOD

Integral Yoga Natural Foods ~ Everyone I know who is into health food told me that Integral Yoga was the largest and best health-food store in New York. I knew they were right when I went to the frozen food section and discovered at least five different kinds of healthful frozen pizza. Integral Yoga is the quintessential nineties health-food store. It prepares a number of dishes for take-out every day, ranging from tofu balls in marinara sauce to stuffed peppers with brown rice filling. None of it tasted like much to me, but I kept looking for the sausage, so I guess I'm no judge. Every day Integral Yoga makes a fresh soup—miso-mushroom on my last visit. I found it practically inedible. The salad bar has seventeen items daily, ranging from seven-grain tempeh to curried potatoes. The fresh produce section had a wide variety of fruits and vegetables, most of them organically grown and in good condition. The juice bar makes all kinds of juice and yogurt combinations. If you want miso, Integral Yoga carries five kinds, including mugi, natto, hatcho, and genmai. Don't ask me what the difference is; I don't know. It also carries all sorts of natural snack foods, breads, and pasta, including items I've never seen anywhere else, such as tofu ravioli. Grains, roots, nuts—Integral Yoga has it all. Just to show you they really are like a full-service grocery store, they also sell health and beauty aids. The prices are inflated, but at least the gel toothpaste they sell is all-natural Nature's Gate.

Integral Yoga Natural Foods
229 West 13th Street (between Seventh and Eighth avenues)
New York, NY 10014
PHONE: (212) 243-2642
SUBWAYS: 14th Street station on the Eighth Avenue A, C, and E lines and
   the Broadway–Seventh Avenue No. 1, 2, 3, and 9 lines.
HOURS: 10 A.M. to 9:30 P.M. Monday through Friday; 10 A.M. to 8:30 P.M.
   Saturday; noon to 6:30 P.M. Sunday.
No deliveries.
All major credit cards accepted.
Mail order available.

HOT DOGS, UPTOWN

Papaya King ~ In 1990 they held a New York hot-dog tasting contest with, among others, Julia Child as a judge. Although it's not clear what Julia Child knows about frankfurters, she and her colleagues settled on Papaya King's as the best. And they *are* superb—wonderfully garlicky and meaty. Taking my young son to Papaya King at ten in the morning and sharing two well-done hot dogs with mustard and sauerkraut and a half-papaya-half-pina-colada drink is a quintessential New York eating experience, although I have to put up with reproving glances from old ladies.

Note: Papaya King dissidents broke away and started Gray's Papaya (at West 72nd Street and other locations). Though Papaya King's owner says only he retained the original hot-dog recipe, I defy anyone to discern the difference between the two joints' hot dogs. Even as I write this, still more papaya-drink-and-hot-dog places are cropping up all over town, with names like Papaya Royalty. I can't vouch for their quality.

Gotta have a hot dog? Katz's Deli has the finest in all of Downtown New York.

Papaya King
179 East 86th Street (corner of Third Avenue)
New York, NY 10128
PHONE: (212) 369-0648
SUBWAYS: 86th Street station on the Lexington Avenue 4, 5, and 6 lines.
HOURS: 8 A.M. to 1 A.M. Sunday through Thursday; 8 A.M. to 3 A.M. Friday
    and Saturday.
No deliveries.
Cash only.

OTHER LOCATIONS:
201 East 59th Street (corner of Third Avenue)
New York, NY 10022
(212) 753-2014

HOT DOGS, DOWNTOWN

Katz's Delicatessen ⌁ If you've gotta have a hot dog (and everyone, even health-food devotees, do get frankfurter urges) and you're downtown, go to Katz's. Not only are the franks very tasty, but they also have that great crisp edge hot dogs get on a grill. The other great Katz's item is the knoblewurst, a garlic sausage that tastes something like a hot dog, only garlickier. Skip the french fries, which used to be fresh and among the city's best but are now puffy frozen masses. Just buy a hot dog or a knoblewurst and soak up the atmosphere in the huge L-shaped dining room, which still has signs like "Send a salami to your boy in the army."

Katz's Delicatessen
205 East Houston Street (corner of Ludlow Street)
New York, NY 10002

PHONE: (212) 254-2246
SUBWAY: Second Avenue station on the Sixth Avenue F line.
HOURS: 7:30 A.M. to 11 P.M. Sunday through Thursday; 7:30 A.M. to 1 A.M.
    Friday and Saturday.
Deliveries throughout the metropolitan area for platters only.
American Express accepted for catering orders only.
Mail order available.

JERK CHICKEN

Vernon's Jerk Paradise --- You've just returned from some R and R in Jamaica, and you get a craving for jerk chicken, the tantalizing grilled and marinated chicken that street vendors barbecue on halved oil drums. Relax, mon. Vernon has brought authentic Jamaican jerk chicken to New York. His version is wonderful—moist and tangy. His jerk pork may even be better, with its satisfyingly crunchy outer edges and reasonably tender meat. The side dish that comes with your jerk pork or chicken is a filling blend of peas, rice, and Caribbean spices. Order a combo jerk platter with a Jamaican fruit punch, and you'll swear you're back in Negril.

Vernon's Jerk Paradise
252 West 29th Street (between Seventh and Eighth avenues)
New York, NY 10001
PHONE: (212) 268-7020 or (800) 287-7020
SUBWAYS: 28th Street station on the Broadway–Seventh Avenue No. 1 and 9
    lines.
HOURS: 11:30 A.M. to 11 P.M. Monday through Thursday; 11:30 A.M. to
    midnight Friday; 3 P.M. to 3 A.M. Saturday; closed Sundays.
No deliveries.
All major credit cards accepted.
Mail order for Vernon's Special Sauce only, which is an incendiary
    concoction.

LATKES (POTATO PANCAKES)

Teresa's --- My mother was a terrific lady, but she couldn't cook to save her life. In fact, she was proud of her lack of culinary skill, which she thought made a strong and forthright feminist political statement. My grandmother, however, also a strong and independent woman, cooked the kind of dishes you dream about. Her latkes were crisp, oniony, and not too thick. Her indomitable spirit lives on in the first-rate latkes served at Teresa's, the true gem of Polish coffeeshops. Teresa's latkes are made to order (an absolute must for anyone serious about making or eating potato pancakes), but waiting fifteen minutes for latkes like these is a small price to pay. They're golden-brown, made with coarsely ground potato, and have just the right amount of onion in them. If they were just a little thinner, I wouldn't miss my grandmother's so much. Teresa's also makes wonderful peasant soups like borscht and mushroom-barley, excellent cheese blintzes (available with fresh blueberries in season), and apple fritters so fine I considered having a separate entry for them.

Teresa's
103 First Avenue (between 6th and 7th Streets)
New York, NY 10003
PHONE: (212) 228-0604
SUBWAYS: Astor Place station on the Lexington Avenue No. 6 line.
HOURS: 6 A.M. to midnight seven days a week.
Deliveries in the neighborhood.
Cash only.

LEMONADE

Lexington Candy Shop ⁓ With its old-fashioned counter and wooden booths, it's somehow appropriate that this establishment makes the best lemonade in town. Every lemonade is squeezed to order using just the right combination of lemons and sugar syrup. A lemonade is $2.95 here, but one sip of this sweet-tart concoction on a summer's day, and you'll know it's one of New York's cheaper summer pleasures. Non-lemonade lovers should try the coffee malteds here, made with coffee syrup, coffee ice cream and plenty of malt powder and served in the old-fashioned metal can straight from the Hamilton Beach mixer. Lexington Candy Shop also makes homey, simple breakfasts and first-rate shrimp-salad sandwiches.

Lexington Candy Shop
1226 Lexington Avenue (corner of 83rd Street)
New York, NY 10028
PHONE: (212) 288-0057
SUBWAYS: 86th Street station on the Lexington Avenue No. 4, 5, and 6 lines.
HOURS: 7 A.M. to 7 P.M. Monday through Saturday; 9 A.M. to 5 P.M. Sunday.
Occasional deliveries.
Cash only.

PANCAKES

Royal Canadian Pancake House ⁓ It was eight o'clock on a Sunday morning, my wife was away on business, and I was desperate for a Manhattan breakfast excursion for my son and me. Then I remembered a friend's telling me about the tasty, humongous chocolate-chip pancakes he had eaten recently at the Royal Canadian Pancake House. William hailed a cab for us (he's been able to do that since he was two—a true Manhattan kid), and fifteen minutes later we found ourselves at RCPH, a long, narrow space with a bar and about thirty tables. I ordered chocolate-chip pancakes for William (thank God, Jane Brody wasn't eating breakfast with us) and an oven-baked apple pancake for myself. The chocolate-chip pancakes arrived a few minutes later, three pancakes the size of manhole covers showered with chocolate chips. Normally there's an inverse relationship between the size of pancakes and how much flavor they have. But these giganto-cakes were actually reasonably light, fluffy, and flavorful. The oven-baked apple pancake was also enormous, loaded with apples, and really good. William pronounced his chocolate-chip pancakes excellent, ate about half a pancake, announced he was finished, and ran out the door. I chased after him, vowing to return to try some of the fifty-two kinds of pancakes they prepare at RCPH.

Note: If you don't like pancakes they also make eggs, omelets, waffles, French toast, and crepes.

Royal Canadian Pancake House
145 Hudson Street (between Hubert and Beach streets)
New York, NY 10013
PHONE: (212) 219-3038
SUBWAYS: Canal Street station on the Broadway–Seventh Avenue No. 1 and
   9 lines.
HOURS: 7 A.M. to midnight seven days a week.
No deliveries.
Cash only.

POTATO CHIPS

U.S. Chips ⟿ I love potato chips. My search for the perfect spud slice has forced me to order by mail from every corner of the country. I've sampled every chip from Burlington, Vermont (Champ Chips), to Rockford, Illinois (Ole Salty's). Now, thanks to U.S. Chips, my search for the perfect potato chip has ended. U.S. Chips fries its potatoes in small batches in canola oil, and they're so fresh they have that half-crunchy, half-pliant texture you find in homemade chips served in high-end restaurants. U.S. Chips come in six varieties: regular salted and unsalted, garlic-and-onion, Cajun BBQ, sweet potato with salt, and sweet potato with sugar and cinnamon. They're all equally addictive, but the sweet potato with sugar and cinnamon are my favorites because they give me an excuse to eat potato chips for breakfast. U.S. Chips' owner Robert Meger even helps me out by calling them breakfast chips.

U.S. Chips
105 East 42nd Street (In Grand Central Station, on the southernmost
   corridor of stores leading to the Lexington Avenue exit)
New York, NY 10017
PHONE: (212) 867-8972
SUBWAYS: Grand Central Station on the following lines: Lexington Avenue
   No. 4, 5, and 6; Flushing No. 7; 42nd Street Shuttle.
HOURS: 7:30 A.M. to 8 P.M. Monday through Friday.
No deliveries.
Cash only.

SCALLION PANCAKES

Ollie's Noodle Shop & Grille ⟿ When the Dumpling House, at the corner of Second Avenue and 13th Street, went out of business, I lost my source for superb scallion pancakes. I spent the next few years searching for someplace that could replicate these thin, crisp, perfectly browned, just slightly greasy delight. Unfortunately all I could find were translucent repositories for onion-flavored fat that were as thick as jelly donuts. Then Ollie's Noodle Shop came to the rescue with its merely perfect scallion pancakes. It's hard to think of a meal I enjoy more than Ollie's spare ribs and scallion pancakes. I figure I counteract the effects of all the fat I'm eating if I also order some steamed bok choy.

Ollie's Noodle Shop & Grille
2315 Broadway (corner of 84th Street)
New York, NY 10024
PHONE: (212) 362-3712 or (212) 362-3111
SUBWAYS: 86th Street Station on the following lines: Broadway–Seventh
    Avenue No. 1 and 9; Eighth Avenue C and Sixth Avenue B.
HOURS: 11:30 A.M. to midnight Sunday through Thursday; 11:30 A.M. to 1
    A.M. Friday and Saturday.
Deliveries in the neighborhood.
All major credit cards accepted.

OTHER LOCATION:
There is another Ollie's at 114th Street and Broadway, but I don't find it to
    be as good as the 84th Street location.

SOUVLAKI AND GYROS

Tony's Souvlaki ⟿ See page 139.

11

ICE CREAM

N ew York is not an exceptional ice cream town. Sure, there are the
ubiquitous Haagen Dazs and Sedutto shops serving first-rate, incredibly rich, high-butterfat ice cream. But in this city of ten million
people, there are precious few idiosyncratic, old-fashioned ice cream stores
with a singular point of view.

One reason for this lack is that ice cream is a seasonal food, and the
ice cream season is not a long one in New York. Given the high cost of
operating a retail business, it makes sense that not too many people risk
starting an ice cream shop. Another reason may be that, given the high
quality of ice creams like Haagen Dazs, Ben and Jerry's, and Sedutto's,
New Yorkers have no need for a non-franchise store that sells only ice
cream.

That said, there are still enough terrific ice cream places in New York
to justify a chapter in this book. Many are outside Manhattan but are
worth a summer-evening adventure. Many of the places mentioned here
are open only seasonally, and I have tried to pin down the exact months
they're open. Some gave me dates but told me they play it by ear, depending
upon the weather, so it's always best to call first if you have any doubt.
Others are pastry shops that serve ice cream and ices only in the summer,
so once again call before you go.

Note: Ice cream afficionados will note that I do not have entries for Ben & Jerry's, Sedutto's, Steve's, and Haagen Dazs. It's not that I don't think these ice creams are first-rate (in fact, I like all of them quite a lot, with a special place in my heart for Haagen Dazs coffee ice cream bars dipped in dark chocolate). It's just that none of them makes ice cream that's truly distinctive.

𝒰PPER WEST SIDE

59TH STREET TO 125TH STREET
CENTRAL PARK WEST TO RIVERSIDE DRIVE

Café La Fortuna ⁓ One of the pleasures of New York is that you can discover wonderful places in your neighborhood years after you've moved there. Café La Fortuna has been around Manhattan's Upper West Side almost as long as I have (it opened in 1976; I came in 1973), and yet I didn't discover its world-class Italian ices until last year. Its lemon ice is so spectacularly tart that there's a pucker in every lick. The coffee ice is made with espresso and will keep you up at night, and the chocolate, unlike every other chocolate Italian ice I've tried, is not too sweet and actually tastes like chocolate. Besides the ices, Café La Fortuna carries an array of desserts and cookies from all over the city. Try the Café Fortuna Supreme, made with pignoli nuts, zabaglione, and Marsala. In the summer, which is the only season they make the ices, there is an extremely pleasant garden where you can sit, drink coffee, eat your dessert, and ponder your fate.

Café La Fortuna
69 West 71st Street (between Central Park West and Columbus Avenue)
New York, NY 10023
PHONE: (212) 724-5846
SUBWAYS: 72nd Street station on the following lines: Broadway–Seventh
    Avenue No. 1, 2, 3, and 9; Eighth Avenue C and Sixth Avenue B.
HOURS: 1 P.M. to 1 A.M. Tuesday through Thursday; 1 P.M. to 2 A.M. Friday;
    12 P.M. to 2 A.M. Saturday; 12 P.M. to 1 A.M. Sunday.
No deliveries.
Cash only.

Godiva Chocolatier ⁓ I'm not very fond of Godiva chocolates (see page 000), so I was prepared to hate Godiva ice cream. I was astonished to find that Godiva makes extremely fresh-tasting, vividly flavored ice cream. However, in keeping with my feeling about their chocolates, I found their vanilla ice cream to be superior to any of their five chocolate flavors. The vanilla has a strong and natural vanilla flavor. The chocolate's okay, as is the chocolate-raspberry cordial, but I found myself wishing after every bite for a more profound chocolate experience.

Note: Be prepared for some unfriendly vibes here. When I asked for a taste, I was told it was against company policy to give tastes. Well, excuuse me!

Godiva Chocolatier
245 Columbus Avenue (between 71st and 72nd streets)
New York, NY 10023
PHONE: (212) 787-5804
SUBWAYS: 72nd Street station on the following lines: Broadway–Seventh
    Avenue No. 1, 2, 3, and 9; Eighth Avenue C and Sixth Avenue B.
HOURS: 10 A.M. to 10 P.M. Monday through Friday; 11 A.M. to 10 P.M.
    Saturday; noon to 7 P.M. Sunday.
No deliveries.
All major credit cards accepted.

OTHER LOCATION:
793 Madison Avenue (between 67th and 68th streets)
New York, NY 10021
(212) 249-9444

$\mathscr{U}$PPER EAST SIDE

59TH STREET TO 96TH STREET
FIRST AVENUE TO FIFTH AVENUE

Godiva Chocolatier — See above.

Sant Ambroeus Ltd. — It's too bad the reception you'll get at Sant Ambroeus is as chilly as the ice cream, because the sorbettos here have no equal in the city. The peach, for example, tastes like what would happen if you put the ripest peach imaginable through a blender. The same could be said for the kiwi fruit or the strawberry or the raspberry. The only way you'll get sorbettos this good is to go to one of those transcendent joints near the Piazza Navona in Rome. The gelati are also excellent, especially the coffee, but it's the sorbetto I keep coming back for again and again.

Sant Ambroeus Ltd.
1000 Madison Avenue (between 76th and 77th streets)
New York, NY 10021
PHONE: (212) 570-2211
SUBWAY: 77th Street station on the Lexington Avenue No. 6 line.
HOURS: 9:30 A.M. to 10:30 P.M. Monday through Saturday; 10:30 A.M. to 6:30
    P.M. Sunday.
Deliveries made all over Manhattan except Sunday.
All major credit cards accepted.

*W*EST VILLAGE

14TH STREET TO HOUSTON STREET
FIFTH AVENUE TO WEST STREET

Pravinie Gourmet Ice Cream ~ See below.

*E*AST VILLAGE

14TH STREET TO HOUSTON STREET
EAST RIVER TO FIFTH AVENUE

Pravinie Gourmet Ice Cream ~ St. Mark's Place is not my favorite Manhattan street for strolling, but when I do find myself anywhere near the East Village, I stop at Pravinie for a mango ice cream cone. They make lots of other flavors here, but on a hot summer's day you can't beat the cool, creamy taste of mango made into a rich, tropical ice cream. If you don't like mango, try another flavor like black bean or coconut or ginger. For something truly different, try the durian ice cream, made from a Southeast Asian fruit so vile-smelling it's banned on many international airlines. Pravinie's durian ice cream, however, doesn't smell bad at all and has an intriguing flavor. All of the Oriental ice creams here are intensely flavored and very different from the vanillas and chocolates of the world.

Pravinie Gourmet Ice Cream
27 St. Mark's Place (8th Street between Second and Third avenues)
New York, NY 10003
PHONE: (212) 673-5948
SUBWAYS: Astor Place station on the Lexington Avenue No. 6 line; 8th
    Street–NYU station on the Broadway R line.
HOURS: Noon to midnight seven days a week.
Cash only.

OTHER LOCATION:
193 Bleecker Street (between Sixth Avenue and Macdougal Street)
New York, NY 10012
(212) 475-1968

Siracusa ~ Forget Haagen Dazs, forget Ben and Jerry's, forget Sedutto's. Siracusa hands down makes the best ice cream in New York. Every flavor is so vivid and bold it's hard to go back to eating any other kind of ice cream. Try the hazelnut or the coffee or the ricotta, their version of vanilla. It doesn't matter what flavor you try, they're all amazing. If you've ever been to Vivoli in Florence, you should know that Siracusa's ice cream is as close as you can get to Vivoli without hopping on a plane. Two things to note about Siracusa: First, it's only marginally less expensive than airfare to Florence. Two small dishes of ice cream cost $10 the last time I went.

Second, Siracusa has closed the gelateria adjoining its restaurant. But you can still order and eat your ice cream at the espresso bar. Or better yet, get a pint to go. It's only $7.00.

Siracusa
65 Fourth Avenue (between 9th and 10th streets)
New York, NY 10003
PHONE: (212) 254-1940
SUBWAYS: Astor Place station on the Lexington Avenue No. 6 line; 8th
    Street–NYU station on the Broadway R line.
HOURS: Noon to 3 P.M. and 5:30 P.M. to 11 P.M. Monday through Saturday;
    closed Sunday.

$\mathcal{D}$OWNTOWN

HOUSTON STREET TO BATTERY PARK

Chinatown Ice Cream Factory ⬿ After stuffing yourself for $10.00 at your favorite Chinatown restaurant, if the thought of eating one of those horrendous bean-paste-dominated pastries at a Chinatown bakery doesn't appeal, head on down to the Chinatown Ice Cream Factory. They make ice cream in flavors you won't find north of Canal Street: green tea, lychee, ginger, and almond-cookie. The ice cream itself is fairly standard low-butterfat stuff, but the unusual flavors make it worth a stop.

Chinatown Ice Cream Factory
65 Bayard Street (between Mott and Elizabeth streets)
New York, NY 10013
PHONE: (212) 608-4170
SUBWAYS: Canal Street station on the following lines: Lexington Avenue No.
    6, Broadway N and R, Nassau Street J, M, and Z; Grand Street station on
    the Sixth Avenue B, D, and Q lines.
HOURS: 11 A.M. to midnight seven days a week.
Cash only.

Ciao Bella Gelato ⬿ For someone like me, who can still recall every bite of every ice cream cone I've had in Italy, it was wonderful to discover the stupendous gelati made at Ciao Bella. The espresso-chip ice cream is one of New York's great ice-cream treats. The lemon sorbetto may put your lips into a semipermanent pucker. Ciao Bella's gelati are very nearly the equal of Siracusa's, and, unlike the treatment of that Noho establishment, the only frostiness you'll experience at Ciao Bella's is in the ice cream. Gelato quality without attitude. I like it.

Note: Ciao Bella's products can also be purchased at Balducci's, Grace's Marketplace, Nature's Gifts, Fraser-Morris, and Dean & DeLuca, among other stores. In fact, Dean & DeLuca's summertime ice cream bar is supplied by Ciao Bella.

Ciao Bella Gelato
262 Mott Street
(between Prince and Houston streets)
New York, NY 10012

PHONE: (212) 226-7668
SUBWAY: Bleecker Street station on the Lexington Avenue No. 6 line.
HOURS: 10 A.M. to 5 P.M. Monday through Friday; closed Saturday and
    Sunday.
No deliveries.
Cash only.

·

$\mathscr{B}$RONX

Hoft's Luncheonette ~ When I was a kid, my buddies and I hung out at the corner candy store a block from my elementary school. Harry's, we called it, after the owner, and there was nothing like going into Harry's, ordering an egg cream, a cherry-lime rickey, a malt, or an ice-cream soda, settling in at one of the red-vinyl counter stools, and watching Harry, the master malt and ice-cream-soda maker, weave his magic. The malts would come in the tall silver can, straight from the Hamilton Beach mixer, so that once you drained your glass, you could refill it yourself with the excess malt left in the can. After moving to Manhattan and watching all the old-fashioned candy stores go the way of the dinosaur, I despaired of ever seeing a real candy store again. Then a friend's tip took me on to Hoft's, an old-fashioned candy store that made the Harry's of my dreams seem like a fast-food joint.

Hoft's is a movie-lot-perfect candy store. Even its location, under the "El," or elevated subway tracks, in the Bronx, is perfect. Its ceilings are tin, painted white, and the candy-counter and soda-fountain fixtures are the original wood variety. There are ten stools at the counter and half a dozen tables at the back. But even thinking of sitting at a table at a place like Hoft's would be candy-store heresy; a stool at the counter is the only way to go.

Hoft's has been run by the Hoft family for more than half a century. It was opened in 1940 by Sadie and Harold Hoft, who made their own ice cream and candy in the basement and whose candy- and ice-cream-making traditions are upheld to this day by Sam Hoft. The ice cream is creamy, homemade-tasting, and not so rich you couldn't eat one of their sundaes *and* drink a malt in one sitting. The sundaes are single scoops of ice cream, topped by real hot fudge, real whipped cream, and a cherry that actually tastes like a cherry. The malts have plenty of malt powder in them and come in those tall metal cans straight from the Hamilton Beach mixer. The orangeade and lemonade are both freshly squeezed to order, and the egg creams are an almost mystical combination of milk, seltzer, and chocolate syrup.

You won't find truffles at the candy counter at Hoft's. They would be out of place, way too upscale. But you will find dark- and milk-chocolate-covered nuts, jellies, mints, and graham crackers. These last are so stupendous that once you've had a Hoft's chocolate-covered graham cracker you'll never be able to go back to Nabisco again. Just like the ice cream here, Hoft's candy is rich, but not sinfully so.

I didn't have a Hoft's cheeseburger, but I loved the tiny little grill that could hold only four patties at a time. They looked terrific—hand-formed and the real deal—and I did notice that I was the only one at the counter not eating one. As I was leaving, I asked the family sitting next to me how their cheeseburgers and egg creams were. "Incredible," they all chimed in together, "we come all the way from New Rochelle for them every Saturday." If they can come ten miles from New Rochelle, I decided, I can travel from Manhattan every Saturday when my son is old enough to appreciate a place like Hoft's. A new Levine family tradition is on the horizon.

Hoft's Luncheonette
3200 White Plains Road (corner of Burke Avenue)
Bronx, NY 10467
PHONE: (212) 654-5291
SUBWAY: Burke Avenue station on the Lexington Avenue No. 5 and
    Broadway–Seventh Avenue No. 2 lines.
HOURS: 7 A.M. to 5:30 P.M. Monday through Saturday; closed Sunday.
No deliveries.
Cash only.

$\mathcal{Q}$UEENS

Eddie's Sweet Shop ∿ With its brown wooden fixtures, tin ceilings, and old-fashioned counter, Eddie's Sweet Shop in Forest Hills hasn't changed much in the more than eighty years it's been in business. Eddie and his family have long since sold out, but the current owner, Giuseppe Citrano, claims he's still making ice cream the way Eddie did. Like most old-fashioned ice creams, Eddie's is less creamy and flavorful than, say, Haagen Dazs. But it's good enough, and when you sidle up to Eddie's on a hot summer's evening, plop down at the counter, devour a hot-fudge sundae, and soak up the old-world atmosphere, you may decide you have to move to Forest Hills.

Eddie's Sweet Shop
105-29 Metropolitan Avenue
Forest Hills, NY 11375
PHONE: (718) 520-8514
SUBWAYS: From the 71st–Continental Avenues–Forest Hills station on the
    Sixth Avenue F, Eighth Avenue E, Broadway R, or Brooklyn–Queens
    Crosstown G line, take the Triboro Coach Q23 bus to the last stop
    (Metropolitan Avenue).
HOURS: 1 P.M. to 11:30 P.M. Tuesday through Friday; noon to 11:30 P.M.
    Saturday and Sunday; closed Monday.
Cash only.

Ben Faremo, the Lemon Ice King of Corona ∿ "I started the lemon-ice business," Peter Ben Faremo explained to me one April afternoon. "In 1944, I started making my ices from real fruit. And I tell you, young man, the secret of staying in business is to be fair and consistent." Well, Ben Faremo's ices are a lot more than fair. They're consistently terrific. Unlike most Italian ices, which taste like a combination of artificial flavoring, water, and sugar, Ben Faremo's ices actually

Peter Ben Faremo, the undisputed Lemon Ice King of Corona.

taste like the real fruit that goes into them. The watermelon tastes like watermelon, the cantaloupe like cantaloupe, and the signature lemon like fresh-squeezed lemonade. Peanut-butter freaks should note that Ben Faremo's makes a peanut butter ice that is as intense a peanut-butter hit as you'll find outside a peanut-butter-and-jelly sandwich.

Ben Faremo, the Lemon Ice King of Corona
52-02 108th Street
Corona, NY 11373
PHONE: (718) 699-5133
SUBWAY: 111th Street station on the Flushing No. 7 line.
HOURS: 10 A.M. to 7 P.M. seven days a week, Memorial Day to Labor Day;
    during other times of the year, call first for hours.
Cash only.

ℬROOKLYN

Karl Droge — Located on a nondescript Bay Ridge block, Karl Droge is the only independent soft-ice-cream vendor I know of left in New York. For more than eighty years, Karl Droge and his successors have been dispensing vanilla soft-ice-cream cones and fruit slushes. Though Karl himself is living on a mountain in Vermont, his credo still keeps the place going: "If you give quality and quantity, you'll never lose your customers." I'm not sure the ice cream here tastes all that different from Carvel's or Dairy Queen's (although it is a little creamier), but that's not the point. Just on principle people should frequent noncommercial, family-run businesses like this. Plus, Karl Droge's has a nifty green-and-red sign that a guy like the late Tom Carvel would never have had the guts to put up in one of his stores.

Karl Droge
6508 Sixth Avenue (at 66th Street)
Brooklyn, NY 11220
PHONE: (718) 833-1407
SUBWAYS: 59th Street station on the Broadway N and R lines.
HOURS: April and October, noon to 5 P.M.; May and September, noon to 8
    P.M.; Memorial Day to Labor Day, noon to 11 P.M.; seven days a week.
Cash only.

Peter's Ice Cream Parlor and Coffee House ~ My wife and son had had it. I
had just dragged them into every Middle Eastern food store on Brooklyn's Atlantic
Avenue. Then I spotted Peter's, and I warily made the suggestion to my wife that
homemade ice cream is the only known antidote to a baklava overdose. Peter
Glick is a throwback, a sixties hipster whose passion happens to be ice cream.
His ice cream is rich and creamy, with not a hint of gum or stabilizers. His flavors
are more fanciful than the standard high-butterfat offerings, my favorite being
the cappuccino-brownie. His sorbets are also first-rate, tasting like fruit and not
much else.

Note: Peter's is one of those incredibly friendly places non–New Yorkers are
surprised to find in the city. The help couldn't be more solicitous. The last time
I was here my son dropped his cone, and they replaced it without charge.

Peter's Ice Cream Parlor and Coffee House
185 Atlantic Avenue (between Court and Clinton streets)
Brooklyn, NY 11201
PHONE: (718) 852-3835
SUBWAYS: Borough Hall station on the following lines: Broadway–Seventh
    Avenue No. 2 and 3; Lexington Avenue No. 4 and 5.
HOURS: Noon to 11 P.M. seven days a week.
No deliveries.
Cash only.

Best of Ice Cream

Best all-around ice cream: Siracusa Gelateria
Best atmosphere: Hoft's Luncheonette; Eddie's Sweet Shop
Best designer-ice-cream flavor: Cappuccino brownie at Peter's Ice Cream
    Parlor and Coffee House
Best hot-fudge sundae: Hoft's Luncheonette
Best gelato: Siracusa Gelateria
Best ice-cream bar: Haagen Dazs coffee-ice-cream bar dipped in dark
    chocolate.
Best ice-cream sodas: Hoft's Luncheonette
Best Italian ices: Ben Faremo, the Lemon Ice King of Corona
Best malts: Hoft's Luncheonette
Best soft ice cream: Karl Droge
Best sorbet: Sant Ambroeus

12

MEAT AND POULTRY

T he butchering and curing of meat seem to be lost arts in America these days. With most people buying their meat in supermarkets and Frank Perdue putting a mediocre chicken in every pot, it's hard to find butchers who truly care about the meat they sell.

New York's melting-pot tradition has brought it a number of butchers and curers who take pride in every piece of meat they sell. A good butcher's prices are generally at least 20 percent higher than a grocer's, but the difference in quality is substantial.

In addition, New York's thousands of restaurants are supplied by a battery of premium-quality wholesalers who sometimes open their doors to the public. I've listed a couple here, but their chief problem is they tend to sell in bulk. My wife often floats me a quizzical look when I bring home a ten-pound filet of beef for our family of three.

The World According to Harry Oppenheimer

In 1973, I graduated from college and came to New York to save the jazz world. I didn't know many people in New York, so the welcome I received at my regular haunts was crucial to my forming a community here. Harry Oppenheimer's butcher shop was just such a place. I would come into Oppenheimer's after work and ask for a pound of ground chuck or one boned

---

and skinned chicken breast or a couple of pork chops. I never got any grief
from Harry or any of his staff about my meager orders. In fact, all
I got was lots of smiles and wisecracks from Lou Lagonia, my regular
counterman, and simple, first-rate instructions on how to cook my meat
from Lou or from Harry Oppenheimer himself. And, of course, I got
impeccable, high-quality meat.

One day in 1991, nearly twenty years later, I walked into Oppenheimer's
to interview Harry for this book. Everything looked the same. The large
counter to the left of the door housed the cold cuts and the sausages. The
counter straight back was for chicken. The simple, old-fashioned white-
lettered sign on a black background telling you Harry's regular stock and
the price of each item was still on the wall. Lou Lagonia was joking with
customers, and Harry Oppenheimer was answering the phone "Harry
Oppenheimer" while simultaneously functioning as cashier for every
transaction at the store.

Harry Oppenheimer opened his store at 98th Street and Broadway in 1946.
A German Jew, he had come to the states in 1934 to escape Hitler. Meat had
run in his family. His father had been a cattle broker, his uncle a butcher.
After serving in the army (the OSS) during World War II, Harry went to
work for a butcher. In 1946, two years later, Harry bought out the butcher
and started Oppenheimer's.

Asked to explain the store's longevity and his success, Harry thought for a
moment and said, "Always treat people the way you like to be treated. You
don't have to be a millionaire to shop here. We offer good service to
everybody. We don't belittle anybody because they buy only a pound of
chopped meat."

At that moment I thought back to the week before, when I had first tried
to interview Harry. He wasn't in the store, but Gilbert Rosado, who has been
with Oppenheimer's for more than thirty-six years, was patiently serving two
elderly women, one of whom was hard of hearing. They asked for a pound of
chopped meat, and Gilbert put a pound and a quarter on the scale. One of
the women asked, "Could you take a quarter of a pound off, please." She
turned to her friend and said, "You have to try everything these days." She
turned back to Rosado and smiled as she said, "If I like it, I'll be back for
more. It looks very good."

Service is indeed the key to Oppenheimer's success. Everything in the
store is geared toward helping the customer. A sign where Harry sits tells
customers how long each kind of meat will last in the freezer. All the meat is
cut to order, not only to ensure freshness, but also, in Harry's words, "so
that people who come in early can't pick through all the meat."

Harry sells you exactly what you want and will patiently explain exactly
how to prepare it. "If you buy a car from somebody," he says, "he should tell
you how to drive it. If you buy meat from me, I should tell you how to cook
it." Of course Harry can take this philosophy to extremes—like the time he
insisted that the boneless pork roast he had just sold my friend Howie was so

The World According to Harry Oppenheimer, continued

good that it should not be stuffed. Harry was wrong. I've had Howie's stuffed pork roast, and it's really tasty.

After being in Harry's store for an hour, I realized that Harry and his merry band of butchers make New York seem like a small town. They, and others like them, provide the city's neighborhoods with fabric and texture. They make New York a welcoming, rather than a forbidding, place. As I was leaving Oppenheimer's, a man walked in, and as soon as Harry saw him he said, "How were those two steaks you bought last week? Good stuff, huh? Did you see how I cut that fat off for you?"

$\mathcal{U}$PPER WEST SIDE

59TH STREET TO 125TH STREET
CENTRAL PARK WEST TO RIVERSIDE DRIVE

Fairway ⁓ See page 221.

H. Oppenheimer Meats ⁓ Harry Oppenheimer has been dispensing cooking advice to neophyte dinner-party givers for nearly five decades (see accompanying sidebar), and the twinkle in his eye suggests he's not ready to slow down yet. His meat is extremely high quality, the service superb; and luckily for him the neighborhood has started to catch up with his prices. Harry can occasionally get a little testy, but that's part of his charm. His pork is the tastiest and most succulent I've found in the city. He carries every cut of meat you could think of, and fresh game as well. How can you not love a store in Manhattan that dispenses free slices of bologna to impatient children waiting with their parents?

H. Oppenheimer Meats
2606 Broadway (between 98th and 99th streets)
New York, NY 10025
PHONE: (212) 662-0246
SUBWAYS: 96th Street station on the following lines: Broadway–Seventh
  Avenue No. 1, 2, 3, and 9; Eighth Avenue C and Sixth Avenue B.
HOURS: 9 A.M. to 6:55 P.M. Monday through Saturday; closed Sunday.
Deliveries only on orders taken before 3 P.M.
Cash only.

Nevada Meat Market ⁓ For more than forty-five years Fred Oppenheimer (no relation to Harry), the owner of the Nevada Meat Market, and his butchers have been treating anyone who walks through the door like a long-lost regular. Which means you can ask for a quarter of a pound of chopped meat without getting a dirty look or ask how to cook the rabbit you just bought without meeting derisive glances. The Nevada Meat Market has a daily display of beautiful aged meat; fresh assorted game in season, including *poussin* and pheasant; and hard-to-find cuts of meat like *osso buco*. It's also the only butcher shop I've found in New York that carries Usinger's liverwurst, a creamy-textured wonder that allows even confirmed non–liverwurst eaters like me to chomp heartily on a liverwurst sandwich. The Nevada Meat Market is expensive ($16.99 a pound for shell steak), but if you're like everyone else these days and eating meat only once or twice a week, why not go for quality?

Nevada Meat Market
2012 Broadway (between 68th and 69th streets)
New York, NY 10023
PHONE: (212) 362-0443
SUBWAYS: 72nd Street station on the following lines: Broadway–Seventh
    Avenue No. 1, 2, 3, and 9; Eighth Avenue C and Sixth Avenue B.
HOURS: 7 A.M. to 6 P.M. Monday through Saturday; closed Sunday.
Deliveries made 8 A.M. to 3 P.M.; $15 minimum.
Cash and personal checks accepted.

Prime Meats and Chick-In ~ Because Prime Meats is my local butcher shop, I sometimes take it for granted. But when I'm strolling around my Upper West Side neighborhood and the urge for red meat comes over me, I drop in on Abe Sonenshine's neighborhood institution. The lamb, beef, and pork are all top quality, although I wish they didn't precut their meat. The Chick-In, or poultry, portion of the store, is actually the other side of the counter. The chicken is Pennfield, and although it's not Bell & Evans, it's cheaper—and it's definitely a cut above Perdue. Chick-In's rotisseried chicken makes a tasty take-home meal, but I've found the rotisseried turkey breast and whole turkeys to be rather dry. Prime Meats is one of the few top-quality butchers to carry Hormel Cure 81 ham, a lightly smoked ham that Paul Prudhomme of K Paul's fame constantly touts.

Prime Meats and Chick-In
2210 Broadway (between 78th and 79th streets)
New York, NY 10024
PHONE: (212) 787-1834
SUBWAYS: 79th Street station on the Broadway–Seventh Avenue No. 1 and 9
    lines; 81st Street station on the Eighth Avenue C and Sixth Avenue B
    lines.
HOURS: 9 A.M. to 6:30 P.M. Monday through Saturday; closed Sunday.
Free delivery.
Cash and personal checks only.

Zabar's ~ See page 237.

$\mathcal{U}$PPER EAST SIDE

59TH STREET TO 96TH STREET
FIRST AVENUE TO FIFTH AVENUE

Grace's Marketplace ⁓ See page 225.

Leonard's ⁓ After researching this book, I developed a law of retail establishments: Any place that's been around for more than fifty years is good, and any place that's been around for more than seventy-five years should be designated a city landmark. Leonard's has been owned and run by the Leonard family since 1910, which more than qualifies the store as a neighborhood institution, a place where New Yorkers can be sure of buying fresh seafood and prime meat as only the Leonard family can provide it. The last time I was here I counted three family members serving customers. John was telling someone how to cook bay scallops, his cousin was cutting me a rib-eye steak, and his mother took my money. You'll find a broad selection of seafood at Leonard's, everything from live crayfish in season to Florida grouper filet. They also make lots of different seafood preparations, everything from fresh crab salad (made with real crab meat, not sea leg) to lobster bisque. The Manhattan clam chowder is bland, but the poached salmon is moist and fresh-tasting. The rib eye I bought was properly aged and marbled, and although it was expensive, prices here don't approach the Lobel's stratosphere. The Leonards sell Bell & Evans chickens and always carry fresh duck and Cornish game hen. Any other fresh game can be ordered on twenty-four hours' notice.

Leonard's
1241 Third Avenue (between 71st and 72nd Streets)
New York, NY 10021
PHONE: (212) 744-2600
SUBWAY: 68th Street–Hunter College station on the Lexington Avenue No. 6
    line.
HOURS: 8 A.M. to 7 P.M. Monday through Friday; 8 A.M. to 6 P.M. Saturday;
    noon to 6 P.M. Sunday.
Free delivery.
All major credit cards accepted.

Lobel's Prime Meats ⁓ Lobel's is the Rolls Royce of meat markets. If you have to ask how much your steak costs here, you can't afford it. Lobel's has absolutely gorgeous aged beef, veal chops that rival the arm-sized ones you get in steak houses, and perfectly trimmed racks of lamb. Though I did gulp when my order of a shell steak and a veal chop came to almost $40, I admit the steak was by far the best-tasting piece of beef I've ever had outside a top-quality New York steak house. Lobel's carries a full line of fresh game, including venison, quail, grouse, and guinea hen. Surprisingly, Lobel's makes very little prepared food. Its barbecued chicken is okay, but the veal and chicken meatballs are oversalted.

Ottomanelli's of the West Village (page 197)—not to be confused with Ottomanelli Brothers (below).

Note: Unless you're a regular, you could be in for a frosty reception, but the Lobels know more than anyone alive about meat. They have written four books on the subject. So anytime you buy meat here it can be an education.

Lobel's Prime Meats
1096 Madison Avenue (between 82nd and 83rd streets)
New York, NY 10028
PHONE: (212) 737-1372
SUBWAY: Nobody who shops at Lobel's takes the subway.
HOURS: 9 A.M. to 6 P.M. Monday through Saturday; closed Sunday.
Delivery available in Manhattan.
All major credit cards accepted.
Mail order available.

Ottomanelli Brothers --- With all the green-awninged Ottomanelli Cafes opening up all over town, it's easy to forget that the Ottomanelli family started its New York food empire in 1900 with this butcher shop. So they're not being precious or pretentious when they describes their store as an "olde fashioned prime butcher shoppe." Besides selling high-quality beef, pork, poultry, and lamb, Ottomanelli's carries an impressive array of wild game—fresh in season, frozen the rest of the year. So if your boss, who loves game, is coming to dinner and you know partridge only when it's located in a pear tree, head to Ottomanelli's. They'll not only sell you a partridge but also tell you how to cook it. Besides meat, Ottomanelli's makes homemade soups, including one of the best lentil soups I've had in Manhattan. It also has a freezer case full of homey southern Italian specialties like baked ziti, lasagna, chicken parmigiana, and pasta sauces. The tomato-based pasta sauces are excellent and the frozen entrees—rich, gooey, and satisfying—are a cut above Celentano's (and it should be noted that I like Celentano's).

Note: This Ottomanelli's is unrelated to the Bleecker Street butcher shop with the same name. Any inquiries into the relationship between the two stores are not encouraged or appreciated. One other thing about the uptown Ottomanelli's: It is definitely a neighborhood store, and it can sometimes take the staff a while to warm up to outsiders.

Ottomanelli Brothers
1549 York Avenue (between 82nd and 83rd streets)
New York, NY 10028
PHONE: (212) 772-7900
SUBWAYS: 86th Street station on the Lexington Avenue No. 4, 5, and 6 lines.
HOURS: 7 A.M. to 6:30 P.M. Monday through Friday; 7 A.M. to 6 P.M.
   Saturday; closed Sunday.
Free delivery.
American Express accepted.

Schaller and Weber
Schaller is *the* source for German deli meats and sausages in New York and perhaps the entire country, for that matter. For nearly one hundred years S & W has been making every kind of wurst, ham, and salami you can think—more than one hundred varieties in all. Try their Westphalian ham, and you may never eat prosciutto again. Their garlic-and-peppercorn salami is impossible to stop eating. To pamper yourself, try the smoked goose breast, which is so rich, so luxuriant, it slides ever so gently into your mouth. The bauernwurst, a coarse, garlicky ham sausage, is my wurst of choice, although you can't go wrong, whichever wurst you choose. Only the bland, somewhat mushy hot dogs disappointed me here. The great thing about shopping at Schaller and Weber is that there's always something new to try. That's the advantage of selling more than one hundred kinds of meat and sausage.

Note: Besides selling sausages, hams, and salamis, Schaller and Weber is also a full-line conventional butcher.

Schaller and Weber
1654 Second Avenue (between 85th and 86th streets)
New York, NY 10028
PHONE: (212) 879-3047
SUBWAYS: 86th Street station on the Lexington Avenue No. 4, 5, and 6 lines.
HOURS: 9 A.M. to 6 P.M. Monday through Saturday; closed Sunday.
No deliveries.
Cash only.
Mail-order catalog available.

Schatzie's Prime Meats
People who live and work in Manhattan's Carnegie Hill neighborhood have their choice when it comes to buying extraordinary prime meats: they can shop at Lobel's, pay astronomically high prices, and get a rather imperious reception, or they can walk a few blocks north, buy meat of the same quality for almost half the price, and be greeted like the long-lost Schatzie son or daughter. Tony Schatzie is the fourth generation of his family in the meat

business, so no one should doubt he knows his stuff. When I asked him to explain the secret of his store's success, he said, "I go to the market every day." What he gets there is gorgeous prime beef that he ages himself, Bell & Evans chickens, free-range chickens, succulent pork, and baby leg of spring lamb that he'll proudly show you hanging in his meat locker. Every kind of fresh game, from mallard duck to venison, is available to order in season. He also makes a mean meat loaf that get its zing from chopped Black Forest ham. Serious chefs should note that Schatzie's has veal, chicken, beef, and lamb stock available every day.

Note: Schatzie prepares entire Thanksgiving dinners, including Bell & Evans fresh-killed turkeys, cranberry sauce, stuffing, sweet potatoes, gravy, and pies for dessert.

Schatzie's Prime Meats
1200 Madison Avenue (between 87th and 88th streets)
New York, NY 10028
PHONE: (212) 410-1555 or (212) 410-1556.
SUBWAYS: 86th Street on the Lexington Avenue No. 4, 5, and 6 lines.
HOURS: 8 A.M. to 6 P.M. Monday to Saturday; closed Sunday.
Delivery available.
All major credit cards accepted.

Tibor Meat ⚊ Tibor Meat is actually a smaller, homier version of Yorkville Packing House, selling the same variety of Hungarian sausages, hams, and pork products. But the one item they provide that Yorkville Packing House doesn't is an incredibly tasty veal-and-pork meatloaf that makes a mean sandwich on dark bread. So if you're daunted by the crowds and hubbub at Yorkville, walk a block and a half down to Tibor Meat.

Tibor Meat
1508 Second Avenue (between 78th and 79th streets)
New York, NY 10021
PHONE: (212) 744-8292
SUBWAY: 77th Street station on the Lexington Avenue No. 6 line.
HOURS: 7 A.M. to 7 P.M. Monday through Friday; 7 A.M. to 6 P.M. Saturday;
    11 A.M. to 5 P.M. Sunday.
No deliveries.
Cash only.
Mail-order price list available.

Yorkville Packing House ⚊ Hungarians are serious carnivores, and Hungarians from all over the tristate area converge on Yorkville Packing House on Saturdays. They come for the wonderful smoked pork chops, the freshly made hot and regular Hungarian sausage laced with paprika, the many varieties of salami and ham, and the Hungarian liver-and-rice sausage, *hurka*, that is definitely an acquired taste. Besides all the pork products, Yorkville Packing House also carries many Hungarian specialty food items, including raspberry syrup and fresh paprika. I've never tried the strudel they sell on weekends, but their little butter biscuits are addictive. For a satisfying lunch on the run, the store provides steamed sausages and a crusty roll that you eat standing up near one of the two little condiment tables. It's not exactly elegant, but it's quick, tasty, and filling.

Yorkville Packing House
1560 Second Avenue (corner of 81st Street)
New York, NY 10028
PHONE: (212) 628-5147
SUBWAY: 77th Street station on the Lexington Avenue No. 6 line.
HOURS: 7 A.M. to 6 P.M. Monday through Saturday; closed Sunday.
No deliveries.
Cash and personal checks only.

*M*IDTOWN WEST

34TH STREET TO 59TH STREET
FIFTH AVENUE TO ELEVENTH AVENUE

Giovanni Esposito & Sons Pork Shop ~ Some people pop vitamins to kickstart their systems in the morning. I prefer sausage, so for me Esposito's Italian sausage is better than an A1 multiple vitamin. The cheese-and-parsley sausage alone will have you mentally sparring with your cardiologist. Don't even bother asking the guys here for their sausage recipe. The Esposito family uses a recipe handed down by their grandparents more than half a century ago. Besides sausage, the store's other specialty is genuine dry-cured Smithfield hams from Gwathmey of Virginia. During the holiday season, they sell nearly a thousand Smithfield or regular smoked hams. Although pork in all its glorious forms is clearly the star attraction here, the store does carry a complete line of meat, from chicken to beef to lamb.

Giovanni Esposito & Sons Pork Shop
500 Ninth Avenue (between 37th and 38th streets)
New York, NY 10018
PHONE: (212) 279-3298
SUBWAYS: 42nd Street–Port Authority Bus Terminal station on the Eighth
    Avenue A, C, and E lines.
HOURS: 8 A.M. to 7:30 P.M. Monday through Saturday; closed Sunday.
Deliveries with a $50 minimum order.
All major credit cards accepted.

Macy's Cellar Marketplace ~ See page 229.

Salumeria Biellese ~ From the outside, Salumeria Biellese looks like just another Italian take-out place with its steam table full of baked ziti, meatballs, and lasagna. You'd never know that in the refrigerated meat case are homemade sausages, salamis, and hams of every variety. They're made every day next door by Mark Buzzio and his staff, who have been making sausage and ham the same old-fashioned way Mark's father did when he opened Salumeria Biellese in 1925. Once you've had Biellese's homemade Genoa and Milanese salami, you'll never go back to Hormel. The homemade prosciutto is so good that it held up against *prosciutto di Parma* in a taste test I conducted. It wasn't as good, but it was close enough. Mark makes special-order French sausages for restaurants like Le Cirque and La Côte Basque and sometimes sells them at the store. Call to ask what he's making for the restaurants that day, and if you're lucky you can pick up some of the most wonderful sausages you'll ever eat, such as the *boudin blanc* with truffles or the sausage with jalapeño, fresh bell pepper, and cilantro. Salumeria Biellese is a little-known New York treasure, one that's worth a trip to this fairly funky neighborhood.

Note: Salumeria Biellese owns a moderately priced restaurant next door, Biricchino, that's useful to know about for a pre–Madison Square Garden meal.

Salumeria Biellese
376-378 Ninth Avenue (between 28th and 29th streets)
New York, NY 10001
PHONE: (212) 736-7376
SUBWAYS: 34th Street–Penn Station on the Broadway-Seventh Avenue No. 1,
    2, 3, and 9 lines and the Eighth Avenue A, C, and E lines.
HOURS: 7 A.M. to 6 P.M. Monday through Friday; 9 A.M. to 6 P.M. Saturday;
    closed Sunday.
All major credit cards accepted.
Mail order available.

ℳIDTOWN EAST

34TH STREET AND 59TH STREET
FIRST AVENUE TO FIFTH AVENUE

Empire Purveyors ~ The trouble with most wholesale-retail meat operations is that they usually make you buy much more meat than you need. I have a family of three, and a whole seven-pound tenderloin of beef would provide us with enough red meat for a month. But Empire Purveyors will sell you a pound of chopped meat, a single steak, or two pork chops, all at prices 30 percent below those at my neighborhood butcher. Last time I was here, I bought aged shell steak for $6.50 a pound, almost four dollars less than I would pay near my home. You can save money on beef, veal, pork, chicken, and duck. If the low prices aren't sufficient incentive to shop at Empire, then maybe Tony and Richard Pinto's warm welcome will sway you. They're friendly, knowledgeable, and willing to tell you more than you want to know about the meat you buy. Don't they know that when they sell meat this good and this cheap they're allowed to be gruff?

Empire Purveyors
901 First Avenue (between 50th and 51st streets)
New York, NY 10022
PHONE: (212) 755-7757
SUBWAYS: 51st Street station on the Lexington Avenue No. 6 line;
    Lexington–Third Avenues station on the Sixth Avenue F and Eighth
    Avenue E lines.

HOURS: 6 A.M. to 4:30 P.M. Monday through Friday; closed Saturday and
   Sunday.
Deliveries in the neighborhood.
Cash only.

*K*IPS BAY/GRAMERCY PARK

14TH STREET TO 34TH STREET
EAST RIVER TO FIFTH AVENUE

Les Halles — Les Halles is the only combination butcher shop and restaurant I
know in New York. Its proprietors are the same people who own Park Avenue
Bistro, and unsurprisingly the butcher shop sells many of the same cuts of meat
served at the restaurant. That means you can get wonderful French bistro preparations and cuts of meat you won't find anywhere else in the city. The pork
stuffed with prunes, for instance, is a delicious and unusual roast that is perfect
for a dinner party. The hangar steak is a flavorful French version of a skirt steak.
The rump steak tastes like a very tender round steak. Of course, you would expect
wonderful pâtés and sausages in a classic French bistro, and Les Halles delivers
in those departments, too. The *pâté Breton* is a delicious pork-and-cognac pâté.
A coarse duck pâté called *rillettes* cries out for a crusty baguette. The *Rosette de
Lyon* is a stupendous, lusty, and unique French sausage. I'm also glad to report
that people in Les Halles were actually solicitous and helpful. None of the pseudo-
Parisian haughtiness here.

Les Halles
411 Park Avenue South (between 28th and 29th streets)
New York, NY 10016
PHONE: (212) 679-4111
SUBWAY: 28th Street station on the Lexington Avenue No. 6 line.
HOURS: 12 noon to midnight Monday through Saturday; closed Sunday.
No retail deliveries.
All major credit cards accepted.

Todaro Brothers — See page 233.

Tom's Meat Market — A Tom's customer and her-two-year-old were awaiting
their order when I saw Tom's co-owner Anthony LoVarco press his nose against
one of his refrigerated cases to look at the child in the carriage. "Can you say
'Anthony'?" the mother was imploring her child. Naturally, the two-year-old
refused to utter Anthony's name, but that's about the only request I've ever seen
refused in this incredibly friendly, high-quality, prime butcher shop. Anthony,
his brother Nick, and everyone who works for them treat every customer as a
long-lost regular. "Eight minutes on each side," Anthony instructed me as he

cut to order my perfect strip steak. A few of Tom's regulars who work in the neighborhood have told me that Anthony and Nick sometimes just throw an extra item into their bag without charge, imploring them to try it. Besides gorgeous prime beef and lamb and Bell & Evans chickens, Tom's has a small fish counter selling a few cuts of whatever their supplier says is freshest. The last time I was here it was tuna and salmon steaks. Tom's also carries whatever fruits and vegetables look good to them that day in the market. I bought some sugar-sweet pencil asparagus to accompany my steak. I didn't buy the huge, bright red strawberries I saw in the case, but I left the store wishing I had.

Tom's Meat Market
214 Third Avenue (between 18th and 19th streets)
New York, NY 10003
PHONE: (212) 475-0395
SUBWAYS: 14th Street–Union Square station on the following lines:
    Lexington Avenue No. 4, 5, and 6; Broadway N and R; 14th Street–
    Canarsie L.
HOURS: 8:30 A.M. to 6:45 P.M. Monday through Friday; 8 A.M. to 5:30 P.M.
    Saturday; closed Sunday.
Deliveries in the neighborhood.
Cash and personal checks only.

*W*EST VILLAGE

14TH STREET TO HOUSTON STREET
FIFTH AVENUE TO WEST STREET

Balducci's ~ See page 205.

Balducci's Veal Braciolette

Baby braciole, or braciolette, are a Sicilian specialty—finger-sized rolls of either beef or veal filled with proscuitto and raisins. They're first skewered tight with a toothpick, then sautéed in onions and oil, and finally simmered in a rich red sauce until fork-tender.

The veal scaloppine for this recipe must be sliced thin to start and then must be pounded even thinner. This makes them easier to roll and creates a more delicate taste. Because the veal is so lean, the braciolette must be cooked briefly over high heat and then slow-cooked in sauce to keep them moist and tender. If this two-stage process seems too time-consuming, do what Mama Balducci used to do: Make enough braciolette to last a few meals.

Balducci's Veal Braciolette, continued

12 small slices veal scaloppine,
  pounded very thin
6 thin slices prosciutto, each cut in
  half
1 large clove garlic, minced
2 tablespoons pignoli nuts
1 tablespoon fresh parsley, minced
2 tablespoons golden raisins
Salt and pepper to taste

2 ounces freshly grated Parmesan
  cheese
½ cup (approximately) olive oil
½ large Spanish onion, chopped
½ cup dry white wine
1 container Balducci's tomato sauce
1 additional handful fresh Italian
  parsley, chopped
Additional salt and pepper to taste

1. Lay veal slices out on a work surface. Place a piece of prosciutto, a pinch of minced garlic, 3 or 4 pignoli nuts, a pinch of parsley, 3 or 4 raisins, and a sprinkle of salt, pepper, and Parmesan on each slice. Roll up lengthwise, holding ends in with the index fingers as you roll. Skewer each brociolette with a large toothpick and set aside.
2. Heat olive oil (enough to cover bottom) in a large skillet over medium-high heat. Add onion and cook about 5 minutes, until golden. Add braciolette and cook for about 10 minutes, turning frequently. Add wine, increase heat slightly, and let evaporate. Reduce heat to low, add tomato sauce, handful of parsley, and salt and pepper. Cook braciolette in sauce for approximately 30 minutes.

Yield: 12 braciolette

Basior Schwartz ~ Located in the bowels of the city's wholesale meat district, Basior Schwartz sells high-quality meat and gourmet foods at half the going rate. Great pâtés from Les Trois Petits Cochons, *parmigiana reggiano*, dried porcini mushrooms, and Bazzini pistachio nuts can all be found here. That's the good news. The bad news is that in many cases you have to buy these foods in huge quantities. A pound of dried porcini mushrooms goes a long way—most recipes call for an ounce or two. The last time I was at Basior Schwartz I found myself staring at a beautiful piece of Parmigiano-Reggiano. Unfortunately it weighed at least three pounds. Four other things to remember about Basior Schwartz: The service is lousy; the selection is limited; its warehouse location makes it seem like you're shopping inside a refrigerator; and there's a lot of inferior food thrown in with the good stuff. That the service is lousy makes some sense, since the store is principally a wholesaler and restaurant supplier that opens its doors to the public. This fact also explains the atmosphere and the limited selection.

Basior Schwartz
421 West 14th Street (between Greenwich and Washington streets)
New York, NY 10014
PHONE: (212) 929-5368

SUBWAYS: 14th Street station on the Eighth Avenue A, C, and E lines and
the Broadway–Seventh Avenue No. 1, 2, 3, and 9 lines; Eighth Avenue
station on the 14th Street–Canarsie L line.
HOURS: 5 A.M. to 10:30 A.M. Monday through Friday; closed Saturday and
Sunday.
No deliveries.

Daniel's Market ∼ With its black-and-white tiled floors and bare brick walls,
Daniel's Market is a little bit of Paris in New York. It's a splendid butcher shop
that sells Bell & Evans chickens and all the standard meats. But what sets this
shop apart is the variety of freshly made French sausages. The *merguez*, a spicy
lamb sausage, the Toulouse, the garlic, the *boudin noir*, and the *boudin blanc*
are all delicious and hard to find elsewhere in New York. Daniel's Market also
makes very good sandwiches on fresh baguettes.

Daniel's Market
179 Prince Street (between Thompson and Sullivan streets)
New York, NY 10012
PHONE: (212) 674-0708
SUBWAYS: Spring Street station on the Eighth Avenue C and E lines;
Houston Street station on the Broadway–Seventh Avenue No. 1 and 9
lines.
HOURS: 11 A.M. to 8 P.M. Monday through Saturday; noon to 6:00 P.M.
Sunday.
Deliveries in the neighborhood.
All major credit cards accepted.

Faicco's ∼ My devotion to this store when I lived in Greenwich Village led my
wife to proclaim that in a former life I was an Italian housewife. Homemade
sweet-and-hot sausages with garlic, cheese, parsley, and anything else that pre-
nouvelle sausage makers stuff into a sausage casing are the main attractions here.
There are other fresh and prepared meats, such as a first-rate ready-to-heat chicken
rollatini, but it's the sausage that makes Faicco's special. Bringing Faicco's sausage
to your hosts in the Hamptons ensures a repeat invitation the following year.

Faicco's
260 Bleecker Street (between Sixth and Seventh avenues)
New York, NY 10014
PHONE: (212) 243-1974
SUBWAYS: Christopher Street–Sheridan Square station on the Broadway–
Seventh Avenue No. 1 and 9 lines; West Fourth Street–Washington
Square station on the following lines: Sixth Avenue B, D, F, and Q;
Eighth Avenue A, C, and E.
HOURS: 8 A.M. to 6 P.M. Tuesday through Saturday; 9 A.M. to 2 P.M. Sunday.
No deliveries.
Cash only.

Florence Meat Market ∼ Florence Meat Market owner Tony Pellegrino listened
intently to opera as he cut to order and trimmed my aged porterhouse steak.

"Don Giovanni, all right," he said to no one in particular as he sawed my meat. I don't know if it's the opera that does it, but somehow Tony's porterhouse steaks deliver on the promise, "It's so buttery, you don't need a knife." In fact, Tony delivers close to Lobel's-quality uptown meat at downtown prices. That doesn't mean it's cheap, but I've found that you get what you pay for in prime meats. If you do want an inexpensive cut of steak, Florence sells what it calls a Newport steak, a mystery cut reportedly invented by Jackie Obaldi, Florence's original owner. Besides the prime aged beef, pork, lamb, and Bell & Evans chickens, Tony sells a few select meat preparations you should seriously think about if you're in a dinner party emergency, for example, chicken à la Perugina, stuffed with prosciutto and herbs, and veal roast à la Parisienne, stuffed with ground veal and herbs. He also sells the only preservative-free, all-natural sausage I've ever liked. Usually I find the nitrites add to the flavor, but his sweet-and-hot Italian pork sausage, his extremely lean veal sausage, and his breakfast links prove me wrong.

Florence Meat Market
5 Jones Street (between Bleecker and West Fourth streets)
New York, NY 10014
PHONE: (212) 242-6531
SUBWAYS: Christopher Street–Sheridan Square station on the Broadway–
   Seventh Avenue No. 1 and 9 lines; West Fourth Street–Washington
   Square station on the following lines: Sixth Avenue B, D, F, and Q;
   Eighth Avenue A, C, and E.
HOURS: 8:30 A.M. to 1 P.M. Monday; 8:30 A.M. to 6:30 P.M. Tuesday through
   Saturday; closed Sunday.
Deliveries in the neighborhood.
Cash and personal checks only.

Jefferson Market ⇝ The Jefferson Market butcher counter is that old-fashioned combination of service and quality that's become increasingly rare in New York. No question is too trivial, no order too insubstantial for the knowledgeable and friendly countermen at this Village institution. Once a month when we lived in the village we would splurge and buy the perfectly trimmed loin lamb chops or the gorgeous aged Delmonico steaks. Prices are high (without reaching the Lobel stratosphere), but I can't remember ever getting a bad piece of meat here. The Bell & Evans chickens, the game, the freshly made sausage—it's all wonderful. Though they don't carry much in the way of prepared food, the meat loaf with chunks of green pepper in it and the homemade German potato salad make one of my favorite take-out meals in all of New York.

Jefferson Market
455 Sixth Avenue (between 10th and 11th streets)
New York, NY 10011
PHONE: (212) 675-2277
SUBWAYS: Christopher Street–Sheridan Square station on the Broadway–
   Seventh Avenue No. 1 and 9 lines; West Fourth Street–Washington
   Square station on the following lines: Sixth Avenue B, D, F, and Q;
   Eighth Avenue A, C, and E.
HOURS: 8 A.M. to 9 P.M. Monday through Saturday; 9 A.M. to 8 P.M. Sunday.
Deliveries made all over Manhattan.
Cash and personal checks only.

The North Pole Meat Market ⁓ I stumbled by accident onto the North Pole Meat Market one Saturday, and now I know how Admiral Peary felt. I discovered a reasonably priced, service-oriented, old-fashioned prime butcher. The owner, Angelo Bonsangue, makes a mean chicken rollatini you just pop into the oven when you get home. He makes his own Italian sausage and ready-to-cook stuffed boneless veal and lamb roasts. He also carries a full line of fresh game. One more thing about the North Pole Meat Market: They make wonderful cooked meat sandwiches in the front of the store. The North Pole $3.50 leg-of-lamb hero would cost four times the price at a chichi uptown restaurant.

The North Pole Meat Market
514 Hudson Street (between Christopher and West 10th streets)
New York, NY 10014
PHONE: (212) 675-6229
SUBWAYS: Christopher Street–Sheridan Square station on the Broadway–
    Seventh Avenue No. 1 and 9 lines.
HOURS: 8 A.M. to 6:30 P.M. Monday through Saturday; closed Sunday.
Deliveries in the neighborhood.
Cash only.

Ottomanelli's ⁓ When my wife and I were newly married and neophyte dinner-party givers, John Ottomanelli's Italian veal roast wrapped in bacon often came to our rescue. Ten years later, Ottomanelli's veal roast is even better, thanks to the *prosciutto di Parma* they now stuff it with. Ottomanelli's is a warm, inviting store, with extremely helpful countermen. All meat is custom cut to order, thereby ensuring freshness. They make their own lamb, veal, pork, and chicken sausage here, and it's very good, though not quite up to Faicco's sausage right across the street. On weekends they sell farm-fresh free-range chickens. In season they sell fresh game and venison sausage. Ottomanelli's is the quintessential neighborhood butcher, selling high-quality meat at a fair price.

Note: The downtown Ottomanelli's is unrelated to the uptown butcher bearing the same name.

Ottomanelli's
285 Bleecker Street (just east of Seventh Avenue)
New York, NY 10014
PHONE: (212) 675-4217
SUBWAYS: Christopher Street–Sheridan Square station on the Broadway–
    Seventh Avenue No. 1 and 9 lines; West Fourth Street–Washington
    Square station on the following lines: Sixth Avenue B, D, F, and Q;
    Eighth Avenue A, C, and E.
HOURS: 8 A.M. to 6:30 P.M. Monday through Friday; 7 A.M. to 6 P.M.
    Saturday; closed Sunday.
Deliveries in the neighborhood.
Cash only.

ℰAST VILLAGE

14TH STREET TO HOUSTON STREET
EAST RIVER TO FIFTH AVENUE

East Village Meat Market ~~ When I visited here one Saturday morning, I was the only person not speaking Polish, so I just followed a Polish customer's lead and ordered some regular and some double-smoked kielbasa. The latter was lean, meaty, and incredibly smoky—as deeply flavored a Polish sausage as I've had. They also sell an array of pork and beef products, including a winning ham salami. Besides meat, the store sells first-rate Polish and Lithuanian breads, which you see in the window as you pass by.

East Village Meat Market
139 Second Avenue (between St. Mark's Place and 9th Street)
New York, NY 10003
PHONE: (212) 228-5590
SUBWAY: Astor Place station on the Lexington Avenue No. 6 line.
HOURS: 8 A.M. to 6 P.M. Saturday, Monday through Thursday; 8 A.M. to 7
    P.M. Friday; closed Sunday.
No deliveries.
Cash only.

Kurowycky ~~ The Kurowycky family came from the Ukraine more than thirty-five years ago to open their store, and thankfully brought along their old-world curing and butchering techniques. They carry ten kinds of ham and home-made kielbasa that had me reconsidering my slavish devotion to Italian sausage, as well

The Kurowycky family (Kurowycky, Sr., is pictured at right) uses old-world curing and butchering techniques brought with them from Ukraine.

as a full line of beef, pork, and chicken. Prices here are amazingly low, perhaps reflecting the values of the working-class Lower-East-Side Eastern-European community they serve. Whatever the reason, prices here are sometimes 50 percent below those of their uptown counterparts for Black Forest ham and the like. Kurowycky also carries wonderful Russian breads and mustards.

Kurowycky
124 First Avenue (between 7th Street and St. Mark's Place)
New York, NY 10003
PHONE: (212) 477-0344
SUBWAY: Astor Place station on the Lexington Avenue No. 6 line.
HOURS: 8 A.M. to 6 P.M. Monday through Saturday; closed Sunday.
No deliveries.
Cash only.
No mail order.

$\mathcal{D}$OWNTOWN

HOUSTON STREET TO BATTERY PARK

Catherine Street Meat Market ～ See page 131.

Daniel's Market ～ See page 195.

Dean & DeLuca ～ See page 214.

Fretta Brothers Sausage ～ John Fretta says that sausage making goes back in his family for ten generations. All that practice explains why their sausage is out of this world. His fresh sausages are as good as New York offers. I am partial to his cheese-and-parsley and fennel sausages. John also makes four kinds of dried Italian sausage, which hang by strings on the wall. The *soppressata* is wonderful, full of pepper, wine, and garlic. I know I'm slowly killing myself when I eat Fretta's sausage (and anybody else's for that matter), but at least I'll die a happy man.

Fretta Brothers Sausage
116 Mott Street (corner of Hester Street)
New York, NY 10013
PHONE: (212) 226-0232
SUBWAYS: Canal Street station on the following lines: Lexington Avenue No.
   6, Broadway N and R, Nassau Street J, M, and Z; Grand Street station on
   the Sixth Avenue B, D, and Q lines.
HOURS: 8A.M. to 6 P.M. Tuesday through Saturday; 9 A.M. to 2 P.M. Sunday.
No deliveries.
Cash only.
Mail order on dried sausages only.

$\mathcal{B}$RONX

Biancardi's ～ See page 134.

Frankie Cappezza makes cheese-and-parsley sausage in the kitchen of the Corona Heights Pork Store.

$\mathcal{Q}$UEENS

Corona Heights Pork Store ~~ I found out about the Corona Heights Pork Store from Patsy Lancieri, the proprietor of perhaps my favorite New York pizzeria, Patsy's, in Brooklyn. I was devouring a sausage pie there one day when I asked Patsy where he gets his sausage. He told me it was from the Corona Heights Pork Store near his house in Queens. I drove out one beautiful April morning with my sidekick and photographer Peter Cunningham. We zigzagged our way through the streets of Queens until we came upon a small park composed of a few benches, several trees and bushes, and a boccie court that seemed to be the nerve center of the neighborhood. I spotted the Corona Heights Pork Store, which overlooked the boccie court. I immediately knew I was going to love this place, because I have an inviolate rule that the quality of a pork store is directly correlated to its proximity to a boccie court. We walked in, and I could tell this was a first-class pork store. Strings of homemade dried sausage were hanging from the ceiling and homemade prosciutto was being cured right next to the sausage. I asked to buy some prosciutto, and co-owner Mary Lou Cappezza told me it wouldn't be ready for ten, maybe twelve, months. This news was disappointing, but I was thrilled to know that someone in New York was still making prosciutto the old-fashioned way. Just then Mary Lou's husband, master sausage maker Frankie Cappezza, came out and saw my obvious disappointment at not being able to buy the prosciutto. He smiled and shrugged his shoulders. "What can I say? Slower is better." Spurned in my quest to buy the prosciutto, I settled for some cheese-and-parsley sausage that I watched Frankie make with beautifully lean pork butt, fresh parsley, and imported Pecorino Romano cheese. While Frankie was making the sausage, Mary Lou lovingly made me a hero with the store's homemade sweet capicolla, fresh homemade mozzarella, and imported sun-dried tomatoes she prepares herself. I vowed to return in a year to try the prosciutto; the hot sausage; the sweet sausage with fennel; and the new-fangled chicken, veal, and lamb sausage the Corona Heights Pork Store was now making.

Corona Heights Pork Store
107-04 Corona Avenue
Flushing, NY 11373
PHONE: (718) 592-7350
SUBWAY: 103rd Street–Corona Plaza station on the Flushing No. 7 line.
HOURS: 9 A.M. to 7 P.M. Tuesday through Saturday; closed Sunday and
    Monday.
No deliveries.
Cash only.

$\mathscr{B}$ROOKLYN

Eagle Foods ⤳ When Ed Schoenfeld, a.k.a. Chop Suey Looey (see page 129), tells me a place near his house in Park Slope has some of the best smoked meats in the city, I go. No questions asked. Eagle Foods turns out to have the best kielbasa I've sampled. It's lean, not too smoky, and loaded with flavor. Eagle also makes world-class liverwurst, tasty smoked turkey, and something they call homemade meat loaf, which looks kind of funky but tastes like a good, coarse country pâté. Besides the smoked meats, Eagle also carries a full line of regular meat and groceries at incredibly low prices, domestic and imported beers from all over, and what they call on their shopping bags "epicurean delights from around the world." I don't know, though; somehow I just couldn't bring myself to buy Korean spring rolls and dumplings in a store that specializes in kielbasa.

Eagle Foods
628 Fifth Avenue (between 17th and 18th streets)
Brooklyn, NY 11215
PHONE: (718) 499-0026
SUBWAY: Prospect Avenue on the Broadway R line.
HOURS: 6 A.M. to 7 P.M. Monday through Saturday; 6 A.M. to 5 P.M. Sunday.
No deliveries.
All major credit cards accepted.

Best of Butchers and Meat Stores

Best all-around butcher: Balducci's
Best beef and veal (price is no object): Lobel's Prime Meats
Best beef (price matters): Florence Meat Market
Best chicken: Bell & Evans (sold in top-quality meat markets all over the
   city)
Best cold-cut selection: Schaller and Weber
Best Eastern European butcher: Kurowycky
Best French and designer sausage: Salumeria Biellese
Best game: Schatzie's Prime Meats; A. Fitz and Sons
Best Italian sausage: Fretta Brothers Sausage; Corona Heights Pork Store
Best pork: H. Oppenheimer Meats
Best prices: Empire Purveyors
Best service: H. Oppenheimer Meats; Jefferson Market; Tom's Meat Market;
   Schatzie's Prime Meats

13

MEGA-STORES

M ega-store is my term for the eight larger-than-life food stores that dot New York. I call them mega-stores because they go way beyond all other food retailers in terms of the quantity and quality of the foods they carry. New Yorkers are spoiled because we take for granted that every neighborhood will have one of these mega-stores; any other city in the United States would be thrilled to have even one store of the stature of Balducci's or Zabar's or Dean & DeLuca's.

I love these stores because they are for me the ultimate adult candy stores. On a quiet weekday I can easily spend an hour meandering through Dean & DeLuca or Zabar's, smelling the coffee, tasting different cheeses, checking out the latest discovery by their indefatigable buyers. Stores like these are engaged in a friendly but spirited competition to come up with the most exotic fresh sausage or California *chèvre*. The result is that there's always something new to try.

Each store has a different and distinct feel. Owners of mega-stores are an idiosyncratic and fanatical lot, and their biases and points of view are reflected not only in the selection of food but also in the way it's presented, the price, the attitude of the staff, and even the speed with which you can get through the checkout line.

The biggest problem facing these stores is providing good service to customers. The owners of each of the stores profiled in this chapter expressed the difficulties of finding, training, and keeping knowledgeable sales help. As a result, service at mega-stores ranges from the almost contemptuous treatment you often get at Zabar's to the sometimes helpful folks at Balducci's. I have found the best way around this problem is to search out department managers and deal only with them. It may mean spending a few minutes extra in the store, but it's worth it.

A note about bread and baked goods wholesalers: Many of the establishments mentioned in the bread and baked goods sections of each mega-store entry are wholesalers that don't have their own retail outlets. In the bread sections, these would include Spiekermann's, Grimaldi, Certified, Old World Bread Company, Central Bakery, Companio, and Tom Cat. Some of the baked goods wholesalers I have mentioned include Erica's, Scot Paris, Cindy Klotz, and Amy Burke. Other sources for bread and baked goods have their own retail outlets, but their stores are located outside the city's five boroughs. Therefore, they are beyond the purview of the book and won't be given their own entry. These include Policastro in Hoboken for bread and The Bakery in Mamaroneck for pies.

Balducci's: The best food store in New York.

BALDUCCI'S: THE BEST FOOD STORE IN NEW YORK

After nearly twenty years of intense New York eating and searching, and after fifteen months of chasing down every stray piece of pasta and fresh mozzarella in the city for this book, I have come to one inescapable conclusion: Balducci's is the best, most important food store in New York. I didn't have this opinion embarking on my research (although I certainly viewed it as one of the handful of great food stores in the city), but I'm quite certain about it now. In terms of its commitment to quality, its breadth of foodstuffs offered under one roof, the variety of the food it makes and sells, the plethora of food-oriented services that it offers, and the passion and zeal with which the people who run the store go about their business, Balducci's simply has no peer in this city of many great food stores.

Balducci's is devoted first and foremost to food. It doesn't get sidetracked by presentation or art or housewares or attitude or pretense or excess. It purely and simply celebrates food in all its glory. That's not to say it doesn't have its artful aspects, its share of pretenses, or its moments of excess. It's just that its essence is food and food alone.

In many ways, Balducci's is the quintessential New York story. The Balducci family came to America from Bari, Italy, and opened their first store in Brooklyn in 1917. In 1947 they opened the original Balducci's, a produce market at 112 Greenwich Avenue. They outgrew that space and moved to the store's present location in 1970. The store has expanded department by department to meet the needs of its immediate community. Although sometimes it's seemed that the store has grown too quickly, eventually each department has come up to snuff. For example, the cheese department for many years was mediocre. Then Steve Jenkins came into the store, upgraded the department in six tumultuous months, and left a cheese section that is now second only to Jenkins's own at Dean & DeLuca. The fish department was floundering (no pun intended) for a long time, but gradually it's been upgraded until now it's one of the handful of great fish stores in New York. Balducci's used to sell a lot of mediocre baked goods. However, in the last couple of years many of the cakes that came from inferior suppliers and merely looked delicious have been replaced with baked goods that actually taste as good as they look.

No New York story would be complete without a family blood feud. In 1980 Andrew Balducci and his sister Grace had a parting of the ways. Grace and her husband Joe left to start their own store. Andrew Balducci then threatened to sue to prevent her from calling it Balducci's. Grace's store is called Grace's Marketplace, and though it's excellent in its own right and very successful, it's no Balducci's.

Even though I think Balducci's is the finest food store in New York, it's by no means perfect. When it's crowded, the store's low ceilings and lack of crowd control make it feel like a crowded rush-hour subway car. Its pretensions—for example, the store's recent decision to carry only *prosciutto di Parma*—occasionally drive me crazy: Many of the domestic prosciuttos such as Volpi and Daniele are perfectly adequate, and besides, maybe not everybody wants to spend the extra money for the imported Italian prosciutto. It can sometimes be hard to find assistance in the store, although its level of service does certainly compare favorably with the city's other mega-stores. The younger salespeoples' lack of knowledge is sometimes glaring, and a few of the stores more knowledgeable counterpeople occasionally fall victim to imperiousness. But I also have to say that when you're in doubt at Balducci's, if you look for any of the many older, wiser heads at the store, you'll be well taken care of.

When I talked to Andrew Balducci, he told me that Balducci's is a "food experience." At the time I thought it was a rather pretentious remark. But after spending literally hundreds of hours in his store, I know he's right. Balducci's *is* a food experience. Indeed, it's the finest food experience you can have in New York.

Appetizers/Smoked Fish/Salads ⎯ Balducci's carries the usual array of Scotch and Canadian smoked salmon; their selection is not as broad as you might expect. I couldn't find my favored Icelandic smoked salmon here, for example. They do, however, have an exclusive on an organically raised Norwegian smoked salmon with the unlikely name of Nordic Light. Though I usually think anything with the word "light" in it is going to be tasteless, Nordic Light turned out to be flavorful and lightly smoked. The homemade *gravlax* is first-rate, and the variety of smoked fish in addition to salmon is impressive. You'll find smoked bluefish, trout, and New Generation's extraordinary smoked scallops and mussels, among many others. Though the smoked fish here is reasonably impressive, it is the marinated Italian preparations in which the store really excels. Try the homemade roasted peppers or the intriguing sliced grilled eggplant with olive oil and mint or the *patate della nonna*, sliced potatoes marinated in olive oil, garlic, and balsamic vinegar. The Giudia artichokes, or grilled artichoke bottoms, are also wonderful, although they're not made on the premises. Pâtés are another highlight of Balducci's appetizer department. Hannelore pâtés are made exclusively for the store by a master pâté chef, Gerhardt Daniels, on Long Island. His *pâté financière*, made with smoked goose breast, foie gras, and truffles, is about as drop-dead great as pâté gets. His vegetable gallantine, made with broccoli, cauliflower, and carrots, is not too shabby, either. If the Gerhardt Daniels pâtés are a little elaborate for your taste, Balducci's also carries the wonderful D'Artagnan and Summer Sweet pâtés and mousses found all over the city.

Baked Goods ⎯ Up until a couple of years ago, I was really down on Balducci's baked-goods department. I felt it suffered from the everything-looks-beautiful-but-tastes-mediocre syndrome that afflicts too many New York stores. But recently Balducci's has improved considerably in its baked-goods department, thanks in part to the efforts of the buyer, Julie Dichiaro. Most of the pies, for example, now come from Kathleen's, the Southhampton-based baker who makes some of the great pies found on this planet. Try her peach crumb or her pumpkin pie. However, some are still being made by a less stellar pie-making concern, Umanoff & Parsons, so ask before you buy. Balducci's is one of the only retail outlet selling Apple Annie's Ritz Diner apple pie, a seemingly hokey confection, complete with a little American flag, that is actually a first-rate apple pie with a partially open fluted crust, sliced instead of chunked apples, and a powdered sugar dusting on top. Among the excellent selection of chocolate-based confections you'll find La Boulange's Chocolate Truffon and Trio cakes. The wonderful cheesecakes and apple tarts are supplied by Mitchell London, Ed Koch's former chef whose confections must have been responsible for most of the weight the former mayor gained while in office. A Balducci's exclusive is a *pêche à la crème*, a gorgeous-looking peach dessert made from sponge cake and triple sec and filled with pastry cream. I didn't care for it, but I admit it's not the kind of pastry I like. Among the cookies, I was crazy about Erica's rugelach. The Italian cookies were the standards found everywhere.

Breads ⁓ Although there's plenty of great bread to be had at Balducci's, it is not one of the store's stronger departments. Unlike most of the other departments at Balducci's, the bread section makes or carries very few items that are exclusive to the store. There are the taralli addictive pretzel-like breadsticks made with oil, water, and flour. They come in fennel, red-pepper, black-pepper, and basil flavors. The store-made prosciutto bread had an odd, hardish texture. They would do better to bring in Morrone's (they do sell Morrone's baguettes). You will find Rock Hill, Tom Cat, Eli's, D & G, Bread Alone, and Old World Bread Company, but except for the tarallis there isn't anything unique or special about Balducci's own bread, and I came to expect something special about every department at the store.

Candy/Nuts/Dried Fruits ⁓ Balducci's carries three lines of chocolates and truffles. Manon chocolates are, of course, among the handful of great chocolates you can buy in this city, and you'll find about a dozen of their varieties here. Champlain chocolates are a high-quality domestic candy made in Vermont; try their capuccino or bittersweet truffles. I was disappointed by the taste and texture of the chocolates from Panel, a French candymaker I've not seen elsewhere in the city. The nuts and dried fruit section is in no way noteworthy. It sells items like raisins, figs, apricots, almonds, and walnuts in prepacked plastic containers.

Cheese and Dairy ⁓ Steve Jenkins came into Balducci's a few years ago and turned around the store's mediocre cheese department. Since then, it's only gotten better. Recently, Balducci's became New York's exclusive purveyor of the cheeses of the Parisian food legend Henri Androuet. Androuet gathers first-rate cheeses from all over the French countryside and then ages them himself in his restaurant. Somehow his cheeses manage to maintain their character even while undergoing a process that is anathema to cheese lovers everywhere, pasteurization. His Crottin, his Livarot, his Petit Noyal are all cheese perfection. The store-made mozzarella is very good, although it can occasionally be oversalted and is certainly not in the league of that of a Village neighbor, Joe's. Balducci's is also the only food store I know of in New York that makes its own Mascarpone, the Italian cream cheese used in making cheese *torte* and tiramisu. The store is not so slavishly devoted to the new generation of great American cheese makers as is Dean & DeLuca (where Steve Jenkins manages the cheese department) but does carry standards like Goat Folks, Coach, and Weininger's. It also carries an excellent sheep's milk cheese made by a farmer, Sally Jackson, in Washington state.

Coffee/Tea ⁓ At any given time you'll find close to fifty different coffees at Balducci's. Recently, the people who work here have been buzzing about their five organically grown Mexican coffees. I tried the organic French roast and could find no difference between it and ordinary coffee. But it was as good, so I guess it's better to avoid those pesticides even as you're killing yourself with caffeine. Other than the organically grown Mexican coffees, you'll find mostly the same range of coffees you find in the other mega-stores. That means everything from Illy Café to La Semeuse to Jamaican Blue Mountain. I did find a Zimbabwean coffee sold in bulk that I had previously seen in New York in bulk bags only at Oren's Daily Roast.

Condiments/Oils/Vinegars/Packaged Items ⁓ Behind the prepared foods counter you'll see bottles of thirty-year-old balsamic vinegar from Modena, Italy. The reason they keep it behind the counter is that it costs $125 for a small 100-milliliter bottle. I'm about as skeptical as a person can be about hyperexpensive foods, but I admit that when they put a sample drop on my hand, it was a transcendent taste experience. It was simultaneously sweet and tart, with resonant flavors coming through long after the drop was gone. I still wouldn't spend the money, but it was wonderful. You'll find cheaper conventional balsamic vinegars here, as well as a fantastic array of Italian, Spanish, and French olive oils. Try the Tenuta San Guido from Italy or the Nuñez el Prado from Spain. Balducci's also carries a full range of aromatic oils from Provence and flavored vinegars.

Deli Meats (Salumeria) ⁓ It's difficult to be on a diet and go past the Balducci's deli counter. I tried it one time and had almost made it to the safe confines of the produce department when I spotted the Speck smoked prosciutto. I'm a prosciutto lover to start with, and if you add the fact that I never met a smoked meat I didn't like, you know that smoked prosicutto called out to me the way Marvin Gaye sang out to Tammi Terrell. Once I stopped for the smoked prosciutto, I had to get some *prosciutto di Parma*. I think it's needlessly snobby for Balcucci's to carry only *prosciutto di Parma*, but I admit you won't find a sweeter, more luxuriant-tasting prosciutto anywhere. Besides the smoked and regular prosciutto, you'll find a full complement of imported and domestic salamis and hams from such quality purveyors as Schaller and Weber and Rapelli. If more exotic fare is what you're looking for, try the smoked Magret, duck breast so rich you can't eat more than a slice or two.

Fish ⁓ In the last couple of years Balducci's fish department has improved to the point that it's now the best fish market in Greenwich Village. Balducci's the only store in New York that carries crab cakes from my favorite Baltimore restaurant, Obrycki's Crab House. They're expensive ($7.95 each as we went to press), but as they're made of crab meat with just enough bread crumbs to bind them together, they're well worth it. Besides the conventional array of fish such as tuna, scrod, and sole, Balducci's also carries things like Idaho trout, marlin steaks, fresh prawns from Hawaii, and fresh shrimp from Florida. It also carries Columbia River wild salmon, a much meatier, less oily alternative to Atlantic salmon. An appealing touch here is the basket offering Balducci's fish recipe of the week. The last time I was there it was soft-shell crabs meunière (see p. 155).

Meat and Poultry ~~ Balducci's is one of only a handful of New York butchers that actually ages its own beef. Balducci's meat is high-priced, but I can't name a butcher other than neighboring Jefferson Market that delivers the breadth of meat and the service that Balducci's butchers provide. The New York strip steak here is every bit the equal of the steaks served at the city's best steak houses. Balducci's is also the exclusive purveyor of Japanese Wagyu beef, from cows that are actually massaged every day until they're slaughtered in order to assure the meat's suppleness and overall quality. I'm not sure what massaging a cow does for the quality of the beef, but I know all those masseuses contribute mightily to Wagyu beef's $125-a-pound price tag. I did buy a very thin (less than a third of a pound) Wagyu steak just for research purposes. It was beautifully marbled, very flavorful, and so rich it would be impossible to eat in American-style portions (even if you could afford it). Balducci's also makes many kinds of sausage, from Italian sweet and hot to the spicy French lamb sausage *merguez*, and carries an unusually large selection of fresh and frozen game, everything from fresh quails to Magret duck breast. Balducci's butchers are unusually helpful and service oriented. Ask for Louis Porco. He'll take care of you.

Pasta/Sauces ~~ Balducci's makes at least twenty kinds of fresh pasta in its huge industrial kitchen in Long Island City. You'll find everything from tricolor cavatelli to squid-ink linguini, and even uncut macaroni sheets for lasagne. Aside from the Ravioli Store (see page 249), Balducci's makes the best designer ravioli in New York. The *broccoli di rapa*, truffle, wild-mushroom, lobster, and *di zucca* (pumpkin and cheese) ravioli are all worthy dinner-party fare. The store also makes and freezes tasty meat ravioli and unusual tomato ravioli with vegetables. Balducci's presents a dozen fresh pasta sauces, but, as could be expected, you'll do best sticking to the simple peasanty sauces like the bolognese, puttanesca, or marinara. Try the pomodoro condito, a garlicky chunked tomato sauce you can even spoon cold from the jar. I found the pestos here timid. Like the fish counter, the pasta department offers a pasta-of-the-week recipe. I've included a recipe for penne with spring dandelion, white beans, and pancetta I first found in the recipe basket at the store.

Balducci's Penne with Spring Dandelion, White Beans, and Pancetta

The first-of-the-season wild dandelion is in—tender, pointed shoots that sprout in early spring. With their sharp flavor and supple texture these greens could move salad-loving Italians to tears. Many would not consider enjoying this baby leaf any other way, for its bitter taste and buttery feel are best savored raw with a dressing.

However, we can't resist turning this seasonal treat into something with entrée status. Thus, our pasta-bean-green dish was born. Navy beans are precooked and combined with sautéed dandelion and crumbled pancetta pieces. If you don't let all the water evaporate while the beans are simmering, there will be enough creamy liquid to serve as a binding sauce.

Although the resulting dish is viscous and dense, the bright, perky flavor of spring dandelion and the spice of pancetta poke through with every bite.

1 cup dried navy beans, presoaked overnight	3 bunches spring dandelion greens
3 cups cold water	2 tablespoons olive oil
1 bay leaf	8 to 12 slices pancetta, diced
½ teaspoon dried thyme	5 cloves garlic, crushed
½ onion, peeled and stuck with 3 cloves	1 pound dried penne pasta

1. Drain presoaked beans and cover with cold water. Add bay leaf, thyme, and onion to pot. Bring to a boil, reduce heat to medium-low, and simmer uncovered for about 1 hour, or until beans collapse against the roof of your mouth. The cooking liquid should be thick; if still too watery, increase heat slightly and continue cooking, monitoring closely, until more water has evaporated. When desired consistency is reached, turn off heat.
2. Rinse and dry dandelion greens and remove stems. Cut leaves in half and set aside.
3. Heat olive oil in large skillet over medium heat. Add pancetta, stirring occasionally, and cook until crisp, about 8 to 10 minutes. Remove pancetta to paper towel and add garlic to same oil in skillet. Cook until garlic starts to "blonde" and add dandelion pieces. Saute for 2 to 3 minutes, stirring until greens are wilted. Turn off heat and set aside.
4. Cook penne in a large pot of boiling, salted water until *al dente*. Drain and add to pot with beans. Add sauteed dandelion (be sure to include all oil and garlic pieces). Combine well and turn into a large serving bowl. Sprinkle with cooked pancetta and serve.

Yield: 6 servings

Prepared Foods ～ It's sometimes overwhelming to shop at Balducci's prepared foods counter. Your eyes may glaze over as you confront the sixty-five oversized platters of food set out every day. My advice is to stick to simple dishes, particularly the ones at the counter called Mama Balducci's Corner. Mama's stuffed peppers, filled with spinach, ricotta, and pignoli nuts, give new life to that humdrum dish. The *broccoli di rapa* with fresh veal sausage is another inspired choice. The *pasta de cecco*, elbow macaroni with chickpeas and pancetta, is an unusual pasta dish I've not found elsewhere. The breast-of-veal roast stuffed with asparagus was tender and flavorful even after being reheated and wasn't fatty like many other breast-of-veal preparations I've had. If you're feeling adventurous, try the *calzone Barese*, stuffed with leeks, sweet onions, golden raisins, anchovies, and black olives. It's not for eating every day, but it is an intriguing blend of flavors. You also can't go wrong with simple salads like the mozzarella, tomato, and onion salad, or the string-bean-and-potato salad. The chicken francese or milanese was lemony but dull, and the stuffed roasted chicken was dry. The grilled polenta with wild mushrooms didn't have much flavor, but in general I'm not a grilled polenta man.

Produce ～ Given the store's history, it's not surprising that produce is the mother of all departments at Balducci's. Nowhere else in the city can you find their range of both regular and designer produce. I spent one April afternoon cruising the produce area for new taste treats and found fresh cactus leaves; ugli fruit; fiddlehead ferns; edible flowers; purple asparagus; red Japanese eggplant; *cardone*, a root vegetable that tastes like a cross between celery and artichoke; and *feijoa*, a fragrant, bright-green-skinned fruit that tastes like a combination of quince and pineapple. The great thing about Balducci's produce is they don't skimp on everyday fruits and vegetables, either. On my last visit I bought superb vine-ripened, Mexican-grown tomatoes that were the best eating tomatoes I've ever had in New York outside the local growing season. Every kind of designer lettuce you can think of is sold here, from mâche to frisée. The same goes for fresh mushrooms. Of course you'll also find a full complement of fresh herbs at Balducci's, although they don't look as fresh here as they do at Fairway or Dean & DeLuca. If you're having trouble finding anything, ask for Gino Roselli. He's been around the store forever, and really knows produce.

Note: Buying produce here, or at Dean & DeLuca or even Fairway, is hardly foolproof. Sometimes even terrific markets sell produce that looks perfect and has no taste. That's not the market's fault. It's nature's.

Miscellaneous Notes ～ Balducci's has a personal shopping service that allows you to eat Balducci's food and never leave your house. All you do is call them and place an order. They do the shopping, and either you pick it up or they'll deliver it anywhere in the five boroughs. Balducci's mail-order catalog requires a $20 minimum order; call (800) 822-1444 for details. They also have a full-scale catering service and do wonderful gift and picnic baskets.

Best Hours to Shop ～ Shopping at Balducci's in the middle of the afternoon on a weekday is a leisurely, extremely pleasant experience. Shopping on a weekend afternoon can feel like a rapid descent into hell. Tuesdays are good days to shop here, as they are elsewhere. After work any other weekday can be difficult, but anything is better than a Saturday or Sunday at Balducci's. The personal shopping service mentioned above proves to be an effective antidote to the Balducci's weekend blues.

Balducci's
424 Avenue of the Americas (between 9th and 10th streets)
New York, NY 10011
PHONE: (212) 673-2600
SUBWAYS: Christopher Street–Sheridan Square station on the Broadway–
    Seventh Avenue No. 1 and 9 lines; West Fourth Street–Washington
    Square station on the following lines: Sixth Avenue B, D, F, and Q;
    Eighth Avenue A, C, and E.
HOURS: 7 A.M. to 8:30 P.M. seven days a week.
Deliveries available all over Manhattan.
All major credit cards accepted.
Mail-order catalog available.

BLOOMINGDALE'S: THE FOOD SHOP WITH ATTITUDE

As in every other department at Bloomingdale's, attitude is of paramount importance at the store's food shops. They don't simply have a coffee department, they have Cafe 59. A mere smoked-fish-and-appetizer department wouldn't be enough at Bloomingdale's; They have a branch of Petrossian. This kind of aspirational food selling has never much appealed to me. I always thought food was supposed to be fun, not a status symbol.

Because Bloomingdale's is such a slave to fashion, it's hard to find constants at the gourmet store, or in any other department for that matter. Cafe 59 was the Michel Guérard boutique just a few years ago. But coffee's in and French nouvelle cuisine is out, so the floor space is devoted to coffee until something replaces *that*.

Despite this retail fickleness, there are a number of departments at Bloomingdale's gourmet store that rank with the city's best. The baked goods, bread, and candy are all constants and all terrific. And if you want a gift basket of food, Bloomingdale's is an excellent place to get it.

Appetizers/Smoked Fish/Salads ⁓ In keeping with its status-conscious orientation, Bloomingdale's has a Petrossian counter. That means you can get the Royal Norwegian smoked salmon for $40 a pound or the Extra Royal, which is fattier and milder, for $47. If those prices seem inflated to you, they are. But since the salmon has the Petrossian name attached to it, some people don't mind paying for it. It's perfectly good salmon, mind you; it's just not worth the premium. Besides the smoked salmon, Petrossian carries meaty smoked trout, smoked eel, smoked sturgeon, and smoked cod's roe. Petrossian's famed caviar and foie gras are, of course, available here. The foie gras is appropriately rich and satiny, but I prefer D'Artagnan's, made in good old Jersey City. Lastly, if you've just been to the Russian Tea Room and fallen in love with the caviar pancakes known as blini, Petrossian sells the buckwheat pancakes you need to make them at home.

Baked Goods ∾ Albert Prato, Bloomingdale's bakery (and candy) buyer, says that the bakery department at the store is the "crossroads of all bakeries." He may be right. Using a combination of great well-known New York bakeries for some things, his own basement ovens for others, and more than a few exclusive-to-Bloomingdale's suppliers makes the bakery department among the best of the city's megastores. A few of the exclusives were real finds for me. Nancy's Fancies are extraordinary buttery cookie cups filled with cheese, fruit, and chocolate. The fruit fillings were particularly good—just fresh, barely sweetened fruit. The two types of Bucks County Gourmet Cookies are large nut-and-chocolate and oatmeal cookies that have a lot more flavor and texture than Mrs. Field's cookies (Mrs. Field's also has a counter at Bloomingdale's). The crumb buns from Hahn's on Long Island are messy, moist, and irresistible. There is a large selection of pound cakes; the butterscotch was amazing, but the almond-lemon was slightly stale. As at all stores of this type, freshness can be an issue. Prato claims that no cake stays on the shelf longer than two days, but the pound cake I tried was clearly more than two days old. The muffins baked in the basement are loaded with high-quality ingredients and flavor. Among Prato's regular cake suppliers are Lanciani, Gindi, Sant Ambroeus, and Guy Pascal. A find for me was La Boulange's trio cake, an incredibly rich combination of chocolate ganache and milk-, dark-, and white-chocolate mousses.

Bread ∾ Bloomingdale's bread department is first-rate. The croissants are baked fresh at the store using Guy Pascal dough. The Orwasher's selections here include raisin-pumpernickel, cinnamon-raisin, and wonderful potato bread. Baguette choices include Boudin's San Francisco sourdough, which are shipped partially baked and then finished in the store's ovens, and Policastro. Other top-rank breads sold here include Eli's raisin-walnut sourdough loaf and rolls, Old World Bread Company's baguettes, and Rock Hill's sourdough peasant breads. The store also sells okay individual pizzas baked on the premises.

Candy/Nuts/Dried Fruits ∾ The candy department ranks with Macy's as one of the city's two best chocolate boutiques. The Gartner Belgian chocolates, a Bloomingdale's exclusive, are superb, heady hits of chocolates. Gartner's Milenka, an absurdly smooth caramel cream, may be one of my favorite pieces of chocolate in the whole city, and usually I'm not much of a cream man. The Laderach Swiss truffles are also excellent. One bite of a Joseph Schmidt oversized chocolate called Chocolate Decadence, and you won't mind that you're biting into the fiftieth thing you've had called Chocolate Decadence. In general, Schmidt, based in California, is one of the few first-rate American chocolate makers. The department also carries a kosher French chocolate, Pierre Koenig, that will make you forget Barton's in a hurry. There's also a Godiva counter here, but it certainly would be a waste to buy Godiva at the expense of all these other clearly superior choices. Besides chocolates by the piece, Bloomingdale's sells boxed chocolate by Perugina and Lindt, as well as lots of gimmicky candy like jelly beans and bubble gum. The dried fruit selection includes pineapple, pears, papaya, raisins, and apricots. Nuts carried here include raw and roasted cashews, pistachios, sliced and raw almonds, and peanuts.

Coffee/Tea ~ The coffee department at Bloomingdale's is called Cafe 59. It sells eighteen kinds of beans ranging from Café La Semeuse, the excellent Swiss coffee served at Lutèce, to Jamaican Blue Mountain, which at $29.50 a pound is definitely a special-occasion purchase. The house blend is full-bodied and excellent. You can also buy a cup of coffee and a pastry here and sit at a small counter overlooking 59th Street. The tea section features Paris's Mariage tea salon, teas sold out of gorgeous large lacquered black containers. You'll find butterscotch and chocolate teas here, in addition to brands from Burma and Indonesia. The teas are very expensive, almost $20 a pound; but they are very good.

Condiments/Oils/Vinegars/Packaged Items ~ The breadth of packaged foods at Bloomingdale's is extraordinary. The last time I was here the salespeople were scurrying around trying to fill all the orders coming in for a Thai peanut sauce mentioned in *New York* magazine that week. The sauce is made in that noted Thai province Hillsdale, New York. The store also carries a full line of Italian and Spanish olive oils, including some with whole olives at the bottom of the bottle. Flavored vinegars are available here by the dozens, including a delightful rosemary vinegar. Also in stock is Cold Hollow's wonderful line of apple sauces. I tried the raspberry apple, which was delicious but a bit overpriced at $4.00 a pint. DeCecco dried pastas are available here in many shapes, as is the Mendocino Spa Pasta, the surprisingly tasty no-cholesterol pasta. You will also find a full line of Silver Palate sauces and vinegars.

Best Times to Shop ~ Other than at holiday times, Bloomingdale's food shops never seem to get crowded. Avoid lunchtime, when people who work nearby tend to shop here.

Bloomingdale's
1000 Third Avenue (between 59th and 60th streets)
New York, NY 10022
PHONE: (212) 355-5900
SUBWAYS: 59th Street station on the Lexington Avenue No. 4, 5, and 6 lines;
    Lexington Avenue station on the Sixth Avenue B and Q lines and the
    Broadway N and R lines.
HOURS: 10 A.M. to 9 P.M. Monday and Thursday; 10 A.M. to 6:30 P.M.
    Tuesday, Wednesday, Friday, and Saturday; noon to 6 P.M. Sunday.
Delivery available.
All major credit cards accepted.
Mail-order catalog available.

DEAN & DELUCA: THE FOOD MUSEUM

I used to hate the idea of Dean & DeLuca. The notion of presentation as the most important element of a food store is enough to make me turn in my taste buds. To me, of course, taste is everything. If the blintzes are asymmetrical, that's okay, as long as they taste great. In fact, I prefer them that way. If somebody's poked a finger in the apple pie, that shows me he's passionate about food. It's not that I mind seeing food presented in an aesthetically pleasing manner. It's just that I don't want taste to be sacrificed in the name of art.

When Joel Dean, a burned-out publishing executive, and Giorgio DeLuca, a frustrated schoolteacher, opened for business almost fifteen years ago, their Soho shop was as much a food museum as a food store. Fed up with the lack of high-quality food available in New York, they decided to open a European-oriented food store where presentation and selection would reign. Artist friends from the neighborhood were brought in to do everything from paint and design the store to put up the food displays. The late Felipe Rojas Lombardi, who introduced tapas to many New Yorkers at the Ballroom, was the original chef.

The result was a visually oriented food store perfectly in tune with its artist-dominated neighborhood. If Zabar's, with its cacaphony and hubbub, was the quintessential Upper West Side food store, then Dean & DeLuca, with its stark and striking food sculptures, was the epitome of its Soho environs. For me the only problem with the original store was that I never felt comfortable touching the food. Every time I grabbed a pear I thought I was removing a limb from a Henry Moore sculpture. I felt as if there should have been a sign in front of the food reading "Please Do Not Touch." Regular, non-artsy customers got lost in the gallery mentality.

All of that began to change somewhat when the store moved to its present, larger, lower-Broadway location in 1988. The new space is gorgeous, its twenty-foot ceilings and wide aisles giving the store a truly European feel. But it is also five or six times larger, and it cost a fortune to build. Many individual departments were created, and department heads were given bottom-line responsibilities for their individual areas. In the ensuing years Giorgio's and Joel's sensibilities were mixed with the more consumer-oriented personalities of the department managers.

Today the D & D cheese department, headed by Steven Jenkins, is at least as much about taste as it is about presentation. The produce department, headed by Michael McGovern, now displays its produce in a way that encourages customers to touch and feel the mâche lettuce or Jamaican ugli fruit they're about to buy. The meat-and-fish department head, John Wasniewski, is a twenty-five-year veteran of the food business who has never shown or worked in a gallery. Joanne Wynkoop, the bread and bakery department head, appears genuinely concerned about serving her customers.

The last time I was here they were having a (perish the thought) sale on a particular brand of balsamic vinegar. Toward closing time the produce department also offers two-for-one sales on perishables that won't last another day. What was once a gallery has become at the very least a crafts guild. Dean & DeLuca has become a more accessible, general, customer-oriented place without losing its Lobro cool.

Appetizers/Smoked Fish/Salads ~ The smoked fish selection is fairly limited at D & D, and it would be hard to recommend as the place to go when provisioning a bagels-and-lox brunch. The Hebrides salmon is silky and rich, as is the house-cured *gravlax*. For a change of pace check out the New Generation smoked scallops with their wonderful nutty flavor. The herring in mustard sauce tasted over-

Dean & DeLuca's coffee bar brings a touch of European style to Lower Broadway.

whelmingly of Dijon mustard and not much else. Two of the store's homemade pâtés, the country-style *poulet*, or chicken pâté, and the smoked-salmon mousse, had me craving more as soon as I left the store.

The salads in the smoked-fish case are a pretty mediocre lot. The baba ghanouj and the hummous have too much garlic and not enough lemon juice. The roasted peppers have a slightly bitter aftertaste. The grilled mushrooms and the grilled eggplant are perfect summer sandwich materials. The new-potato salad is prepared with scallions, mustard, and mayonnaise, and it tastes rather ordinary. The rémoulade is crunchy and delicious, and the eggplant salad has a mellow tang. For some reason, D & D doesn't carry cole slaw.

Baked Goods ⁓ It's not a surprise that the cakes, cookies, and pies look better at Dean & DeLuca than anywhere else. What *is* somewhat surprising is that so many of them taste as good as they look. Head buyer Joanne Wynkoop (and her predecessor, Brigitte Weil) has assembled an extraordinary collection of the best baked goods available from bakeries and kitchens all over the New York area. From Faith's in Park Slope come irresistible cream-lime, chocolate-velvet, and mixed-fruit tarts, along with a coconut angel food cake that has no equal in New York. Scot Paris supplies a walnut cake with cappuccino icing, which has a terrific combination of flavors and textures, as well as cayenne ginger snaps with a real kick to them. Amy Burke provides barely sweetened poppy rounds and delicate thumbprint cookies that taste as good as they look. Products of other purveyors include The Little Pie Company's superior pies and Black Hound's ethereally light chocolate creations. Two notes about D & D's cakes: First, prices for cakes, pies, and cookies are extremely high here. Large versions of some of the better, richer cakes can cost almost forty dollars. Second, because they're all brought in from the outside, freshness can be a problem. You'll be more than annoyed if you pay twenty-five dollars for a stale cake, as I have in the past. So when you buy a cake here, ask when it arrived at the store. If the person you ask doesn't know, insist that he or she find someone who does.

Bread ⸺ This is hands down the best bread department in the city. Joanne Wynkoop (and her predecessor, Brigitte Weil) has assembled a collection of bread from all over the New York area, and everything tastes as good as it looks. You'll find breads from almost every star-quality New York baker represented here: Orwasher's pumpernickel-raisin bread; Tom Cat's baguettes and rolls; Companio's savory and sweet focaccias; Policastro's Italian rolls and baguettes; Old World Bread Company's pepperoni bread, rolls, and baguettes; Bread Alone's currant bread and rolls; Soutine's sourdough-cheddar rolls; and Rock Hill Bakehouse's sourdough boule. They also carry things I've not seen elsewhere, like an incredibly dense and flavorful green-pepper-and-onion focaccia from a Brooklyn bakery, Royal Crown.

Candy/Nuts/Dried Fruits ⸺ Committed candy lovers will be temptingly tormented at Dean & DeLuca's candy counter. It's not enough that the store carries Manon's celestial creations as well as chocolates made by a lesser-known but almost-as-good Belgian chocolatier, Bruyerre. No, they take their chocolates to another level by utilizing the artistry of Orstrud Carstens, a German-born woman who decided she'd rather make chocolates than be an architect. So now she tempts all of us with her creations made with Vahlrona chocolate she imports herself. Her milk cappuccino may keep you up for a few hours, but you'll be so pleased savoring the taste you won't mind. Besides ultrasophisticated, superexpensive chocolates, D & D carries a surprising amount of silly candy like raisinettes and gummi bears (note the exclusive D & D spelling). The dark-chocolate-covered pistachio nuts are a devilish treat you don't see much around the city. Surprisingly, the dried fruits and nuts section here is filled with generic items. You'll find the expected peanuts, hazelnuts, pistachios, and macadamia nuts—although it must be noted that the macadamias here come from Costa Rica rather than Hawaii. The dried mango and dried tangerine were the most intriguing items in the dried fruits category; otherwise, it's the usual golden raisins, apricots, figs, and the like. Also, anybody looking for glaced fruit should know that D & D carries glaced peaches.

Cheese and Dairy ⸺ Steven Jenkins (see page 65) is without question the most passionate and knowledgeable cheese purveyor in the city. He's opinionated, outspoken, and acerbic, but you'll notice that even when he's making his most cutting comments there's a hint of a twinkle in his eye. At Dean & DeLuca, he's constructed his best cheese department yet. His selection of the new high-quality American cheeses is unparalleled, and his Italian, French, Spanish, and Dutch cheese choices aren't far behind. Simply put, look for Steve Jenkins and you'll find the best cheese counter in the city.

Note: When you ask Steve Jenkins for suggestions, be aware that he likes assertively flavored, strong-tasting cheese. His cheese tastes are not for the timid.

D & D, like Zabar's, Grace's Marketplace, and Balducci's, has the Glensfoot Farm line of milk and cream products. My son is a devotee of Glensfoot Farm chocolate milk. The store also carries Hollow Road Farms' tangy sheep's-milk yogurt.

Coffee/Tea ⁓ Dean & DeLuca's bulk coffee section is small, but the twenty-two varieties you do find are impeccably fresh and are roasted by two high-quality roasters, Schapira's and First Colony. Try the intriguing and flavorful Yemen mocha. D & D also has the most extensive packaged coffee section I've seen in New York. I had never even seen or heard of Zimbabwean coffee before, but there it was on the shelf at Dean & DeLuca (I subsequently saw it in bulk at Oren's Daily Roast). You won't find any bulk or loose teas here, but there are plenty of unusual packaged teas such as Kousmichoff Russian and Mariage from Paris.

Condiments/Oils/Vinegars/Packaged Items ⁓ Joel Dean and Giorgio DeLuca are passionate about olive oil and have perhaps the most extensive collection in the city. Italian, French, Spanish—you name it, they have it. The same goes for flavored vinegars. You'll also find every jam, preserve, and barbecue sauce imaginable. Try the Asbell's South Carolina barbecue sauce, but be forewarned that it's absolutely incendiary. There are numerous varieties of flour, and for all the homesick northern Californians doing time in New York, they even carry Alice Waters's Cafe Fanny Granola. It's delicious but ridiculously expensive. Bean fans should note that D & D packages many kinds of unusual legumes—everything from fava beans to Maine yellow eyes. If you're looking for any kind of flour or pancake mix, chances are Dean & DeLuca has it. The last time I was here I counted fifty kinds of exotic flours, ranging from Lund's Swedish pancake mix to Indian chapati flour.

Deli Meats (Charcuterie) ⁓ D & D's charcuterie doesn't carry many meats, but those it does carry are excellent. Try the three New York State hams cut straight off the bone: the Woodland ham is salty, the Serrano ham has a sweet prosciutto-like quality, and the regular has a pleasant, meaty flavor. The *prosciutto di Parma* sold here actually has the Dean & DeLuca logo imprinted on it. I don't know what that means, but it is first-rate prosciutto. The store also carries the complete line of Molinari salamis from San Francisco; I'm partial to the toscano with its mellow flavor.

Espresso Bar ⁓ The espresso bar at Dean & DeLuca carries minisandwiches, muffins, Danish, and, of course, strong and bracing espresso, cappuccino, and regular and decaffeinated American coffee. The brownies, made by the former D & D baked-goods buyer Brigitte Weil, are richly satisfying. Most of the muffins are mediocre, with the exceptions of Cindy Klotz's celestial carrot and chocolate muffins. Both are topped with her cream-cheese icing. The croissants and Danish are serviceable, nothing more. The sandwiches at the espresso bar are tiny and overpriced. The country biscuit with ham that I tried had the world's mushiest, thickest biscuit.

In summer the espresso bar has gelati supplied by one of New York's premiere gelato makers, Ciao Bella (see page 177). As warm weather approaches, D & D makes tangy, not-too-sweet homemade lemonade and a refreshing cooler of orange juice, mint, and Driscoll strawberries.

Fish ⁓ Although the fish department here isn't up to the rest of the store, friends of mine who live in the neighborhood say it is the best source for fresh fish in the area. On my last visit, the whole-fish selections included clear-eyed bluefish, pompano, red snapper, and striped bass. There were also fresh clams, oysters, and mussels, which weren't identified by particular type. You'll find standard Manhattan fish-market selections such as tuna and swordfish steaks, mahi-mahi, and salmon, as well as less-common fish like baby coho salmon and rainbow trout. The lobsters in the tank here are particularly lively and feisty, always a good sign in live crustaceans.

Housewares ⁓ As you'd expect, almost all the housewares at Dean & DeLuca are beautiful, expensive, and imported. You'll find lots of white porcelain from France, hand-painted ceramic dinnerware from Italy, and their own line of copper cookware. Then there are the wonderful Sitram and Paderno lines of stainless-steel cookware from France and Italy, respectively. According to Fred Bridge, these two companies make the best stainless-steel cookware, and their price tags will certainly support that notion. The most downscale, common brand I've found here is Le Creuset, and that's hardly the people's cookware. Dean & DeLuca's housewares are for serious cooks only, and frankly most of those people know they can get the same quality down the street at Broadway Panhandler for much less.

Meat and Poultry ⁓ John Wasniewski, the meat buyer, doesn't wear an earring or skinny ties (nothing about the huge Wasniewski is skinny), but he really knows his meat. He carries what may be the broadest selection of sausages in the city. Last time I was here I counted twenty-six varieties from purveyors such as Salumeria Biellese, Bruce Aidell, and D'Artagnan. Try the duck sausage with Grand Marnier from Salumeria Biellese or the Italian sausage with tomato and cheese. As well as sausage, the store carries a full line of beef, lamb, and chicken. John also makes a superior marinade with olive oil, garlic, coriander, rosemary, and thyme that he uses on chicken breasts, lamb chops, and boneless leg of lamb. These marinated meats are perfect for weekend barbecuing. Those who swear by free-range birds should note that D & D carries D'Artagnan free-range, organically fed chickens and *poussins*.

Pasta/Sauces ⁓ Cheese man Steve Jenkins is also in charge of the pasta department at D & D, and although his noodle knowledge doesn't equal his cheese acumen, he still knows enough to assemble a first-rate selection. It's the only store I know in New York that carries the wondrous ravioli made by the Ravioli Store. You'll be able to tell which ones they are by their size (huge), their price (high), and their flavors (they're the only shrimp, jalapeño-pepper, and grilled-corn ravioli in the store). The other intriguing pasta I've found here and nowhere else is papadini, a dry Indian pasta made with lentils and flavored with cilantro. You'll also find a full line of fresh and dry pastas.

The imported Crespi Grand Pesto is so pungent and strong that the store recommends diluting it, and rightfully so. The bolognese sauce has a pleasant tang, as does the marinara sauce. The yellow tomato sauce is eminently skippable.

Prepared Foods — Over the years I have found much of Dean & DeLuca's prepared food to be timidly seasoned and overly fussy. But on my last few visits I have been impressed by most of the food sampled here. The kitchen appears to have made the wise decision to go for less elaborate, more peasant-oriented dishes. Try the papadini with tomato, cilantro, and parmesan cheese or the French navy beans with mild Italian sausage. Every take-out kitchen in New York has a grilled chicken dish, but the one made here with wild mushrooms, peas, and pearl onions is my personal favorite. They even manage to pull off an unusual dish like roasted barley and smoked trout. Only the chicken salsina, which needed another flavor to complement the puree of sun-dried tomatoes it came in, and the dullish cavatappi with radicchio, arugula, and smoked bacon, disappointed me.

Produce — Produce has always played a substantial role in D & D's business, and even in the new huge space it is still the highest-grossing department in the store. Under Michael McGovern, the produce department has become a bona fide user-friendly, customer-oriented place. The fruits, vegetables, and herbs still look terrific; they've just been made more approachable. Only Dean & DeLuca could make me talk about lettuce the way we used to talk about girls in high school. You'll find at least ten kinds of fresh mushrooms in the store at any one time. The last time I visited, I sampled an unusual and delicious wine-cap mushroom. There's a separate lettuce case where you'll find everything from Italian frisée to Baby Lolla Rosa to edible flowers. At the fresh-chilies section there's a sign explaining that chili growers measure hotness in Scoville Units, ranging from 200,000 units on down. The last time I was at the store they were selling 200,000-Scoville-unit Habanero chilies that could literally burn a hole in your pocket. I've also found D & D to be the best source for wonderful and unusual varieties of fruits. Last summer I found the most wonderful-tasting Babcock peach there, which had luscious reddish-pink flesh.

Sandwiches — The sandwich bar at D & D is nothing special. Conventional designer fillings such as ham, fresh mozzarella, spinach, basil, and roasted peppers are done in by the mediocre Voilà baguettes on which they're placed. The grilled eggplant with roasted red peppers, mozzarella, and fresh basil is a rewarding combination, however. For some reason D & D also sells mushy, dull-tasting wursts and frankfurters steamed in beer. Not even the store's own honey mustard can save these sausages. The soups sold in concert with the sandwiches range from a mellow and satisfying white bean to an underseasoned Manhattan Clam Chowder that tastes like a bad pasta sauce.

Best Times to Shop — Dean & DeLuca has a large neighborhood following that stops in after work. So like most of the other mega-stores, you'll do best going before five on weekdays. Saturdays and Sundays you're on your own, but even when the store is very crowded, the wide aisles and high ceilings make it feel far less claustrophobic than Zabar's, Balducci's, or Fairway.

Dean & DeLuca
560 Broadway (corner of Prince Street)
New York, NY 10012
PHONE: (212) 431-1691
SUBWAYS: Broadway–Lafayette Street station on the Sixth Avenue B, D, F,
     and Q lines; Bleecker Street station on the Lexington Avenue No. 6 line;
     Prince Street station on the Broadway R line.
HOURS: 9 A.M. to 7 P.M. seven days a week.
No deliveries.
All major credit cards accepted.
Catering and picnic baskets available.

FAIRWAY: THE PEOPLE'S MEGA-STORE

I have a soft spot in my heart for Fairway. It's my neighborhood mega-store, one I have frequented a hundred times a year for the last fifteen years. To say I know it intimately doesn't even begin to tell the story. Store clerks in Fairway refer customers to me when they can't answer a question. So I am biased on the subject of mega-stores in the city: Fairway is my favorite. I say that not because of its produce, which is beyond reproach, or its service, which is most assuredly not. No, Fairway is my favorite because of its utter lack of pretense.

Ever since it opened in 1975, Fairway has been a vibrant, raucous, neighborhood joint where anarchy reigns. Regular shoppers know that Fairway on weekends is not for the timid. They must be prepared for fending off shopping carts coming at them like bumper cars gone amok, for protecting their turf from West Side senior citizens who know exactly which comice pear they want, and for standing on so many lines they think they've been transported to the Soviet Union. Fairway shoppers adopt an almost cheerful, Zen-like demeanor to deal with all this craziness. They have to, or they themselves would go crazy. In fact, some people do. My wife, for one, refuses to go into Fairway on a weekend.

Although I love the place, service can be a problem at Fairway. The checkout lines, for example, can be intimidating for the uninitiated. Also, other than store manager David Grotenstein, deli manager Adrianna Arvelo, and a couple of cheese-counter clerks, it's hard to find Fairway employees knowledgeable and passionate about the food they sell. If you do ever run into trouble here, David G. (as he's known in the store) is the man to turn to. But, in general, it's best to know what you want and what it looks like before venturing into Fairway.

Appetizers/Smoked Fish/Salads — Tucked between the bread counter and the gourmet take-out section, the smoked fish counter at Fairway has a pretty standard array of smoked fish preparations. It's clear that nobody is really focusing on smoked fish at Fairway, because if someone were paying attention they'd spruce it up a bit. I did find perhaps my favorite smoked salmon here, the delightfully smoky Icelandic variety. They also have Gaspé, regular Western Nova, Scotch, and Norwegian salmon here, along with smoked tuna, bluefish, sable, whitefish, and the like. They do carry the intriguing Homerus pastrami salmon, which has a peppery, garlicky black crust. Although it's not one of the featured counters at

Fairway: Like no other market.

the store, the turnover in the smoked fish department is fast enough to ensure freshness.

Salads have been a problem at Fairway for as long as I can remember, but there have recently been some encouraging signs. The Mardi Gras coleslaw, made with red and white cabbage, is fresh and tangy. The homemade potato salad made with lots of mayonnaise, eggs, and onion, makes a wonderful picnic-basket stuffer. The regular coleslaw and potato salad are the same fare you get all over town. I have yet to detect any blue cheese in the blue-cheese–new potato salad.

Baked Goods ∿ Surprisingly, desserts are not one of Fairway's strong points. The chocolate-chip and oatmeal cookies baked on the premises are fresh and moist, but there's nothing particularly special about them except that they're significantly cheaper than Mrs. Field's. The Danish and sticky buns, from Suzy's Bake Shop in Flushing, are boring and too sweet. The pound cakes from the Connecticut Muffin Company are okay, but I wish they were more vividly flavored. Grogan's marble pound cake, on the other hand, is as good a pound cake as I've had on the West Side. The small cookies—Florentines and the like—are very standard. The Umanoff & Parsons crumb pies are good, filled with fresh fruit and topped by a first-rate streusel topping. The other Umanoff & Parsons pies have a heavy, nonflaky crust. Chocoholics will be comforted at Fairway only by the David Glass chocolate cakes in the freezer case.

Bread ∿ The bread counter is sensational at Fairway. The bagels are from H & H and sell for a third the price as at H & H's own store; and even if they're not hot, they're still fresh. You can buy bread from such first-rate suppliers as D & G,

Zito's, Spiekermann's, and Eli's. Try the rolls or baguettes from Old World Bread Company. They also carry wondrous garlic knots, Eli's raisin-nut rolls, and terrific rosemary-laced focaccia from Central Bakery in Jersey City. The muffin selection is pretty standard, though the minimuffins baked on the premises are a wonderful alternative to the six-ounce monsters, especially for little kids.

Candy/Nuts/Dried Fruit — Chocolate lovers should check out the Cailler chocolate bars. I think they're superior to Lindt (which Fairway also carries), and cheaper besides. The Fairway bars are small and pricey, but they do taste like the world's greatest chunky. If you're looking for a box of chocolates to bring as a house gift, Fairway sells decent Lindt truffles for $7.98 per pound. Surprisingly, you'll also find a selection of bulk penny candies that are perfect, inexpensive treats for children. Lastly, the store carries Callebaut chocolate, the cooking chocolate of choice among experienced dessert makers.

Nuts and dried fruits, sold next to the coffee bins, are one of Fairway's strengths. Try the Monukah raisins or the dried jumbo peaches or pears. At the cheese counter you'll find irresistible dried cherries and cranberries. The almond-raisin granola from the Bread Shop is a favored breakfast at our house. Nuts like cashews and almonds are invariably fresh at Fairway, the result of the store's rapid turnover.

Cheese and Dairy — Steven Jenkins (see page 65) made the Fairway cheese department one of the best in the city when he worked there in the mid 1980s. Though it's still excellent, there does seem to be more precut cheese now. Also, with the exception of the new Steve Jenkins, David Grotenstein, the cheese-counter folks at Fairway don't seem terribly knowledgeable, or forthcoming with what information they might have. Those caveats aside, Fairway still is a cheese-lover's paradise. Try the Neal's Yard line of cheeses from England, especially the farmhouse cheddar, or buy a ripe, runny, smelly piece of Taleggio, one of the world's most satisfying cheeses. Fairway is also a fine source for all the great new crop of American cheeses. Try the earthy, tangy Laura Chenel goat cheeses from California, or the fresh *chèvre* from Goat Folks in New York State. The latter is my wife's goat cheese of choice, which she uses like cream cheese. You'll also find Ben's amazing cream cheese at the cheese counter. Fairway also carries a full line of low-fat cheeses, including goat cheeses from Coach that actually have flavor and texture. In the dairy case you'll find things like kefir, a yogurt drink, and first-rate Hollow Road Farms sheep's-milk yogurt.

Coffee/Tea — Fairway's coffee counter is supplied by Gillies 1840, one of the city's leading coffee roasters. Turnover, while nowhere near Zabar's, is good enough to ensure freshness. The store carries thirty-eight kinds of regular and decaffeinated coffees, including delicious and hard-to-find Lavazza Bar Espresso. No loose teas are sold here, only the celestial Seasonings and Twinings packaged varieties.

Condiments/Oils/Vinegars/Prepared Foods — Fairway carries a wide range of Italian olive oils and flavored vinegars. The Da Raccolto olive oil from Umbria is excellent and a very good buy. Try the Olio Trevi, a light, fragrant, fruity extra-virgin olive oil. The Da Raccolto from Bari is no better than Colavita or any other inexpensive olive oil. Fairway also carries the terrific homemade Krutons, which are so good I munch them like potato chips. By the Raffetto pasta you'll find Tomato Plus and Garlic Plus, sauces that are fine all-purpose condiments for use on meat or pasta.

Deli Meats (Charcuterie) ～ Don't let Fairway's inelegant deli-meat presentation fool you. This is one serious charcuterie counter. It has the city's largest selection of sausages from Bruce Aidell, whose duck sausage will put you in summer grilling heaven. Aidell's smoked duck-and-turkey sausage is a real treat, and his smoked chicken-and-apple creation makes an excellent breakfast sausage. Fairway also carries excellent nitrite-free smoked meats from Nodine's and Jugtown Mountain Smoke House. They carry half a dozen kinds of prosciutto, from domestic Volpi to the satiny, sweet *prosciutto di Parma* from the town of Langhorina, Italy. The Fairway baked ham is excellent, but their herb-roasted turkey is dry and the homemade roast beef doesn't have much flavor. You'll also find the usual array of Hansel and Gretel, Boar's Head, and Schaller and Weber products.

Pasta/Sauces ～ There are two Fairway pasta sections, one next to the dairy case to the far left as you walk into the store, the other by the cheese department. Why the pasta and sauces are in two different places is a mystery to me, because it doesn't make much sense. Near the cheese department you'll find various tortellini imported from Italy. Try the sweetish pumpkin, the tangy Gorgonzola, or the earthy porcini-mushroom-filled ones. You'll also find good, if not great, spinach and potato gnocchi. The cheese department itself carries an excellent pesto made under Fairway's own Da Raccolto brand in Italy. The pasta case on the far left features Raffetto's products. Try the garlic-and-parsley fettucine, or the excellent meat, cheese, or spinach ravioli, or the manicotti. The sauces are mostly Contadina (formerly Pasta and Cheese), and they're surprisingly good. The Forestiera sauce, made with prosciutto and zucchini, is a particular Levine family favorite. They also carry an excellent Tutta Pasta sauce, Salsa Forte. Finally, Fairway arranged a marriage between Riviera Pasta and Coach Goat Cheese that has produced a goatcheese and sun-dried tomato ravioli that's already taken its place in my ravioli pantheon.

Prepared Foods ～ The prepared foods department is probably Fairway's weakest. The soups are okay, nothing more, and they're all underseasoned with the exception of the creditable gazpacho. The vegetarian lasagna is appropriately tangy and cheesy, the sesame noodles are nothing special, and the chicken antignano, prepared with basil, tomato sauce, and Parmesan cheese, tastes like airline food. You'll do best sticking to simple preparations such as the meat loaf and the meatballs. The sesame chicken is mostly wings, and the turkey Marsala is an ill-conceived attempt at healthful cooking.

Produce ～ Unlike Balducci's, Fairway has remained true to its produce-store roots and kept the majority (approximately 60 percent) of its shelf space and square footage devoted to fruits, vegetables, and fresh herbs, all sold at very fair prices. Fairway carries everything from mundane iceberg lettuce and tasteless Florida winter tomatoes to Royal Gala apples from New Zealand and baby mâche lettuce. Humming away in one aisle or another is every fresh herb imaginable, from chervil to cilantro. Latin American food devotees know that Fairway is a great place to shop for yucca roots, plaintains, and fresh and dried peppers. Fairway is mecca for mushroom lovers, carrying half a dozen varieties at any one time, including cremini, shitake and portobello. The mushroom prices are lower here than at other comparable stores in the city.

Note: The produce sold outside the store is different from that sold inside. The oranges are smaller, the pineapples are from Puerto Rico or Costa Rica instead of Hawaii, and the pears are less ripe. So although prices are lower for these items, so is the quality. Some items, such as the grapes, berries, and mangoes, are available only outside. Don't bother trying to cheat Fairway by telling your checkout person the oranges you picked up inside the store were actually gotten outside. First, it's a sleazy thing to do. Second, the checkout people at Fairway don't miss a trick, and you could end up in produce prison.

Best Time to Shop — As you might expect, the best time to shop at Fairway is weekdays from 9:00 to 4:00. Get there any earlier in the morning, and you'll find that half of the checkout lines haven't opened yet. Weekday evenings from 7:30 to midnight are also very good times to shop at Fairway. On Saturdays and Sundays, the only window of opportunity is from 8:00 to 9:00 A.M., or after 8:00 P.M. Otherwise you just have to throw yourself into the fray.

Fairway
2127 Broadway (between 74th and 75th streets)
New York, NY 10023
PHONE: (212) 595-1888
SUBWAYS: 72nd Street station on the following lines: Broadway–Seventh
   Avenue No. 1, 2, 3, and 9; Eighth Avenue C and Sixth Avenue B.
HOURS: 7 A.M. to midnight, seven days a week.
No deliveries.
Cash only.

GRACE'S MARKETPLACE: A STORE OF SURPRISES

I expected to write a scathing entry for Grace's Marketplace. My few visits prior to starting the research for this book had left me with the distinct impression the store was overpriced, poorly laid out, and staffed by rude people who didn't know anything about what they were selling. But after repeated trips to check out every department, I can report that Grace's is a first-rate store worthy of mention along with Balducci's, Zabar's, and Fairway.

The only initial impression that stuck with me was the poor layout. Even when the store was not crowded I found myself bumping into the two other people shopping there at the time. There's no attempt made at controlling the flow of traffic between the various departments. As you enter, you're confronted by the bread department. Directly to the left of the entrance are the sweets, cookies, cakes, pies, and chocolate. On the far left is the produce and on the far right the cheese and appetizing departments. Crammed into the back are the dairy, coffee, and pasta departments. So although you don't get the old ladies of Fairway fighting

The sprawling Grace's Marketplace on New York's Upper East Side.

you for pears, you do often find yourself tangled up with an East Side matron trying to get to the produce department from the bread area.

The price of the prepared food is very high, but certainly no more so than at Dean & Deluca; and compared to Eli Zabar's E.A.T., it's a bargain. I found the staff to be reasonably helpful and polite, with some departments better than others.

Appetizers/Smoked Fish/Salads ⁓ Grace's carries seven different kinds of smoked salmon, including Balik, a Grace's exclusive that's a very delicately smoked Scotch salmon priced at a mere $72 a pound. I'm a fairly discerning smoked-salmon eater, and although I thought it was very good salmon, I wouldn't pay that price for anything short of diamond-studded Nova. It also carries a deliciously different barbecued salmon and a wide assortment of domestic smoked fish such as trout and bluefish. There is an excellent selection of pâtés from the likes of D'Artagnan, Petrossian, and Les Trois Petits Cochons. Grace's also carries the widest selection of truffle and truffle products in the city. You'll find fresh Italian black truffles in season (astronomically priced, of course), canned truffles, rabbit terrine with truffles, and truffle oils, which are the the most cost-effective way of flavoring your pasta with truffle.

Grace's homemade cole slaw and potato salad both need a shake of salt to come to life. The shrimp salad thankfully is made with very little mayonnaise, and the marinated mushrooms would spruce up any cold antipasto plate.

Baked Goods ⁓ Although Grace's doesn't make any of its own baked goods, it does get deliveries thrice weekly (Tuesday, Thursday, and Saturday) from some of the city's best bakeries. Like all the other mega-stores that use this system (Dean & DeLuca, Zabar's, Balducci's) this means that on occasion you will be purchasing a less-than-fresh cake at a very steep price. Even when you ask when a particular pie or cake arrived at the store, you don't get a straight answer. "Everything's fresh" is the stock response. Would that it were so. That said,

Grace's carries first-rate pies from The Little Pie Company, superior Mitchell London cheesecake, and extraordinary rugelach from Erica's. Also, ask at the counter what they're carrying from Yura. She's one of the city's great unsung bakers.

Bread ~~ Grace's bread department is first-rate. The house-made foccacia is excellent. The rest of the breads are supplied by many of the best bread bakers in the tristate area. You'll find baguettes, raisin-nut rolls, and pepper brioches from Eli's; terrific sausage bread from New Jersey's Old World Bread Company; and amazing cheddar rolls from Soutine. There's also rye bread and raisin pumpernickel from Orwasher's, semolina baguettes from Morrone's, and Swiss peasant bread from Joe Speikerman. Grace's also carries an eggy Italian breakfast muffin filled with apples, cherries, blueberries, or apricots and called a Pandorino, which I've not seen elsewhere in the city.

Candy/Nuts/Dried Fruit ~~ Grace's carries Neuhaus chocolates. Try the Soprano, made with coffee-flavored fresh cream, or the Tentation, toffee filled with coffee and fresh cream. The store also carries the oversized Champlain truffles made in Vermont. Schwartz chocolate-covered marshmallows are the Rolls Royce of that prosaic candy, and Grace's is the only shop I know of in New York that sells them.

The dried fruit selection is fairly extensive. Try the delicious dried mango, which doesn't even need its sugar coating. The nut selection is quite large; I found some delicious cinnamon almonds that had me wishing I'd bought more.

Cheese and Dairy ~~ Grace's cheese counter is fairly small but carries more than one hundred kinds of cheese at any given time. Italian and French varieties are the specialty, and I've found the counterpeople more knowledgeable than at most of the other mega-stores. One day I was buying cheeses for a dinner party, and a staff member steered me toward four superb cheeses: a Fontina Val D'Aosta that bore no resemblance to conventional Fontina cheese; a perfectly ripe Reblochon; a Vacherin-style French cheese called a Clerol de Cleron that was wrapped in birch leaves; and a wonderful Italian sheep cheese, Rosselino Pienza Pecorino. Every Wednesday the store gets a shipment of Italian buffalo mozzarella, a worthwhile indulgence for any food lover. The store also carries two kinds of freshly made sheep's-milk yogurt: Hollow Road Farms and Vermont. Grace's also carries Glensfoot Farm milk, delivered every Tuesday and Friday. It's both pasteurized and homogenized, and I'm not sure it tastes any better than the milk you buy in a supermarket, but I buy it because it comes in a nondescript plastic bottle with a black-and-white label. Gelati devotees should note that Grace's carries Ciao Bella's sensational ice cream (see page 177).

Coffee/Tea ~~ Grace's coffee department carries more than forty coffees roasted by White House, one of the standard coffee roasters in the city. Try the mellow house blend. No loose teas are sold here, only the fairly standard Grace's, Bigelow, Wagner, and Celestial Seasonings varieties.

Condiments/Oils/Vinegars/Packaged Items ~~ You'll discover more than thirty varieties of olive oil at Grace's. Try the organically grown, delicately flavored

Lerida brand from Spain, or the slightly nutty-tasting French olive oil, Louis de Regis. The Rothschild Estate blueberry vinegar makes a delicious vinaigrette. To its credit, Grace's also carries Sarabeth's fabulous preserves and the Silver Palate line of outrageously rich dessert sauces.

Deli Meats (Salumeria) — Grace's sells a wide assortment of deli meats and sausages, again from the best suppliers around the city, country, and world. It carries a wonderful array of sausages, everything from conventional Italian sweet sausage from the Calabria Pork Store on Arthur Avenue in the Bronx to porcini-mushroom sausage made by Salumeria Biellese. Grace's also carries five kinds of fresh and smoked turkey, including delicious apple-smoked and honey-cured varieties. It has a broad selection of Schaller and Weber meats, such as smoked veal, as well as domestic and imported Italian hams and salamis. Try the sweet but not cloying maple-cured ham.

Pastas/Sauces — Grace's carries a wide selection of fresh and dried pastas and ready-to-heat sauces. Besides standard brands like DeCecco, it also carries the dried imported Cipriani pasta made by the family that owns the famed Harry's Bar in Venice. It's a wonderful light and flavorful pasta, but I'm not sure any pasta is worth $8 per half pound. The fresh pastas, made by Durso and Pastosa, include whole-wheat, spinach, egg, and tomato noodles of various thicknesses. Near the make-your-own salad bar you'll find agnolotti, or half-moon-shaped pasta, stuffed with either olives, porcini mushrooms, or Mascarpone cheese and salmon. On the sauce front, stick to the basic tomato, marinara, and meat sauces, and you'll do fine. The tomato sauce in particular is probably the best ready-to-heat tomato sauce I've had in New York. The non-tomato-based sauces like pesto and Alfredo are bland and uninspired.

Prepared Foods — On any given day Grace's offers more than a hundred different dishes in its prepared-foods department. Most have a distinctly Italian accent, which makes sense given Grace Balducci's southern Italian heritage. It's best, then, to stick with Grace's simple, peasant-type foods. The pasta with cauliflower sauteed in red onions is extraordinary: The cauliflower is crunchy, the shell pasta firm. The rigatoni with *ricotta salata* and tomatoes had firm, flavorful tomatoes even in the middle of winter.

Simple pastas with tomato sauce or white clam sauce are extremely well-prepared. More than ten grilled or baked fish entrées are put out every day, and although I thought most of the preparations were dull and underseasoned, the fish was impeccably fresh. Another low-cal alternative, a spa salad made with elbow macaroni, chicken, scallions, and snow peas, was good for that kind of thing, although I did miss a hit of olive oil. Meat was an iffier proposition. Calves liver with bacon and onions was delicious, but the chicken *sacchetto*, a whole chicken breast stuffed with spinach and cheese, tasted like airline food, and the pot roast was tasty but dry. Smoked chicken with honey-mustard sauce was flavorful but oversmoked. This was the only department in which my previously held opinion about rude, uninformed sales help turned out to be true.

Produce — Rusty, Grace's son-in-law and the manager of the store, says produce is the store's cornerstone. On a cold February day, I found five different kinds of mushrooms (white portabello, enoki, cremini, shitake, and oyster mushrooms) and five kinds of designer lettuce (radicchio, mâche, lolarosa, mesclun, and frisée). I also found things I haven't seen many other places in the city, like Italian bitter onions called *campascioni*. On the fruit side, I found Italian blood oranges that were absolutely delicious. There's also plenty of conventional produce at Grace's, all very carefully picked. One affirmation of the quality of the produce here is that Le Cirque buys a lot of its produce from Grace's. Prices here are higher than at Fairway and lower than at Dean & DeLuca.

Best Times to Shop ∼ Grace's always seems crowded to me because of the way it's laid out. Weekends are a zoo, but Grace's has a personal-shopper service that allows you to call in an order and have it delivered. Weekday mornings seem relatively peaceful, but come 4:00 P.M., gridlock sets in and lasts through the evening rush.

Grace's Marketplace
1237 Third Avenue (between 71st and 72nd streets)
New York, NY 10021
PHONE: (212) 737-0600
SUBWAY: 68th Street–Hunter College station on the Lexington Avenue No. 6
    line.
HOURS: 7 A.M. to 8:30 P.M. Monday through Saturday; 8 A.M. to 7 P.M.
    Sunday.
Deliveries made throughout Manhattan.
All major credit cards accepted.
Catering and picnic baskets available.
Mail-order catalog available.

MACY'S CELLAR MARKETPLACE:
THE NOT-SO-LITTLE MEGA-STORE
THAT COULD

I don't know why, but nobody takes Macy's Cellar seriously. Ask committed food lovers about Macy's, and they'll say, "Oh, yeah, it's a good place," in a voice that tells you it's a store they'd visit only if caught in a violent thunderstorm stepping out of Penn Station. Maybe it's because the store is associated with Kris Kringle in *Miracle on 34th Street* instead of with Paul Prudhomme and the late James Beard. Maybe it's because it's Macy's, the clothing store, or because it's in the basement, and the lack of natural light casts a pall over the food.

It's true that the food looks a lot better in Dean & DeLuca, with the light pouring in, but Balducci's with its low ceilings and crowded aisles doesn't exactly have an airy feel. Anyway, we're talking about cheese and Nova and croissants here, not ficus plants or diefenbachia or mums. I guess the real reason is there's nothing alluring about Macy's in general or the Cellar in particular; there's no cachet associated with shopping at the store.

There may not be anything sexy about shopping at the Cellar Marketplace, but I can tell you there's a heckuva lot of good food down there. It has a remarkably comprehensive cheese section, an excellent smoked-fish counter, a charcuterie/

deli section I would put in a league with just about anybody's, and a caviar case supplied by Iron Gate that wages yearly battle with Zabar's in the famed holiday price war in which both stores and their customers win.

Almost two years ago Macy's Cellar Marketplace attempted to increase its visibility and stature by bringing in noted southern chef and cookbook author Gene Hovis to be the creative director of the marketplace. I'm not sure what a creative director at a food shop does, but I can tell you the man knows how to cook. His pies, lemon pound cake, hams, fried chicken, chicken salad, and macaroni and cheese are all top-quality efforts.

There are other knowledgeable and colorful characters populating the Cellar Marketplace. At the smoked-fish counter there's Jim White, a soft-spoken, dignified man with the hands of a surgeon. At the deli/charcuterie counter there's Anthony Atillio, who really knows his stuff. The last time I was in the store, I learned more than I ever wanted to know about the prosciutto business in Parma, Italy.

Granted, there are some shaky departments at the Cellar Marketplace. Why a food store this good would lease its baked goods section to a truly mediocre New York bakery, Eclair, is beyond me. The same goes for using a mediocre croissant and Danish maker, Vie de France. Ten years ago Vie de France may have seemed like an attractive vendor, but today I can think of at least ten better croissant makers in the city.

Despite these lapses, the Cellar is a top-ranking New York mega-store. So go to Macy's Cellar Marketplace, the gourmet store for the average Joe, and enjoy —or Ze Gezundt, as my grandmother used to say in Yiddish. And if it will make you feel any better, just bring a Dean & DeLuca shopping bag to carry your purchases. I promise you nobody will know the difference.

Appetizers/Smoked Fish/Salads ~ Macy's has a competitive selection of smoked fish at very reasonable prices. It's the only store I've seen in New York that carries both cold- and hot-smoked tuna. Usually hot-smoked tuna is dry and leatherlike, but the version I tasted here was moist and flavorful. The cold-smoked tuna was excellent too, with the satiny, delicate texture of a good smoked salmon. The store also carries New Generation's wonderful and exotic smoked fish preparations. Try the smoked scallops in garlic and olive oil, or the strong-tasting smoked mussels. Macy's selection of smoked salmons is also extraordinary. The hot-smoked Norwegian salmon was so buttery I wanted to spread it, and the peppered Norwegian salmon had the lusty taste of pastrami. Macy's caviar case is supplied by Iron Gate, probably the best-known high-quality caviar importer in the city. Every year at Christmas, Macy's engages in a high-spirited caviar price war with Zabar's, which may be the first war in which there are truly no losers.

Baked Goods ~ The baked goods at Macy's can be easily divided into two categories. There are the Gene Hovis baked goods, which are simply extraordinary. Try his lemon pound cake, and you'll never be able to eat Sara Lee again. His apple pies, available only at Thanksgiving, are piled high with fresh apple slices, and his sweet-potato pie is redolent of cinnamon and vanilla. The other category of baked goods are in concessions, one leased by Eclair, a truly mediocre New York bakery; one leased by Mrs. Field's cookies (ho-hum); and a third leased by T. J. Cinnamon's, which happens to make the most wonderful, goopy, messy cinnamon buns around. I know T. J. Cinnamon's is a chain and I'm not supposed to like them, but I just can't resist. They're that good.

Bread ~ The bread department at Macy's is supplied by Featherstone, a bread wholesaler used by many of the city's best restaurants. Though Featherstone carries dozens of varieties, he supplies Macy's with breads from only a few sources, notably Rock Hill and Eli's. Eli's breads and rolls are, of course, wonderful. His raisin-nut rolls have single-handedly filled me up at many restaurants around the city. Rock Hill makes high-quality, country-style sourdough and regular breads. Try any of its Italian-style breads. Macy's croissants are supplied by Vie de France, a mediocre French baker that seemed okay when it was one of the only croissant makers in New York.

Candy/Nuts/Dried Fruit ~ Candy is one of the highlights at Macy's. Neuhaus has a counter here, as does Godiva. Neuhaus's *truffe café*, or butter-cream coffee, is one of my favorite chocolates in the city. Its Mousmé, enrobed chopped nuts and toffee, is not far behind. Godiva chocolates are simply not very good, and with Neuhaus around, who needs them. Macy's also carries Joseph Schmidt's oversized chocolates from California. They're excellent, although one will easily fill you up. Macy's has a sugar-free candy counter, and although I'm not a fan of sugar-free anything, it's good to know about anyway. The bulk candy counter is huge, filled with things like raisinets, M&Ms, peanut brittle, nuts, and jelly beans. And if that's not enough, there's a concession just outside the Cellar called Candy & Company that allows you to fill your own bag with penny candy of every variety. I brought a bag of their jelly sours to a meeting, and all the participants were puckering their lips from the tartness.

Cheese and Dairy ~ In its own quiet way Macy's has put together one of the best cheese departments in the city. If it lacks the panache of the Dean & DeLuca cheese department, it's just because there's no dominant personality involved. Wisely, Macy's divides its cheese cases by country of origin. Last time I was there I tried a terrific Alsatian goat cheese, called Banon, which is wrapped in chestnut leaves and then coated with cumin, curry, herbs, or pepper. I also tried an extraordinary Italian cheese, a Taleggio-like Bartella that you'll be able to smell a mile away. Like many of the mega-stores Macy's did seem to be a little light on the new American cheeses.

Coffee/Tea ~ First Colony supplies Macy's with seventy-two kinds of fresh-roasted coffee beans. In addition to the traditional South and Central American and African coffees, you'll find lots of the gimmicky flavored coffees, including chocolate-raspberry-truffle and chocolate-cinnamon. Recently the store added First Colony's line of dark coffees, in which the beans have been roasted a bit longer. Try the Greenwich Village blend, a pleasant combination of espresso and regular beans. Macy's also carries a wide variety of herbal, fruit, and English teas.

Condiments/Oils/Vinegars/Packaged Items ~ Although it is haphazardly organized, Macy's packaged-goods section features more varieties of crackers, condiments, and sauces than I've seen anywhere else. There are also preserves from high-quality purveyors like Sarabeth's Kitchen and Tiptree, along with the requisite olive oils and flavored vinegars.

Deli Meats (Charcuterie) ⸺ Don't tell anybody, but this is another absolutely first-rate department at Macy's. Start with three hams prepared by Gene Hovis and carved off the bone. The bourbon-baked ham is mellow and sweet and makes great sandwiches. His Arkansas peppered ham has a potent kick to it, and the Virginia red-eye ham has that salty, almost dry quality that lets you know its inspiration was the classic Smithfield hams. You'll also find a broad selection of meats by Schaller and Weber, Boar's Head, and Hebrew National. Try the Bunderfleisch, a dry-cured prosciutto-like meat from Germany, which, sliced thinly, makes an elegant appetizer. The store also has a comprehensive selection of pâtés from three superb pâté manufacturers: D'Artagnan, Michel's Magnifique, and Summer Sweet. You can't go wrong with either the spinach-and-smoked-salmon mousse from Summer Sweet or D'Artagnan's quail terrine with foie gras.

Fish ⸺ Macy's fish department is actually leased by Ottomanelli's. Although Ottomanelli's is better known for its butcher shops, the fish did appear to be fresh (and the basement lighting certainly didn't show it off to its best advantage). Selection is limited to fifteen varieties; the last time I visited, they included salmon, tuna, swordfish, and cooked crayfish.

Meat and Poultry ⸺ The meat department at Macy's is an Ottomanelli's outlet. That means you'll find first-rate beef, chicken, lamb, and pork along with a full line of game (fresh in season, frozen the rest of the year). Try the meaty smoked pork chops or the well-seasoned Italian sausage. The prepared meats, such as the rotisseried chickens and the spare ribs, looked kind of scrawny. Behind the meats you'll find Ottomanelli's line of prepared foods. These include chicken pot pie, frozen hamburger patties, and Italian dishes including lasagna and manicotti.

Pasta/Sauces ⸺ Macy's is the only store in Manhattan that carries Morisi pasta (see page 250). Although it would be impossible for any store to carry all 250 varieties, Macy's does carry a broad cross-section including the bizarre fruit pastas, which make a zippy summer salad with fresh fruit and yogurt. Macy's also makes its own pasta in egg, spinach, tomato-and-garlic, and herb flavors. Its tortellini are the excellent Bertagni line (also carried at Fairway and Zabar's) imported from Italy. If your taste runs to simple dried pasta, Macy's carries the ubiquitous but nonetheless excellent DeCecco brand from Italy.

Prepared Foods ⸺ Gene Hovis, a southern chef and a cookbook author, came to Macy's in 1990 to lend some much-needed pizzazz to Macy's Cellar. Though there are other prepared foods to be had at Macy's, his signature dishes are clearly the stars of the show. His savory meatloaf has a terrific, crunchy glaze, his regular and cheddar buttermilk biscuits are addictive, and his macaroni and cheese is a one-dish cholesterol binge. His Maryland crab cakes are lightly spiced and delicious, although heating them in a microwave doesn't do them much good. His buttermilk fried chicken was certainly crisp and greaseless, but bought cold it was kind of dry. The non–Gene Hovis foods, like the grilled vegetables, were competently prepared, but didn't have the oomph of the Hovis dishes.

Best Hours to Shop/Miscellaneous Information ⁓ Weekday mornings before eleven and then after the lunchtime crowd leaves at two are the best times to shop at Macy's Cellar. Weekends are of course fairly crowded, and on preholiday shopping days it's a madhouse. One terrific aspect of the Cellar is its proximity to Macy's kitchenware section. It's great to be able to shop for food and for pots and pans in the same place. Macy's has a frozen-yogurt-and-ice-cream concession in the Cellar. The frozen yogurt was standard Columbo, and the ice cream is an okay, no better, brand of gelato, Grangelato. The gelati are not strongly flavored the way great gelati should be. Only the lemon was to my liking, and even that was a tad too sweet.

Macy's Cellar Marketplace
151 West 34th Street at Herald Square (the entire block between Broadway
    and Seventh Avenue)
New York, NY 10001
PHONE: (212) 736-5151
SUBWAYS: 34th Street station on the Sixth Avenue B, D, F, and Q and the
    Broadway N and R lines; 34th Street–Penn Station on the Broadway–
    Seventh Avenue No. 1, 2, 3, and 9 and the Eighth Avenue A, C, and E
    lines.
HOURS: 9:45 A.M. to 8:30 P.M. Monday, Thursday, and Friday; 9:45 A.M. to
    6:45 P.M. Tuesday, Wednesday, and Saturday; 10 A.M. to 6 P.M. Sunday.
Deliveries available.
All major credit cards accepted.
Mail order available by calling 1 (800) 446-2297.

TODARO BROTHERS: AN ITALIAN, NEIGHBORHOOD KIND OF PLACE

When you walk into Todaro Brothers, the first thing you notice is that it feels and sounds like a neighborhood Italian grocery store. One customer is complaining that his wife will be angry because the store hasn't stocked pocket-sized pita breads for a week. Counterpeople are bantering among themselves, and the store's regulars are shopping for staples like milk and bread. Workers from the nearby hospitals come in to buy sandwiches. Of all the mega-stores in New York, Todaro Brothers feels the homiest.

But just because the store doesn't take itself overly seriously doesn't mean this isn't a very serious food store. For seventy-five years the Todaro family have been distributing and selling high-quality imported and domestic Italian foodstuffs out of their unprepossessing storefront in their not-very-fashionable Kips Bay neighborhood. It's the kind of store where gourmet-food-business competitors come to steal ideas.

In terms of square footage, Todaro Brothers is by far the smallest mega-store in New York, yet it's surprisingly complete. Within its crowded environs you'll find fresh fish, meat, bread, baked goods, prepared foods, pasta, and perhaps the

Todaro Brothers, New York's smallest mega-store, is full of surprises.

best Italian cheese selection in New York. They don't carry many things you can't find somewhere else, but there are enough surprises and oddities to keep a food lover interested. There is a small produce section that carries staples such as iceberg lettuce along with a limited selection of fresh herbs and designer produce, including miniature white eggplants and Swiss red chard.

Appetizers/Smoked Fish/Salads ～ The smoked fish selection is the standard array of Norwegian, Scotch, and eastern salmons, along with items like smoked tuna and trout that you're beginning to see all over the city. But the store's olive selection is first-rate, ranging from the huge purple Chilean Alfonsos to French niçoises. They also have delicious hot marinated peppers stuffed with prosciutto and cheese that are both incendiary and addictive. You'll also find a wide selection of pâtés and mousses, including the Summer Sweet smoked-salmon-and-spinach mousse that I can't seem to get enough of. Todaro's also has a full-scale fish counter with filets, whole fish, and shellfish.

Baked Goods ～ In the last year Todaro Brothers has gone to great lengths to improve the quality of their baked goods. I'm not much of a carrot-cake fan, but Cindy Klotz's carrot muffins with sour-cream icing could easily make me a convert. Cindy also makes a dense, chocolaty blackout cake. The Bakery in Mamaroneck supplies Todaro Brothers with pies that are so good I've started checking out house prices in the area. The sugar-free apple pie is the best sugar-free desert I've ever tasted. A woman named Margaret Palka supplies wonderful, old-fashioned buttery rugelach that taste even better than my grandmother's, and hers were great. Mitchell London supplies the store's excellent cheesecake, and the Italian cookies are supplied by the mothers of all Italian cookies: Ferrara's and Veniero's.

Even the apple strudel was surprisingly good, filled with big chunks of apples, raisins, and cinnamon.

Note: This is one store where you should definitely inquire when a cake or pie has arrived.

Bread ~~ The bread department here is solid, if unspectacular. Italian loaves and baguettes of every variety imaginable come from two major New Jersey sources: Central and Certified bakeries. The semolina loaves are excellent and come from Grimaldi, a brick-oven Italian bakery in Brooklyn. From Orwasher's you'll find that bakery's signature pumpernickel-raisin bread and rolls. The ubiquitous Eli's bread has found its way to Todaro Brothers in the form of his plain and onion *ficelles* and addictive raisin-nut rolls. The mediocre croissants are from Dumas, as are the good, buttery Danish.

Cheese and Dairy ~~ Todaro Brothers may have as good a selection of Italian cheeses as I found in New York. The last time I was there I tasted a handful of Italian cheeses, each better than the next. Try the Robiola Valsassini, a soft-ripened cheese with a creamy texture and strong taste. Or the Caprella, a soft-ripened goat Brie that has so much character you'll never be able to eat conventional Brie again. Or the torta San Gaudenzio, a delicious Gorgonzola-and-Mascarpone-layered cheese. Although the selection of French cheese here is limited, you will find classic French *chèvres* like the mild but flavorful Taupinière. They also make their own mozzarella on the premises. It's sometimes a little hard, and although it's not among the city's best, it's definitely better than Polly-O. About the only thing you won't find at this cheese counter is a large selection of the new American cheeses. They carry Coach and a few others, but that's about it.

Coffee/Tea ~~ Todaro's sells between seven and eight hundred pounds of coffee a week supplied by Gillie's and White House. They carry thirty varieties of coffee, including combinations of special beans like Hawaiian Kona and gimmicky flavored beans like vanilla-hazelnut. Try Todaro's Golden Blend, a sweetish, almost mocha-java-like mellow roast, or Luciano's Blend, a strong but not bitter combination of beans.

Condiments/Oils/Vinegars/Packaged Items ~~ Lou Todaro is also an importer and distributor, so it makes sense he would carry a wide selection of olive oils and flavored vinegars. He carries Raineri olive oil, which was rated number one in a taste test conducted by, among others, Gael Greene and the late James Beard. He also has bizarre gift-packaged Raineri olive oil packed in tubes labeled with the exact tree and branch locations where the olives used in making that particular tube of oil were picked. It doesn't make the olive oil taste any better, but it's a great marketing gimmick. Todaro's own Bel Aria brand is a solid budget choice for both olive oil and wine vinegar.

Deli Meats (Salumeria) ~~ I expected Todaro Brothers to have a terrific Italian salumeria so was disappointed to find a pretty standard selection of domestic and imported hams and salamis. You'll find Boar's Head and Volpi products, along with first-rate imported items such as *prosciutto di Parma* and Hungarian Pick salami.

Fish ∼ The store recently installed a fish counter with the aid of Bill Bowers, the former fish-department head at Balducci's. Every day Bowers goes to the Fulton Fish Market and returns with tuna, salmon, shrimp, mussels, littleneck clams, and soft-shell crabs in season. The store also puts up tuna, salmon, and swordfish kebobs that make perfect summer grilling material. Todaro's fish is usually impeccably fresh, but I have seen some soft-shell crabs here that looked comatose and definitely past their prime.

Meat and Poultry ∼ The Todaro Brothers meat counter is presided over by Italian butchers right out of central casting. They make five kinds of fresh Italian sausage, ranging from cheese-and-parsley to *luganega*, a mild Italian breakfast sausage. You'll find good-looking, reasonably priced club steaks, but as the meat is choice, it won't have the rich, marbled look of prime meat. Of course, it won't have the price tag, either. In keeping with the store's Italian orientation, I found *braciole* and *osso buco* available every day. The chicken is Bell & Evans. One very nice touch here is the minibooklet of fresh meat recipes. It tells you how to cook virtually every cut of meat available at the store.

Pasta/Sauces ∼ Todaro Brothers has one of the largest fresh and dried pasta selections in New York. From a little-known fresh pasta maker, Durso, come six kinds of noodles, including a sweet-red-pepper fettucini that barely needed sauce. It's also one of the few stores in New York that carries fresh rather than dry ziti, radiatore, and tricolor fusilli. Todaro Brothers is the New York distributor for the line of Bertagna imported filled pastas you see all over New York, so it's not surprising to find virtually the entire line of tortellini and agnolotti. The dried pasta choices are seemingly endless, ranging from the staples DeCecco and Del Verdi to lesser-known high-quality brands like Misura and Lucio Garofallo. In the freezer case you'll find a full range of store-made pasta sauces. You'll fare best with the simplest ones, like the pomodoro or the marinara sauce. One unusual sauce I'd not seen elsewhere is the *mala femmina*, a delicious marinara-type sauce made with olives, capers, and a touch of anchovy.

Prepared Foods ∼ Though prepared foods are not Todaro Brothers' strong suit, there are enough good dishes that you can eat well if you choose carefully. Stick to simple, peasanty dishes like the barley with vegetables and bacon or the delicious chicken pesto made with moist chunks of chicken breast and imported pesto sauce. I loved the special potato salad with bacon, scallions, and egg, although I admit I love anything made with bacon. The fried sesame chicken tasted great straight from the fryer, but I have doubts about what it would taste like reheated. The agnolotti with vegetables was way too garlicky even for a confirmed garlic lover like myself. The veal chops looked dry as the desert.

Sandwiches ∼ Unlike many of the other mega-stores, Todaro Brothers doesn't consider sandwich making an unworthy pursuit. Among the intriguing and satisfying sandwiches they make here are two I'd take on any picnic, anywhere: The Angelina contains olive paste, balsamic vinegar, roast beef, and smoked mozzarella; The Ferrara is composed of chicken breast stuffed with mozzarella and thin slices of *prosciutto di Parma*. I am also extremely fond of Todaro's tuna salad, made with plenty of mayonnaise and shredded carrots. It won a *Daily News* prize a few years back for best tuna salad in the city.

Best Hours to Shop ～ During the day Todaro Brothers has a relatively steady stream of traffic, with a lull occuring between 2:00 and 4:00 P.M. On Saturdays and Sundays the store can get quite crowded, and because it's small, it might feel a bit claustrophobic.

Todaro Brothers
555 Second Avenue (between 30th and 31st streets)
New York, NY 10016
PHONE: (212) 532-0633
SUBWAY: 33rd Street station on the Lexington Avenue No. 6 line.
HOURS: 7:30 A.M. to 9 P.M. Monday through Saturday; 8 A.M. to 8 P.M.
   Sunday.
Deliveries throughout Manhattan.
All major credit cards accepted.
Catering and picnic baskets available.
Mail-order catalog available.

ZABAR'S: THE QUINTESSENTIAL NEW YORK STORE

In its nearly six decades of existence, Zabar's has become the Kleenex of the gourmet food business. That is, its name has become a generic term for "gourmet store." So, when people from out of town are describing the latest and greatest food store in Chicago or Seattle, they say, "It's like Zabar's." Unfortunately, they're wrong. Nothing is like Zabar's.

Zabar's celebrates gluttony like no other food store in New York. The store itself and, consequently, the people who shop there revel in its excess. No matter how hard I try, I can't seem to buy one thing at Zabar's. If I go in to buy coffee, I end up with cole slaw and a chicken pot pie. I can't help it. I've tried shopping there right after I've eaten. Nothing works.

Unfortunately, like all institutions based on excess, at Zabar's sometimes matters of taste fall by the wayside. There are certain things sold in Zabar's that are unconscionably awful. The boxed apple and pecan pies are of such inferior quality that they make the store look bad. I don't care how cheap they are, they're not worth it.

That said, I love shopping at Zabar's. For every inferior item they mistakenly sell, there are five wonderful ones to offset them. It has the best combination of selection and price of any of the mega-stores covered in the book.

Zabar's also has the best people-watching opportunities of any store in the city. New Yorkers who haven't seen each other for years are constantly running into each other there. Yet it's also become a must stop for both American and foreign tourists visiting New York. Recently my wife walked into Zabar's only to find a group of Japanese tourists snapping photographs of the smoked fish counter. First cars, then computers, now lox: I know I'm soon going to be eating smoked salmon from Osaka.

The world-famous, the one-and-only, Zabar's.

A personal plea to Murray Klein and Saul Zabar: Please stop the insufferably obnoxious sale announcements on the P.A. system in the store. There's enough going on at Zabar's without having to be harangued into buying a croissant on sale.

Appetizers/Smoked Fish/Salads ― Zabar's has become synonymous with smoked fish in New York, and for good reason. Zabar's sells extraordinarily high-quality smoked fish at reasonable prices. Notice I didn't say low prices, because no good smoked salmon is going to be cheap, unless you visit one of the wholesalers like Homerus in Mamaroneck or Marshall's in Greenpoint in Brooklyn. But Zabar's does offer terrific value on its smoked fish, to go along with its huge selection. Besides smoked salmon from every conceivable corner of the world, Zabar's sells smoked bluefish and trout, homemade gefilte fish and pickled herring, sturgeon, sable, whitefish, and many other smoked and cured fish items. If it swims and can be smoked, Zabar's carries it. And because they sell so much (over three thousand pounds of smoked salmon a week), the smoked fish at Zabar's is always fresh. Of course Zabar's also sells nonsmoked items like caviar and poached salmon. Every Christmas Zabar's engages in its celebrated caviar price war with Macy's. As far as I'm concerned, this is truly the first war with no loser. The poached salmon is fresh-tasting but dry, perhaps because the store preslices the individual steaks.

Note: The smoked fish line at Zabar's can be agonizingly long. It's discouraging to walk into the store and take a number only to realize there are fifty people ahead of you. But wisely, Zabar's has begun to sell high-quality presliced smoked salmon in one of its dairy cases. You'll miss the kibitzing countermen, but you won't miss the wait.

Zabar's also packages and refrigerates its wonderful salads. Zabar's shrimp salad, made with shrimp, celery, mayonnaise, and a pinch of sugar, is perhaps my favorite version in the city. Its lobster salad, made with langostinos, and crab salad are nearly as good. Zabar's has made its own first-rate oniony potato salad and cole slaw for years, in contrast with many of its competitors, who sell the generic prepackaged variety.

Baked Goods — In the main store, desserts and baked goods are limited to the sensational rugelach sold at the bread counter, a selection of awful boxed pies, David Glass's wonderful chocolate-mousse cake, Mitchell London's extraordinarily creamy yet light cheesecake, and the store's signature Russian coffee cake. In the annex just south of the main store you can find rich cakes and tarts, Danish and sticky buns, and napoleons and éclairs made by a Long Island City bakery, Exquisities. With the exception of the nut Danish, everything I've tried here has been too sweet and boring.

Bread — Zabar's bread department is okay but nothing more. Among the first-rate breads it sells are Orwasher's raisin-pumpernickel; bagels from Columbia Hot Bagels; Eli's baguettes, raisin-nut sourdough, and farm bread; and Soutine's cheddar rolls. It also carries Spikermann's Swiss peasant bread, which is perfect for making sandwiches, and Scripps's European five-grain bread, which remarkably is good for you and good-tasting. But the rye bread is nothing special, the corn bread from Moishe's lacks the density great Jewish corn breads should have, and the croissants are heavy and greasy.

Candy/Nuts/Dried Fruit — After years of experimenting with candy, dried fruit, and nut counters, Zabar's has settled into selling boxed chocolates and prepackaged dried fruits and nuts. Name-brand discounted chocolates sold include Perugina, Droste, Lindt, and Toblerone. The store also sells the extraordinary Kopper's brand of chocolate espresso beans and cordials.

The dried fruit and nut selection is pretty meager. Try the unsulfured, unsweetened, dehydrated pineapple. It's ugly, but it tastes sensational. The nuts sold are the standard almonds, cashews, walnuts, pecans, and the like. Pistachio lovers should note that Zabar's sells five-pound bags of California pistachios for $23.98.

Cheese and Dairy — Zabar's sells three million dollars' worth of cheese every year, so they must be doing something right. You can find 350 kinds of cheese here, with the accent on French and Italian varieties. Try the marinated buffalo mozzarella with sun-dried tomatoes, herbs, and cracked peppercorns; or Cacio Peperino di Pienza, a wonderfully earthy Italian Rosselino sheep's-milk cheese; or, if you're watching your cholesterol, a surprisingly tasty low-fat Tomme de Savoie called Coeur Légère. In fact, Zabar's has one of the broadest selections of low-fat cheeses in the city. I was a little surprised not to find more of the new high-quality American cheeses here. You can find Goat Folks and Coach, but there's no sign of Westfield Farms or Craigston cheeses.

Coffee/Tea ⸺ Zabar's has a noteworthy and sound approach to coffee. It carries only eleven coffees, six regular and five decaffeinated, ranging from French and Italian roasts to Colombia Supremo. Zabar's doesn't carry any of the expensive beans like Jamaican Blue Mountain or Hawaiian Kona, so it can keep its coffee prices ridiculously low. No coffee in the store costs more than six dollars a pound. The combination of the limited selection and the fact that the store sells thirty thousand pounds of coffee a week ensures incredible turnover and therefore freshness. It sells another five to eight thousand pounds of coffee a week by mail. In addition to the coffee, Zabar's sells ten kinds of loose tea, including Ceylon, black currant, and decaffeinated Earl Grey.

Condiments/Oils/Vinegars/Packaged Items ⸺ Zabar's sells its own brand of extra-virgin California olive oil, which has a fruity, gentle olive taste. It also carries an array of Italian and Spanish olive oils, including a wonderfully strong Spanish brand called Nuñez de Prado. Also available are the requisite balsamic vinegars as well as grapefruit and orange vinegars bottled by the Chic Ma Maison restaurant in Los Angeles. Even though I was predisposed to dislike them, both made extraordinary vinaigrettes for salads. Try the Inner Beauty sweet papaya mustard; it does wonders for hot dogs. In general, Zabar's has the largest and best selection of sauces and condiments in the city.

Deli Meats (Charcuterie) ⸺ Zabar's has a superb deli-meat and charcuterie department. It's one of the few retailers in the city that carries Usinger's liverwurst and garlic beef salami, they sell a host of Schaller and Weber products, and their own wine-and-garlic salami is perfect Central-Park-picnic material. Try the Pick imported Hungarian salami or the Rapelli pepper salami. My wife swears by the Virginia-style corned beef, which has a bizarre-looking but tasty red fruit glaze. Zabar's is also one of the few stores in New York that carries Weaver's Lebanon bologna, a dark, sweet variety that's popular in the Midwest and Pennsylvania.

Pasta/Sauces ⸺ You'll find pasta all over the place at Zabar's. Next to the cheese counter you'll find a variety of Riviera tortellini including the sweet, nutty pumpkin ones my son loves. In other parts of the store you'll find DeCecco and Al Dente dried pastas, which are excellent, and Trio fresh pasta, which I don't think is up to Raffetto's standards. The Trio sauces, including pesto and marinara, are boldly seasoned and lustily flavored. You'll also find the standard Tutta Pasta and Contadina sauces here.

Prepared Foods ⸺ Zabar's chef is a Russian named Boris, and he lays out so much food every day it looks like his previous gig was with the Red Army. Unfortunately, I've never found much of it to be very good. Most of it is just too heavy for my taste, either doused in way too much sauce or wrapped in phyllo dough or puff pastry. You'll do best with hearty, peasanty foods. The Chinese loin of pork is tasty and lean, the knishes and the kugel are excellent, and the tortellini with spinach and feta cheese has a nice tang to it. My wife is crazy about the chicken pot pies, wrapped in the ubiquitous puff pastry and not too goopy. The slow-roast brisket is dry, the roast shell steak tastes no better than okay roast beef, and the Dijon-mustard chicken is dry and uninteresting. Zabar's soups are generally excellent, especially if you stick to the heartier ones such as vegetable chowder and mushroom-barley.

Best Hours to Shop — Weekdays before 5 P.M. are the best times to shop at Zabar's, but what's surprising is how empty the store is between, say, 6:45 and 7:30 P.M. on weekday evenings. If you have to shop on weekends, go Saturday night after 8 P.M. (the store is open until midnight Saturday). During the day on Saturday and Sunday you're on your own, although you'll do okay getting there between 8:00 and 9:00 A.M. During the holiday season there is no good time to shop at Zabar's.

Zabar's
2245 Broadway (between 80th and 81st streets)
New York, NY 10024
PHONE: (212) 787-2000
SUBWAYS: 79th Street station on the Broadway–Seventh Avenue No. 1 and 9
  lines; 81st Street station on the Eighth Avenue C and Sixth Avenue B
  lines.
HOURS: 8 A.M. to 7:30 P.M. Monday through Friday; 8 A.M. to midnight
  Saturday; 9 A.M. to 6 P.M. Sunday.
Delivery available for large orders only.
All major credit cards accepted.
Catering and picnic baskets available.
Mail-order catalogue available.

Best of Mega-Stores

Best all-around store: Balducci's
Best baked goods: Dean & DeLuca
Best bread counter: Dean & DeLuca
Best butcher: Balducci's
Best charcuterie/deli: Grace's
Best cheese: Dean & DeLuca (or wherever Steve Jenkins is)
Best chocolates/candy department: Macy's, Bloomingdale's
Best coffee: Zabar's
Best exotic produce selection: Balducci's; Dean & DeLuca
Most expensive: Dean & DeLuca
Best fish counter: Balducci's
Best fruit: Balducci's
Best olive oils/vinegars: Balducci's; Dean & DeLuca
Best packaged foods: Dean & DeLuca
Best pasta (fresh): Balducci's
Best pasta (dried): Todaro Brothers
Best prepared foods: Balducci's
Best prices: Zabar's
Best produce: Balducci's
Best produce on a budget: Fairway
Best sandwiches: Todaro Brothers
Best service: No one
Best smoked fish: Zabar's
Best value (over-all): Fairway
Best vegetables: Balducci's; Fairway

14

PASTA

Growing up on the outskirts of the city (just over the Queens line in Nassau County) I, like everybody else I knew, thought that pasta came only in dry form in boxes. It was Mueller's or Buitoni or, on a good day, Ronzoni ("Ronzoni sono buoni, Ronzoni is so good"). The idea that pasta could be made fresh and could actually have some flavor independent of the sauce you ladled over it was unheard of.

Then in the early 1980s, along came Henry Lambert, who introduced many New Yorkers to fresh pasta through his Pasta and Cheese line of pastas and sauces. Busy urbanites looking for a reasonably priced, tasty, and nutritious meal quickly embraced fresh pasta and sauce as a way of life. Lambert became so successful that the Campbell's Soup Company bought him out and launched Lambert's products nationally under its Contadina brand name.

These days, if you admit to eating Ronzoni pasta, anyone who is passionate about food will shoot you a look that could charitably be described as horrified. Fresh pasta in New York is now the rule rather than the exception.

Once fresh pastas in conventional and spinach varieties became available, it was only a matter of time before bored and restless New Yorkers welcomed every flavor of pasta imaginable. Now there's whole-wheat pasta and black-squid-ink pasta and artichoke pasta, among a score of flavored pastas. Some originated in Italy; others were the product of ever-imaginative American chefs and retailers. Some have a discernable flavor; some don't.

Today, New York is truly a pasta lover's town, with neighborhood outlets for not only fresh pastas but also many brands of superior Italian dried pastas such as the nutty-tasting DeCecco.

But even with locally made fresh pasta and imported dried pastas available in every supermarket and gourmet store, it's still the most fun to head down to Raffetto's or Bruno the King of Ravioli and watch them make and cut the product they're about to sell.

𝒰PPER WEST SIDE

59TH STREET TO 125TH STREET
CENTRAL PARK WEST TO RIVERSIDE DRIVE

Bruno the King of Ravioli ⸺ See page 245.

Fairway ⸺ See page 221.

Zabar's ⸺ See page 237.

𝒰PPER EAST SIDE

59TH STREET TO 96TH STREET
FIRST AVENUE TO FIFTH AVENUE

Grace's Marketplace ⸺ See page 225.

Milano Gourmet ⸺ See page 119.

*M*IDTOWN WEST

34TH STREET TO 59TH STREET
FIFTH AVENUE TO ELEVENTH AVENUE

Bruno the King of Ravioli — Jim Puliatte, Bruno's co-owner and the third generation of his family to be involved in the store, claims that when his grandfather opened the store in 1888 it was the first time ravioli was commercially available in America. I don't know if that's true, but it's a nice story. At any rate, Bruno's traditional ravioli are excellent. The cheese ravioli have a firm outer texture and a creamy ricotta cheese filling. The shitake-mushroom ravioli have a subtle mushroom taste, and the vegetable ravioli (made with carrots, spinach, and mushrooms) are so tasty you forget they're actually good for you. The manicotti is also first-rate. The sun-dried-tomato ravioli don't taste like much of anything, and the lasagnas are eminently skippable. Besides pasta, the store also carries terrific Policastro breads from Hoboken.

Note: Bruno's makes its ravioli in an adjoining storefront, and if you're lucky you can see them making the items you're buying.

Bruno the King of Ravioli
653 Ninth Avenue (between 45th and 46th streets)
New York, NY 10036
PHONE: (212) 246-8456
SUBWAYS: 42nd Street–Port Authority Bus Terminal station on the Eighth
   Avenue A, C, and E lines.
HOURS: 7 A.M. to 5:30 P.M. Monday through Friday; 8 A.M. to 5 P.M.
   Saturday; closed Sunday.
Delivery with $50 minimum order.
All major credit cards accepted.

OTHER LOCATION:
2204 Broadway (between 78th and 79th streets)
New York, NY 10024
(212) 580-8150

Macy's Cellar Marketplace — See page 229.

*K*IPS BAY/GRAMERCY PARK

14TH STREET TO 34TH STREET
EAST RIVER TO FIFTH AVENUE

Todaro Brothers — See page 233.

*W*EST VILLAGE

14TH STREET TO HOUSTON STREET
FIFTH AVENUE TO WEST STREET

Balducci's ~ See page 205.

Mama Balducci's Pasta e Fagioli

Mama Balducci had a singular fancy for fresh cranberry beans. When they came in particularly plump and firm she'd cook them into a thick and starchy pasta casserole steaming under a coverlet of grated Parmesan. She preferred tubetti or conchiglie pasta cuts but would readily use broken spaghetti pieces if that's all that was available.

From start to finish, the entire preparation takes no more than thirty minutes.

1 pound fresh cranberry beans
½ cup olive oil
2 whole garlic cloves
1 pound fresh plum tomatoes diced very small
Salt and fresh-ground pepper to taste

1 pound dried tubetti or conchiglie pasta
¼ cup fresh parsley
Freshly grated Parmesan cheese to taste

1. Shell beans and rinse. Place in a Dutch oven, add 8 cups water and salt to taste, and bring to a boil. Lower heat and boil gently for 30 minutes. Drain beans.
2. *Prepare marinara sauce*: Heat olive oil and add the cloves of garlic. When garlic turns "blonde," add diced tomatoes, salt, and pepper and cook over medium-low heat for 20 minutes, stirring occasionally. Remove whole cloves of garlic.
3. Cook pasta in a large pot of boiling salted water until *al dente*. Drain and add to sauce along with beans. Add fresh parsley and simmer 5 minutes more. Serve sprinkled with fresh Parmesan cheese.

Yield: 6 servings

Raffetto's ~ When I lived in the village I used to love to go to Raffetto's to watch them cut the pasta by hand on a guillotinelike pasta cutter that had been in use since the store opened in 1906. Since then, Andrew Raffetto, the grandson of the founder, has added an automated guillotine pasta cutter to the operation. As far

Raffetto's on West Houston sells more than fifty kinds of fresh and dry pasta.

as I can tell, the pasta's just as good. Raffetto's simple spinach or plain pastas are flavorful and well-textured. Its cheese and spinach ravioli are wonderful, and its garlic-parsley fettucine barely needs sauce. Raffetto's sells more than fifty kinds of fresh and dry pasta. The most recent addition to the Raffetto's line is the pesto-filled ravioli, one of my son's favorite all-time dinners. Raffetto's also sells okay Italian breads, cheese for grating, and canned imported Italian tomatoes and olive oil.

Raffetto's
144 West Houston Street (between Sullivan and Macdougal streets)
New York, NY 10012
PHONE: (212) 777-1261
SUBWAYS: Spring Street station on the Eighth Avenue C and E lines;
    Houston Street station on the Broadway–Seventh Avenue No. 1 and 9
    lines.
HOURS: 8 A.M. to 6 P.M. Tuesday through Saturday; closed Sunday and
    Monday.
No deliveries.
Cash only.

Tutta Pasta ⸺ Tutta Pasta makes superb sun-dried-tomato ravioli that don't skimp on the sun-dried tomatoes. The company also makes twenty-six varieties of flat pasta and twenty-five kinds of filled pasta at its factory in Brooklyn. Of the ones I've tried, the standouts have been the delicate saffron ravioli and the pumpkin ravioli and tortellini, which have a delightfully sweet and nutty flavor. Tutta Pasta also makes a line of ready-made pasta sauces that are assertively seasoned and fresh tasting. The white clam sauce with porcini mushrooms would be perfect if it weren't for the rubbery clams. Tutta Pasta has another store and restaurant on Laguardia Place and a restaurant next door to the Carmine Street location. You can find their sauces and pasta at Fairway, Nature's Gifts, East Village Cheese, and Sal's Gourmet.

Tutta Pasta
24 Carmine Street (just south of Bleecker Street)
New York, NY 10014
PHONE: (212) 242-4871
SUBWAYS: Christopher Street–Sheridan Square station on the Broadway–
    Seventh Avenue No. 1 and 9 lines; West Fourth Street–Washington
    Square station on the following lines: Sixth Avenue B, D, F, and Q;
    Eighth Avenue A, C, and E.
HOURS: 8 A.M. to 7 P.M. Monday through Saturday; closed Sunday.
$15 delivery minimum.
Cash only.

OTHER LOCATION:
504 La Guardia Place (between Bleecker and 3rd streets)
New York, NY 10012
(212) 420-0652

*E*AST VILLAGE

14TH STREET TO HOUSTON STREET
EAST RIVER TO FIFTH AVENUE

Pasta Place ⏤ When I asked Joe Chilleri, the owner of the Pasta Place, how long his store had been open, he said, "At this location, one year. Before that we were around the corner for three years and two blocks down for another seven years. They keep raising my rent; I keep moving my store." I hope the burgeoning East Village rents don't drive Chilleri out of business, because his homemade pasta is a silky delight. His garden pasta, a combination of beet, spinach, and egg fettuccini, is terrific. His spinach ravioli, with flecks of spinach surrounded by creamy ricotta cheese, melt in your mouth. His meat tortellini are stuffed with a tasty combination of mortadella, Genoa salami, and prosciutto. His marinara sauce was bland and dull, but his mushroom sauce was full of sliced mushrooms and fresh chopped garlic. Besides pasta and sauce, Joe makes his own mozzarella. His *bocconcini*, little balls of marinated mozzarella, were superb, redolent of garlic and red pepper.

Pasta Place
247 East 10th Street (between First Avenue and Avenue A)
New York, NY 10009
PHONE: (212) 460-8326
SUBWAY: Astor Place station on the Lexington Avenue No. 6 line.
HOURS: Noon to 7 P.M. Monday through Saturday; closed Sunday.
No deliveries.
Cash only.

$\mathcal{D}$OWNTOWN

HOUSTON STREET TO BATTERY PARK

Dean & DeLuca — See page 214.

Piemonte Ravioli Company — At an all-Piemonte-product dinner party we had, the oohs and ahhs were reserved for the cannelloni, which had just the right combination of cheese, spinach, and veal. Piemonte makes twenty-five kinds of fresh flat and filled pasta. The flat pastas I've sampled are just fine, but it's the filled pastas I keep coming back for. The porcini-mushroom ravioli actually have enough porcini in them so you can taste the mushroom. Piemonte also makes wondrous *panzotti*, half-moon-shaped pasta filled with a combination of spinach, Parmesan, and ricotta cheeses. Skip the bland pesto sauce.

Piemonte Ravioli Company
190 Grand Street (between Mott and Mulberry streets)
New York, NY 10012
PHONE: (212) 226-0475
SUBWAYS: Spring Street station on the Lexington Avenue No. 6 line; Grand
    Street station on the Sixth Avenue B, D, and Q lines.
HOURS: 8 A.M. to 6 P.M. Tuesday through Saturday; 8 A.M. to 3 P.M. Sunday.
Deliveries throughout Manhattan on large orders.
Cash only.
Mail order available.

OTHER LOCATION:
3436 65th Street
Woodside, NY 11377

The Ravioli Store — Even if your grandmother was Italian and a great cook, she never made ravioli like these. Owner John Zaccaro (yes, he's the son of the former Democratic vice-presidential nominee Geraldine Ferraro) make fifteen kinds of exotic ravioli. The standouts include blue-corn ravioli with a black-bean-and-Monterey-Jack filling, tomato ravioli with a five-cheese filling, and tomato-basil pasta with a walnut-pesto filling. I found a number of the other ravioli, including a version made with tequila-marinated shrimp, to have fillings so pureed they lost much of their individual character and flavor.
  Note: Dean & DeLuca also carries Ravioli Store products.

The Ravioli Store
75 Sullivan Street (between Spring and Broome streets)
New York, NY 10002
PHONE: (212) 925-1737
SUBWAYS: Spring Street station on the Lexington Avenue No. 6 line; Grand
    Street station on the Sixth Avenue B, D, and Q lines.
HOURS: 10 A.M. to 7 P.M. Monday through Friday; 11 A.M. to 4 P.M. Saturday;
    closed Sunday.
$50 minimum on deliveries.
Cash only.

ℬRONX

Borgatti's Ravioli and Egg Noodles ⁓ See page 134.

ℬROOKLYN

Morisi Pasta ⁓ I knew I had arrived at Morisi Pasta in Park Slope when I spotted an American flag made out of dried pasta in the window. Inside I found bin after bin of dried pasta in every shape, size, and flavor imaginable—250 varieties in all. The pasta shapes had names like gemelli, bumbola, zitoni, and creste di galli. The linguini was made old-world style with beveled edges. The flavors included goat-cheese-and-walnut, salmon, carbonara (bacon), and cheddar-cheese. I found later the cheese and meat-flavored pastas don't have a very strong taste, although they do taste vaguely of whatever they're flavored with. But the truly unusual flavors are the fruit pastas: pineapple, prune, blueberry, and peach, among others. These go well in fruit salads or with yogurt. When I asked Christine Morisi who had come up with the flavors, she just smiled knowingly and said, "Most come from my father's wicked imagination."

Note: Morisi's pasta is denser and chewier than store-bought pastas and requires more cooking time.

Morisi Pasta
647 Fifth Avenue (between 18th and 19th streets)
Brooklyn, NY 11215
PHONE: (718) 788-2299
SUBWAY: Prospect Avenue station on the Broadway R line.
HOURS: 8 A.M. to 6 P.M. Monday through Saturday; closed Sunday.
Cash and personal checks only.
Mail-order catalog $2.50 (deducted from the price of the first order).

Pastosa Ravioli ⁓ I stumbled onto Pastosa in the midst of an unsuccessful search for the definitive prosciutto-bread (or lard-bread) bakery in Brooklyn. While the lard bread turned out to be disappointing, Pastosa's ravioli (especially the spinach), manicotti, fresh pastas, and fresh sauces (try the prosciutto and basil) were a revelation. The smoked-Gouda-and-sun-dried-tomato ravioli had me thinking about moving to Carroll Gardens, and the artichoke-and-sausage sauce was so good that I came back to check out schools in the neighborhood for my son. My bags were so full I couldn't try the seafood ravioli, but I suspect it would be stellar.

Pastosa Ravioli
347 Court Street (between Union and President streets)
Brooklyn, NY 11231
PHONE: (718) 625-9482
SUBWAYS: Carroll Street station on the Sixth Avenue F and Brooklyn–
   Queens Crosstown G lines.

HOURS: 9 A.M. to 7 P.M. Monday through Friday; 9 A.M to 6 P.M. Saturday; 9
A.M. to 12:30 P.M. Sunday.
No deliveries.
All major credit cards accepted except American Express.

OTHER LOCATIONS:
Note: Pastosa Ravioli has thirteen other stores in Brooklyn and on Long
Island.

Best of Pasta

Best all-around pasta store: Raffetto's
Best canneloni: Piemonte Ravioli Company
Best designer ravioli: The Ravioli Store
Best dry pasta selection: Morisi Pasta
Best fresh pasta: Borgatti's Ravioli and Egg Noodles; Raffetto's
Best sun-dried tomato ravioli: Tutta Pasta

15

~~

PIZZA

City people across the country have very strong feelings about their local pizza. Chicagoans swear by the deep-dish or double-crusted pizzas served up in places like Giordano's or Edouardo's. New Havenites swear by the superb thin, blister-crusted pizza made in huge coal-fired brick ovens at Pepe's, Sally's, and Modern Apizza.

But New York is the city of the pizza slice. When you're in a hurry and need something to eat there is nothing better than discovering a pizzeria with a fresh pie just waiting for you on one of those metal pans. Although the last ten years have seen the proliferation of individual designer pizzas served in upscale restaurants like Orso and La Bohème, New Yorkers still hold their local pizzerias close to their hearts. A pizzeria primarily serves pizza, but it will invariably have heros, lasagna, and other southern Italian fare as well.

I've included pizzerias in this book because New Yorkers are just as likely to pick up a pizza and take it home or to have it delivered as they are to eat it in the pizzeria. Plus, a slice of pizza is the perfect antidote for shopper's malaise. Besides, I love pizza. I've passed this pizza passion on to my young son, and I'm proud to say he can tell the difference between a slice from Tom's and one from Vinnie's, two of our local pizza joints.

EAST HARLEM

ABOVE 96TH STREET
FIRST AVENUE TO FIFTH AVENUE

Patsy's Pizza ~~ Patsy Lancieri, uncle of Patsy Grimaldi (of the Brooklyn Patsy's), opened New York's first coal-stoked brick-oven pizzeria in 1932. Patsy Lancieri died a few years ago, but his widow, Carmella, has carried on the pizza-making tradition. Her pizza is so good that Frank Sinatra has on occasion flown Patsy's pies to Los Angeles to enjoy on his birthday. After tasting my first Patsy's pizza I can conclude that Ol' Blue Eyes knows pizza as well as he knows how to sing. The crust is not too thin, and it's blistered and chewy, the way great coal-stoked-oven crusts get. The sauce is homemade, the sausage is first-rate, and only the store-bought mozzarella mars this pizza's perfection. Patsy's East Harlem location just south of the Triboro Bridge makes it a perfect pit stop for a trip to Long Island. If you have a Patsy's pizza in the car, you won't even mind the traffic jams on the way to the Hamptons. Patsy's sells slices at an alcove adjoining the restaurant. The slices are okay, but nothing like the whole pies next door. To truly experience Patsy's you have to order a whole pie.

Patsy's Pizza
2287 First Avenue (between 117th and 118th streets)
New York, NY 10029
PHONE: (212) 534-9783
SUBWAYS: 116th Street station on the Lexington Avenue No. 6 line.
HOURS: 11 A.M. to 2 A.M. Tuesday through Sunday; closed Monday.
Delivery in the neighborhood.
Cash only.

UPPER WEST SIDE

59TH STREET TO 125TH STREET
CENTRAL PARK WEST TO RIVERSIDE DRIVE

La Traviata Pizza ~~ I don't know anything about opera, and neither do the guys who run this pizzeria, but I do know pizza, and so do the guys at La Traviata, because the pizza here has one of the more intriguing crusts in the city—chewy but not thin, and loaded with garlic. La Traviata makes a lot of would-be exotic pizzas like artichoke and broccoli, but, as many theologians have pointed out, God meant pizza to be eaten with nitrite-laden meats, fresh mushrooms, and maybe clams (if they're fresh).

La Traviata Pizza
101 West 68th Street (between Broadway and Amsterdam Avenue)
New York, NY 10023
PHONE: (212) 721-1101

SUBWAYS: 66th Street station on the Broadway–Seventh Avenue No. 1 and 9 lines; 72nd Street station on the Sixth Avenue B and Eighth Avenue C lines.
HOURS: 11 A.M. to 11 P.M. seven days a week.
Deliveries in the neighborhood.
Cash only.

Sal and Carmine's — In 1973, when I first moved to the city and took a job paying $111 a week, my friend Bob and I ate approximately half our meals at a pizza-by-the-slice joint on 95th and Broadway called Sal's. Sal's always had fresh slices with a billowy but tasty crust, fresh tomato sauce, and gobs of mozzarella cheese. Now, almost twenty years later, I've moved, Sal's moved (eight blocks north), and he's taken on a partner, Carmine. But the pizza here is still so elementally satisfying I wouldn't mind again eating half my meals here. Sal's mushrooms are canned, but his onions and peppers are fresh, as are the slices in general.

Sal and Carmine's
2671 Broadway (between 101st and 102nd streets)
New York, NY 10025
PHONE: (212) 663-7651
SUBWAYS: 103rd Street station on the following lines: Broadway–Seventh
    Avenue No. 1 and 9; Eighth Avenue C and Sixth Avenue B.
HOURS: 11:30 A.M. to 11 P.M. seven days a week.
No deliveries.
Cash only.

Tom's Pizzeria — Tom makes some of the best pizza in the city. He uses whole-milk mozzarella, homemade sauce, Romano cheese, and fresh additional ingredients like mushrooms in making an absolutely superior pie. The imported romano cheese gives the pizza its distinctive tang. That's the good news. The bad news is that Tom can be nasty and vituperative at times, making eating here a less-than-wonderful experience. But thankfully Tom is not around much these days, and the other counterpeople are friendlier.
Note: No matter how busy business gets, Tom's always seems to use reheated pizzas for its slices, meaning you often get the resultant cardboard crust.

Tom's Pizzeria
510 Columbus Avenue (between 84th and 85th streets)
New York, NY 10024
PHONE: (212) 877-6954 or (212) 877-9792
SUBWAYS: 86th Street station on the following lines: Broadway–Seventh
    Avenue No. 1 and 9; Eighth Avenue C and Sixth Avenue B.
HOURS: 11 A.M. to midnight Monday through Saturday; 2 P.M. to 11 P.M.
    Sunday.
Cash only.

V & T Pizzeria and Restaurant ⁓ When I was growing up, for some reason we had steak and pizza every Sunday in the summer. I know it's a bizarre combination, but I was a kid—I didn't know any better, and it seemed like a righteous combination to me, given that steak and pizza were two of my favorite foods. The steak was cooked outside on a grill, and the pizza came from Cairo's. Cairo's pizza was incredibly gooey, messy, and tasty, with a thick crust, plenty of cheese, and a spicy sauce. V & T's pizza, my brother Gil recently pointed out, is almost identical to Cairo's. He realized that when a V & T pizza he had just picked up collapsed under its own weight, soaking the box and his pants, just like Cairo's used to. V & T makes a first-rate pizza, with tangy homemade tomato sauce, whole-milk mozzarella, and a thick if not deep-dish crust. The sausage has a nice fennel flavor, but the canned mushrooms haven't seen the ground in years. Cairo's is long gone, so anyone interested in this kind of pizza has to go to V & T. The steak comes separately.

V & T Pizzeria and Restaurant
1024 Amsterdam Avenue (between 110th and 111th streets)
New York, NY 10025
PHONE: (212) 663-1708
SUBWAYS: 110th Street–Cathedral Parkway station on the following lines:
    Broadway–Seventh Avenue No. 1 and 9; Eighth Avenue C and Sixth
    Avenue B.
HOURS: 11:30 A.M. to 11:45 P.M. Tuesday through Thursday; 11:30 A.M. to
    12:45 A.M. Friday and Saturday; 11:30 A.M. to 10:30 P.M. Sunday.
No deliveries.
Cash only.

Vinnie's Pizza ⁓ In 1989 Vinnie's closed for three months for renovation, and I prayed the owner, Sal Carlino, wouldn't simultaneously tamper with the decor and the pizza. My prayers were answered. Vinnie's is a little cheerier, a little cleaner, and its phone number is now listed, but the pizza by the slice remains among the city's best. Vinnie's uses whole-milk mozzarella, and his pizza dough makes a dense, chewy crust. The great thing about going to Vinnie's for a slice is that the slice turnover is so rapid you get a fresh, unreheated slice every time. If Vinnie's would just use fresh mushrooms instead of canned, everything would be perfect.

Vinnie's Pizza
285 Amsterdam Avenue (between 73rd and 74th streets)
New York, NY 10023
PHONE: (212) 874-4382
SUBWAYS: 72nd Street Station on the following lines: Broadway–Seventh
    Avenue No. 1, 2, 3, and 9; Eighth Avenue C and Sixth Avenue B.
HOURS: 11 A.M. to 1 A.M. seven days a week.
Delivery hours 11:30 A.M. to 11 P.M.
Cash only.

*U*PPER EAST SIDE

Mimi's Pizzeria ~ My friend Bob first put me on to Mimi's, and he's so finicky about his pizza slices that he claimed it should be included in the book only if I mentioned that Mimi's quality depends on who's making the pizza. I think that's a bit much (but I love him for saying it), so I'll just report that Mimi's makes a mean slice of pizza, with a chewy crust and just the right amount of real mozzarella cheese. Some people think they go a little light on the sauce, but I for one don't really miss it. Neither, apparently does Paul McCartney. According to Mimi's lore, a couple of years ago McCartney himself called up and asked that ten Mimi's pies be delivered to the Newark Airport for him and his entourage to enjoy.

Mimi's Pizzeria
1248 Lexington Avenue (between 84th and 85th streets)
New York, NY 10028
PHONE: (212) 861-3363
SUBWAYS: 86th Street station on the Lexington Avenue No. 4, 5, and 6 lines.
HOURS: 11 A.M. to 11 P.M. seven days a week.
Free local delivery.
Cash only.

OTHER LOCATION:
Madison Avenue (between 91st and 92nd Streets)
New York, NY 10128
(212) 369-1800

Steve's Pizza ~ Steve's Pizza is named for Steve Lamanus, who moved his Bronx-based pizzeria to this Second Avenue location nearly thirty years ago. His grandson Dimitrius now owns the place and still maintains his grandfather's standards for making pizza. The homemade dough turns into a brown, slightly crunchy base for his homemade sauce and whole-milk mozzarella. I don't know if I'm ready to nominate Steve for pizza immortality, as the copy on the take-out menu here seems to suggest, but in this age of "pizza cheese" and premade crusts Steve's is a worthwhile slice joint to know about.

Steve's Pizza
1386 Second Avenue (between 71st and 72nd streets)
New York, NY 10021
PHONE: (212) 628-8854
SUBWAY: 68th Street–Hunter College station on the Lexington Avenue No. 6
    line.
HOURS: 11 A.M. to 10 P.M. seven days a week.
Deliveries in the neighborhood.
Cash only.

ℳIDTOWN WEST

34TH STREET TO 59TH STREET
FIFTH AVENUE TO ELEVENTH AVENUE

Angelo's ~~ Angelo's has dubbed itself the "pizza king," and although its pizza is very good, I think "pizza duke" might be more appropriate. I love Angelo's thin but chewy and flavorful crust and their great fennel sausage, but I wish they would add a little bit more sauce and skip the canned mushrooms. Still, for its crust alone Angelo's deserves a spot in pizza's royal family.

Angelo's
859 Ninth Avenue (between 55th and 56th streets)
New York, NY 10019
PHONE: (212) 586-0159
SUBWAYS: 59th Street–Columbus Circle station on the following lines:
Broadway–Seventh Avenue No. 1 and 9, Eighth Avenue A and C, Sixth
Avenue B and D.
HOURS: 11 A.M. to midnight seven days a week.
Deliveries in the immediate neighborhood only.
American Express accepted.

Mangia ~~ See page 286.

𝒲EST VILLAGE

14TH STREET TO HOUSTON STREET
FIFTH AVENUE TO WEST STREET

Arturo's ~~ The only way to describe Arturo's accurately is to call it a neighborhood family bar. It's incredibly dark inside, it has live music performed by outré amateurs, and it has a coal oven that turns out very good pizzas. The crust—chewy, slightly charred, and delicious—is the best part of an Arturo's pie. The sauce is nothing special, the mushrooms are canned, and the mozzarella is assuredly store-bought. Arturo's is also the only pizzeria I know of in New York that serves breakfast sausage laced with sage on its pizza. One bite and you'll be looking for the orange juice and coffee.

Arturo's
106 West Houston Street (corner of Thompson Street)
New York, NY 10012
PHONE: (212) 677-3820 or (212) 475-9828
SUBWAYS: Spring Street station on the Eighth Avenue C and E lines;
Houston Street station on the Broadway–Seventh Avenue No. 1 and 9
lines.

HOURS: 4 P.M. to 1 A.M. Sunday through Thursday; 4 P.M. to 2 A.M. Friday
   and Saturday.
Delivery in the neighborhood.
All major credit cards accepted.

John's Pizza ⁓ Hands down, John's pizza is the best to be found in Manhattan.
The crust is thin and charred from the coal-fired brick oven, the mozzarella is
creamy and rich, the tomato sauce is homemade, the sausage is homemade and
wonderful, and the mushrooms are fresh. Have them add fresh garlic to your
sausage-and-mushroom pizza, and you will surely be in pizza heaven. It's true
you always have to wait on line at John's (except at weekday lunch and off-hours
on weekends), but believe me, it's worth it. They don't deliver, but they will put
a pizza in a taxi if you order a cab. However, I have heard numerous stories of
cabbies not being able to resist the smell of John's pizza and digging in.
   Note: Another John's opened up a few years ago on the East Side. Even though
they built another coal-fired brick oven to make the pizzas, for some reason the
pizza just doesn't taste the same. Still, it turns out excellent pizza.

John's
278 Bleecker Street (between Sixth and Seventh avenues)
New York, NY 10014
PHONE: (212) 243-1680
SUBWAYS: Christopher Street–Sheridan Square station on the Broadway–
   Seventh Avenue No. 1 and 9 lines; West Fourth Street–Washington
   Square station on the following lines: Sixth Avenue B, D, F, and Q;
   Eighth Avenue A, C, and E.
HOURS: 11:30 A.M. to 11:15 P.M. Monday through Thursday; 11:30 A.M. to
   12:15 A.M. Friday; 1 P.M. to 12:15 A.M. Saturday; noon to 11:15 P.M.
   Sunday.
No deliveries.
Cash only.

OTHER LOCATION:
John's of Bleecker Street
408 East 64th Street (between First and York avenues)
New York, NY 10021
PHONE: (212) 935-2895

*E*AST VILLAGE

14TH STREET TO HOUSTON STREET
EAST RIVER TO FIFTH AVENUE

Stromboli Pizzeria ⁓ In the mid 1970s I underwent what seemed like an endless
series of career crises. Career number 432 was audio engineering, and every day
I would ride my bike forty-five blocks to audio engineering classes that were
absolutely incomprehensible to me. What kept me sane during that period was
discovering Stromboli pizza. Every evening after class I would have two Stromboli
slices—heavy, with lots of mozzarella, a pinch of Romano, a chewy and flavorful

crust, and Stromboli's unique sweet-but-tangy sauce. Stromboli slices are so tasty they don't need toppings, except perhaps some fresh garlic. The countermen here are extremely friendly in a pizza-place kind of way. That means they may give you some grief just for the hell of it, but in the end they come through. The last time I was there somebody ordered a slice and the guy at the counter gave him two for the price of one, saying the first slice was too small.

Stromboli Pizzeria
112 University Place (between 12th and 13th streets)
New York, NY 10003
PHONE: (212) 255-0812 or (800) 698-9878
SUBWAYS: 14th Street–Union Square station on the following lines:
    Lexington Avenue No. 4, 5, and 6; Broadway N and R; 14th Street–
    Canarsie L.
HOURS: 11:00 A.M. to 2 A.M. Monday through Saturday; 11 A.M. to 11 P.M.
    Sunday.
Free delivery in Manhattan.
One pie minimum.
Cash only.

Two Boots to Go ⬳ Because of its Italian Cajun orientation, Two Boots makes the only barbecued shrimp pizza (and crawfish pizza, for that matter) that I've found in the city. Two Boots' exotic toppings are complemented by incredibly tangy tomato sauce and fresh-tasting mozzarella and Romano cheeses. If only the thin crust had some real flavor, Two Boots would enter my top-ten-pizzas-of-all-time list.

Note: The Two Boots restaurant is right across the street from the take-out storefront and serves the same pizza.

Two Boots to Go
36 Avenue A (between 2nd and 3rd streets)
New York, NY 10009
PHONE: (212) 505-5450
SUBWAY: 2nd Avenue station on the Sixth Avenue F line.
HOURS: Noon to 1 A.M. seven days a week.
Delivery in the neighborhood.
Cash only.

OTHER LOCATION:
514 Second Street (between Seventh and Eighth avenues)
Brooklyn, NY 11215
(718) 499-3253

OWNTOWN

HOUSTON STREET TO BATTERY PARK

Ray's Pizza ⬳ Forget the Famous Original Ray's, One and Only Ray's of Greenwich Village, Ray Bari, or any other pizzeria with Ray in its name. This Ray's Pizza is the original Ray's Pizza in New York. It's somehow fitting that it was opened in

Paul Rizzo (left) with a tray of his specialty, Sicilian pizza.

1959 and is still owned by a guy named Ralph. Ralph makes a first-rate slice with a crispy crust, not-too-sweet tomato sauce, and fresh mozzarella. If you want one of those slices laden down with so much white "pizza cheese" it needs a piece of bone china to properly hold it, go to one of the zillion other pizzerias with Ray in its name. If you want a high-quality slice of pizza, come here.

Ray's Pizza
27 Prince Street (between Mott and Elizabeth streets)
New York, NY 10012
PHONE: (212) 966-1960
SUBWAY: Spring Street station on the Lexington Avenue No. 6 line.
HOURS: Noon to 11 P.M. seven days a week.
Free delivery in the neighborhood.
Cash only.

$\mathcal{Q}$UEENS

Rizzo's ～ Most Sicilian pizza is just too thick for me. The two-inch-thick crust should be used for insulation, and the mass of cheese on top could serve as a space blanket. But Rizzo's in Astoria is the home of the wondrous thin-crusted Sicilian slice. For forty years Joe Rizzo has been making thin-crusted Sicilian pizza the way his father learned in Sicily. That means he uses homemade sauce, full-cream mozzarella, and just enough Romano cheese to give his pizza a little zing. When you walk into Rizzo's all you'll see on the counter is rectangular trays of fresh-out-of-the-oven Sicilian pizza. If you want a slice of conventional round Neapolitan pizza, you'll have to go elsewhere, because they don't make it at Rizzo's.

Rizzo's
30-13 Steinway Street
Long Island City, NY 11103
PHONE: (718) 721-9862
SUBWAYS: Steinway Street station on the Broadway R and Brooklyn–Queens
Crosstown G lines; 30th Avenue (Grand Avenue) station on the Broadway
N line.
HOURS: 11 A.M. to 8 P.M. seven days a week.
Delivery in the neighborhood.
Cash only.

$\mathscr{B}$ROOKLYN

Patsy's ⸺ Patsy Grimaldi discovered his love for pizza as a thirteen-year-old working for his uncle at the East Harlem pizzeria that still bears his uncle's name (also Patsy). Thirty-five years later, Patsy Grimaldi's love for the art of coal-stoked brick-oven pizza making could be ignored no longer, and he opened Patsy's in Brooklyn Heights.

After tasting one of his sausage-and-mushroom pies, I could only thank God that Patsy decided to follow his muse. I don't say this casually, but Patsy makes the best pizza in all of New York. His crust is medium-thin, chewy, and just charred enough without being burned. The sauce is deceptively simple, made from imported fresh tomatoes, extra-virgin olive oil, and a few spices. The mozzarella is made fresh every day by a friend of Patsy's. The mushrooms are fresh, the sausage is big chunks of fennel-laced perfection, and this round masterpiece's *pièce de résistance* is the fresh basil atop every pie. He even roasts his own peppers, an unheard of practice in a pizzeria. I thought I would never admit this about any New York pizzeria, but the great New Haven pizzerias Sally's and Pepe's have nothing on Patsy's.

Patsy's
19 Old Fulton Street
Brooklyn, NY 11201
PHONE: (718) 858-4300
SUBWAYS: Clark Street station on the Broadway–Seventh Avenue No. 2 and
3 lines.
HOURS: Noon to 11 P.M. Monday, Wednesday through Friday; 2 P.M. to
midnight Saturday and Sunday.
No deliveries.
Cash only.

Totonno's ⸺ There are a few things you should know before trekking to Coney Island to sample Jerry Totonno's pizza artistry. The first is that he's open only on Fridays, Saturdays, and Sundays from 1:00 P.M. on. The second is that he makes his pizza dough fresh every morning, and when he runs out of dough, he closes shop. According to our waitress, who was definitely familiar with the inner workings of the Totonno operation, this can be as early as 6:00 P.M. some days.

Since there was a short line at 2:45 P.M. on a nonholiday Friday the last time I was here, I would tend to believe her. So call before you go to get a dough count. The third thing you should know is that Totonno's has no identifying marks on its exterior or interior. Those in the know look for a Miller High Life neon sign that doesn't work; a picture of Jerry Totonno's father, Anthony, who started Totonno's sixty-five years ago; an autographed black-and-white glossy of what must be a local band; and a photo of the 1955 Brooklyn Dodgers. There is no sign and no address; there are no napkins with the Totonno's logo. In fact, Totonno's has no logo—only pizza, wondrous pizza, with creamy, fresh-sliced mozzarella, fresh tomato sauce, homemade sausage, and a perfect, blistered and charred crust that comes from baking the pizza in a very hot, coal-fired brick oven. Being serious about pizza and not experiencing Totonno's is like being serious about modern art and not going to MOMA.

Totonno's
1524 Neptune Avenue (between West 15th and West 16th streets)
Brooklyn, NY 11224
PHONE: (718) 372-8606
SUBWAYS: Stillwell Avenue–Coney Island station (last stop) on the following
    lines: Broadway N; Sixth Avenue B, D, and F.
HOURS: 1 P.M. until they run out of dough, Friday through Sunday only.
No deliveries.

Two Boots to Go ⸺ See page 259.

Best of Pizza

Best all-around pizza: Patsy's (Brooklyn)
Best neopolitan slice (Upper West Side): Tom's Pizzeria
Best neopolitan slice (Village): Stromboli Pizzeria
Best pizza (Manhattan): John's (Bleecker Street location)
Best Sicilian slice: Rizzo's

16

PRODUCE

Produce markets have been a part of the New York City landscape for centuries now. There is a terrific bit of folklore in my family about how my Uncle Izzy told his wife he was going out for a pack of cigarettes, then slid down the awning of the produce market they lived over in the Bronx, and came back twenty years later.

These days there are a number of different kinds of produce markets in the city. Korean markets have added color and life to New York's landscape. The individual markets vary widely in terms of the quality of merchandise. Some are quite discerning about what they pick up at the Hunts Point wholesale market. Others don't make that effort and sell whatever is cheapest at the market that day.

Then there are the upscale produce-only markets (like the Paradise markets), which make a point of selling only fruit and vegetables that look perfect, at a price that could hardly be called perfect. The last time I was at a Paradise market, I saw the owner scolding one of his workers for not picking carefully enough the fruit he was putting on display. By the way, just because produce looks terrific doesn't mean it tastes terrific. The taste of fruit and vegetables depends on many factors: rain patterns, the method of farming, how much sun they received, and so on.

There are also upscale markets, like Balducci's and Fairway, that have evolved from their fruity beginnings to become gourmet mega-stores. Generally, the produce I've bought in stores like these has been very good, but that doesn't mean you can't get bad apples and tomatoes there. Whenever and wherever you shop for produce, you have to pick and choose very carefully. There's a reason the fruit at your grandmother's house was always so good. She was the one picking through all the apples and oranges at the market.

Note: Although produce at some New York supermarkets has gotten better, I haven't yet seen a supermarket produce department with the quality of produce found in the city's better produce markets.

*U*PPER WEST SIDE

59TH STREET TO 125TH STREET
CENTRAL PARK WEST TO RIVERSIDE DRIVE

Fairway ⁓ See page 221.

*U*PPER EAST SIDE

59TH STREET TO 96TH STREET
FIRST AVENUE TO FIFTH AVENUE

Annie's ⁓ Although it's in the same neighborhood as the two Paradise markets, Annie's manages to sell impeccably fresh conventional and designer produce at prices you don't need a loan to afford. You won't find exotica like mâche lettuce and baby artichokes, but if you're just looking to make a classy salad with ingredients like oyster mushrooms and radicchio, Annie's is the place to buy them.

Annie's
1204 Lexington Avenue (between 81st and 82nd streets)
New York, NY 10028
PHONE: (212) 861-4957
SUBWAYS: 86th Street station on the Lexington Avenue No. 4, 5, and 6 lines.
HOURS: 8 A.M. to 7:30 P.M. Monday through Saturday.
Deliveries in the neighborhood.
Cash and personal checks only.

Grace's Marketplace ~ See page 225.

Nature's Gifts ~ Nature's Gifts is one of the few Manhattan produce markets that's managed to become a mini–gourmet store without sacrificing the inordinately high quality of their produce. Their fruits and vegetables are very fresh looking and tasting, and they carry unusual items like tomatillos and poblano peppers to go along with the requisite regular and designer lettuces, bananas, tomatoes, and the like. Their take-out counter has lots of appetizing Middle Eastern items. Unusual items to try include two types of couscous, one with pesto, the other with sun-dried tomatoes. They're very tasty, if a tad oily. Nature's Gifts also carries fresh and dried pasta, Eli's Breads, and Ciao Bella gelati.

Nature's Gifts
1297 Lexington Avenue (between 87th and 88th streets)
New York, NY 10128
PHONE: (212) 289-6283
SUBWAYS: 86th Street station on the Lexington Avenue No. 4, 5, and 6 lines.
HOURS: 24 hours a day, seven days a week.
Deliveries within a fifteen-block radius.
Visa and MasterCard accepted.

OTHER LOCATIONS:
320 East 86th Street (between First and Second avenues)
New York, NY 10128
(212) 734-0298

1174 Lexington Avenue (between 80th and 81st streets)
New York, NY 10028

Paradise Market ~ The good news is that the Paradise Market has row after row of perfect, impeccably fresh designer produce like baby zucchini and mesclun lettuce. The bad news is you might have to direct-deposit your paycheck to the store to pay for the privilege of shopping here. I paid $3.75 for two normal California tomatoes here in April. I wouldn't mind paying ridiculously high prices for perfect produce if the place was friendlier, but if you're not a regular, be prepared for a chilly reception.

Paradise Market
1100 Madison Avenue (corner of 83rd Street)
New York, NY 10028
PHONE: (212) 737-0049
SUBWAYS: 86th Street station on the Lexington Avenue No. 4, 5, and 6 lines.
HOURS: 8 A.M. to 7 P.M. Monday through Saturday; closed Sunday.
Deliveries in the neighborhood.
Cash only.

OTHER LOCATION:
Paradise Market II
1081 Lexington Avenue (between 76th and 77th streets)
New York, NY 10021
(212) 570-1190

*W*EST VILLAGE

14TH STREET TO HOUSTON STREET
FIFTH AVENUE TO WEST STREET

Amazing Foods ～ Amazing Foods supplies many of the city's best restaurants with exotic fruits, vegetables, and fish. On Fridays Amazing Foods reluctantly opens its doors to consumers. This means that one of the three guys working there will take you into their warehouse, where you'll see boxes of newly arrived designer lettuce and baby vegetables you don't recognize. You'll also see sides of smoked fish and boxes of fish such as orange roughy and lotte. What all this means is that you can buy at very low prices the foods you normally see in chic restaurants and stores. The last time I was here I bought a pound of Oregon morels for $14.95. Balducci's was selling the same mushrooms for $40.

Note: Don't expect attentive service, as serving retail customers is not really this store's business. But I've found the folks here to be friendly and helpful overall.

Amazing Foods
805 Washington Street (between Horatio and Gansevoort streets)
New York, NY 10014
PHONE: (212) 645-4166
SUBWAYS: 14th Street station on the Eighth Avenue A, C, and E lines and the Broadway–Seventh Avenue No. 1, 2, 3, and 9 lines; Eighth Avenue station on the 14th Street–Canarsie L line.
HOURS: 10 A.M. to 5 P.M. Friday only.
Deliveries on large orders only.
Cash only.

Balducci's ～ See page 205.

Integral Yoga ～ See page 167.

Jefferson Market ～ The Jefferson Market is one of those rare New York establishments that make this immense city seem like a small town. Babies are fawned over, no request is too insignificant, and regulars and nonregulars alike are treated like family. The last time I was there I saw one of the counterpeople look through an entire bin of Idaho potatoes trying to find two that would satisfy his elderly customer. No complaints, no grumbling, just a stream of friendly patter even as he reached the bottom of the bin. Although the Jefferson Market has been selling high-quality produce, meats, and groceries of all kinds to New Yorkers for more than six decades, it has managed to stay contemporary without losing its old-fashioned low-key feel. This means that alongside the iceberg lettuce you'll find frisée and radicchio and endive. It means that now you'll find five kinds of mushrooms and Jerusalem artichokes and patti-pan squash. Of course you'll also find plain old red pears and Temple oranges and Indian River grapefruits. Maybe the best thing about Jefferson Market is that if you ask the workers there to find you a perfectly ripe pineapple to serve the day you buy it, they're happy to do it. If you just can't face the Balducci's craziness, and produce and meat is what you need, Jefferson Market can come to your rescue.

Jefferson Market
455 Sixth Avenue (between 10th and 11th streets)
New York, NY 10011
PHONE: (212) 675-2277
SUBWAYS: Christopher Street–Sheridan Square station on the Broadway–
    Seventh Avenue No. 1 and 9 lines; West Fourth Street–Washington
    Square station on the following lines: Sixth Avenue B, D, F, and Q;
    Eighth Avenue A, C, and E.
HOURS: 8 A.M. to 9 P.M. Monday through Saturday; 9 A.M. to 8 P.M. Sunday.
Deliveries made all over Manhattan.
Cash and personal checks only.

$\mathcal{E}$AST VILLAGE

14TH STREET TO HOUSTON STREET
EAST RIVER TO FIFTH AVENUE

The Egg Store ⁓ Really fresh eggs are hard to come by in New York. But at the Egg Store, the eggs you buy on Wednesday, Thursday, Friday, or Saturday (the only days the store is open) were laid the previous Monday by the chickens at Shady Hollow Farm. Three days from the chicken to me: That's what I call fresh. Now if you think it's odd that a store is open only four days a week, consider that until a few years ago, the store was open only on Thursdays. In fact, the old hand-stenciled sign in the window reads, "Fresh Jersey Eggs Open Thursday Only." For more than thirty years The Egg Store (formerly the Thursday Store) has been supplying fresh eggs to whoever is lucky enough to get there before the eggs are gone. The new owner of The Egg Store, Olga Worobel, has broadened the product line considerably. For a tasty, quick dinner, try one of Olga's chicken pot pies. Then when you've polished that off, have one of her orange-coconut-custard pies for dessert. Wash it all down with some fresh cider from the farm. Then get a good night's sleep, and have a couple of fried eggs for breakfast.

The Egg Store
72 East 7th Street (between First and Second avenues)
New York, NY 10003
SUBWAYS: Astor Place station on the Lexington Avenue No. 6 line.
HOURS: 7 A.M. to 7 P.M. Wednesday through Friday; 10:30 A.M. to 7 P.M.
    Saturday; closed Sunday through Tuesday.
No deliveries.
Cash only.

Manhattan Fruitier ⁓ I don't know about anyone else, but I've always found Harry & David's fruit gifts to be filled with dull, unripe fruit that's so heavily waxed it should be used as candles. So I was thrilled to discover Manhattan Fruitier, a tiny gem of an East Village store that makes up the most extraordinary fruit gift baskets I've ever seen. Manhattan Fruitier's baskets vary with the season, but in the course of a year you'll find fresh medjool dates, gorgeous red-blushed New Jersey miniature apricots, Asian pear apples, champagne grapes, and, in the fall, Spitzenberg apples, an antique apple variety apparently favored by Thomas Jefferson. The store's more expensive baskets include a choice of chocolates, biscotti, or cheese sticks. Manhattan Fruitier Jehv Gold will deliver his baskets anywhere within a fifty mile radius of Manhattan. Because his fruit is so perishable, he will not ship his baskets. He does, however, ship what he calls a Good Traveler Box, a collection of dried, candied, and pickled fruits and sundries, packaged to look like an antique grocery hamper. Inside the box you'll find items like Australian crystallized ginger, which is so intensely flavored it'll cause your whole face to pucker, and Californian pear wafers, a paper-thin slice of dried pear that puts other dried pear I've tasted to shame. Manhattan Fruitier's baskets and boxes are expensive ($50 to $200), but unlike a lot of other expensive food gifts in New York, they're worth it.

Note: Jehv Gold actually cares that the fruit tastes as good as it looks. The last time I was in the store I found him picking out pieces of unripe or overripe fruit that his workers had just put into finished baskets waiting to be shipped out.

Manhattan Fruitier
210 East 6th Street (between Second and Third avenues)
New York, NY 10003
PHONE: (212) 260-2280
SUBWAY: Astor Place station on the IRT Lexington No. 6 line.
HOURS: 9 A.M. to 5 P.M. Monday through Friday.
Deliveries made within a fifty mile radius of New York City.
Mail order available.
All major credit cards accepted.

Native Farms Organic ⁓ Organic, schmorganic is what I usually have to say about the relative merits of organic produce. I always figured pesticides somehow added to the flavor. Then I went down to Native Farms Organics. It has the freshest, best-looking produce in New York, regardless of how it's grown. At any given time they have half a dozen kinds of lettuce, each one fresher looking than the next. They sell a premixed-greens combination so good it passed my wife's unbelievably high salad standards. In December I bought some of the store's yellow cherry tomatoes, which actually had some legitimate tomato flavor in them, a real rarity for that time of year. They carry anywhere from six to ten kinds of potatoes depending upon the season, and that doesn't include the sweet potatoes or yams. Of these, try the purple peruvians; they're so moist and flavorful they don't even need butter. Native Farms' unwaxed cucumbers don't have that greased watermelon feel to them and they taste delicious, although they'll last only two days without the wax. The store has root vegetables such as parsnips and beets as well as more unusual produce—for example, Meyer lemons, the thin-skinned, very juicy, almost sweet California lemons preferred by pastry chefs. Most items come with descriptions of where they came from and how they were grown. In addition to vegetables and fruits, the store carries Bread Alone breads

Native Farms Organics: Fresh organic produce at reasonable prices.

and locally produced cheeses. Amazingly, prices are more reasonable than you'd think, given the quality and the organic spiel.

Native Farms Organic
332 East 11th Street (between First and Second avenues)
New York, NY 10003
PHONE: (212) 614-0727
SUBWAYS: First Avenue station on the 14th Street–Canarsie L line; Astor
    Place Station on the Lexington Avenue No. 6 line.
HOURS: 10 A.M. to 10 P.M. seven days a week.
No deliveries.
Cash only.

Tom the Honest Boy ⟿ If the Paradise Market with its two-dollar tomatoes is the yang of New York produce markets, then Tom the Honest Boy is the yin. Tom (nobody has ever ascertained his last name) has been selling fruits and vegetables at ridiculously low prices on the same corner of Houston and Broadway for more than forty years. The last time I was here I bought a bag of eight large yellow peppers for $1.25. That same day I went into Fairway (by no means the most expensive produce market in town) just to get a comparative price. Fairway was selling them for $2.98 a pound, which translated to twice as expensive as Tom's. Tom's peppers admittedly had some dark spots, and one was slightly soft, but at these prices who's complaining. Handsome asparagus were 99¢ a bunch, again less than half the price of any uptown produce market. Seedless grapes (a few did have pits) were a ridiculously low $1 per pound in the middle of March. In addition to selling standard fruits and vegetables Tom caters to his Hispanic customers by selling items like fresh yucca, hot peppers, and all sorts of plaintains.

Note: Somebody has to tell Tom to get a new sign. I've never met anybody who could read the sign on his stall that tells you you're shopping at Tom the Honest Boy.

Tom the Honest Boy
A street produce market located on the southeast corner of Broadway and
    Houston streets
PHONE: None
SUBWAYS: Broadway–Lafayette Street station on the Sixth Avenue B, D, F,
    and Q lines; Bleecker Street station on the Lexington Avenue No. 6 line;
    Prince Street station on the Broadway R line.
HOURS: 7 A.M. to 6 P.M. Monday through Friday; 7 A.M. to 4 P.M. Saturday
    and Sunday.
No deliveries.
Cash only.

$\mathcal{D}$OWNTOWN

HOUSTON STREET TO BATTERY PARK

Aux Délices Des Bois ⤳ With its high ceilings, beige tones, exposed pipes, and Tribeca location, Aux Délices Des Bois could just as easily be a gallery as the city's only store devoted to mushrooms. On a given day, owners Amy and Thierry Farges carry six to twelve kinds of fresh mushrooms displayed neatly on shelves in a single refrigerated case. The last time I was here I walked away with three kinds of mushrooms: cauliflower, honey, and chanterelles. The cauliflower mushrooms came in an oblong slab that looked like cauliflower and had to be sliced like bread before being sauteed. The honey mushrooms were small, almost petite, and had

Aux Délices Des Bois: The City's only store devoted to mushrooms.

a subtle, sweet flavor. The chanterelles tasted woodsy, earthy, and wonderful. All the fresh mushrooms come from either Pennsylvania or Oregon, and Amy is more than happy to tell you anything you want to know about her growers and suppliers. The store also carries a limited assortment of dried Chinese and porcini mushrooms, as well as a few other specialty foods such as French organic sea salt.

Aux Délices Des Bois
4 Leonard Street (between Hudson Street and West Broadway)
New York, NY 10013
PHONE: (212) 334-1230
SUBWAYS: Franklin Street station on the Broadway–Seventh Avenue No. 1
   and 9 lines.
HOURS: 10 A.M. to 7 P.M. Monday through Thursday; 10 A.M. to 6 P.M.
   Friday; closed Saturday and Sunday.
Cash only.
Mail order available.

Dean and DeLuca ~ See page 214.

Kam Kee ~ See page 131.

GREENMARKETS

Having gone to college in Iowa, I have a soft spot in my heart for farmers. Notice I said heart and not stomach, because Iowa farmers grow mostly feed corn for pigs, and soybeans. You don't find too many people saying, "Boy, nothing tastes better than a fresh-picked soybean." And you don't overhear one pig saying to another, "Man, that sugar corn we had for dinner tonight was delicious. It didn't even need butter."

So when I came to New York in 1973 following graduation, I thought my immediate proximity to farmers was history. Like everybody else, I shopped at grocery stores and local fruit stands, buying usually mediocre produce.

Then in 1976, at 59th Street and Second Avenue, appeared the first Greenmarket, the brainchild of an obsessed architect turned foodie, Barry Benepe. Seven growers showed up in vans and pickup trucks one March morning, and an institution took root.

Now, fifteen years later, there are eighteen thriving greenmarkets operating in the five boroughs. An estimated forty thousand shoppers yearly spend more than nine million dollars at these markets. The purpose, according to the consumer fact sheet handed out, "is to support farmers and preserve farmland by providing an opportunity for growers to sell their produce and farm products directly to the consumer."

These days, it is not just farmers who sell the fruits of their labor. Fishermen sell fish, sausage makers sell sausage, pretzel makers sell pretzels, bread bakers sell bread, and free-range-chicken farmers sell chickens. In fact, it's now possible to do all of one's household food shopping at the Union Square Greenmarket, held year-round on Wednesdays, Fridays, and Saturdays. Other markets are smaller, but almost all of them sell more than produce.

A shopping foray to the Union Square Greenmarket is the quintessential New York Greenmarket experience, a sea of tie-dye and flannel and overalls—clothing worn by farmers and New Yorkers alike. The market is an oasis of civility, where New Yorkers are actually kind and reasonably courteous to one another. Perhaps it's a form of therapy for harried, jaded city dwellers.

All kinds of farmers bring food to the Greenmarkets, from third-generation farming families to recent hipster refugees from urban life. But perhaps no farmer better represents the Greenmarket than Vincent D'Attolico and his wife, Joan. Vincent sells his ninety-six varieties of organic produce, including fifty kinds of lettuce, at the Union Square Greenmarket on Wednesdays and Saturdays. He and Joan also sell wonderful herbs, including the best garlic I've ever tasted. Vincent is a crusty, good-hearted, unconventional soul who always wears his jeans perilously close to what could only be called the fault line. Until 1976 he was an electrical contractor, operating out of a Brooklyn office. But he tired, he says, of "spending three days out of five trying to collect money" and moved his family ninety miles from the city, to Pine Island, New York, where he had bought a dilapidated farm with forty-five acres of land five years earlier. "I didn't trust banks," he recalled, "so I bought the farm as an investment. A lotta people thought I was a radical when I did that, and I am. I kept telling people the banks didn't know what they were doing, nobody listened, and now look what's going on," he said, referring, I suppose, to the Savings and Loan crisis and the numerous banks that have gone under recently. Now, more than fourteen years of trial-and-error farming later, Vince is one of the mainstays of the Union Square Greenmarket. He's the kind of rural sophisticate who tells you with a twinkle in his eye, "If I call shallots sha-*lots*"—he uses the French pronunciation—"I can get a lot more money for them."

Vince told me that in the two businesses he's had, he's seen the best and worst New Yorkers have to offer. "A guy who owed me money from my electrical contracting days was buying some lettuce from me. All of a sudden he says, 'Vince, is that you?' I said, 'Yup, it's me, and you still owe me money.' He says, 'Why didn't you just call and come over and get it?' " Laughing knowingly Vince added, "Like I didn't call him a hundred damn times looking for that money."

As he was telling me the story, a man dressed in a dashiki with an elaborately knitted, multicolored hat on his head and a bamboo quiver on his back came over and asked Vince a question about his moon squash. Vince discussed the whys and wherefores of that squash for a minute or so, and I left, knowing that he liked farming, even with all its hardships, a heckuva lot more than electrical contracting.

Shopping at the Union Square Greenmarket is a refreshing experience, but don't assume that because a piece of fruit or a vegetable is purchased at a farmer's market it's going to be of high quality. I've bought my share of tasteless apples and mealy tomatoes at Greenmarkets all over the city. Sometimes it's not the grower's fault. Like our moods, a farmer's goods are directly affected by the weather. Too much rain or not enough rain or a cold spell at the wrong time can mean all the difference in the world to a produce farmer's crop. But even though all the farmers in a given region are subject to the same weather conditions, some are simply better at what they do and produce better-tasting produce.

There are some items that just shouldn't be bought at New York's Greenmarkets. Baked goods, for example, are for the most part mediocre or worse at Union Square and the other sites. I've tasted more bad pies, bread, and cookies at the Greenmarkets than I care to remember. There are a few wonderful pie, bread, and cake bakers at the various locations, and with one or two exceptions that's all they sell. Farmers should farm, and bakers should bake. Mrs. Bonté shouldn't sell lettuce, and Greenmarket farmers, in general, should stick to produce.

Although farmers and purveyors at the Greenmarkets do come and go, there is remarkably little turnover, considering the nature of the business. The Greenmarket purveyors included in this book have all been coming to the markets for at least five years. They bring the same goods every week, subject to weather limitations, and even set up in the same place year after year.

Mountain Sweet Berry Farms has extraordinary day-neutral strawberries, a small, sweet strain of berry that adapts to whatever amount of daylight it receives and therefore can be grown and harvested from June to October, even in the East. These folks also sell wonderful fresh and smoked brook trout cultivated at a pond on their farm, as well as tasty gray-jacketed Peruvian potatoes. They're at the Union Square Greenmarket on Wednesdays and Fridays and at 77th Street and Columbus Avenue on Sunday.

Wondervue Orchards, located in Lebanon, New Jersey, has huge, incredibly sweet white and regular peaches, as well as amazing white nectarines, something I've never seen before. See them at the World Trade Center Greenmarket on Tuesdays, the Union Square market on Wednesdays and Fridays, and the market at 57th Street and Ninth Avenue on Saturdays.

Wildhive Apiaries produces first-rate honey and delicious honey-fruit spreads that taste as good as any store-bought jam. The apiary people also sell a greenish-blue-shelled Chilean egg called an Arukana that's very tasty and supposedly lower in cholesterol than other eggs. Wildhive is at Union Square on Fridays and Saturdays.

Quattro's Game Farm sells delicious fresh and smoked wild turkeys, pheasants, and ducks. Three generations of the Quattrociocchi family have been raising these birds for more than fifty years. Sal or Frank will tell you anything you want to know about the birds, from how they taste to how to prepare and cook them. The Quattrociocchis also sell extraordinary, extremely lean pheasant sausage. They're at Union Square on Saturdays.

Ted Blew and his family raise organically fed pigs that turn into some of the best bacon, fresh and smoked sausage, and smoked pork chops I've ever eaten. To me, "organic" and "sausage" don't belong in the same sentence, but maybe I'll be convinced. The Blews have an unfair advantage: When they cook up their smoked sausage, the smell makes it impossible to walk by their stand without sampling and then buying some. They also sell organic grains and, in season, forty kinds of hot peppers. They're at Union Square on Wednesdays and Saturdays from June to November.

The Bulich Family sells basket after basket of absolutely perfect mushrooms that taste even better than they look. Mushrooms are a religion to the Buliches, and they love to make mushroom converts. So when you ask a question about either the cultivation or preparation of their mushrooms, be prepared for a lengthy answer. The Buliches are not equally devoted to ginseng, but ginseng lovers I know swear by theirs. They are at Union Square on Wednesdays, Fridays, and Saturdays, and at the World Trade Center Greenmarket on Thursdays.

Martin's handmade Amish-country pretzels are to Mr. Pretzel what a BMW is to a Yugo. These pretzels are so good they satisfy even my very picky oldest brother. They are crunchy and flavorful and are made of nothing but flour, water, yeast, and salt. The pretzel salespeople are more than happy to give you a sample and also have a better-than-even-money chance of making you laugh. The last time I stopped at their stand, they were calling their whole-wheat unsalted pretzels their dog-biscuit flavor. You can buy these perfect pretzels at Union Square on Wednesdays, Fridays, and Saturdays; at 77th Street and Columbus Avenue on Sundays; at Cadman Plaza on Tuesdays; and at City Hall on Fridays.

Mary Nemeth is hands down the best baker at the Union Square Greenmarket. Her perfect little biscuits (plain or bacon) will never make it out of the Greenmarket uneaten, no matter what your intentions are. Ditto her wonderfully moist and flavorful chocolate-pistachio cake and her plain chocolate cake, which don't have any icing because they don't need any. Her pies aren't up to the level of her cakes and biscuits, but they are pretty good in their own right. They're not too sweet, are packed with fruit, and have pretty lattice crusts. Mary Nemeth and her husband, Julius, are at Union Square every Saturday.

The Nemeth Orchards folks make superb unsweetened plum-apple and pear-apple sauce. Their fruit crumb pies are good, but their other pies are eminently skippable. The fillings are fine, but the crust is often soggy. Nemeth Orchards is at the Union Square Greenmarket on Wednesdays and Saturdays.

Breezy Hill Orchards is my stop for apples, raspberry-apple sauce, and the most extraordinary raspberry-apple juice in the land. Also for sale are many varieties of fresh-picked apples, displayed in a way that's convenient for shoppers. The raspberry-apple sauce, sold in old-fashioned mason jars, compares favorably with the Nemeth Orchards sauces. The raspberry-apple juice tastes like no other juice I've had, with the simultaneous flavor of juicy apples and ripe raspberries. Breezy Hill is at Union Square on Wednesdays and Saturdays.

I had perhaps the best yellow peach of my life at **Stone Arch Farms**. Actually, it had me as much as I had it: It was so juicy much of it landed on my shirt. Stone Arch also makes wonderful, fresh grape juice that puts Welch's to shame. The juice comes from two of the twenty-nine kinds of grapes grown at Stone Arch Farms and sold in the course of the year at the Greenmarket. Stone Arch is at Union Square on Wednesdays and Fridays in the spring and summer, and at Grand Army Plaza in Brooklyn on Saturdays.

There are many other treats at the Union Square greenmarket. **Northern Bourne** sells a hydroponically grown seedless cucumber that's a little sweeter than and just as crunchy as its seeded, grown-in-soil counterpart. You find these cukes at Union Square on Wednesdays and Saturdays. Every Wednesday in season **Blooming Hill Organic Farm** sells their small but sweet peach tomatoes, which have a peachlike color and fuzz.

Coach Farms and its lesser-known counterpart, **Little Rainbow Chèvre**, sell wonderful *chèvres* at Union Square on Wednesdays, Fridays, and Saturdays. A more unusual and equally superb local cheesemaker is **Hollow Road Farms**, which sells its delectable sheep cheeses and sheep yogurt on Fridays and Saturdays at Union Square. You can find some of these cheeses at places like Fairway, but Fairway won't carry the entire line of Coach Farm products that you'll find here. Besides, it's more fun to shop for them here, and who wants to go into Fairway on a Saturday?

For maple syrup, try **Tony Van Glad's Wood Humestead** maple syrup. He'll gladly explain what all the grades and different ambers mean, and once you've tried his syrup you'll never be able to eat commercial syrups again. He's at Union Square on Fridays and Saturdays.

Good fresh corn can be bought in New York only at the Greenmarkets, and the best Greenmarket corn I've found is grown by the **Samascotts** from Dutchess County. My wife, who loves corn, ate eight ears of a strain of yellow corn the Samascotts sold me one rainy morning in September. They're at Union Square on Fridays and at the World Trade Center site on Tuesdays and Thursdays.

The best bread to be found at the Greenmarkets is brought in by **Daniel Leader**, the proprietor of **Bread Alone** of Boiceville, New York. It wasn't enough that Leader had his hearths and internal oven bricks sent over from France. No, he took bread fanaticism one step further and actually imported master French mason André LeFort to supervise the laying of forty-five thousand bricks. The results are in the tasting, and Leader's traditional French-style sourdough bread (called *pain levain*), sour rye, walnut bread, and currant rolls, are about as good as bread gets in New York. His bread can be found at Union Square on Wednesdays and Fridays, at 57th Street and Ninth Avenue on Wednesdays and Saturdays, and at Grand Army and Cadman Plazas on Saturdays, and at Federal Plaza on Fridays.

You'll also find his bread at Dean & DeLuca, Balducci's, Fairway, Jefferson Market, Grace's Marketplace, Native Farms Organics, and Aux Délices Des Bois.

Hugh W. Nelms of **Hoedown Sweets** looks suspiciously like Famous Amos of cookie fame, but one bite of his coconut cake will tell you he's moved well beyond Amos in the baking department. His rum-raisin bread pudding, his savory muffins, and his chocolate cake are all, as his business card states, "better than good." Hugh calls himself a "corn-bread-ologist," yet I've never seen any corn bread at his table. He's at the 77th Street and Columbus Avenue Greenmarket on Sundays.

The Washington Market Greenmarket is smaller and calmer than its Union Square counterpart, but there is no sacrifice in quality. The morning I was there, David Bouley, chef and proprietor of Bouley and Drew Nieporent of the Tribeca Grill and Montrachet had been shopping for produce for their restaurants at the **Frank Wilklow** family stand. The Wilklows carry wonderful Concord and Niagara grapes, first-rate apples, and delicious pears. The Wilklows come to Washington Market on Wednesdays in May through December and Saturdays year-round. They're also at the Grand Army Plaza market in Brooklyn on Saturdays.

The Greenmarket at 57th Street and Ninth Avenue on Wednesdays and Saturdays is in a tiny park that can easily go unnoticed. But thankfully I've noticed that the people at Hoboken's **Buon Pane** bring their brick-oven baked breads there on Wednesdays. Their semolina bread is quite good, and the garlic and rosemary focaccia breads make terrific, inexpensive lunches with some fresh mozzarella. They're also at the Gansevoort Street location on Saturdays.

Getting to the Greenmarket

No matter where you live or work in New York, there's usually a greenmarket within walking distance. While locations and dates remain fairly stable from year to year, it may be wise to check before heading out the door with market basket or string bag in hand. For information call the Council on the Environment of New York City at (212) 566-0990. The following schedule is reprinted with their permission.

MARKET	DAY	DATES
Manhattan		
City Hall (Park Row)	Tuesday, Friday	Year Round Year Round
World Trade Center (Church & Fulton streets)	Tuesday, Thursday	June–December Year Round
Federal Plaza (Broadway & Thomas Street)	Friday	Year Round
Washington Market Park (Greenwich & Reade streets)	Wednesday, Saturday	Year Round Year Round
St. Mark's Church (10th Street & 2nd Avenue)	Tuesday	June–November
West Village (Gansevoort & Hudson streets)	Saturday	June–November
Union Square (17th Street & Broadway)	Wednesday, Friday, Saturday	Year Round Year Round Year Round
Roosevelt Island (Bridge Plaza)	Saturday	Year Round
Sheffield Plaza (57th Street & 9th Avenue)	Wednesday, Saturday	Year Round Year Round
IS 44 (77th Street & Columbus Avenue)	Sunday	Year Round
West 102nd Street (102nd Street & Amsterdam Avenue)	Friday	June–November
West 125th Street (Adam Clayton Powell Boulevard)	Tuesday	July–November
West 175th Street (Broadway)	Thursday	June–December
Bronx		
Poe Park (Grand Concourse & East 192nd Street)	Tuesday	June–November

Brooklyn

Cadman Plaza West (Montague Street)	Tuesday, Saturday	Year Round Year Round
Grand Army Plaza	Saturday	July–November
Albee Square (Fulton Street & Dekalb Avenue)	Wednesday	July–November

The Union Square Greenmarket provides fresh and organic produce every Wednesday, Friday, and Saturday.

Taste of the Season

The Greenmarket farmers' market enables New Yorkers to enjoy the fresh taste of hundreds of different fruits and vegetables throughout the growing season. To enable consumers to better plan their menus, the Council on the Environment of New York City has prepared this seasonal harvest calendar. Since farmers come from within a 200-mile radius and weather can be extremely variable, the seasons can vary from the calendar by a week or more. The following calendar is reprinted with permission from the Council on the Environment of New York City.

	January	February	March	April	May	June	July	August	September	October	November	December
Arugala					◗	●	●	●	●	●		
Asparagus					●	●	●					
Basil						◗	●	●	●	◖		
Beans							●	●	●	●		
Beets	○	○	○			◗	●	●	●	●	●	○
Broccoli							●	●		●	●	●
Cabbage	○	◖				●	●		●	●	●	○
Carrots	○	○	○				●	●	●	●	●	○
Cauliflower						●	●		◗	●	●	
Celery							●	●	●	◖	○	
Collards					●	●	●	●	●	●	●	
Corn							◗	●	●	◖		
Cucumbers						◗	●	●	●	◖		
Eggplant							◗	●	●	◖	◖	
Leeks	○	○	○	●	●	●			●	●	●	○
Lettuce						◗	●	●	●	●	●	◖
Lima Beans								●	●	●	●	
Jerusalem Artichoke								●	●	●	●	○
Onions	○	○	○	○	○	◖	◗	●	●	●	●	○
Okra								●	●	●		
Parsley						◗	●	●	●	●	●	
Peas						●	◖		◗	●		

● In season   ○ In storage

	January	February	March	April	May	June	July	August	September	October	November	December
Peppers							◑	●	●	◐		
Potatoes	○	○	○	○			●	●	●	●	●	○
Pumpkins	○	○	○							●	●	○
Radishes					●	●	●	●	●	●		
Rhubarb					●	●						
Scallions					●	●	●	●	●	●		
Spinach					●	●	●		●	●	●	
Squash-Summer							◑	●	●	●	◐	
Squash-Winter	○	○	○					◑	●	●	○	○
Sweet Potatoes	○	○	○	○				●	●	●	●	○
Tomatoes							◑	●	●	◐		
Turnips	○	○	○				●	●	●	●	○	○
Apples	○	○	○	○	○	○	◑	●	●	●	○	○
Blueberries						●	●					
Cantaloupe							◑	●	●	◐		
Cherries						●	●					
Grapes									●	●		
Peaches						●	●	●				
Pears								◑	◑	●	○	
Plums								●	●	◐		
Raspberries							●		●			
Sour Cherries							●					
Strawberries						●						
Watermelon								●	●	◐		

17

SANDWICHES

Ask twelve New Yorkers where to get the best pastrami on rye in the city, and you'll get thirteen different answers. That's how particular and serious New Yorkers are about sandwiches. New York is a wonderful sandwich town, filled with terrific sandwich joints of every variety—from pastrami-on-rye specialists like Bernstein-on-Essex or Pastrami King to gourmet establishments like Melampo Imported Foods that create sandwich poetry with prosciutto and mozzarella and sun-dried tomatoes on freshly baked focaccia.

Half the fun of eating a sandwich is watching the sandwich maker assemble it. A first-rate sandwich maker is an artist, or at the very least an architect, and New Yorkers like Alessandro Gualandi at Melampo Imported Foods and all the guys at the Italian Food Center are the I. M. Peis of sandwiches. In fact, Gualandi says the secret of making a sandwich customer happy is to convince him the sandwich is being made especially for him. Sounds like an architect to me.

A great sandwich maker in a sandwich joint never uses a scale to measure the amount of meat or cheese for a sandwich. That would be like asking Julia Child to use a measuring cup. After all, no one ever asked Leonardo Da Vinci to paint by numbers.

All the sandwich places mentioned in this book either are exclusively take-out places or at the very least do a substantial amount of take-out business. I rationalize including certain establishments with dining rooms (such as Bernstein-on-Essex) because they are convenient places to go when you've been shopping on the Lower East Side and need a rest.

One tip about ordering sandwiches: If possible, order your sandwich meat hand-sliced. With its craggy edges and rough-hewn texture, a hand-sliced pastrami sandwich really brings out the flavor of the meat in a way a machine-sliced one never could.

Note: New York is home to many old-fashioned Jewish-style delis that I haven't included in this chapter. Places like the Stage, Fine & Schapiro, and Wolf's all serve some very good food. I just didn't find anything at those places distinctive enough to be included here.

$\mathcal{U}$PPER WEST SIDE

59TH STREET TO 125TH STREET
CENTRAL PARK WEST TO RIVERSIDE DRIVE

Amir's Falafel --- Though Amir's falafel is just fine, the store is actually misnamed, because Amir's shish kebob is merely perfect. Five or six cubes of lean, marinated lamb, grilled to order, lettuce, tomato, and tahini dressing are stuffed into a fresh pita. Ask the counterman to put dressing throughout the pita, and you've gotten the ultimate Middle Eastern sandwich.

Note: I was worried a few years ago when Amir moved from his very funky original location to spanking new quarters complete with a post-modern neon sign two blocks north. I shouldn't have been. The sandwiches are just as good. Also, Amir's has opened a second branch at A & S Plaza.

Amir's Falafel
2911A Broadway (between 113th and 114th streets)
New York, NY 10025
PHONE: (212) 749-7500
SUBWAYS: 116th Street–Columbia University station on the Broadway–
    Seventh Avenue No. 1 and 9 lines.
HOURS: 11 A.M. to 11 P.M. seven days a week.
No deliveries.
No mail order.

OTHER LOCATION:
A & S Plaza
100 West 33rd Street (between Sixth and Seventh avenues)
New York, NY 10001
(212) 594-2667

Galaxie Deli and Restaurant ⏤ In the mid-1970s I used to eat lunch every day with the two guys I worked for at a great little hole-in-the-wall deli named Linda's. Linda's had huge fresh-roasted turkeys from which your sandwich would be hand-carved. Linda sold the place to a guy named Teddy, who in turn sold it to Gus Michaels. Thankfully, every owner kept up the fresh-turkey tradition. Then the gentrification of the neighborhood began, the rent went sky-high, and Linda's went out of business. Two years ago I was walking past the storefront Linda's formerly occupied, and there in the window was one of those long-absent turkeys. Linda's was back. They had gussied it up a bit, and it was called the Galaxie, but everything else was the same. Same turkey sandwiches, same first-rate brisket, same good-but-not-great pastrami, same lousy French fries.

Note: I actually prefer the Galaxie's turkey sandwiches to those at Viand. The meat is a little more moist and has a bit more flavor. You can't go wrong with either one, though.

Galaxie Deli and Restaurant
2244 Broadway (between 80th and 81st streets)
New York, NY 10024
PHONE: (212) 580-7064
SUBWAYS: 79th Street station on the Broadway–Seventh Avenue No. 1 and 9
    lines; 81st Street station on the Eighth Avenue C and Sixth Avenue B
    lines.
HOURS: 6 A.M. to 9 P.M. Monday through Saturday; 6 A.M. to 8 P.M. Sunday.
Deliveries in the neighborhood.
Cash only.

Mama Joy's ⏤ I'm convinced that these days most roast beef used in sandwiches in New York delis is made from recycled paper products. Ecologically correct, I suppose, but gastronomically horrifying. At Mama Joy's you actually get roast beef that is juicy and flavorful and tastes like roast beef. A roast-beef hero from Mama Joy's would be sheer perfection if it weren't for the fresh but flavorless hero rolls the sandwich comes on. In fact, I often think about sending an anonymous note to Mama suggesting she check out Morrone's as a possible bread source. Oh yes, Mama Joy's sells a wide range of salads and other sandwiches. I've tried a number of others, like a Cure 81 ham and Swiss, which is a good combination, but I usually end up with the roast beef. It's just too good to pass up.

Note: At lunchtime the line can be daunting here. It moves quickly, but patience is required.

Mama Joy's
2892 Broadway (between 112th and 113th streets)
New York, NY 10025
PHONE: (212) 662-0716
SUBWAYS: 110th Street–Cathedral Parkway station on the following lines:
    Broadway–Seventh Avenue No. 1 and 9; Eighth Avenue C and Sixth
    Avenue B.
HOURS: 8 A.M. to 1 A.M. seven days a week.
Deliveries in the neighborhood.
Cash only.

$\mathcal{U}$PPER EAST SIDE

59TH STREET TO 96TH STREET
FIRST AVENUE TO FIFTH AVENUE

Canard and Company ∼ See page 299.

E.A.T. ∼ See page 300.

La Fromagerie ∼ La Fromagerie's owner, Daniele Grosjean, has singlehandedly elevated the ham sandwich from its humdrum status to the realm of the sublime. La Fromagerie's version has tasty, sliced-to-order, house-baked ham on a baguette from the East Harlem bread bastion Morrone's (see page 44). They must sell other sandwiches here, but I've never seen anybody order one. True to its name, La Fromagerie carries a fine if limited selection of properly ripened French cheeses. It also has one of the city's first-rate chicken pot pies in both a regular and a curried version.

La Fromagerie
1374 Madison Avenue (between 95th and 96th streets)
New York, NY 10128
PHONE: (212) 534-8923
SUBWAY: 96th Street station on the Lexington Avenue No. 6 line.
HOURS: 9 A.M. to 7:30 P.M. Tuesday through Saturday; 9 A.M. to 6:30 P.M.
   Sunday. Closed mid-August through Labor Day.
Delivery in the neighborhood.
Cash only.
Mail order available.

Viand Coffee Shop ∼ Most turkey sandwiches around New York are made either from turkey roll, which even stray dogs reject, or from turkey breast, which savvy eaters reject out of hand because turkeys, like people, should never be subjected to breast augmentation procedures. The Viand Coffee Shop actually carves your turkey sandwich off a real turkey, one that has all its relevant body parts intact. The craggy, moist pieces of meat are piled high enough on the sandwich to be a filling and hearty lunch, without the unnecessary Carnegie Deli height, which is most assuredly not desirable in turkey sandwiches. A Viand turkey sandwich, along with some of their rice pudding, is a terrific New York lunch. Everything else I've tried here is pretty standard coffee-shop fare.

Note: The guys who work at the Viand are classic "Cheeseburger, cheeps" Greeks who are hip enough to have seen the humor in those classic John Belushi "Saturday Night Live" sketches.

Viand Coffee Shop
673 Madison Avenue (between 61st and 62nd streets)
New York, NY 10021

PHONE: (212) 751-6622

SUBWAYS: 59th Street station on the Lexington Avenue No. 4, 5, and 6 lines; Lexington Avenue station on the Sixth Avenue B and Q lines; Fifth Avenue station on the Broadway N and R lines.

HOURS: 6 A.M. to 10 P.M. Monday through Saturday; 7 A.M. to 10 P.M. Sunday.

Deliveries in the neighborhood.

Cash only.

Note: This is the original Viand Coffee Shop. There are two other locations, one at Madison Avenue and 78th Street, the other at Second Avenue and 86th Street. There appears to be some sort of Viand Coffee Shop civil war going on. I could not get a straight answer as to who was affiliated with whom.

*M*IDTOWN WEST

34TH STREET TO 59TH STREET
FIFTH AVENUE TO ELEVENTH AVENUE

Carnegie Delicatessen ～ I was concerned when Leo Steiner, the Carnegie Deli's owner and chief of the pastrami-and-corned-beef police, died tragically and prematurely in 1987. With his death, the Carnegie lost not only one of the world's great pastrami-and-corned-beef curers but also its guiding spirit. So I'm thrilled to report that after a suitable period of mourning, during which the cured meats did suffer, the Carnegie Deli's corned beef and pastrami are back to being world-class quality. A hand-carved pastrami sandwich from the Carnegie is sandwich perfection personified: peppery, garlicky, tender, with the requisite amount of fat necessary to make a pastrami sandwich great.

Note: Getting your pastrami sandwich hand-carved not only makes your sandwich more flavorful, but also makes it a more manageable size. This is because when they hand-carve your sandwich, it doesn't attain the Eiffel Tower size of the machine-sliced meat sandwiches at the Carnegie. The other must-trys at Carnegie Deli are the corned-beef hash, made-to-order with onions and pepper, and the matzo-ball soup, which, when not too greasy, would put a lot of Jewish grandmothers out of business. Don't, repeat, don't ever order a turkey sandwich or the French fries at the Carnegie. The turkey is usually dry, and when they pile it six inches high on a sandwich you feel like you're biting into the Sahara Desert. The French fries are flavorless, frozen logs.

Carnegie Delicatessen
854 Seventh Avenue (between 54th and 55th streets)
New York, NY 10019

PHONE: (212) 757-2245

SUBWAYS: 57th Street station on the Broadway N and R lines; 7th Avenue station on the Eighth Avenue E and Sixth Avenue B and D lines; 50th Street station on the Broadway–Seventh Avenue No. 1 and 9 lines.

HOURS: 6:30 A.M. to 3:45 A.M. seven days a week.

Deliveries within a five-block radius.

Cash only.

Mail order available for cheesecake only.

Corrado Kitchen ~ Corrado Kitchen is an outgrowth of the adjoining Italian restaurant called, not surprisingly, Corrado. I've never eaten at Corrado, but if the focaccia sandwiches are any indication of the kitchen's overall skill, I plan to make a reservation soon. The focaccia sandwich with imported prosciutto, home-made mozzarella, tomatoes, and fresh basil is one of midtown Manhattan's superior take-out treats. The focaccia is flavorful and chewy without being too crunchy, and each component of the filling is impeccably fresh. A sandwich of grilled vegetables and provolone on focaccia is also just about perfect. The other specialty sandwiches here, like the grilled breast of chicken with shredded carrots and honey mustard, sound more interesting than they taste. The pasta salads are fresh and don't have that pickled taste that most pasta salads around town do, but they lack character. Desserts here are another triumph. The chocolate-nut brownies are fudgelike in texture, with enough bittersweet chocolate in them to satisfy even the most ardent chocoholic. The pecan bars are loaded with pecans layered on a buttery crust. No goopy pecan filler here. I haven't tried the mini fudge mousse or the carrot cake, but they both look wonderful. Based on the brownie and pecan bar, I'm sure they taste terrific, too.

Corrado Kitchen
1375 Sixth Avenue (between 55th and 56th streets)
New York, NY 10019
PHONE: (212) 333-7696
SUBWAYS: 57th Street station on the Sixth Avenue B and Q lines and the
   Broadway N and R lines.
HOURS: 7:30 A.M. to 9 P.M. Monday through Friday; 9 A.M. to 5 P.M.
   Saturday; closed Sunday.
Free delivery in the immediate area.
All major credit cards accepted ($20 minimum).

DiLuca Dairy ~ See page 68.

Focaccia Fiorentina ~ It was Wednesday, around lunchtime. I had just had knee surgery the day before, and my colleagues and I were bemoaning the lack of interesting lunch places that delivered to our office. All of a sudden I remembered the menu from Focaccia that I'd stuffed into my drawer. Focaccia had seemed kind of odd to me because it was a delivery-only sandwich place that had no actual address on its menu flyer. All it said on the front of the sheet was "Focaccia, Firenze and New York, 58th Street, east of 6th Avenue," with a phone number and fax number. In short order I persuaded five of my colleagues to order sandwiches, and I ordered another five sandwiches (covering almost everything on the menu) for tasting purposes. Although it took nearly an hour for the order to arrive, once my coworkers took a bite of their sandwiches (and gave me a sliver for research purposes), nobody was complaining. First of all, the focaccia the sandwiches were on was impeccably fresh, not too oily, and had a wonderful crunch. The fillings, ranging from prosciutto, salami, and roast beef to mozzarella, provolone, and Parmigiano-Reggiano, were all terrific and not too thickly piled on the bread. The extra-virgin olive oil was poured on with a judicious hand.

Even the container of take-out *tiramisu* was superb, with its intense coffee flavor and chunks of the requisite ladyfingers. Only the cold Florentine tomato soup disappointed, as it tasted like mediocre gazpacho. I've tried to find Focaccia by walking along West 58th Street, but haven't had any luck. So I called a friend in Florence, who got out the Florentine version of Focaccia's flyer. It read, "Focaccia, Firenze, New York, just east of La Strada Boulevard." Foiled again.

Focaccia Fiorentina
(A delivery and catering store only)
58th Street off Sixth Avenue
New York, NY 10019
PHONE: (212) 765-2222
FAX: (212) 765-1716
HOURS: 9 A.M. to 6 P.M. Monday through Friday; closed Saturday and
    Sunday.
Cash only.

Mangia --- I thought of Mangia as just another generic midtown-Manhattan designer sandwich shop until I tasted its roasted-eggplant sandwich served with tomatoes and watercress on a French baguette. The eggplant was wonderfully smoky and the baguette excellent, but what made the sandwich was the tomato-basil-Parmesan dressing. The other designer sandwiches here, such as the *chèvre* with sun-dried tomatoes and the basil-parmesan chicken, are good and solid, although the roast beef with horseradish dressing doesn't have very much beef flavor. Mangia's minipizzas, called *pizzetas*, are wonderful. Try the one with Gruyère, bacon, and mushrooms. Although many people talk up Mangia's baked goods, I found the cookies and the Maida Heater's chocolate brownies to be disappointing.

Mangia
54 West 56th Street (between Fifth and Sixth avenues)
New York, NY 10019
PHONE: (212) 582-3061
SUBWAYS: 57th Street station on the Sixth Avenue B and Q lines; Fifth
    Avenue–53rd Street station on the Sixth Avenue F and Eighth Avenue E
    lines.
HOURS: 7:30 A.M. to 6:30 P.M. Monday through Friday; 9 A.M. to 5 P.M.
    Saturday; closed Sunday.
Delivery available.
All major credit cards accepted.

OTHER LOCATION:
16 East 48th Street (between Fifth and Madison avenues)
New York, NY 10017
(212) 754-7600

Piatti Pronti --- The ideal designer sandwich has the perfect confluence of ingredients, just the right combination of flavors and textures. Piatti Pronti's Lucca is such a sandwich, with its combination of prosciutto, sliced chicken, sun-dried tomatoes, rosemary sprigs, and olive oil on Italian brick-oven bread. Piatti Pronti's twelve other sandwich choices are put together just as carefully, with faultlessly fresh ingredients and all the right touches. PP also makes very good but not great individual pizzas and calzones, and first-rate soups. There's also an espresso bar where you can get those great grilled sandwiches with ham and/or cheese you'd find in Italy.

Note: Expect long lines and a crowded store if you go to pick up your lunch between 12:30 and 1:45. The best time to come is during off-peak hours, when the store has an airy, very pleasant feel. Piatti Pronti does deliver, but during peak lunch hours they take forever.

Piatti Pronti
34 West 56th Street (between Fifth and Sixth avenues)
New York, NY 10019
PHONE: (212) 315-4800
SUBWAYS: 57th Street station on the Sixth Avenue B and Q lines, Fifth
  Avenue–53rd Street station on the Sixth Avenue F and Eighth Avenue E
  lines.
HOURS: 8 A.M. to 5 P.M. Monday through Friday; closed Saturday and
  Sunday.
Deliveries in the neighborhood.
All major credit cards accepted.
OTHER LOCATIONS:
8 Maiden Lane
New York, NY 10038
(212) 233-1500

37 West 46th Street (between Fifth and Sixth avenues)
New York, NY 10036
(212) 575-4820

Remi to Go ⋯ See page 307.

IDTOWN EAST

34TH STREET TO 59TH STREET
FIRST AVENUE TO FIFTH AVENUE

Mangia ⋯ See page 286.

HELSEA

14TH STREET TO 34TH STREET
FIFTH AVENUE TO ELEVENTH AVENUE

Amir's Falafel ⋯ See page 281.

$\mathscr{K}$IPS BAY/GRAMERCY PARK

14TH STREET TO 34TH STREET
EAST RIVER TO FIFTH AVENUE

Eisenberg Sandwich Shop ⋯ Most tuna sandwiches you get in coffee shops taste as if the tuna and the mayonnaise were mixed together sometime in the previous decade and left to ferment. Unfortunately, unlike wine, tuna doesn't age well. But the folks at Eisenberg's have been making the absolutely perfect tuna sandwich for more than six decades. All it contains is solid white tuna from a can and mayonnaise whipped together fresh every morning. No celery, no onions, no apples, no kiwi fruit. An Eisenberg's tuna sandwich on rye toast and a cherry-lime rickey are one of Manhattan life's simple pleasures. Eisenberg's itself is just as classic as its tuna sandwich—a long, narrow room with a wooden counter that runs almost the entire length of the joint, with a simple white tin ceiling. It hasn't changed since it opened, and Eisenberg devotees who were worried when the Eisenbergs sold out a few years ago to a Korean family need not have concerned themselves. It still has the same friendly counterpeople, the same old rectangular wooden signs listing the sandwich options, and, thank God, the same tuna.

Note: Eisenberg's makes lots of other good sandwiches, like chicken salad, egg salad, corned beef, and roast chicken, but Eisenberg neophytes should start with the tuna sandwich.

Eisenberg Sandwich Shop
174 Fifth Avenue (between 22nd and 23rd streets)
New York, NY 10011
PHONE: (212) 675-5096
SUBWAYS: 23rd Street station on the Broadway N and R lines and the
    Lexington Avenue No. 6 line.
HOURS: 6 A.M. to 4 P.M. Monday through Friday; closed Saturday and
    Sunday.
Deliveries in the neighborhood.
American Express accepted.

Eisenberg's Tuna Salad

1 can Bumble Bee solid white tuna
Hellman's mayonnaise

Mash the tuna and the mayonnaise with a big spoon. If you use a fork, it won't turn out right. All the tuna salad must be eaten the day you make it.

Todaro Brothers ⋯ See page 233.

$\mathcal{E}$AST VILLAGE

14TH STREET TO HOUSTON STREET
EAST RIVER TO FIFTH AVENUE

Second Avenue Kosher Delicatessen & Restaurant ⁓ Unlike the glitzy delis in Midtown, the Second Avenue Deli still feels like a deli when you walk in. There's hubbub all around you, the countermen are kibbitzing with the customers and one another, and every exchange seems to be a negotiation. What isn't up for discussion is owner Abe Lebewohl's hearty mushroom-barley soup, the lean and flavorful corned beef that he cures himself, and the fresh French fries he makes, which are properly oniony, crisp, and golden brown. Unfortunately, what I've just described is lunch for two or three, for the portions are very large here. The pastrami is very good, if not among the city's best, and the turkey, as at most delis around town these days, is pretty dry.

Second Avenue Kosher Delicatessen & Restaurant
156 Second Avenue (corner of 10th Street)
New York, NY 10003
PHONE: (212) 677-0606
SUBWAY: Astor Place station on the Lexington Avenue No. 6 line; 8th Street–
    NYU station on the Broadway R line.
HOURS: 10 A.M. to midnight Sunday through Thursday; 10 A.M. to 2 A.M.
    Friday and Saturday.
Deliveries all over Manhattan.
Cash only.
Mail order available.

$\mathcal{M}$ushroom and $\mathcal{B}$arley $\mathcal{S}$oup from the $\mathcal{S}$econd $\mathcal{A}$venue $\mathcal{K}$osher $\mathcal{D}$elicatessen & $\mathcal{R}$estaurant

½ cup dried mushrooms   1 stalk celery, chopped
2 cups medium barley   1 carrot, chopped
4 quarts stock   ½ parsnip root, chopped
2 tablespoons olive oil   Salt and pepper to taste
2 onions, diced

1. Soak mushrooms in water for a few hours. Drain well and chop.
2. Place barley and stock in a large, 6- to 8-quart soup pot. Bring to a boil, reduce heat to low, cover, and simmer for 40 minutes.
3. Heat oil in a saucepan over medium heat and sauté onions to a light golden brown. Drain excess oil.
4. Add sautéed onion, celery, carrot, parsnip, and mushrooms to soup pot and cook for another 20 minutes. Add salt and pepper to taste and enjoy!

Yield: 10 servings

$\mathscr{D}$OWNTOWN

HOUSTON STREET TO BATTERY PARK

Barocco Alimentari ⁓ See page 311.

Bernstein-on-Essex ⁓ Don't be put off that this Lower East Side institution slings kosher Chinese food when it's not dishing out deli. The Chinese food is not quite so horrible as you'd imagine, but the pastrami is the real deal here, the authentic Romanian-style preparation not served in the Midtown delis. They cure it themselves, and it's so good and peppery and garlicky that it's difficult (although not impossible by any means) for me to order a pastrami sandwich anywhere else in Manhattan. The French fries are also terrific here, fresh and crisp and oniony. The rest of the deli sandwiches are fairly standard.

Bernstein-on-Essex
135 Essex Street (between Stanton and Rivington streets)
New York, NY 10002
PHONE: (212) 473-3900
SUBWAYS: Delancey Street station on the Sixth Avenue F line; Essex Street
    station on the Nassau Street J, M, and Z lines.
HOURS: 8 A.M. to midnight Sunday through Thursday; 8 A.M. to 2 P.M.
    Friday; closed Saturday.
Deliveries available all over Manhattan.
All major credit cards accepted.
Mail order available.

Dean and DeLuca ⁓ See page 214.

Donald Sacks ⁓ You're wandering around Soho on a beautiful spring morning, and you don't want to waste any of the day by going inside for lunch. The solution: Go to Donald Sacks, one of the original New York designer-sandwich joints. His Brie and Westphalian ham with Bermuda onion on black bread is the perfect combination of flavors and textures. His smoked-chicken salad on semolina really hits the spot, and his Black Forest ham, smoked turkey, and cheese with sweet peppers is as intense a confluence of flavors as you'll find on one sandwich. If you don't feel like a sandwich, they make very good soups and salads at Donald Sacks as well. Finally, if you've got a sweet tooth, buy a Donald Sacks chocolate-pecan wedge. It's sinfully rich, buttery, and chocolaty. The only problem with buying your lunch at Donald Sacks is you have to be willing to sit on a stoop to eat it. There's simply no other public sit-down spot in Soho.

Note: This is a tiny store, and when there are more than six people inside, it can seem like a subway car at rush hour. Also, be prepared for a heavy dose of Soho attitude from the help here.

The sandwiches are fantastic at the Italian Food Center, which also carries a wide range of Italian imported foods.

Donald Sacks
120 Prince Street (between Greene and Wooster streets)
New York, NY 10012
PHONE: (212) 226-0165
SUBWAYS: Broadway–Lafayette Street station on the Sixth Avenue B, D, F,
    and Q lines; Bleecker Street station on the Lexington Avenue No. 6 line;
    Prince Street station on the Broadway R line.
HOURS: 8 A.M. to 6 P.M. Monday through Friday; 10 A.M. to 6 P.M. Saturday
    and Sunday.
Deliveries in Manhattan.
American Express accepted ($50 minimum).

OTHER LOCATION:
3 World Financial Center
220 Vesey Street (between Hudson River and West Street)
New York, NY 10281
(212) 619-4600
Note: This is a much bigger Donald Sacks. It's really an overpriced sit-
    down restaurant, but it does have a take-out section with soups, salads,
    sandwiches, and sweets.

Italian Food Center ⁓ Until 1987, anyone ordering a sandwich at the Italian Food Center got to pick out his or her own piping-hot hero bread and hand it to one of the guys making sandwiches. Now they keep the breads behind the counter, and I really miss the bread selection ritual. Thankfully, the sandwiches themselves

Alessandro Gualandi takes sandwich making to a new level at Melampo Imported Foods.

are the same wonderful, greasy, lip-smacking messes. Try the New Yorker, a combination of prosciutto, Genoa salami, marinated mushrooms, and provolone. The Italian Food Center also carries a wide range of Italian imported foods and prepares more-than-creditable versions of southern Italian specialties such as chicken rollatini and eggplant parmigiana to take home. The last time I was here, they put out a tray of still-hot bruschetta, which I proceeded to munch on while they made my sandwich.

Italian Food Center
186 Grand Street (corner of Mulberry street)
New York, NY 10012
PHONE: (212) 925-2954
SUBWAYS: Spring Street station on the Lexington Avenue 6 line; Grand
    Street station on the Sixth Avenue B, D, and Q lines.
HOURS: 8 A.M. to 7 P.M. seven days a week.
Deliveries in the neighborhood.
All major credit cards accepted.
Mail order available.

Melampo Imported Foods ⟶ Watching owner Alessandro Gualandi make my prosciutto-and-smoked-mozzarella sandwich with sun-dried tomatoes on home-made focaccia, I knew I was in the presence of genius. First he takes a quarter of Manhattan's best focaccia and slices it in half lengthwise. He then slices the prosciutto and places it ever so carefully on the bottom of the bread. Next he takes his fresh, handmade smoked mozzarella, cuts off four or five generous slices by hand, and fans them ever so carefully on top of the prosciutto. Then he takes some tongs and plucks a whole bunch of his sun-dried tomatoes and places them atop the cheese. Last, he splashes on some extra-virgin olive oil. He hands you your sandwich, you ask for one of the terrific Italian lemon sodas he stocks, and you leave the store. Knowing that you can't wait to eat this work of art, you go to the playground next door, hoping one of the concrete tables with benches on both sides is available. You sit down, take a bite, and realize you're eating one of New York's best lunches.

Note: To buy a whole focaccia bread to take home, you must order it one day in advance. It's a pain but worth it. Order two, because the first one won't make it home intact.

Melampo Imported Foods
105 Sullivan Street (between Spring and Prince streets)
New York, NY 10012
PHONE: (212) 334-9530
SUBWAYS: Spring Street station on the Eighth Avenue C and E lines;
   Houston Street station on the Broadway–Seventh Avenue No. 1 and 9
   lines.
HOURS: 11 A.M. to 8 P.M. Monday through Saturday; closed Sunday.
No deliveries.
Cash only.

Piatti Pronti ～ See page 286.

$\mathcal{Q}$UEENS

Pastrami King Restaurant ～ I admit to being a sucker for any establishment that refers to itself as the king of whatever it specializes in. Maybe it's because the five places I know of that use this convention—Angelo the Pizza King; Bruno the King of Ravioli; Ben Faremo, the Lemon Ice King of Corona; Barney Greengrass the Sturgeon King; and Pastrami King—all put out superior products. Pastrami King's garlic-infused, dry-cured Romanian pastrami is a dark, almost burnished, reddish-brown in color and is much drier and leaner than, say, the Carnegie Deli's. There is just enough fat on the meat to keep the sandwich from being dry. A Pastrami King pastrami sandwich, an order of their superthick, four-inch-long, fresh-cut French fries, and a Doctor Brown's cherry soda is the quintessential New York lunch. I can't tell you about any of the other sandwiches at Pastrami King; I've never figured out a reason to order anything other than the pastrami.

Note: Pastrami King's Queens Boulevard location in Kew Gardens makes it an ideal pit stop for any Long Island foray. It's literally a five-minute detour off the Grand Central Parkway.

Pastrami King Restaurant
124-24 Queens Boulevard (at 82nd Avenue)
Jamaica, NY 11415

PHONE: (718) 263-1717
SUBWAYS: Union Turnpike–Kew Gardens station on the Broadway R, Sixth
   Avenue F, and Eighth Avenue E lines.
HOURS: 8 A.M. to 9 P.M. Sunday through Friday; 8 A.M. to 10 P.M. Saturday.
Deliveries in the neighborhood.
American Express accepted.
Mail order available.

Best of Sandwiches

Best designer sandwiches: Piatti Pronti
Best corned-beef sandwich: Carnegie Delicatessen; Second Avenue Kosher
   Delicatessen
Best focaccia sandwiches: Melampo Imported Foods
Best focaccia sandwiches (Midtown): Focaccia Fiorentina
Best ham sandwich (French-style): La Fromagerie
Best old-fashioned Italian hero sandwiches: DiLuca Dairy, Italian Food Center
Best pastrami sandwich (Midtown): Carnegie Delicatessen
Best pastrami sandwich (Downtown): Bernstein-on-Essex
Best pastrami sandwich (Queens): Pastrami King
Best tuna sandwich: Eisenberg Sandwich Shop
Best turkey sandwich: Galaxie Deli and Restaurant

18

TAKE-OUT AND PREPARED FOOD

My absolute passion is take-out. Though my wife complains bitterly about the amount of take-out we eat, I am just not willing to deal with planning and cooking a meal when I get home at 7:30 or 8:00.

The best gourmet take-out, and it's not all that common, is as good as great restaurant food. At its worst, it's overpriced swill that tastes like college-food-service fare. Gourmet take-out can be divided into a number of categories. First, there are the small take-out shops run by one or two partners. These include such standouts as Neuman & Bogdonoff, Yura, and the Park Avenue Gourmandises. Because they are small and usually the result of one person's vision, they tend to be consistent, with their food coming from a singular point of view.

Then there are the hallowed halls of the larger gourmet stores like Balducci's, Dean & DeLuca, Zabar's, and Todaro Brothers, which have huge selections of prepared foods but tend to be less consistent in quality. Finally, there are the newest breed of gourmet take-out places, the outgrowths of successful restaurants. Places like Barocco Alimentari and Remi to Go in a certain way have greater pressure to sell top-quality food because their failure to do so would reflect badly on their restaurants.

There are a couple of caveats to buying gourmet take-out. One is to know that prepared food often looks better than it tastes. This is especially true at the larger establishments like Zabar's and Grace's Marketplace. So ask for a taste of whatever you're contemplating buying. Two, get clear instructions on how to heat whatever you've bought. I can't tell you how many times I've bought delicious-looking things only to discover I had forgotten to ask anyone at the store how to prepare them—and usually the store has closed by the time I get home. Three, ask when the food you're contemplating buying was made. You shouldn't have to buy yesterday's food that's been stored in the refrigerator.

$\mathcal{U}$PPER WEST SIDE

59TH STREET TO 125TH STREET
CENTRAL PARK WEST TO RIVERSIDE DRIVE

Adriana's Bazaar ⬿ See page 116.

Azteca Deli Grocery ⬿ See page 116.

Bennie's ⬿ Dr. Bennie, a Lebanese plastic surgeon, started Bennie's in 1982. I don't know how he does with tummy tucks, but he has a magic touch with salads and vegetables. The lentil salad, made with parsley, lemon juice, and olive oil, breathes new life into that tired dish. His nontraditional sesame noodles, made with tahini and soy sauce, are a welcome change from the usual peanut-butter drenched globs you get from most Chinese restaurants. Both the curried chicken salad and the lemon chicken are very good, made with tender white-meat chicken and an assortment of spices. Perhaps my favorite dish here is the garlic-roasted potatoes, pungent quartered new potatoes roasted in garlic and olive oil.

Bennie's
321 ½ Amsterdam Avenue (between 75th and 76th streets)
New York, NY 10023
PHONE: (212) 874-3032
SUBWAYS: 72nd Street station on the following lines: Broadway—Seventh
   Avenue No. 1, 2, 3, and 9; Eighth Avenue C and Sixth Avenue B.
HOURS: 11 A.M. to 10 P.M. seven days a week.
Deliveries in the neighborhood.
American Express accepted.

Cleopatra's Needle ⬿ Most Middle Eastern take-out food I've had has been so oily and pasty it would be better utilized as mortar to help rebuild Beirut. But Cleopatra's Needle's baba ghanouj and hummous are so spritely and fresh-tasting I no longer have to go to Atlantic Avenue in Brooklyn to satisfy my Middle Eastern eating urges. The Egyptian owner, Mohamed Hussein, and his Haitian chef, Nelson William, prepare a tangy feta cheese with tomatoes and green peppers so good my young son prefers it to peanut butter. The Egyptian vegetarian moussaka is wonderful hot or cold, and the cumin-accented breadsticks can be used instead of pita for his dips. Besides all the appetizers, they make five or six hot entrées daily, including a creditable couscous and Cleopatra snapper. If you have any room, there are lots of traditional sweet, syrupy Middle Eastern desserts as well, including a decent whole-wheat baklava.

Cleopatra's Needle
2485 Broadway (between 92nd and 93rd streets)
New York, NY 10025
PHONE: (212) 769-6965
SUBWAYS: 96th Street station on the following lines: Broadway–Seventh
    Avenue No. 1, 2, 3, and 9; Eighth Avenue C and Sixth Avenue B.
HOURS: 11 A.M. to midnight seven days a week.
Deliveries in Manhattan.
All major credit cards accepted.
Mail order available.

Fairway ～ See page 221.

International Poultry Company ～ See page 302.

The Silver Palate ～ The Silver Palate was the first creditable gourmet take-out store on the Upper West Side. Its founders, Julie Rosso and Sheila Lukin, have written three best-selling cookbooks and became so successful that they sold the store in 1987 to Peter Harris. He's opened a branch in Tokyo and broadened the distribution of the line of packaged Silver Palate dressings, dessert sauces, and exotic nuts. Oh yes, they still sell food at the Silver Palate, but when you walk into the store these days it feels like a brokerage house instead of a food-lover's paradise. However, if you stick to their desserts, salads, and vegetables you'll do fine. Scrumptious pies, cookies, and cakes; terrific potato salads; and a wonderful asparagus with prosciutto in a garlic vinaigrette are all guaranteed hits. The Silver Palate also carries wonderful, chewy Policastro and Tom Cat Bakery baguettes. The chicken and pasta dishes I've tried here have been bland and uninspired. Prices are exceptionally high, even for gourmet take-out, and the help can sometimes be uninterested and uninformed. Two good things about the Silver Palate: they always put out one or two interesting foods to try, and they prepare satisfying picnics for Central Park events.

The Silver Palate
274 Columbus Avenue (between 72nd and 73rd streets)
New York, NY 10023
PHONE: (212) 799-6340

SUBWAYS: 72nd Street station on the following lines: Broadway–Seventh
   Avenue No. 1, 2, 3, and 9; Eighth Avenue C and Sixth Avenue B.
HOURS: 7:30 A.M. to 9:30 P.M. Monday through Friday; 7:30 A.M. to 8:30 P.M.
   Saturday; 8:30 A.M. to 8:30 P.M. Sunday.
Deliveries in the neighborhood.
All major credit cards accepted.
Mail-order catalog available.

Williams Bar-B-Que ⁓ My mother was a goddawful cook (hence my keen take-out palate), but she did make one thing well: a kind of Jewish soul-food side dish with egg barley, mushrooms, onions, and enough chicken fat to send heart specialists into apoplexy. About ten years ago I discovered a duplicate of this dish in the window at Williams Bar-B-Que, the leader in New York Jewish soul food. Williams makes creditable fried chicken, a fairly greaseless rotisseried duck, and plump rotisseried chickens. Williams also carries a complete selection of Jewish-style side dishes. Skip the soggy, leaden potato pancakes, but don't miss the kasha varnishkes, made with bow-tie noodles, buckwheat groats, onions, and, yes, the ubiquitous chicken fat. Williams also makes a wonderful homemade cranberry sauce.

Williams Bar-B-Que
2350 Broadway (between 85th and 86th streets)
New York, NY 10024
PHONE: (212) 877-5384
SUBWAYS: 86th Street station on the following lines: Broadway–Seventh
   Avenue No. 1 and 9; Eighth Avenue C and Sixth Avenue B.
HOURS: 8 A.M. to 8 P.M. seven days a week.
Deliveries from 59th to 100th Streets.
Cash only.

Zabar's ⁓ See page 237.

𝒰PPER EAST SIDE

59TH STREET TO 96TH STREET
FIRST AVENUE TO FIFTH AVENUE

Akemi Japanese Gourmet Deli ⁓ One look at the array of delicacies found in Akemi's salad bar, and you'll know you're not in Kansas anymore. Instead of standard salad bar fare such as soggy cut-up fruit and tired-looking tuna, you'll find things like clam salad, lotus root and chicken, pickled cucumber, fishcakes and yamcakes, and butterfish. The lotus root and chicken had that combination of sweetness and saltiness many Japanese food preparations do, but I wished it had more chicken in it. The fishcake and yamcake combination was more sweet than anything else, with a few sesame seeds adding some crunch. My favorite item at the salad bar is a simple shredded chicken preparation that tasted like one of those gratis appetizers served at many Japanese restaurants. Akemi also sells standard Japanese fare like tempura, dumplings, teriyaki, and sushi. My son liked the shrimp dumplings so much he was popping them into his mouth like M & Ms. But the truth of the matter is, so were his parents.

Akemi Japanese Gourmet Deli
1128 Third Ave (between 65th and 66th streets)
New York, NY 10021
PHONE: (212) 734-1532 or 734-3180
SUBWAY: 68th Street-Hunter College station on the Lexington Avenue No. 6
   line; Lexington Avenue station on the Sixth Avenue B and Q lines.
HOURS: 10:00 A.M. to 9 P.M. Monday through Saturday; Closed Sunday.
Free delivery in neighborhood with $10.00 minimum order.
All major credit cards.

Canard and Company ⸺ Even on stodgy Madison Avenue there are food shops like Canard and Company that actually feel like neighborhood joints. Canard is genuinely customer-friendly and community-oriented. It has tastings and a newsletter and exudes lots of good vibes. Good food, too. The chef, Peter Ivy, has a way with Santa Fe–style dishes. Try the black bean chile with chipotle salsa. It manages to have a kick without sounding a fire alarm in your mouth. The jicama salad with an orange and cilantro vinaigrette will have you singing the praises of this root seldom seen on the East Coast. The guacamole is chunky and fresh, made with just enough lime juice. The designer sandwiches are wonderful. Try the white-fronted goose sandwich (ignore the silly sandwich names), which has glazed apple-smoked baked ham, smoked mozzarella, tomato, fresh mixed greens, and herb mayonnaise. Canard's owner, Roy Wade, is also smart enough to carry bread and baked goods from the best bakeries in the New York area. He has the largest selection in the city of baked goods from the legendary Kathleen's in Southhampton. Her pies are extraordinary, her coffee cake's just as good, and her chocolate-chip cookies and doughnut holes shouldn't be wasted on small children. The moist and rich crumb buns here, made by Hahn's, are the best I've found in the city. Bread fans should rejoice that Canard carries Morrone and Policastro baguettes. The cheesesticks are tangy and insanely buttery, so if you eat one and you're on Weight Watchers, you're finished with eating for the day.

Canard and Company
1292 Madison Avenue (corner of 92nd Street)
New York, NY 10128
PHONE: (212) 722-1046
SUBWAY: 96th Street station on the Lexington Avenue No. 6 line.
HOURS: 7 A.M. to 9 P.M. seven days a week.
Deliveries in Manhattan.
American Express accepted.
Mail order, catering, and gift baskets available.

David's ⸺ If Williams Bar-B-Que is the Jewish soul-food king of the West Side, then David's can lay claim to that title on the East side. David's leaves its rotisseried chickens on the spit until somebody orders one, so they're always piping hot. The meat is tender and the skin crispy. David's, in addition to chicken, rotisseries other poultry like duck, turkey, capon, and Rock Cornish hens. David's kasha varnishkes may be my favorite take-out version in the city. It has plenty of onions and enough chicken fat to grease a football stadium. His egg barley with mushrooms is almost as good. The string beans and other salads are decent, but the rice pudding's a loser.

David's
1323 Third Avenue (corner of 76th Street) New York, NY 10021
PHONE: (212) 535-6104
SUBWAY: 77th Street station on the Lexington Avenue No. 6 line.
HOURS: 9 A.M. to 8:30 P.M. Monday through Friday; 9 A.M. to 7:30 P.M.
    Saturday and Sunday.
Free delivery.
All major credit cards accepted.

E.A.T. --- Yes, the rumors are true. You have to fill out a credit application before you can buy anything at E.A.T. It's that expensive. But I have to applaud owner Eli Zabar. In a city where ridiculously high prices by no means guarantee quality, he consistently delivers the goods. Almost everything I've tasted here has been sublime. The sandwiches on his superb baguettes are sinful perfection. Try a trio of mozzarella, basil, and tomato drizzled with a mustard vinaigrette—or perhaps the simple grilled eggplant sandwich. For more elaborate fare, try the blackened salmon stuffed with herbs. Eli's breads are distributed city wide and are among the city's best. End your meal with one of his wondrous old-fashioned desserts, like his marble cake or his carrot cake, and you'll be a blissfully happy person as you file for Chapter 11. Only the legendary brownies, which I found a little dry, and the sodden ham-and-cheese croissants disappointed me here. Oh, yes, the Parmesan toast, flat bread baked with *parmigiano reggiano*, was wonderful, but $30.00 a pound for crackers is too much, no matter how good they are.

Note: When my wife was in the hospital after giving birth, my cousins Bob and Meryl sent over an amazing basket of goodies from E.A.T. It had brownies, cookies, a rattle, and a stuffed bunny. Vicky got mad at me for eating all the food in the basket; I countered that at least I didn't eat the rattle and bunny.

E.A.T.
1064 Madison Avenue (between 80th and 81st streets)
New York, NY 10028
PHONE: (212) 772-0022
SUBWAY: 77th Street station on the Lexington Avenue No. 6 line.
HOURS: 7 A.M. to 10 P.M. seven days a week.
Deliveries available for a fee.
American Express accepted.
Catering and picnic baskets available.

El Pollo --- The grilled, rotisseried, and roasted chicken craze in New York has produced a lot of generic-tasting chicken, but El Pollo's "secret" twenty-four-hour marinade distinguishes this store from all its competitors. Although the owner, Lucio Medina, won't say exactly what's in the marinade, I taste garlic, paprika, soy sauce, white wine, and vinegar. Half of an El Pollo chicken, along with an order of Medina's fresh, crispy French fries, is one of New York's most satisfying cheap meals. The chicken is so flavorful it doesn't need either of the sauces that come with it, but if you order the hot sauce, be forewarned: It's incendiary. Skip the *papa relleno*, a lump of fried mashed potatoes stuffed with ground meat.

El Pollo
1746 First Avenue (between 90th and 91st streets)
New York, NY 10128
PHONE: (212) 996-7810
SUBWAYS: 86th Street station on the Lexington Avenue No. 4, 5, and 6 lines.
HOURS: 11 A.M. to 11 P.M. seven days a week.
Free delivery.
Cash only.

Fraser-Morris ⬩ Before New York became a center for passionate food lovers, Fraser-Morris must have seemed like the real thing. Today, however, it seems almost like a caricature of a gourmet store. You know—snooty service, indifferently prepared food, and lots of ridiculously expensive imported packaged goods. For example, Fraser-Morris is currently the exclusive importer for a line of packaged items from the legendary Parisian gourmet shop Fauchon. This means you can get two white peaches packed in syrup for nine dollars. They definitely taste better than Del Monte, but not that much better. I don't look forward to going back to Fraser-Morris any time soon. Maybe they treat regulars better.

Note: I feel compelled to mention that Fraser-Morris does make wonderful homemade apple sauce.

Fraser-Morris
1264 Third Avenue (between 72nd and 73rd streets)
New York, NY 10021
PHONE: (212) 288-2727
SUBWAYS: 68th Street station on the Lexington Avenue No. 6 line.
HOURS: 8:30 A.M. to 7 P.M. Monday through Saturday; 10 A.M. to 5 P.M.
   Sunday.
Deliveries made anywhere.
All major credit cards accepted.
Mail order, picnic and gift baskets, and catering available.

Grace's Marketplace ⬩ See page 225.

Hale & Hearty ⬩ Admittedly, I have a bias against take-out food stores that make health claims about their food. So I was unabashedly skeptical when I passed Hale & Hearty and saw a pledge on the wall and on the menu that read, "Wholesome and delicious food that is naturally low in fats, cholesterol, and sodium. . . . Hale & Hearty is for people who want to stay healthy and eat well." Imagine my surprise when it turned out that some of Hale & Hearty's food was quite tasty. The lentil soup was flavorful and well-seasoned, though a little ham or sausage would have done wonders for it. The twice-cooked baked potato stuffed with mushrooms, broccoli, and Parmesan cheese was filling and tangy. The lemon-chicken cutlet was moist and crisp, even after being microwaved. Equally satisfying were the roasted potatoes with lemon aoli, and an intriguing combination of white beans, apple, tomato, and grilled corn. For dessert, try the hazelnut cake with a chocolate frosting made with Callebaut chocolate and milk. It's so moist and chocolaty you won't even miss the butter in the frosting. I still like pork an awful lot, but I must admit that Hale & Hearty's offerings convinced me that healthy take-out can be tasty and nutritious.

Hale & Hearty
849 Lexington Avenue (between 64th and 65th streets)
New York, NY 10021
PHONE: (212) 517-7600
SUBWAYS: 68th Street–Hunter College station on the Lexington Avenue No.
   6 line; Lexington Avenue station on the Sixth Avenue B and Q lines.
HOURS: 8 A.M. to 8 P.M. Monday through Friday; 11 A.M. to 6 P.M. Saturday;
   closed Sundays.
Delivery available within a ten-block radius.
All major credit cards accepted.

International Poultry Company ⚊ I am always (or never) on a diet, and therefore I'm constantly looking for places that have tasty low-cal foods. I don't find many, so it was a revelation to discover IPC's Santa Fe chicken, a grilled chicken breast accompanied by tangy, non-oily salsa. IPC also makes succulent rotisseried free-range chickens and a wonderfully flavored and virtually fat-free duck. Their skin-less fried chicken is good, although don't think it's dietetic just because the skin's been removed. Lastly, IPC's soups range from very, very good to sublime. Their chicken soup with lots of fresh dill and bow-tie pasta may force Jewish grand-mothers all over the city to revisit their recipes. The black-bean soup may do the same for Cuban grandmothers.

Warning sign: Two other IPC stores have opened in Manhattan, and the last time I had the Santa Fe Chicken, it was kind of dry. So it's possible the owners are spreading themselves too thin.

International Poultry Company
1133 Madison Avenue (between 84th and 85th streets)
New York, NY 10028
PHONE: (212) 879-3600
SUBWAYS: 86th Street station on the Lexington Avenue No. 4, 5, and 6 lines.
HOURS: 10 A.M. to 9 P.M. Monday through Friday; 9 A.M. to 8 P.M. Saturday
   and Sunday.
Delivery available.
All major credit cards accepted.
Picnic baskets and catering available.

OTHER LOCATIONS:
983 First Avenue (corner of 54th Street)
New York, NY 10022
(212) 750-1100

2151 Broadway (at 76th Street)
New York, NY 10023
(212) 721-7000

Lorenzo & Maria's Kitchen --- It's hard to imagine prepared food looking any better than the glistening, pristine platters placed in the window of Lorenzo & Maria's Kitchen. Thankfully for all of us, much of what Maria Armendariz cooks tastes as good as or better than it looks. The marinated shrimp with fresh dill is so fresh I can practically hear the surf from the Gulf of Mexico when I eat them. Her leg of lamb is properly rare and tender in its rosemary-suffused gravy. Her liberal use of fresh herbs makes her vegetables and side dishes even better than her main courses. The steamed sugar snap peas and carrots are marinated in almond oil with thyme and coriander, and the carrot puree isn't overwhelmed by cream or butter the way so many vegetable purees are. The sauteed wild rice with pignoli nuts and mushrooms is the best wild-rice preparation I've tasted. Even Maria's homemade applesauce is made special by her use of apple juice as a sweetener. But save room for dessert. Maria makes a *crème caramel* that would put many New York restaurant versions of this dessert to shame. Her poached pear with caramel sauce is so good that I growled at my son when he asked me for a bite. I have tasted a few items here that are not up to the kitchen's high standards. The chicken marengo and the beef bourguignon are dull and uninteresting versions of these classic dishes. The angel food cake is heavy and dry. The pies are okay, but are certainly not among the city's best.

Note: Lorenzo & Maria's food doesn't come cheap. In fact, it may be (along with E.A.T.) the most expensive store of its kind in New York. The applesauce is $4.25 for half a pound, the sauteed wild rice $10.00, and the sugar snap peas and carrots $6.50. There's a reason they don't put the price tags on the gorgeous platters of food in the window. It would scare too many people away. For more on Lorenzo & Maria's Kitchen, see Thanksgiving Trot on page 315.

Lorenzo & Maria's Kitchen
1418 Third Avenue (between 80th and 81st streets)
New York, NY 10021
PHONE: (212) 794-1080
SUBWAYS: 77th Street station on the Lexington Avenue No. 6 line.
HOURS: 9 A.M. to 8 P.M. Monday to Saturday; closed Sunday.
Deliveries made all over the city.
No credit cards.
Catering available.
Shipping available.

Neuman & Bogdonoff --- It's not surprising that Paul Neuman, having been brought up in the fish business (his father owns the Rosedale Fish Market) has a way with fish. But what I want to know is who taught Paul and his wife, Stacy Bogdonoff, how to cook and bake all the other terrific items in their store. I've sampled almost a hundred different dishes from N & B, and almost everything has been absolutely first-rate. Pastas such as radiatore with pancetta are assertively flavored and impeccably fresh, as are the wide variety of cold salads, such as the cold shrimp in lemon sauce. Even old standbys like chicken salad are lent an added dimension here. The chicken marengo is hearty and good, and the soups are all assertively seasoned. Try the cucumber. Save room for N & B's extraordinary baked goods. The muffins (see the entry for Taylor's on page 33) set the standard for moisture, flavor, and relative lightness. The sour-cream pecan coffee cake alone is worth a detour to N & B, and the apple cobbler is the best I've had north of the Mason-Dixon line. I *have* tried a couple of losers here. Potato pancakes were burned on one side, and a piece of chocolate cake had dry edges from being left out presliced all day.

Neuman & Bogdonoff
1385 Third Avenue (between 78th and 79th streets)
New York, NY 10021
PHONE: (212) 861-0303
SUBWAY: 77th Street station on the Lexington Avenue No. 6 line.
HOURS: 7 A.M. to 7:30 P.M. Monday through Friday; 7 A.M. to 7 P.M.
    Saturday; closed Sunday.
Delivery available.
All major credit cards accepted.
Mail order, gift and picnic baskets, and catering available.

Neuman & Bogdonoff's Cucumber Soup

4 cucumbers, peeled, seeded, and grated	1 dash Tabasco
1 cup yogurt	Salt and white pepper to taste
1 quart buttermilk	1 tablespoon sugar, or to taste
	1 bunch fresh dill

1. Sprinkle a little salt on grated cucumber and let stand for 1 hour.
2. Using cheesecloth or a towel, squeeze all the water out of cucumber.
3. In a large bowl, stir together cucumbers and remaining ingredients except dill. Chill thoroughly and then serve, garnished with fresh dill.

Yield: 6 to 8 servings

Neuman & Bogdonoff's Chicken Salad

½ cup julienned carrots
½ cup julienned celery, cut on a 45°
   angle
½ cup sliced red onion
½ cup sliced red pepper

½ cup sliced green pepper
½ cup sliced yellow pepper
2 cups champagne vinegar
½ pound sliced poached chicken
   breast per person

DRESSING

1 cup margarine
½ cup Dijon mustard
10 ounces champagne vinegar

½ ounce lemon juice
Salt and pepper to taste
Chopped parsley for garnish

1. Keep all vegetables separate as you prepare them.
2. In a heavy-bottomed saucepan, bring 2 cups champagne vinegar to a boil.
   Add carrot and celery and cook for 1 minute. Add onion and cook for 1
   minute. Add peppers and cook for 1 minute, or until all vegetables are just
   crunchy. Drain off liquid and set aside vegetables to cool.
3. *Prepare dressing*: In a medium-sized bowl, stir together margarine,
   mustard, 10 ounces champagne vinegar, lemon juice, salt, and pepper.
4. In a large bowl, toss together chicken breast and cooled vegetables. Add
   desired amount of dressing, garnish with parsley, and serve.

Word of Mouth — Word of Mouth was one of the city's first important gourmet
take-out stores, and it's still one of the best. As is true at virtually all the good
take-out places, you will be rewarded by sticking to the simplest, most elemental
foods. Word of Mouth's meat loaf, for instance, is faultless—crusty on the outside,
tender on the inside, and intensely seasoned. The lamb stew accented with saffron
is tasty, but I've occasionally gotten a tough piece of lamb. Eating Word of Mouth's
unbelievably rich and creamy rice pudding has become a religious experience for
some members of our household. The store is famous for its chicken salads, but
I find its classic version with dill, walnuts, and apples rather boring. Try the one
with bacon instead. Word of Mouth makes terrific baked goods, including lemon
pecan bars, peanut cup bars, and irresistible Mexican wedding cookies my mother-
in-law brings over to win the affection of her grandson. They often get intercepted
by me.

Word of Mouth
1012 Lexington Avenue (between 73rd and 74th streets)
New York, NY 10021
PHONE: (212) 734-9483
SUBWAYS: 77th Street station on the Lexington Avenue No. 6 line.
HOURS: 10 A.M. to 7 P.M. Monday through Friday; 10 A.M. to 6 P.M. Saturday;
   11:30 A.M. to 5:30 P.M. Sunday.
Delivery for a fee.
American Express accepted.
Picnic baskets arranged.

Yura — According to Yura herself, her "main interest is in food that people can eat every day. That kind of food can and should taste great. The tunas and BLTs of this world are so bad and can be so good." I've never had a BLT from Yura, but her fresh tuna salad was the very essence of this most New York of New York salads. As for eating her food every day, count me in. Yura makes some of the best takeout food in all of New York, and her baked goods aren't far behind. Her food is unquestionably fresh, simple, and, with one or two exceptions, boldly seasoned. Her moussaka has a satiny béchamel, big tender slices of eggplant, and tasty morsels of lamb. Her pinwheel sandwiches, made with smoked turkey, arugula, and tomato, are a perfect combination of flavors and textures. The exceptions: Fried chicken here was properly crisp and peppery, but the skin on one side was virtually uncooked; her meat loaf had a crunchy edge, but a too-rare center; and the macaroni and cheese was surprisingly dull. Yura's soups are at least as good as her main courses. Her tangy tomato soup contains just enough cream to make it satiny smooth. Her yellow-squash-and-rosemary soup is a work of art, and I don't even like rosemary or yellow squash very much.

It's hard to believe, but Yura may be a better baker than she is a chef. Her angel food cake with a bittersweet chocolate icing made me an angel-food-cake convert. Her apple crisp belongs on my short list of apple-crisp heavy hitters, that's saying something because apple crisp is one of my all-time favorite desserts. Teddie's Apple Cake is moist, flavorful, and loaded with fresh apples. Yura's chocolate turtles with nuts are as dense a chocolate cookie as I've ever had. They're much more fudgelike than cookielike, but that's okay with me. However, the excessively sweet Yankee pudding, made with chocolate, bananas, meringue, and custard, was unremarkable, and the fresh pear sauce was a good idea ruined by too much clove. One thing more: Yura's breakfast muffins rank right up there with Taylor's (see page 33) as the city's best, and I may prefer Yura's because they're lighter and smaller. Try her coffee-cake muffin or her farmer's muffin made with devil's food cake with a cheesecake center.

Service can be a real problem at Yura. When the store is crowded, customers fly by in all directions. The counterpeople, meanwhile, get harried and a little huffy. But still, with food this good, it's worth the hassle. Yura is one of New York's unheralded food masters. Check her out now so you can say you knew her when.

Yura
1650 Third Avenue (between 92nd and 93rd streets)
New York, NY 10128
PHONE: (212) 860-8060
SUBWAY: 96th Street station on the Lexington Avenue No. 6 line.
HOURS: 7 A.M. to 8 P.M. Monday through Saturday; 8 A.M. to 6 P.M. Sunday.
Delivery available.
All major credit cards accepted.
Catering and picnic baskets are available.

*M*IDTOWN WEST

34TH STREET TO 59TH STREET
FIFTH AVENUE TO ELEVENTH AVENUE

Good & Plenty to Go — Eileen Weinberg, owner of Good & Plenty to Go, is a New York food pioneer, having been one of the original owners of one of the first gourmet take-out stores in the city, Word of Mouth. Her food is hearty and assertively seasoned and, unlike much take-out food, often tastes *better* than it looks. Her vegetarian chili puts most variations of that basically forgettable dish to shame, and her smoked-chicken salad with bacon is quite special, although it has too much mayonnaise in it. The barbecued brisket is tangy and tasty but bears little resemblance to true Kansas City–style or Texas-style barbecue. Her tamale pie is very good, and she sells Tom Cat baguettes to accompany your meal. Her macaroni and cheese is the best version I've had in New York, but even an avowed cholesterol lover like me thinks it's just a tad too rich.

Good & Plenty to Go
410 West 43rd Street (between Ninth and Tenth avenues)
New York, NY 10036
PHONE: (212) 268-4385
SUBWAYS: 42nd Street–Port Authority Bus Terminal station on the Eighth
    Avenue A, C, and E lines.
HOURS: 8:30 A.M. to 8 P.M. Monday through Friday; 10 A.M. to 6 P.M.
    Saturday; 8 A.M. to 6 P.M. Sunday.
No deliveries.
American Express accepted.

Macy's Cellar Marketplace — See page 229.

Remi to Go — We descended on Remi to Go en masse, three hungry carnivores, two starving vegetarians. I had gathered the tasting troups because I figured that a take-out joint affiliated with one of midtown Manhattan's hottest Italian restaurants would have lots of interesting offerings. I was right. The pasta salads were fresh and tasty and didn't have that unpleasant pickled taste many pasta salads get from sitting around too long. Try the penne with salami or with mixed grilled vegetables. The sandwiches were hearty and delicious, with unusual touches. The country ham and Taleggio cheese on a baguette was an intense sandwich, the pungent cheese bumping up against the strong taste of the ham. The focaccia with grilled vegetables had a delicious vinaigrette, and the one with grilled marinated eggplant was exceptional, although the goat cheese that was supposed to be on it was barely in evidence. The tuna with white beans was unusual but dull. Be sure to save room for dessert here. The apple-Mascarpone cheesecake with a *crème brûlée*-like top was so wonderful I had to fight off my colleagues just to get the last bite. The chocolate soufflé cake was very good, but not up to the level of the cheesecake. The brownies were prosaic and uninspiring. Remi to Go has quite a few tables set up in the atrium it shares with its parent restaurant. It is one of the few pleasant, reasonably priced places to eat outside in midtown.

Note: As could be expected, you might experience some heavy-duty attitude here. Some of the staff are extremely solicitous and friendly, but others, like the manager, think they're still working the line at the old Studio 54.

Remi to Go
145 West 53rd Street
(in the atrium between Sixth and Seventh avenues)
New York, NY 10019
PHONE: (212) 581-7115
SUBWAYS: 57th Street station on the Broadway N and R lines and the Sixth Avenue B and Q lines; 7th Avenue station on the Eighth Avenue E and Sixth Avenue B and D lines; 50th Street station on the Broadway–Seventh Avenue No. 1 and 9 lines.
HOURS: 7:30 A.M. to 7 P.M. Monday through Friday; closed Saturday and Sunday.
Free delivery.
All major credit cards accepted.
Catering is available.

*M*IDTOWN EAST

34TH STREET TO 59TH STREET
FIRST AVENUE TO FIFTH AVENUE

International Poultry Company ~ See page 302.

*C*HELSEA

14TH STREET TO 34TH STREET
FIFTH AVENUE TO ELEVENTH AVENUE

Kitchen Food Shop ~ I've always thought a good burrito was basically a Mexican version of a blintz. But since there are a lot more Jewish grandmothers than Mexican grandmothers in New York, finding a good burrito in New York was next to impossible before Stewart Tarabour opened Kitchen in 1985. His puebla pork-stew burrito boasts generous chunks of tender pork that's been stewed for hours, along with pinto beans, fresh cilantro, rice, mixed green salsa, and the house hot sauce (which is not all that hot), all wrapped in a twelve-inch flour tortilla. On any given day Kitchen offers six kinds of burritos, including at least two vegetarian choices, such as three-cheese or Indian-vegetable-stew. The black-bean redneck chili is superb, and not all that incendiary. Kitchen makes two kinds of cornbread. The Oaxacan blue-cornmeal cornbread has Mexican white cheese, roasted sweet peppers, various chilies, and more. It's terrific and very filling. The smoky chile cornbread packs a real kick, although it's not as intriguing as the Oaxacan variety. The black-bean soup is rather bland, the chocolate bread pudding is uninteresting, and the toasted-almond cake is moist but dull. Kitchen has the most intriguing array of sodas carried by any store I've been to in New York. The Mexican tamarind soda tastes like a carbonated, fruity, but not too sweet iced tea. The Mexican Apple soda was refreshing and nonsyrupy. There are half a dozen other Mexican sodas, along with four flavors of a New Mexican line of soda called Blue Sky.

Note: In the front of the store are various dried and fresh chilies, including *ancho, pasilla,* and *chipotle* varieties. With the unfortunate demise of Casa Moneo some years ago, the city has lacked a good outlet for dried and fresh chili peppers. Kitchen, along with Stop One Supermarket on the Upper West Side, has started to take up the chili slack. If your interest in chilies borders on obsession, you'll be happy to know that Kitchen carries current and back issues of *Chili Peppers* magazine.

Kitchen Food Shop
218 Eighth Avenue (between 21st and 22nd streets)
New York, NY 10011
PHONE: (212) 243-4433
SUBWAYS: 23rd Street station on the Broadway–Seventh Avenue No. 1 and 9
    lines and the Eighth Avenue C and E lines.
HOURS: 11:30 A.M. to 9:30 P.M. Monday through Thursday; 11:30 A.M. to 10
    P.M. Friday; noon to 9:30 P.M. Saturday and Sunday.
Deliveries in the neighborhood.
Cash only.
Mail order available.

$\mathscr{K}$IPS BAY/GRAMERCY PARK

4TH STREET TO 34TH STREET
EAST RIVER TO FIFTH AVENUE

Curry in a Hurry ··· Although the curry here is quite fine, if a bit oily, it is the tandoori chef, Anwar Malik, and his delectable array of tandoori meats that makes this cheerless little place stand out. His tandoori chicken, either on the bone or off, is a masterpiece—juicy, tender, and heady with flavor. It's hard to believe that microwaving tandoori chicken to heat it up doesn't ruin it, but I guess nothing could ruin Mr. Malik's handiwork. The vegetables, rice, and Indian breads here are also tasty, although the microwave doesn't do the bread justice.

Note: Curry in a Hurry is a dark, dingy place, but it does have a few tables you can sit at if you're having a bite to eat after shopping for Indian and Middle Eastern specialties in "Little India."

Curry in a Hurry
130 East 29th Street (between Lexington and Third avenues)
New York, NY 10016
PHONE: (212) 889-1159
SUBWAY: 28th Street station on the Lexington Avenue No. 6 line.
HOURS: 11:30 A.M. to 9 P.M. Monday through Saturday; 11:30 A.M. to 8 P.M.
    Sunday.
No deliveries.
All major credit cards accepted.

Park Avenue Gourmandises ⤳ With its painted tin ceilings, mahogany walls, and Provençal-inspired food, PAG has added a distinctively French flavor to its rapidly changing neighborhood. Park Avenue Bistro chef Jean Michel Diot, one of the owners here, produces some of the best take-out food available in the city. The terrific individual appetizer tarts are like Provençal pizzas, made with a delicious puff pastry dough and topped with either tomatoes and basil, spinach and ham, anchovies, or tomato, goat cheese, and roasted pepper. Perfectly cooked slices of leg of lamb in a light, garlic-infused sauce could be taken for homemade, and the accompanying ratatouille has diced zucchini mixed in with the eggplant and tomatoes. For lunch, PAG makes worthwhile sandwiches, including a pro-sciutto-and-mozzarella on country sourdough bread I have yet to resist. The Gourmandise cake, made with Grand Marnier–soaked chocolate sponge cake, chocolate ganache, and chocolate mousse, is a tempting dessert choice. So is the mixed fruit tart, enlivened by slices of blood oranges in season. The Opera cake squares, layers of chocolate and mocha cream on almond pastry, are very good, although a little sticky for my taste.

Note: PAG carries a variety of French breakfast pastries and rolls. The croissants are very good, the brioches are dry, and the Danish are merely serviceable.

Park Avenue Gourmandises
47 East 29th Street (between Park and Madison avenues)
New York, NY 10016
PHONE: (212) 447-1822
SUBWAY: 28th Street Station on the Lexington Avenue No. 6 line.
HOURS: 8 A.M. to 8:30 P.M. Monday through Friday; 10 A.M. to 7 P.M.
   Saturday and Sunday.
Deliveries in the neighborhood.
All major credit cards accepted.
No mail order.

Todaro Brothers ⤳ See page 233.

$\mathcal{W}$EST VILLAGE

14TH STREET TO HOUSTON STREET
FIFTH AVENUE TO WEST STREET

Balducci's ⤳ See page 205.

Benny's Burritos to Go ⤳ Anytime I'm confronted with enough food to fill a serving platter, I suspect somebody's trying to cover up poor quality with quantity. So I felt sure, when presented with a Benny's beef Bay burrito the size of a sleeping bag, that it was going to be lousy. I was wrong. The beef was tender and shredded, the pinto beans were soft without being pasty, the guacamole was spritely, and the shredded coriander was a nice touch. Since each twelve-inch-long Benny's burrito is stuffed with beef or chicken, pinto or black beans, Monterey Jack cheese, guacamole, and sour cream, they don't have combination plates. But if burritos aren't your thing, they have enchiladas, soft tacos, and chili. Beware the enchilada casings sticking to the top of the take-out container.

Note: Benny's likes to think of itself as one-stop party-shopping headquarters, so it sells everything it makes in bulk, from shredded beef and chicken to commercially made tortilla chips and its own coriander-laced salsa.

Benny's Burritos to Go
112 Greenwich Avenue (between Jane and West 13th streets)
New York, NY 10014
PHONE: (212) 633-9210
SUBWAYS: 14th Street station on the Eighth Avenue A, C, and E lines and
    the Broadway–Seventh Avenue No. 1, 2, 3, and 9 lines; Eighth Avenue
    station on the 14th Street–Canarsie L line.
HOURS: Noon to midnight seven days a week.
Deliveries in the neighborhood with a $10 minimum order.
Cash only.

OTHER LOCATION:
93 Avenue A (at 6th Street)
New York, NY 10009
(212) 254-3286

$\mathscr{E}$AST VILLAGE

14TH STREET TO HOUSTON STREET
EAST RIVER TO FIFTH AVENUE

Benny's Burritos to Go — See page 310.

$\mathscr{D}$OWNTOWN

HOUSTON STREET TO BATTERY PARK

Barocco Alimentari — I was upset a few years ago when Tavola Caldo Alfredo closed on Bleecker Street, leaving the city without a first-rate take-out lasagna. Enter Alimentari, the nifty sliver of a take-out shop adjoining the Italian restaurant Barocco. Alimentari's lasagna is rich and satiny, filled with porcini mushrooms and sausage in a béchamel sauce. Buy some of the country-style bread they bake here, some fennel and parmigiana salad, and some lasagna, and you've got a homey take-out meal. And don't forget to buy some bread pudding for dessert. It makes Paul Prudhomme's seem like My-T-Fine. One other thing about Alimentari: It has wonderful sandwiches, including a roast-pork-and-spinach sandwich I've traveled from the Upper West Side to Tribeca for. Only the extremely chocolaty but dry brownies aren't up to snuff.

Tiny Barocco Alimentari is a slice of take-out heaven, located on Church Street near the edge of Tribeca.

Barocco Alimentari
297 Church Street (between Walker and White streets)
New York, NY 10013
PHONE: (212) 431-0065
SUBWAYS: Canal Street station on the following lines: Broadway—Seventh Avenue No. 1 and 9; Eighth Avenue A, C, and E; Broadway N and R; Lexington Avenue No. 6; Nassau Street J, M, and Z.
HOURS: 9 A.M. to 8 P.M. Monday through Friday; 10 A.M. to 6 P.M. Saturday; closed Sunday.
Deliveries in the immediate neighborhood, from Houston to Chambers streets.
Catering and picnic baskets available.
All major credit cards accepted ($25 minimum).

Barocco Alimentari's Classic Lasagna al Forno

1 ounce dry porcini mushrooms
1 pound canned Italian plum
  tomatoes
½ red onion
2 small celery stalks
1 small carrot
2 cloves garlic
1 sprig fresh rosemary
2 to 3 leaves fresh sage
2 tablespoons olive oil
2 tablespoons butter
⅓ pound ground beef

½ pound ground chicken breast
1 mild Italian veal (or pork) sausage
½ cup dry red wine
1 tablespoon tomato paste
1 cup meat stock
Salt and pepper to taste
1 pound fresh lasagna noodles
2 cups dense bechamel sauce (use your
  favorite French or Italian recipe)
1 cup fresh grated Parmesan cheese
1 stick unsalted butter

1. Soak porcini mushrooms in a cup of warm water until soft, about 15 minutes. Remove from water and clean stems of any dirt. Strain the soaking water carefully and reserve the water. Set aside.
2. Coarsely chop canned tomatoes, discarding seeds and allowing excess liquid to drain. Set tomatoes aside.
3. Finely chop the onion, celery, carrot, and garlic. Chop together the rosemary and sage.
4. Heat oil together with 2 tablespoons butter in a heavy, deep saucepan large enough to contain all the ingredients. Add the chopped vegetables (except for the chopped tomatoes and the mushrooms) and herbs and gently simmer until lightly browned.
5. Chop the softened porcini mushrooms and add to the cooking vegetables. Simmer 1 minute. Add ground meats and sausage, raise heat, and, using a fork, break up the meat, exposing it all to the heat as it cooks. When the meat has lost its rawness, add the wine combined with the tomato paste, along with liquid reserved from soaking the mushrooms, stock, and the chopped tomatoes. Allow liquids to come to a boil, then reduce heat and simmer gently, uncovered, for one hour or more, yielding a dark, rich sauce. Add salt and pepper to taste. Remove pan from heat and set aside.
6. *Prepare pasta*: In a large kettle bring lightly salted water to a rapid boil. Meanwhile, set several clean dishtowels onto a counter where the cooked pasta will dry. Cook the sheets of pasta one at a time, very briefly (3 to 4 seconds if it is fresh) after the water returns to the boil. Remove with tongs, drop into a bowl of cold water to stop the cooking, rinse under running water, and lay flat to dry on the towels. Repeat until all pasta is cooked.
7. Preheat oven to 375°F.
8. *Assemble lasagna*: Lightly grease the bottom of your lasagna dish with a little oil from the meat sauce. Cover bottom of pan with the first layer of pasta, overlapping the sheets slightly. Spoon a thin layer of bechamel over the noodles and then, over this, spoon a few tablespoons of meat sauce— lightly enough to create a somewhat translucent layer of sauce. Sprinkle with Parmesan cheese. Place the second layer of pasta in the dish and repeat process. Continue layer by layer (six layers maximum), reserving some bechamel for the top. Spoon a light coating of the bechamel over the final sheet of pasta, dot with butter, and sprinkle with cheese.
9. Bake until top is bubbly, swelling, and golden brown in color, about 25 minutes.

Yield: 6 to 8 servings

Barocco Alimentari's Bread Pudding

4 cups milk	1 cup rum
⅓ cup sugar	12 egg yolks
2 tablespoons ground cloves	1 cup sugar
2 large loaves day-old Italian bread	4 cups milk
sliced approximately ⅜ inch thick	3 cups heavy cream
and with crust removed	1 tablespoon vanilla extract
3 cups raisins	Ground cinnamon

1. Warm 4 cups milk together with ⅓ cup sugar and clove. Lay the bread flat on trays and pour the warm milk mixture over all the slices. Set aside.
2. Stir together raisins and rum and set aside to soak.
3. In a large bowl and using an electric mixer set at low speed, beat together egg yolks, 1 cup sugar, 4 cups milk, heavy cream, vanilla, and a dash of cinnamon.
4. Preheat oven to 350°F.
5. Gently squeeze excess milk out of bread. Cover the bottom of a rectangular baking dish (deep enough to hold three layers of bread) with a layer of the soaked bread. Spoon on half of the raisins and sprinkle with cinnamon to taste. Pour one third of the cream-and-egg mixture over this layer. Repeat with second layer of bread, the second half of the raisins, cinnamon, and another third of the cream mixture. Finish with the third layer of bread and the last third of the cream, omitting raisins and cinnamon for the top.
6. Bake until golden brown, about 50 minutes.

Yield: 6 to 8 servings

Dean and DeLuca — See page 214.

Whole Foods of Soho — I thought I had taken a wrong turn when I arrived at the prepared foods counter of Whole Foods of Soho. Instead of the tamari-laced gruel I had seen at other health-food stores, I found myself staring at an array of food that actually looked and smelled appetizing. So it didn't surprise me that the potato-cheddar pocket I bought tasted like a great knish. (The unhealthful connotations of knishes probably prevented the store from actually calling it one.) Even more amazing was the wedge of pumpkin pie I bought. Most health-food sweets taste like pegboard mixed with bran and honey, but this pumpkin pie was delicious; it can't be good for you. The chicken salad made with raisins, walnuts, and egg-free mayonnaise was delicious. I didn't try the shepherd's pie, but it sure looked good. Next to the prepared foods was a case containing organically raised poultry and a small selection of fish. The poultry looked okay, but the fish had clearly seen better days. Besides the prepared foods and the meat and fish, Whole Foods of Soho has a complete salad bar, loads of bins of bulk items like nuts and grains, a small organic produce section, the largest selection of healthful snack foods I've encountered in New York, and a floor-to-ceiling hydraulic press that squeezes all kinds of juices daily.

Whole Foods of Soho
117 Prince Street (between Wooster and Greene streets)
New York, NY 10012
PHONE: (212) 673-5388
SUBWAYS: Broadway–Lafayette Street station on the Sixth Avenue B, D, F,
    and Q lines; Bleecker Street station on the Lexington Avenue No. 6 line;
    Prince Street station on the Broadway R line.
HOURS: 9 A.M. to 9:30 P.M. seven days a week.
Delivery available on large orders.
All major credit cards accepted.

Thanksgiving Trot

Another Thanksgiving was upon us, and our little family was descending on my mother-in-law. So in the name of art (namely, this book), I proposed to my mother-in-law that I do take-out shopping from a number of stores to fill our Thanksgiving table full of food. Now mothers-in-law, like mothers, fathers, grandparents, aunts and uncles, and anyone over forty, regard with extreme prejudice the idea of a family ritual dinner prepared by outsiders. But a few deftly negotiated phone calls later, we had struck a deal: I would supply the turkey, gravy, stuffing, cranberry sauce, and pie, and she would supply the appetizers, peas, carrots, and sweet potato–marshmallow soufflé.

Before I embarked on this project, I set a few ground rules. Having subjected myself to the insanity that besets every mega-take-out store on Thanksgiving Eve, I decided that all food other than pies had to be ordered on the phone and delivered to my mother-in-law's apartment on Manhattan's East Side no later than Thursday at 1:00 P.M. My mother-in-law wanted the cutoff point to be 9:00 A.M. on Thanksgiving in order to have sufficient time to deal with any no-shows, but I pacified her by securing the home phone numbers of the owners of every store I ordered from.

The turkey was item number one. From reading the newspapers, I knew that virtually every serious butcher and take-out emporium prepared Thanksgiving turkeys for delivery. The prices varied widely, from four to twelve dollars a pound, depending on what the turkey had been fed (organic grain or just plain swill), and how much it had been allowed to exercise before its untimely demise (whether it was free-range or pen-fed). I decided on Lorenzo & Maria's Kitchen (see page 303), which had organically fed, fresh-killed turkeys for $5.00 a pound. They not only would cook the unstuffed (for health reasons) bird with my choice of sage, rosemary, or

Thanksgiving Trot, continued

thyme but also were the only store I called that would deliver the turkey hot and ready to be served on Thanksgiving Day at 1:00 P.M. sharp.

Stuffing was the next hurdle. I thought about ordering one kind of stuffing from Lorenzo & Maria's, but they were getting a minimum of thirteen dollars a pound for even a meatless stuffing, and I drew the line at double-digit stuffing prices. I opted for three kinds of seven-dollar-a-pound stuffing from Grace's Marketplace (page 225): chestnut-scallion, walnut-raisin cornbread, and sausage-and-herb. I also ordered the cranberry sauces from Grace's, whose cranberry-orange sauce and cranberry conserve with pecans sounded intriguing enough.

Finally there was the matter of the pies. Having sampled dozens of pies for the last ten months in researching this book, I knew I could get first-rate ones from places like The Little Pie Company, Taylor's, Better Pie Crust, and Briermere Farms out on Long Island. But in the interests of art and science, I opted to try new places. I ordered an apple pie and a pumpkin pie from Pâtisserie Les Friandises (see page 16), a French bakery in my neighborhood, and a plum pie from Lorenzo & Maria's. I was going to limit myself to those three and was about to starting to pat myself on the back for restraint, when I remembered that a famous southern chef, Gene Hovis, had just become creative director at Macy's Cellar Marketplace (see page 230). His pies were famous, so I flew to 34th Street and picked up a pumpkin pie and a sweet-potato pie. Pie purists know it's a sin to pick up pies baked on a Wednesday and eat them on Thursday, but Macy's is not about to be open on Thanksgiving morning. However, please note that serious pie places like The Little Pie Company (see page 27) open Thanksgiving morning just to sell absolutely fresh pies.

We arrived at my mother-in-law's at about 12:45 on Thanksgiving Day, laden with five pies and eighteen of Gene Hovis's justifiably famous buttermilk biscuits. The stuffings and cranberry sauces had arrived from Grace's on schedule the day before, with complete, easy-to-follow serving instructions.

All we needed was the turkey. Of course, that's like saying all you need at a funeral is the coffin. I assured my mother-in-law that the turkey was on its way. At 1:15 I placed my first phone call to Lorenzo & Maria's. Don't worry, they said, the turkey had just left the store in a truck, and the store was a mere seven blocks from my mother-in-law's. "Don't worry," I told my mother-in-law, "the turkey's on the truck." By 1:45, the remaining guests had arrived, we still had no turkey, and I was starting my fortieth lap around the apartment. I put in another call to the store around 2:00 P.M., and was assured the bird would arrive any moment. Finally, at 2:15, just as I was about to leave to pick up ten Swanson Hungry-Man TV dinners from the supermarket, the turkey arrived, brown and beautiful and hot, as promised.

After carving the turkey, we sat down to eat. The turkey was superb, moist, flavorful, and perfectly done. The cranberry conserve with pecans was the best cranberry preparation I've ever had in my life. The three stuffings, for all their varied and exotic ingredients, tasted like, well, stuffing. I kept taking little portions of each and nibbling them one by one in a desperate effort to distinguish one from the other. Alas, I couldn't. My mother-in-law's sweet-potato–marshmallow soufflé was excellent. Gene Hovis's butter-milk biscuits were tasty, light, and richer than sin. Les Friandises' apple pie was gorgeous to look at and had lots of tender, not-very-sweet Granny Smith apples in the filling, but it had a hard, glazed, nonflaky crust and was simply a mediocre pie. Their pumpkin pie was not to my taste at all. Lorenzo and Maria's plum pie had a delicious plum filling but a strange English-style lard crust that just didn't make it. Gene Hovis's pumpkin pie was a triumph, light and full of pumpkin goodness. I must admit, however, that neither I nor anyone else at the table could distinguish his sweet-potato pie from his pumpkin pie. I decided they had given me two pumpkin pies by mistake.

My finicky criticisms aside, everyone agreed that it was a first-rate Thanksgiving dinner. We all groaned that we had eaten too much and vowed to practice restraint next year. Most important to me, my mother-in-law genuinely appeared to be satisfied with the results of my telephone skills. But she is a very polite and dignified woman, so I knew I would have to wait until we got home for the post-festivities mother-daughter phone call to get the real scoop. The phone rang around 8 P.M., and I began to pace nervously around our apartment. When my wife hung up the phone, I faced her expectantly.

"Well," I queried, with only a slight tremor in my voice. "What's the verdict?"

"She said it was a triumph," came the reply, "but she thought we didn't really need five pies for nine people."

Turkey; Plum Pie:
Lorenzo & Maria's Kitchen
1418 Third Avenue (between 80th and 81st streets)
New York, NY 10021
PHONE: (212) 794-1080
SUBWAYS: 77th Street station on the Lexington Avenue No. 6 line.
HOURS: 9 A.M. to 8 P.M. Monday through Saturday; closed Sunday.
Deliveries available throughout the metropolitan area.
Cash, personal checks, and charge accounts only.
Catering, gift, and picnic baskets available.
Mail order available.

Stuffing:
Grace's Marketplace
1237 Third Avenue (between 71st and 72nd streets)
New York, NY 10021
PHONE: (212) 737-0600
SUBWAY: 68th Street–Hunter College station on the Lexington Avenue No.
    6 line.

Thanksgiving Trot, continued

HOURS: 7 A.M. to 8:30 P.M. Monday through Saturday; 8 A.M. to 7 P.M. Sunday.
Deliveries made throughout Manhattan.
All major credit cards accepted.
Catering and picnic baskets available.
Mail-order catalog available.

Pumpkin and Apple Pies:
Pâtisserie Les Friandises
665 Amsterdam Avenue (between 92nd and 93rd streets)
New York, NY 10025
PHONE: (212) 316-1515
SUBWAYS: 96th Street station on the following lines: Broadway–Seventh Avenue No. 1, 2, 3, and 9; Eighth Avenue C and Sixth Avenue B.
HOURS: 8 A.M. to 6 P.M. Tuesday through Saturday; 8:30 A.M. to 3 P.M. Sunday.
Deliveries in the neighborhood.
American Express accepted.

Pumpkin and Sweet Potato Pies:
Macy's Cellar Marketplace
151 West 34th Street at Herald Square (the entire block between Broadway and Seventh Avenue)
New York, NY 10001
PHONE: (212) 736-5151
SUBWAYS: 34th Street station on the Sixth Avenue B, D, F, and Q and the Broadway N and R lines; 34th Street–Penn Station on the Broadway–Seventh Avenue No. 1, 2, 3, and 9 and the Eighth Avenue A, C, and E lines.
HOURS: 9:45 A.M. to 8:30 P.M. Monday, Thursday, and Friday; 9:45 A.M. to 6:45 P.M. Tuesday, Wednesday, and Saturday; 10 A.M. to 6 P.M. Sunday.
Deliveries available.
All major credit cards accepted.
Mail order available by calling 1 (800) 446-2297.

Best of Prepared Food

Best bread: E.A.T.; Barocco Alimentari
Best bread pudding: Barocco Alimentari
Best coffee cake: Neuman and Bogdanoff
Best cookie: Yura (chocolate turtles); Word of Mouth (Mexican wedding cookies)
Best desserts: Yura (apple cobbler, chocolate angel-food cake); Remi to Go (apple-Mascarpone cheesecake)
Best grilled chicken: El Pollo
Best Italian food: Barocco Alimentari
Best kasha varnishkes: David's
Best lamb dish: Park Avenue Gourmandises (leg of lamb)
Best lasagna: Barocco Alimentari
Best macaroni and cheese: Good & Plenty to Go
Best meat loaf: Word of Mouth
Best Mexican take-out: Kitchen Food Shop
Best Middle Eastern take-out: Cleopatra's Needle
Best rice pudding: Word of Mouth
Best sandwiches: E.A.T.
Best soups: International Poultry Company (black bean, chicken); Yura (tomato, yellow squash, and rosemary)
Best Tandoori chicken: Curry in a Hurry

19

WINE

As a kid the only wine I knew was the kosher Manischewitz consumed at Passover dinner every spring. I wondered what all the fuss was about wine because, to me, it seemed like a perfect substitute for professional motor oil. In college I graduated to Boone's Farm and Mogen David 20-20, which the French Appelation Board might generously classify as wine-flavored beverages.

Even now, I would hardly call myself a wine connoisseur. But for some reason I seem to be attracted to people who regard wine as the holy grail. My friends Howie and Mitchell, my brother Mike, and my cousin Sam are all passionate about wine and are certainly responsible for whatever wine knowledge I possess.

Serious wine stores in New York are a varied lot. Some, like Acker Merrall or Rosenthal, alert you to their dedication and intent as soon as you walk into the store. The stores are quiet, airy, and spacious, with wines carefully laid out on wooden racks that invite browsing and discussion. Others, such as Quality House and Park Avenue Liquors, look like New York neighborhood liquor stores, with naked flourescent lighting and nip bottles on the counter. In these latter stores, it is only after browsing the aisles and talking to the salespeople that you realize you're in a store where wine is regarded as a religion.

The variables in high-end wine stores are price, selection, service, and attitude. The difference in price between two stores for the same bottle of wine can be staggering; so if you are looking for a specific bottle of expensive wine, call a couple of stores and get price quotes. Some good wine stores, like K & D and Garnet, display the same respect to California wines as they do to French and Italian wines. Others tend to specialize: Quality House, for example, clearly focuses on French wines, whereas Gotham concentrates on champagnes and leaves wines in general to other stores. Service also varies widely in wine stores. At some places, such as Park Avenue Liquors, salespeople seem to understand the importance of building loyalty by treating customers well no matter how much they know about wine. Salespeople at other stores, like Crossroads, seem to treat customers as annoyances until they become regulars. Even two experiences at the same wine store can vary widely, depending on the salesperson you get. For example, Garnet is a great store to go to if you know exactly what you want; otherwise, depending on who you get as a salesperson, you may get rushed, brusque treatment. So it's best to develop a relationship with a particular salesperson in a store and then stick with him or her. That way you'll know that when you walk in or call with questions, you'll get a straight, helpful response.

$\mathcal{U}$PPER WEST SIDE

59TH STREET TO 125TH STREET
CENTRAL PARK WEST TO RIVERSIDE DRIVE

Acker Merrall and Condit --- Acker Merrall can seem intimidating to wine neophytes and nonregulars. The wines are very carefully laid out according to where they're from; there's plenty of space to walk around in; and it never seems to get noisy, no matter how many people are shopping. Yet I have found the salespeople to be consistently helpful, no matter how much I was spending on a bottle of wine. I have had other friends complain about snooty salespeople here, but I've never had a reason to complain. Acker Merrall has very strong California, German, and Alsatian sections, and its other French and Italian sections aren't far behind.

It also has a fairly wide selection of half-bottles, something many other good wine stores in the city don't. Considering the tone of the store and the number of bottles it carries, Acker Merrall's prices are reasonable.

Acker Merrall and Condit
160 West 72nd Street (between Broadway and Columbus avenues)
New York, NY 10023
PHONE: (212) 787-1700
SUBWAYS: 72nd Street station on the following lines: Broadway–Seventh
    Avenue No. 1, 2, 3, and 9; Eighth Avenue C and Sixth Avenue B.
HOURS: 8:30 A.M. to 11:30 P.M. Monday through Saturday; closed Sunday.
Deliveries all over the New York area (and the entire country).
All major credit cards accepted.
Mail-order catalog available.

Gotham Liquors ⁓ Most consumers' knowledge of champagne starts with Freixinet and ends with Dom Perignon. But talk to Jack Battipaglia, Gotham Liquor's irrepressible owner, and he'll be glad to give you a seminar in champagne on the spot. He'll tell you how chamnpagne makers like Krug and Paul Roger represent a much better value than their bigger-name counterparts, and he'll sell you a good bottle of champagne at a lower price than almost any other store in the city. But champagne is the only reason to make a special trip to Gotham, and if Jack is not around or in the back, no one else has the requisite knowledge to steer you right. I should also note that Jack's knowledge does not extend to wine. The store's wine selection is limited, but you can find some bargains if you already know your wines and are willing to cruise the racks.

Gotham Liquors
2519 Broadway (at 94th Street)
New York, NY 10025
PHONE: (212) 876-4120
SUBWAYS: 96th Street station on the following lines: Broadway–Seventh
    Avenue No. 1, 2, 3, and 9; Eighth Avenue C and Sixth Avenue B.
HOURS: 9 A.M. to 9 P.M. Monday through Saturday; closed Sunday.
Deliveries all over Manhattan.
Visa and MasterCard accepted.
Mail order available.

67 Wine & Spirits Merchants ⁓ I almost overlooked 67 Wine & Spirits (as a reliable if unexciting neighborhood standby) until an oenophile in my health club locker room informed me in no uncertain terms that it would be a mistake to do so. He was right. Not only does 67 have a first-rate selection of French, Californian, and other wines at (gasp) reasonable, uninflated prices, but also its salespeople are informed, friendly, courteous, and absolutely unpretentious. The store's lack of snobbishness is a reflection of owner Bernie Weiser, whose mission in life is to treat every customer well, no matter what their level of wine expertise. What a pleasure to find a wine store in Manhattan whose salesclerks don't try to make you feel like a fool if you don't know the difference between a Chardonnay and a Sauvignon Blanc. It's not that Weiser and company don't have a lot to be snobbish about. The store carries almost 3500 bottles of wine and champagne at a given time, including a superb collection of champagnes, an equally impressive selection of Californian and French wines, and a growing section of Australian and Italian wines. In shopping for a wine to serve a humongous Thanksgiving gathering at our house, Bernie turned me on to an under-ten-dollar 1988 Zinfandel from California's Caymus Vineyards that impressed even the wine snobs in our group.

67 Wine & Spirits Merchants
179 Columbus Avenue (between 67th and 68th streets)
New York, NY 10023
PHONE: (212) 724-6767
SUBWAY: 65th Street on the Broadway–Seventh Avenue No. 1 and 9 lines.
HOURS: 9 A.M. to 9 P.M. Monday through Thursday; 9 A.M. to 10 P.M. Friday
    and Saturday.
Free delivery.
All major credit cards accepted.

*U*PPER EAST SIDE

59TH STREET TO 96TH STREET
FIRST AVENUE TO FIFTH AVENUE

Garnet Wines & Liquors ⟶ Garnet has a noteworthy selection of California, French, and Italian wines, and a great champagne selection as well. It has reasonable if not rock-bottom prices. So why isn't it everyone's favorite wine store? Because service can be brusque and, depending upon who your salesperson is, not particularly helpful or knowledgeable. There are a number of people at Garnet who are solicitous, helpful, and not condescending, and if you find one you like, stick with him because you won't find a better combination of selection and price anywhere in the city. Needless to say, if you are already knowledgeable and don't want to schmooze with the salesperson about wine, Garnet is the place for you.

Note: On many Saturdays and on all major holidays, as well as the day before them, Garnet has a line for the registers that extends out the door. Though they really do try to keep things moving, the wait can be exasperatingly long.

Garnet Wines & Liquors
929 Lexington Avenue (between 68th and 69th streets)
New York, NY 10021
PHONE: (212) 772-3211
SUBWAYS: 68th Street–Hunter College station on the Lexington Avenue No.
    6 line.
HOURS: 9 A.M. to 9 P.M. Monday through Saturday; closed Sunday.
Visa and MasterCard accepted ($25 minimum).
Telephone orders accepted.

K & D Liquors ⟶ K & D looks like a disaster area. It's poorly laid out, has the feel of a local liquor store, and in general feels out of control when you walk in.

But don't let the chaos fool you. K & D has one of the best overall selections of wine in the city. Its California section is first-rate, its Italian section is pretty good, and its French and German sections are solid even if not up there with the best in the city. It also has a terrific selection of wines from the lesser-known wine-producing countries of Chile, Greece, and Australia. One of the salesmen here, a young man named Joel, really knows his stuff, and doesn't make you feel like a boob no matter how elementary your questions are. K & D's prices are competitive, if not rock-bottom, and they seem to go out of their way to engender customer loyalty with friendly, nonpatronizing service.

K & D Liquors
1366 Madison Avenue (between 95th and 96th streets)
New York, NY 10128
PHONE: (212) 289-1818
SUBWAYS: 96th Street station on the Lexington Avenue No. 6 line.
HOURS: 9 A.M. to 10 P.M. Monday through Saturday; closed Sunday.
Visa and MasterCard accepted.
Delivery and mail order available.

Morrell & Company — With its vaulted ceilings, exposed beams, and huge watercolor posters on the walls, Morrell looks more like a wealthy person's library than a liquor store. The accoutrements and the store's snooty reputation had me braced for a rough, patronizing ride. So I was both surprised and delighted when the young man who waited on me ten days before Christmas turned out to be incredibly friendly and concerned that I get the right wines. I asked him to recommend two bottles of white wine for under ten dollars each, and he came up with a California and an Australian wine that were both winners. Morrell's prices are high, but their inventory is huge, and it's pleasant to walk into a liquor store that feels like a library.

Morrell & Company
535 Madison Avenue (between 54th and 55th streets)
New York, NY 10022
PHONE: (212) 688-9370
SUBWAYS: Fifth Avenue–53rd Street station on the Sixth Avenue F and
    Eighth Avenue E lines; 51st Street station on the Lexington Avenue No.
    6 line.
HOURS: 9 A.M. to 7 P.M. Monday through Friday; 9:30 A.M. to 6:30 P.M.
    Saturday; closed Sunday.
Deliveries made all over the tristate area.
All major credit cards accepted.
Mail-order catalog available.

Rosenthal Wine Merchant — (formerly Ardsley Wines & Spirits): When you walk into Rosenthal, you wonder if the store is a front. With its immaculate interior, carefully painted tin ceilings, mauve-colored fixtures, and beautiful wooden fixtures, it feels like a library or a restaurant rather than a wine store. Then you notice that there are only about 150 bottles of wine and champagne in the whole store, most of them unrecognizable even to serious oenophiles, and you wonder what the deal is. So here's how owner Neil Rosenthal operates. He goes to France, makes deals with small estates to gobble up their entire U.S. allotment, and then charges a fortune per bottle, figuring he's the only wine store in town playing this game. If you want the cachet of buying or bringing a bottle of French wine or champagne, smug in the knowledge that you're toting a very good, if not terrific, expensive bottle of French wine no one's ever heard of, this is the place for you. Other than his little-known French wines, Rosenthal carries literally a handful of standard California and Italian wines.

Rosenthal Wine Merchant
1200 Lexington Avenue (between 81st and 82nd streets)
New York, NY 10028
PHONE: (212) 249-6650
SUBWAYS: 86th Street station on the Lexington Avenue No. 4, 5, and 6 lines.
HOURS: 9:30 A.M. to 7 P.M. Monday through Friday; 9:30 A.M. to 6 P.M.
   Saturday; closed Sunday.
Deliveries throughout Manhattan.
Visa and MasterCard accepted.
Mail order available.

Sherry Lehmann ⁓ Sherry Lehmann is the Rolls Royce of liquor stores. Just as Rolls Royce salespeople can be imperious and patronizing, so can the people at Sherry Lehmann. The last time I walked into the store, however, I received prompt, courteous attention, particularly noteworthy because it was two weeks before Christmas and the store was jammed with customers. Sherry Lehmann has a phenomenal selection of wines and champagnes at what even the store's owners would admit are very high prices. Although at one time its selection of California wines was limited, that is no longer the case. Its French and Italian wine stocks are enormous, as is its champagne stock. What surprised me on a recent visit was the variety of inexpensive wines (under $10) it carries. It's as if a Rolls Royce dealer had decided to sell Toyotas.

Sherry Lehmann
679 Madison Avenue (between 61st and 62nd streets)
New York, NY 10021
PHONE: (212) 838-7500
SUBWAYS: 59th Street station on the Lexington Avenue No. 4, 5, and 6 lines;
   Lexington Avenue station on the Sixth Avenue B and Q lines; Fifth
   Avenue station on the Broadway N and R lines.
HOURS: 9 A.M. to 6:45 P.M. Monday through Saturday; closed Sunday.
Deliveries made throughout the tristate area.
All major credit cards accepted.
Mail-order catalog available.

IDTOWN EAST

34TH STREET TO 59TH STREET
FIRST AVENUE TO FIFTH AVENUE

Park Avenue Liquors ⸺ The first interesting fact about Park Avenue Liquors is that it's on Madison, not Park, Avenue. The second noteworthy thing is that, from the outside, it looks like a typical neighborhood liquor store, with naked flourescent lighting and nip bottles on the counter. But don't let its humdrum appearance fool you. The store is nicely laid out and easy to walk through, and it's one heckuva wine store. They have a fine selection of vintage port, lots of rare, hard-to-find California wines, and a good selection of champagnes at not-so-friendly prices. The wine prices are fairly standard for a store of this type. Their French selection is good, not outstanding, but they have Manhattan's best selection of the new Italian wines that have forced oenophiles to revise their thinking on Italian wines in general. Unlike many other serious wine stores, Park Avenue seems genuinely customer oriented. There are free pamphlets all over the store that explain the essentials of different French regional wines, something I haven't seen elsewhere. And the service is sincerely helpful, whether you're an absolute beginner or a wine expert. Ask for Scott, a knowledgeable, friendly, and unpretentious guy. He'll steer you right and won't make you feel foolish in the process.

Park Avenue Liquors
292 Madison Avenue (between 40th and 41st streets)
New York, NY 10017
PHONE: (212) 685-2442
SUBWAYS: 42nd Street–Grand Central on the following lines: Lexington
    Avenue No. 4, 5, and 6; Flushing No. 7; 42nd Street Shuttle.
HOURS: 8 A.M. to 7 P.M. Monday through Friday; 8 A.M. to 5 P.M. Saturday;
    closed Sunday.
Deliveries throughout Manhattan.
American Express accepted ($40 minimum).
Mail order available.

*C*HELSEA

14TH STREET TO 34TH STREET
FIFTH AVENUE TO 11TH AVENUE

Crossroads Wines ⸺ My brother, who's a big guy, was trying to negotiate his way through Crossroads' unbelievably narrow aisles when he accidentally knocked over a couple of twelve-dollar bottles of California wine. Miraculously he managed to snare one before it hit the ground, but the other tumbled unceremoniously to the floor and broke. Although he graciously apologized, the Crossroads staff merely frowned contemptuously and went to get a mop and broom to clean up the mess. I know retailers are never happy to lose unpaid inventory, but I felt the people at Crossroads could have been a lot more gracious about the whole thing. It's unfortunate they are so unfriendly because they have one of the largest selections of wine in the city—and at reasonable prices. French, California, Italian, Port, Australian, Oregonian—the store has everything. For some reason these same wine experts display their okay selection of champagnes upright in a refrigerated case—a definite no-no. I've heard the salespeople at Crossroads are nice to you once they've gotten to know you, but unfortunately not everyone gets the chance to become a regular.

Crossroads Wines
55 West 14th Street (between 5th and 6th avenues)
New York, NY 10011
PHONE: (212) 924-3060
SUBWAYS: 14th Street station on the Sixth Avenue F line; 14th Street–Union
    Square station on the following lines: Lexington Avenue No. 4, 5, and 6;
    Broadway N and R; 14th Street–Canarsie L.
HOURS: 9 A.M. to 9 P.M. Monday through Saturday; closed Sunday.
Deliveries all over Manhattan.
Visa and MasterCard accepted.
Mail order available.

𝒦IPS BAY/GRAMERCY PARK

14TH STREET TO 34TH STREET
EAST RIVER TO FIFTH AVENUE

First Avenue Wines & Spirits ⤳ Although it's lesser known than the stars of the wine world such as Crossroads and K & D, First Avenue has an unbeatable combination of selection, price, and service. The owner, Ira Weiner, can help you choose from more than 2,500 wines, some of which are stored in what he claims is the largest temperature-controlled vintage room in the city. He has lots of wines from small, idiosyncratic wine growers, and he is more than happy to explain what each one of them is. Although he is very strong in all wine categories, he claims to have 500 different German wines, by far the largest selection of German wines in New York.

First Avenue Wines & Spirits
383 First Avenue (between 22nd and 23rd streets)
New York, NY 10010
PHONE: (212) 673-3600
SUBWAY: 23rd Street station on the Lexington Avenue No. 6 line.
HOURS: 9 A.M. to 8:30 P.M. Monday through Saturday; closed Sunday.
Delivery available throughout the New York metropolitan area.
All major credit cards accepted.
Mail-order catalog available.

Quality House ⤳ Gary Fradin, the owner of Quality House, takes his wine seriously. Very seriously. The last time I was here with my brother Mike and his friend Alan, Gary Fradin got so involved in a discussion of vintage years for

Bordeaux wines and questions of price and value raised by Krug Champagne's pricing structure that he followed us out the door and up the street until one of the other salespeople implored him to return. Gary and his cohorts are extremely knowledgeable about their vast collection of French wines and champagnes and, if you show any interest at all, will talk to you for hours about it. Gary is very opinionated, but if you don't agree with him, he doesn't make you feel like an idiot. And if you're a relative wine neophyte, he is wonderfully helpful and solicitous. His prices are reasonable, considering the level of service. Although French wines are their specialty, their selection of Italian and California wines is more than adequate.

Quality House
2 Park Avenue (between 32nd and 33rd streets)
New York, NY 10016
PHONE: (212) 532-2944
SUBWAY: 33rd Street station on the Lexington Avenue No. 6 line.
HOURS: 9 A.M. to 6:30 P.M. Monday through Friday; 9 A.M. to 4 P.M.
   Saturday; closed Sunday; closed Saturdays during July and August.
Deliveries throughout the New York area.
Cash and personal checks only.
Mail order available.

$\mathcal{W}$EST VILLAGE

14TH STREET TO HOUSTON STREET
FIFTH AVENUE TO WEST STREET

Burgundy Wine Company Limited ⟿ If you want to know how seriously Burgundy Wine Company proprietor Al Hotchkin takes wines from Burgundy and the Rhone (the only wines he sells in his store), go no further than the opening line of a recent newsletter he sent his customers: "As many of you know I spent a good part of April and May visiting producers in Burgundy and the Rhone." Anywhere from one to three times a year Hotchkin visits the growers and producers of every bottle of wine sold in his store. His regular customers (equally serious oenophiles unable to take off three months a year to taste wine) are the grateful recipients of Hotchkin's legwork. At any given moment Hotchkin carries 500 bottles of wine (because he often gets only a few cases of a particular vintage, his inventory is constantly changing), and he can tell you more than you want to know about every single bottle in the place. Though neighborhood customers do come in looking for a bottle of wine to drink with dinner that night, Hotchkin admits his store is really not for the uninitiated. "We spend an average of anywhere from half to three quarters of an hour with a customer, so we are not geared up for volume." That said, I walked into the store a few months ago, and minutes later walked out with a wonderful bottle of 1989 Cote du Rhone made by Dom Brusset. So though it sounds like a pretentious, stuffy place, I found the folks at Burgundy to be surprisingly friendly and accommodating.

Burgundy Wine Company Limited
323 West 11th Street (between Greenwich and Washington streets)
New York, NY 10014
PHONE: (212) 691-9092
SUBWAY: 14th Street station on the Broadway-Seventh Avenue 1, 2, 3 and 9
   lines.
HOURS: 10 A.M. to 7 P.M. Tuesday through Saturday. Closed Mondays.
Delivery available.
Mail order catalogue and newsletter available.
Cash and personal checks only.

$\mathcal{E}$AST VILLAGE

14TH STREET TO HOUSTON STREET
EAST RIVER TO FIFTH AVENUE

Astor Place Wines & Spirits ⁓ Astor Place is the Kiddie City of the wine world—that is they carry a huge inventory of wines from all over the world, but finding what you want is difficult and finding anyone from whom you can successfully solicit advice is next to impossible. Astor Place has strong South American wine, champagne, and French wine sections, and if you do happen to find an informed salesperson, you can do very well here. Astor Place wants to be taken seriously as a wine store. The owners just have no idea how to do it.

Astor Place Wines & Spirits
12 Astor Place (corner of Lafayette Street)
New York, NY 10003
PHONE: (212) 674-7500
SUBWAYS: Astor Place station on the Lexington Avenue No. 6 line; 8th Street–
   NYU station on the Broadway R line.
HOURS: 9 A.M. to 9 P.M. Monday through Saturday; closed Sunday.
Deliveries throughout Manhattan.
Visa and MasterCard accepted.

$\mathcal{Q}$UEENS

Goldstar Wines and Spirits ⁓ In 1971 Lou Iacucci opened Goldstar, hellbent on proving the Italian wine naysayers wrong. Today, with the reputation of Italian wines intact, even soaring, Goldstar is *the* store for Italian wines in the city. You'll find hundreds of bottles of Tuscan, Piedmontese, and Veneto wines, ranging in price from eight to three hundred dollars. Very special bottles, like the wonderfully rich and full-bodied 1971 Tignanello, are kept in the temperature-controlled Chateau Room. Though Lou Iaccuci passed away in 1989, his wife, Lucy, has maintained both the store's terrific inventory and its warm, unpretentious feeling. Goldstar's knowledgeable staff never makes you feel foolish the way some other wine salespeople do. Besides the Italian wines, Goldstar has an excellent Port selection, and, in keeping with its feel for the neighborhood, a superior selection of kosher wines.

Goldstar Wines & Spirits
103-05 Queens Boulevard (between 68th Road and 68th Drive)
Forest Hills, NY 11375
PHONE: (718) 459-0200
SUBWAY: 71st Avenue-Continental Avenue station on the E, F, R, and G
  lines.
HOURS: 9 A.M. to 9 P.M. Monday through Thursday; 9 A.M. to 10 P.M. Friday
  and Saturday.
Delivery available.
Mail order catalogue.
MasterCard and Visa accepted.

Best of Wine Stores

Best all-around wine store (if you know what you're doing): Garnet Wines & Liquors

Best all-around wine store (if you don't know what you're doing): Park Avenue Liquors, 67 Wine & Spirits Merchants

Best California wine selection: Park Avenue Liquors; First Avenue Wines & Spirits Merchants

Best champagne prices: Gotham Liquors; Garnet Wines & Liquors

Best champagne selection: Garnet Wines & Liquors

Best French wine selection: Quality House; Park Avenue Liquors

Best German wine selection: First Avenue Wines & Spirits

Best for hard-to-find bottles: Park Avenue Liquors

Best Italian wine selection: Park Avenue Liquors

Best service: Park Avenue Liquors; 67 Wine & Spirits Merchants

Best value: Garnet Wines & Liquors

INDEX BY CUISINE

Index by Neighborhood

Open sunday

Open late

(AFTER 8 P.M. MONDAY THROUGH FRIDAY)

Mail orders accepted

WE DELIVER

Bargain prices

GIFTS AND GIFT BASKETS

PLACES TO SIT

(ON PREMISES OR IN AN ADJOINING RESTAURANT)

Note: Every Pizza and "Gotta Have It"
entry has seating as well.

Special Indices

Rest in peace

The following stores are unfortunately no longer with us. I miss them terribly.

Barking Fish: Real New Orleans Po' Boys
Casa Moneo: Chilies; Mexican foodstuffs
Cheese of All Nations: Cheese
Chocolates by M: Caramels (still available by mail)
Dave's Luncheonette: Egg creams
The Eat Shoppe: Waffles
A. Fitz & Sons: Meat
Garden Cafeteria: Blintzes
Geffen's: Blintzes
Gitlitz: Combination sandwiches
Harvey's Coffee Shop: Meatballs and potatoes; fresh grapefruit juice.
Louis Lichtman's: Babka
Mary Elizabeth's: Doughnuts and doughnut holes; roast chicken sandwiches on
    homemade bread
Moisha's Luncheonette: Egg Creams
MOM's Pies: Pot pies
Mrs. Herbst's: Strudel
Schwartz's Candies: Chocolate-covered marshmallows (still available by mail and
    at Grace's Marketplace)
Tavola Caldo Alfredo: Italian food
Trinicria: Italian sandwiches

General index

FREE NEW YORK EATS UPDATE

New food stores are opening all the time in New York. To help you keep up with the latest food finds, get a free *New York Eats* update. Just send a self-addressed stamped envelope to Ed Levine, New York Eats, PO Box 782, Ansonia Station, New York, NY 10023. Please allow three to four weeks for processing.